THE INTOKU CODE

Delta Force's Intelligence Officer—Doing Good in Secret

WADE ISHIMOTO

CASEMATE
Pennsylvania & Yorkshire

Published in the United States of America and Great Britain in 2024 by
CASEMATE PUBLISHERS
1950 Lawrence Road, Havertown, PA 19083
and
47 Church Street, Barnsley, S70 2AS, UK

Copyright 2024 © Wade Ishimoto

Hardback Edition: ISBN 978-1-63624-469-3
Digital Edition: ISBN 978-1-63624-470-9

A CIP record for this book is available from the British Library

All rights reserved. No part of this book may be reproduced or transmitted in any form or by any means, electronic or mechanical including photocopying, recording or by any information storage and retrieval system, without permission from the publisher in writing.

Printed and bound in the United Kingdom by CPI Group (UK) Ltd, Croydon, CR0 4YY

Typeset in India by Lapiz Digital Services, Chennai.

For a complete list of Casemate titles, please contact:

CASEMATE PUBLISHERS (US)
Telephone (610) 853-9131
Fax (610) 853-9146
Email: casemate@casematepublishers.com
www.casematepublishers.com

CASEMATE PUBLISHERS (UK)
Telephone (0)1226 734350
Email: casemate@casemateuk.com
www.casemateuk.com

All photographs from author's collection unless otherwise indicated.

First and foremost, I dedicate this book to my wife Bobbi (Mi Hye), who has stood by me for over 50 years through both good and bad times. Secondly, my thanks go to the hundreds of mentors that I have had both in the military and civilian life with special credit to those who taught me how to be a soldier and to do well in Special Forces. My martial arts teachers, Moon Yo Woo, Masaichi Oshiro, and Shizuo Imaizumi, also deserve my sincere thanks. To my extended family and those I served with, I thank you for all you have done to spread *Intoku*. I also respect those serving our country today who embody the *Intoku* spirit through military, national, and public service.

Just as the number one can never be reduced to zero, once we act or speak, our action or speech is never completely erased.

An old Oriental saying tells us, "Sow good, and the harvest will be good. Sow evil and reap evil." We must understand that everything we do comes back to ourselves.

Therefore, before wishing for our own happiness and welfare and that of our children, we must do good in secret. To do good in secret means to act without seeking attention and praise, to act without any hope of reward. This is called *Intoku*.

Among the various ways of performing *Intoku*, to walk the way of the universe and to lead others along this way is best.

Koichi Tohei

Intoku is a Japanese word that translates to "good done in secret." The noted Aikido master Koichi Tohei wrote about *Intoku* in his book *Ki Sayings*. *Intoku* is what this book is about. You will find my recollections of good done in secret. What you won't find are spy techniques despite my years in clandestine operations. Those techniques are best left truly secret to prevent evil oppressors from understanding how they can be demolished.

Good done in secret means being humble but at the same time being filled with a spirit of wanting to help others in both routine and highly stressful situations. It requires a steadfast dedication. I make no claims about being perfect. I have certainly had my share of "bad" days where the reader could question my ability to live up to *Intoku*. Regardless, I trust you will enjoy my sojourn through life and profit from many of the lessons I have learned.

Contents

Prologue: Eagle Claw   vii

1	The Forging of a Warrior	1
2	A Rebel Finds Independence	11
3	The Army Calls!	19
4	Learning the Craft of Intelligence and Leadership	29
5	Hawaii—Finding and Losing	41
6	Vietnam and Resilience	47
7	5th Special Forces Group and Detachment B-57	53
8	The Green Beret Case	67
9	Special Action Force Asia	85
10	New Challenges and Opportunities	113
11	The Beginning of the Delta Force	127
12	Rice Bowl—Initial Preparations	159
13	Eagle Claw—The Final Plan	173
14	Conducting the Rescue Attempt	181
15	Back to Business	195
16	Valuable Lessons	201
17	A Second Career Begins	211
18	The Land of Enchantment—Albuquerque, New Mexico	219
19	The Branch Davidian Incident Review	227
20	The Khobar Towers Review	235
21	Anti-terrorism	245
22	Fighting Terrorism in the Corporate Sector	257
23	Life in the Pentagon	267

Epilogue   293

Prologue

Eagle Claw

"What else can go wrong tonight?" I thought to myself. I was on the back of a Yamaha motorcycle heading down a dirt road in the middle of the Great Salt Desert of Iran with one of my assigned Rangers, Specialist Robert Rubio.

It had been a rough four-and-a-half-hour ride on the first MC-130 aircraft leading the mission to rescue 53 American hostages in Tehran, Iran, in April 1980. Immediately after we landed, Staff Sergeant Littlejohn and I were the first off the airplane and set up our initial security, with Littlejohn moving to the front of the aircraft and myself to the rear. Rubio drove his motorcycle up to me a few minutes after landing, and I asked him, "How are Massey and McGirr doing?"

"Sir, they're sick."

I asked how sick they were and Rubio replied that they were okay, just a little slow because they got air sick on the ride into Iran from Masirah Island off the coast of Oman.

"Keep the engine running, I'll get on the back."

As soon as I got on the motorcycle, Rubio and I were illuminated by the lights of a Mercedes bus with some 40 passengers on board.

Kaboom!

Staff Sergeant Littlejohn fired a 40-millimeter grenade at the bus. The bus came to a halt, and I said to Rubio, "Let's go, we can't wait on the others. We've got to see if any other vehicles are coming."

Rubio gunned the motorcycle, and we took off down the desert floor. Just as I was thinking about what else could go wrong, Rubio turned his head and said, "Sir."

Instantly, I replied, "I see it, get off the road." We were communicating on ESP (extrasensory perception) and had both seen the lights of a vehicle coming towards us.

"Which way, Sir?"

"Go left, to the south," I replied.

Rubio veered the motorcycle to the left and I said, "Stop! Put the bike behind the berm [a road grader had scraped a foot-high berm on the side of the road], grab a LAW [light antitank weapon] and come up on me."

I got off the motorcycle and stood in the middle of the road while Rubio was getting the LAW off the motorcycle handlebars. The height and spread of the headlights told me that this was a truck coming at me. I took the safety off my M-16 rifle and held up my hand in a gesture to have the vehicle stop. That did no good—it kept coming at me.

As I started firing my rifle at the truck, my mind was flashing back to Vietnam. I had been in this kind of situation before, except in Vietnam it had been Dai Uy Trieu, a Vietnamese Special Forces captain who shot an M-60 machine gun at a truck near Bu Dop, Vietnam.

I knew there was no way I was going to stop this truck with an M-16 rifle, which fires 5.56 mm bullets compared to the 7.62 mm bullet of an M-60 machine gun. Nonetheless, I kept firing. The truck kept coming.

"Rubio!"

"Yes Sir."

"Cock your LAW. Ready?"

"Yes Sir."

"Fire!"

Whooosh! Rubio had fired at the truck.

Boooom! It hit the truck—a 3,000-gallon gasoline tanker! Well, that certainly brought the truck to a halt. There was no explosion—instead, a jet of ignited fuel was going at least 100 feet into the air from the top rear of the truck.

Rubio was in a prone position behind the road berm. I told him to keep me covered, and I began circling in to avoid being highlighted by the light coming from the fire. As I approached the truck, I heard a loud noise, it turned out it was the truck's radio blaring Persian music into the middle of the desert night. Suddenly, I saw another fuel truck pulling up behind the one that Rubio and I had stopped.

What the hell else could go wrong was going through my mind. I doubled back towards Rubio and told him that there was another truck behind. He told me that someone had jumped out of the cab of the first truck and was running backwards. I said, "Rube, grab the motorcycle, let's see if we can catch them."

Rubio got the motorcycle and I climbed on the back. It was a kick-start Yamaha dirt bike, and Robert had to kick-start it at least nine times before the darn engine finally turned over. Then Robert started fumbling with his night vision goggles. I asked him, "What's the matter?" He replied that his night vision goggles weren't functioning. We had infrared paper taped over the motorcycle headlight, so it was imperative that he had night vision goggles to be able to see. I immediately reached up to my head and it dawned on me—doggone it, we were so short of equipment that I had given up my night vision goggles to another member of the rescue force, stupidly thinking that I would find a way to do without them. Now I didn't have any when we needed them.

Making a quick decision, I got off the rear of the motorcycle to lighten the load and directed Rubio to try his best to catch up to the second truck and try to take it out. I told him that if he went 10 minutes without catching the truck to turn around and come back. My assessment of the situation was that the occupant of the first truck, at best, only saw an Oriental-looking person wearing a watch cap, nondescript jacket, blue jeans, and sneakers. If he had caught a glimpse of Robert Rubio, he would only have seen someone in a non-standard camouflage uniform who, again, would not look like a typical Caucasian American. Perhaps the truck driver would have thought we were the second coming of Genghis Khan!

Robert took off. He returned about 20 minutes later and reported he was unable to catch up with the other vehicle. I reassured him that it was not his fault and to take up a position to block any other vehicles, along with Curt Massey, Mike McGirr, and seven others who were sent to reinforce us. This was going to be a long night. Fortunately, we did not encounter any more vehicles over the next few hours. There was plenty of time to reflect on what had brought me to this point in my life. My thoughts went all the way back to my childhood.

CHAPTER I

The Forging of a Warrior

I was born a few months before the attack on Pearl Harbor, to Paul and Sumi (Tamagawa) Ishimoto. Both my parents came from large families. My dad had three brothers and three sisters, and my mother had three sisters and one brother. My dad's father, Tetsuhei Ishimoto, had migrated to Hawaii in the 1880s and was a skilled worker in stone. He helped to construct a water catchment tunnel through the Koolau Mountains that irrigated the pineapple and sugar cane fields in the Wahiawa area. My grandfather married Yone Akimoto who lived about a mile away from him in Yamaguchi Prefecture in Japan. My grandfather was a hard worker, and I can remember being with him when he was well into his 70s, as he literally broke rocks in the heat of the day. He would size up a boulder, find a fissure, pour a little water from a flask, fracture the boulder with a chisel, and then take a sledgehammer to break it apart. He built free-standing stone walls to include a wall at Punahou School and another at Saint Louis High School.

My dad and his older brother were about five feet two inches tall. In contrast, the two younger brothers were over six feet in height. His older brother, Tamotsu, was a skilled fisherman who would bring in over 50 pounds of fish with one cast of his net. He was also an amateur Sumo champion in Hawaii and a fireman. My dad was also a battler, twice winning Amateur Athletic Union boxing championships as a flyweight and bantamweight and making it to the semi-finals of the National Amateur Athletic Union Championships in the 1930s. There were three sisters: Grace (Hironaka), Fumiko (Okamoto), and Marilyn (Peterson). The two youngest were Uncle Arthur and Rikio. Aunt Fumiko's husband, William, served in World War II along with Uncle Arthur who was a member of the Military Intelligence Service and saw action in the Philippines. Uncle Rikio also served in the Army at the end of World War II.

My mother was the second born in her family, with her older sister being Mitsu (Aihara), and the two younger sisters being Ruth (Brighter) and Marjorie (Rose), along with one brother, Paul Tamagawa. Aunt Ruth's husband David served during World War II and was wounded in action and Uncle Paul also served in the Army at the end of World War II.

Both families were close and would get together at various times during the year. Neither family had much money, but they all valued work ethic so there was always food on the table. I began to understand that hard work can, in fact, pay dividends. I also began to understand the lessons of humility when my dad told me of how his mother bleached rice bags and then sewed them into shirts for him and his siblings.

At the onset of World War II, one third of Hawaii's population consisted of Americans of Japanese ancestry. They played a vital role in Hawaii's economy and proved their loyalty to America. Of those 160,000, some 2,000 were incarcerated—in sharp contrast to the 120,000 incarcerated on the mainland. The military governor of Hawaii, Lieutenant General Delos Emmons, and the head of the FBI in Hawaii, Robert Shivers, strongly opposed the incarceration of Japanese Americans. Their beliefs were proven correct when President Franklin Roosevelt authorized the formation of the 442nd Regimental Combat Team. Two thirds of its original members came from Hawaii, and the 442nd became the most highly decorated regiment of the war.

Also at the start of World War II, my parents and I were living on Lukepane Street in the Kapahulu area of Honolulu. One of the early "good done in secret" acts that I learned about later happened on December 7, 1941. My Grandfather Tamagawa saw a neighbor's home set on fire by one of our antiaircraft rounds being fired at the Japanese planes attacking Hawaii. He ran to that house and doused the fire with a garden hose. Ironically, the home belonged to the Ellis family whose son was a fireman at Pearl Harbor and would become the Fire Chief of Honolulu later in life.

We moved to the rectory of St. Mark's Episcopal Church on Campbell Avenue in Kapahulu thanks to the kindness of Father Kenneth Bray who chose to live at the Nuuanu campus of 'Iolani School. Our next-door neighbors were the Fuchise family, and they had a very strong influence on my early years. Because both my parents worked, the Fuchises raised me. They had a dry-cleaning business, and they looked after me. I called the matriarch of the family *obachan*, grandmother in Japanese. Her children were Ne, Robert, Helen, Margaret, Aki, and Frank. Ne and Margaret particularly looked after me and taught me to read at two years of age. I will always remember their kindness and how they embodied *Intoku*.

One of the oddities was Mr Fuchise. He became almost a recluse during World War II as he still revered the Emperor of Japan and could not bring himself to believe that Japan would attack the United States. He fully supported his adopted country but kept a picture of the Japanese Emperor in his bedroom. Both Aki and Frank served in the military and Aki became one of my heroes when he was decorated while fighting in the battle of Taejon during the early days of the Korean War. Aki was a corporal, and my respect for him caused me to name my dog Corporal in his honor.

My dad wasn't quite sure what he wanted to do after graduating from McKinley High School in Honolulu. He tried working on an interisland ship transporting cattle from the island of Hawaii to Honolulu and found that was not for him. He thought about becoming a professional boxer but felt that his vision was not good enough for him to really make a go of that. He had been an Eagle Scout and was fortunate enough to have met Wade Warren Thayer who was the Scout Executive in Honolulu. Mr Thayer (after whom I am named) offered my dad a job as an office boy and later brought him on as a professional Scouter. My father tried to enlist during World War II but was told he was too old. So, he stuck with his Scouting job and was also an air raid warden. The area he covered for the Boy Scouts included the major Army installation on Oahu, Schofield Barracks, and he was able to befriend many in the Army, who would give him military items that he would pass on to me.

After the end of World War II, we moved to the family home of my mother's father on Catherine Street in Kapahulu. My mother's father had passed away, but his desire was that his home be open to all in the family. So, for a period of time, there were three families living in the house, along with Aunty Marjorie and Uncle Paul. I slept with four of my cousins in a small 8 × 6 foot room. Times were hard, but no one complained, and we found ways to make up for the lack of money. Uncle David Brighter raised pigeons that we used to eat, and there were mango trees, a fig tree, and pear trees on the property that gave us fruit. We couldn't afford paste for school, so my mother used to help me mash leftover rice and use that as a paste.

The Catherine Street home was in a cosmopolitan neighborhood, and that was an important part of growing up and understanding how to get along with others and the value of diversity. Our next-door neighbors were the Leong family of Chinese heritage; at the back of us was the family of Sam Kapu, who was a skilled Hawaiian musician who played in the Hawaii Calls radio program. His wife, Aunty Juanita, used to take care of myself and my cousins. Across the street was the Wallace family of Hawaiian ancestry.

I began to learn some military skills while growing up on Catherine Street. During World War II, Balsa rafts had been placed outside Waikiki Beach for whatever reason. After the war, they were brought ashore and placed alongside the fence surrounding the Honolulu Zoo for storage. The beachboys learned how to make better surfboards using balsa wood and fiberglass, and they saw the rafts as an excellent source of balsa. There were a couple of occasions when they picked me up and placed me in a tree as a lookout to warn them of any policemen coming down Kapahulu Avenue or Ala Wai Boulevard. I guess that was my introduction to reconnaissance!

Tongue in cheek, I also incurred my first parachute injury. My Tamagawa grandfather had erected a clothesline that had one end anchored on a dirt mound. I would shinny up the pole and then go hand over hand down the clothesline and then pretend I was jumping out of an airplane and shouting "Geronimo." Unfortunately, I never learned what a parachute landing fall or PLF was, so one day I came down on my elbow and dislocated it!

Living in the St. Mark's rectory and my granddad's home gave my dad the ability to save enough to make a down payment on a home. Just before the start of the Korean War, we moved to Kuliouou Valley on the eastern side of Oahu. I can't think of a better place to grow up. In 1950, the valley still had a truck farm, Costa's Dairy a block away, two chicken farms, and another small dairy at the upper end of the valley. There were still undeveloped lots that were filled with trees called *koa haole* and underbrush. This made for perfect terrain to "play soldier." I would take a helmet liner that my dad had gotten along with a pistol belt, a canteen, a cast-iron Walther P38 replica pistol, and a demilitarized Springfield '03 rifle and pretend that I was on a combat patrol. I recruited my neighbors, Tommy Kaulukukui and his brother Donald, along with Wayne Ho to go on "patrol" with me. My dog Corporal played a K9 role!

There was an Army National Guard firing range at the upper end of Kuliouou Valley. One of my dad's friends was Francis Takemoto. Mr Takemoto had been commissioned as a second lieutenant in 1935 and served with the 100th Infantry Battalion during World War II. He was an educator and became a school principal, but he continued his duties with the Hawaii Army National Guard. During the Korean War, he had command of a battalion as a lieutenant colonel and would stop by our house and take me to the firing range in Kuliouou Valley. I was taught how to shoot an M-1 carbine and even a Garand rifle, despite my age. Mr Takemoto became one of my heroes, and in 1964, I was pleased to learn that he became the first brigadier general of Asian descent.

Our back-door neighbor was Tommy Kaulukukui, who had also served in World War II but never talked about his service. Like the Fuchise family in Kapahulu, I was fortunate to be part of the Kaulukukui extended family. The Hawaiian word to describe that is *hanai*. I learned to respect my elders at a very early age, and Mr Kaulukukui was always "Uncle Tommy" to me. His wife, Felice (Wong), was a nurse, and she along with their three children, Carol or Malina, Tommy Jr. or Banjie, and Donald, were very close to me. Uncle Tommy was an inspiration in more ways than one. He had been the University of Hawaii's first All-American football player in the 1930s and was extolled by the sportswriter Grantland Rice for having returned a kickoff for over 100 yards against UCLA. He sold insurance for a living but was known as a community leader and inspiration to many. Among his many accomplishments were bringing Pop Warner football to Hawaii, being the U.S. Marshal for the District of Hawaii, and being in the Office of Hawaiian Affairs.

Kuliouou was as diverse a neighborhood as one could ever expect to find. The Buffins family lived next door to the Kaulukukuis. Mr Buffins was a Black American who headed the National Association for the Advancement of Colored People in Hawaii and whose wife was Asian. Next door to us was the Ho family (Chinese Hawaiian descent) with Punchy, Arlene, Sharon, Wayne, and Whitney. Everyone got along, and other neighbors and friends were named Young, Aiwohi, Reeves,

Correa, Brash, Pascoe, Higa, Del Rosario, Quemado, Wise, Krueger, Stillman, Ching, Kekoa, Searle, Silva, Arakaki, Perry, and Kurihara. It was like living in the United Nations. I learned the value of diversity early on while living in Kuliouou.

The best example of diversity was Aunty Abigail. She was part of the Reeves *ohana* (family) and was married four times. Her first marriage was to a Taylor and she had a son, John, from that marriage. Then West Vannatta was born from her second marriage. Then Bernard, Lola, and Witt Akana came from her third. Finally, she married Nelson Ching and had Herbert, Gail, Nelson, and Deborah with him! The Reeves clan was noted for their large families. Aunty Rose Reeves had 12 children; Aunty Sister Correa had 13! Yet they always opened their arms to others in the neighborhood. You could always count on getting something to eat if you were around their homes at dinner. The elders were always looking after the younger children, and I learned to respect them and to know that there was always someone to support you, no matter what.

The elders included those a few years older than me. Two stand out. James Arakaki and Joe Kekoa made me a mascot of theirs. Both had 1946 Ford coupes. James's car was immaculate with naugahyde leather upholstery, chrome parts in his engine, a custom paint job. His was a show car. Joe's car was all beat up with paint peeling off it and holes in the upholstery. But Joe loved to drag race. They both often worked on their cars together as the engines were the same. I would be the tool boy for them, handing them a wrench or whatever tool they needed. James had me help him wash and wax his car. They took me on rides all over the island, and we would often gather at Joe's aunt's house to play music and sing. The only mischief they ever got me into was stealing watermelons in Waimanalo one night. The farmer fired a shotgun at us. Joe kept saying that we didn't need to worry because it was only filled with rock salt. Somehow, I didn't care but just ran faster!

Living in Kuliouou Valley also helped to develop my independence. As both of my parents worked, I would come home after school and have time to myself. There were all kinds of fun things to do besides playing soldier. With my friend Melvin Higa and his older brother, we built an outrigger canoe out of corrugated metal roofing and lumber that we scrounged. We set sail down Kuliouou Stream, headed for the ocean. We made it down the stream for about 400 yards all the way to Kuliouou Park. There were small waves where the stream met the ocean, and we started taking on water. We weren't smart enough to have brought something to bail the canoe out, so it ended up sinking, and we swam to shore satisfied that we had a good time.

My independence was fostered during a two-week-long bus strike. The elementary school I attended in the fourth grade was six miles from home. My dad admonished me that I needed to walk home and not accept any rides from strangers. The first day of the bus strike I followed his directions. It took me almost two hours to walk home, and I was beat from the hot weather and dehydrated. The next day and for the duration of the strike, I said the hell with what my dad said and at nine years of age started hitchhiking home!

With that independence came a great sense of mischief. The Hawaiian word is *kolohe*. I could fill volumes with the crazy things I did, but here are a couple.

One night a few of my friends were just chatting when I heard and saw a car without its lights come barreling up Kuliouou Road. I instinctively knew it was a policeman and that a neighbor had probably complained. I told my friends to stand fast until the cop started to put on his brakes. I then flipped him "the bird" and we ran away. A couple of my buddies got scared and went home, but Wayne Ho stuck with me. We played this game with the cop where Wayne and I would pop out on the road and yell at him, "Cuckoo, cuckoo, fuck you!" He would jump back in his car and try to chase us down and couldn't catch us. In frustration he took off up the valley, only to see our innocent friend nicknamed "Otsu" (Spencer Kurihara) riding his bike down the road. The cop pulled him over and threw him in the back of his car. He parked it and was talking to the neighbor who had complained. Wayne and I crawled up to the car, opened the door, and tried to get Otsu to run away. Otsu was too afraid, so Wayne and I snuck off and went home to sleep.

I also had an early sense for guerrilla warfare. This was illustrated one night when I saw a party going on at the Makino residence. The Makinos were rich from starting the *Hawaii Hochi* Japanese language newspaper. The guys and gals were dressed in tuxedoes and gowns and were dancing on a gazebo in the middle of a small fishpond. I gathered up a few of my friends and laid out a plan of action. We sneaked up on the pond with some artillery simulators that we had "found" at the National Guard range in Kuliouou. I figured out that there was a little current and that the firecrackers would float towards the gazebo. I also knew that the fuzes were waterproof, so once lit, they would stay lit. The plan worked like a charm. Puffing on my Pall Mall cigarette, I lit the fuzes and my gang threw them towards the gazebo. About six of them landed in the water, and they started going off. Water was sprayed from the blast and drenched the partygoers. We were laughing as they panicked, and they heard and saw us. The guys came running after us, but we already had a tactical advantage and a head start. As we ran down the road, I was lighting off more simulators and throwing them behind. Knowing the neighborhood far better than those chasing us, we cut across some back yards and ended up hiding at the Crozier residence as Mike Crozier was one of the gang.

Bodysurfing became a passion for me, and that was an important part of growing up and learning about myself. Kuliouou Valley was known for having some of the best bodysurfers in Hawaii. The Krueger brothers (Frank, Harold, and Rene), Richard (Black) Perry, "Fat" Ishii, "Punchy" Ho, and others were role models. So, one of the challenges was to maintain Kuliouou's reputation. That was an important lesson in life which I didn't fully understand at the time. The translation later in life was that of honor, of camaraderie, of maintaining a tradition. I may not have been as good as those before me, but it was important to try and maintain the standards that they had set. Just as importantly, there were those who were younger than me who also tried to live up to the standard. Folks like Wayne Ho, Gordon "Chico" Rosa and his brother Marshall kept up the tradition.

There were other challenges important to building character and becoming a man that were associated with bodysurfing. Unlike those who surfed the shore break, my friends and I ventured out into deeper waters further from shore. We had to be strong swimmers and willing to take the chance of being in deeper water and currents. One had to overcome a certain amount of fear to be able to do that. It also meant that the size of the waves we would catch would be much larger. My three favorite spots were Portlock Point, Sandy Beach, and Makapuu. There were times when Portlock would have waves up to 15 feet and Makapuu saw 20-foot waves at times. Sandy Beach was never that big, but the challenge there was currents that could sweep you out to sea. I had to learn to overcome fear and to deal with the rush of adrenaline that came from catching a really big wave and not getting smashed in the sand or on rocks along with not panicking when I was held underwater by a crashing wave. I also learned that there are times when no one else can know of an exhilarating experience—times when it is yourself and only yourself that can experience something remarkable. Normally, a great ride on a wave would be less than 100 yards, but there was one day when I caught a wave that kept going on and on at Portlock. I later measured the distance on a map and found that I had gone over half a mile, but that there was no one that could verify that as I was surfing alone. On another day at Makapuu, no one was on the beach. It was sunset and the waves were rolling in. At times, sharks would come close to shore at Makapuu, so my challenge to myself was to prove that I could go alone into the ocean, with darkness falling, in rough waters, and catch a wave. I did it and overcame whatever fear I had, but once more, there was no one around to share that experience. The lesson in life for me was that I could individually overcome fear, that I did not need to seek recognition, but only to prove to myself that I could do something challenging.

In my age group, there were four of us considered to be the best bodysurfers at Makapuu. My best friend from Kuliouou, Darryl Aiwohi, along with Jerry Waiolama and Charley Lum King from Waimanalo. Charley was an amazing guy who showed what perseverance and attitude can do. He lost his leg in Vietnam to a mine and was in a funk for a while. His sister, Iwalani, had married the noted Puerto Rican professional golfer Chi Chi Rodriguez. Chi Chi bought Charley a set of golf clubs and got him to start playing. Although I was not there, I heard and read of the day that Charley shot a hole-in-one. Even more remarkable was his determination to bodysurf again. He would show up at Makapuu, remove his prosthesis, and swim out away from shore. He showed what determination can do to make a difference in one's life. I've seen the same kind of determination shown by amputees coming out of Afghanistan and Iraq recently. They prove what determination and the power of the mind can do.

Another lesson learned was the value of hard work. Because both of my parents worked, I usually had a few hours by myself after school was over before they arrived home. There was time for play, but there was also work that could be done. One of the reasons I worked was because Jimmy Hudnall got me into smoking cigarettes. Jimmy was a couple of years older than me and his nickname was "Gobi" because he was as big as the Gobi Desert! He picked me up by the neck one day at Costa's Dairy, stuck a cigarette in my mouth and said, "Smoke!" I got hooked and now had to earn money to buy cigarettes. There was plenty of work in Kuliouou Valley. I picked beans for the dairy cows, shined shoes, harvested chicken eggs and candled them (referring to the practice of seeing whether an embryo had formed inside the egg by holding a candleflame up to it), delivered newspapers, worked at a trap and skeet range, did yard work, and dove for lead sinkers to melt down and resell. So hard work was bred into me at an early age.

Another positive influence came about through religion. My parents were devout Episcopalians and joined the Holy Nativity Church when we moved to Kuliouou. The rector was Reverend John Morrett. He was really a nice man and an inspiration. Before World War II, he had joined the National Guard and left his seminary studies when he sensed that war was imminent. He was captured in the Philippines and survived the Bataan Death March. After being moved four times to different prison camps, he was able to escape. After he left the Army, he finished his seminary studies and became a priest. I struck up a bond with him when I was 10 years old and hospitalized with encephalitis. I had been in a coma for a couple of days. I came out of the coma and heard my father and Reverend Morrett talking about what would be done if I died. I reached over and touched Reverend Morrett's hand and surprised him! I often say that was the first time I died and got to know God. From that point on, I lost my fear of dying. I later became an acolyte at Holy Nativity along with my buddy Fred Brown. Ironically, when I took my father to be admitted to a hospice facility in Honolulu in 2004, one of the nurses there was Reverend Morrett's son. He brought me up to date on Reverend Morrett and had him send me a copy of his book, *Soldier Priest*.

As I reflect on my life, I've thought about the importance of experiences learned by oneself, strictly on your own, that can help mold you as a person. These experiences may help you understand how to overcome fear, achieve higher goals than you thought possible, or prove something of value to you. Most often, they will not be witnessed by anyone, and therefore it may be difficult to share their value because others might think you are exaggerating or lying. Regardless, they will help mold you as a person for the rest of your life.

Here are a few of those such experiences I have had. The lessons I took away dealt with overcoming fear, understanding the feeling of exhilaration and accomplishment that can come from doing something by oneself, and understanding that one can think through situations and make choices—there are always options. Years later, it also reminded me of how I resonated with the Special Forces motto of *De Oppresso Liber* (to free the oppressed) and how I had learned early in life to deal with oppressors.

I was riding my bicycle up Kuliouou Road one day when the dogs of a hunter and taxidermist named Lee got out of their yard. They chased me and I jumped into a tree to avoid them. I sat in the tree crying with no one around. After some minutes, the dogs got tired of harassing me and went away. I came down from tree, and vowed revenge. I filled my water gun with witch hazel and went back the next day to lure the dogs to me and then shot them with witch hazel. They never harassed me again! There was another dog incident where the son of a Japanese family living at the end of Wakine Place in Kuliouou had their spitz dog bite me one day. I borrowed Melvin Higa's brother's pellet gun, crossed Kuliouou Stream and hid in the bushes on the other side overlooking where the dog was. I shot him 10 times and hoped that the son would come out so I could shoot him in the butt!

The ocean can be both a humbling and exhilarating experience. Punchy Ho, my next-door neighbor, came up with all kinds of ways to make money. That included diving for lead sinkers off Portlock Point (now known as China Walls) where surf casters used to frequently lose their sinkers. We used to dive and recover them, melt them down and sell them without regard to lead poisoning! One day I was diving with Punchy and was having a hard time coming to the surface. At first, I thought I was weak, and then it dawned on me—stupid, it's the weight of the lead that is making it hard to surface! So, I figured the solution was to cache the lead in one shallow spot and then return later to retrieve it on a manageable basis!

The last story for now is about a newspaper circulation manager who was giving Wayne Ho a hard time one day. The manager was a fat, foul-smelling guy who was threatening Wayne for not having done all his collection to turn over to the manager. He swore at Wayne and threatened to beat him up if Wayne didn't have the money for him in a few hours. While he was doing this, I spotted some big nails, retrieved them, and propped them up against all four of the manager's car tires. Somehow the manager never made it back to see Wayne that evening!

CHAPTER 2

A Rebel Finds Independence

Schooling and education certainly play a role in determining a person's future along with their character. As I reflect on my experiences, I believe that there are different parts of schooling and education that are involved in what a person becomes and how they live their lives. Importantly, those experiences may not totally be related to academics and to teachers. Sports, extracurricular activities, coaches, other students, and friends can play important roles. In addition, education can come from places other than formal schools and through people who are not formal teachers. These are the kinds of people that embody *Intoku*—they are mentors, champions, and informal teachers because they care about others and are not seeking self-gain.

I previously mentioned that my informal schooling began early in life with the Fuchise family teaching me how to read and write from the time I was two years old. I was a good student through the ninth grade, always ranking at the top of my class academically. But that changed and I became disenchanted with school. The change started when I was in the eighth grade in a public school and was suspended for fighting. Uncle Tommy Kaulukukui came to my rescue after he heard about my plight.

Uncle Tommy quietly arranged for me to get "interviewed" by Jimmy Clark, who had played for the Washington Redskins and was the football coach at St. Louis School. In addition, he had me meet with the 'Iolani School baseball coach, Ted Shaw, who had played in the Negro Major Leagues. Coach Shaw was a quiet, humble man, and that resonated with me. Coach Shaw arranged for me to meet two of his star players, Norm Matsushima, and Edwin Oshiro whose nickname was "Kengo," who talked to me and had me show them my baseball skills. That committed me to 'Iolani School and I started my ninth grade there. I should mention that high school sports in Hawaii were a big deal and the old Honolulu Stadium used to frequently see over 25,000 attendees at some of the high school football games. Recruiting for both the public and private schools was a very common thing.

I had a working scholarship at 'Iolani that required me to work for two hours a day in the cafeteria. One of the hours was at lunch and the other hour was when the rest of my classmates had a study period. For whatever reason, my father would never tell me what the tuition was at 'Iolani, but he made me feel like I was in danger of breaking the bank. As I learned years later, the tuition was slightly over $400 a year at the time, which meant that I was working in the cafeteria for less than $1 an hour—less than the minimum wage! But I enjoyed working in the cafeteria as it gave me a reprieve from the classroom and an opportunity to sneak out behind the cafeteria to have a cigarette!

The cafeteria workers were all ladies and somehow, they took a liking to me. They included Mrs Chang, the mother of one of my classmates (Dick Chang) that later in life would become the Episcopal Bishop of Hawaii; Mrs Sing, whose son Gary was a year behind me at 'Iolani; Mrs Eng, whose husband was the financial director for 'Iolani; and Mrs Takei, whose sons played football for St. Louis High and who would always admonish me not to beat up on her sons. All of them treated me like I was part of their family.

Two things happened to me in the ninth grade that had a profound effect on me. In the classroom, I got all "A"s for my grades. I also was the starting catcher for the ninth-grade baseball team. The first thing that happened was that 'Iolani was playing Mid-Pacific Institute at Ala Wai field. I had a big lead off second base when my teammate hit a line drive towards the first baseman. I slid back into second base to avoid a double play and felt as if I were punched in my eye. I jumped up and started swinging my fists but realized I could not see. Then I heard the voice of Coach Chuck Halter who calmed me down. As I learned later, the first baseman had thrown the ball trying to get a double play and it was the ball that hit me in the eye. I lost depth perception for almost a year after that.

Later that summer, even though my depth perception had not recovered, we were playing for the Hawaii championship of the Babe Ruth League. For whatever reason, Coach Halter put me in as a pinch hitter and then sent me to right field. I misplayed two balls because of my loss of depth perception, which led to a tied game and a co-championship. Coach Halter knew I was really down on myself. I got back to the dugout, and he just put his arm around my shoulder and patted it. That was another lesson learned about *Intoku*. He could have ranted and raved and chewed me out, but instead, he chose to reassure me.

That injury effectively ended my baseball days as I could not regain the hitting prowess that I had before. At the same time, I expected that my parents would reward me for my academic grades. I saw my classmates showing up with new clothes, driver's licenses, and other rewards. All I received were verbal congratulations from my parents. My father would not allow me to get a driver's license and I had to earn my own money to buy clothes. There was never any explanation for that, and it troubled me. I lost interest in getting good grades and became a lackadaisical student from that point.

Nonetheless, my education continued. There were only a few teachers who inspired me or whom I respected. Football became the only meaningful thing for me in high school. Fortunately, there were coaches who I respected, along with those who set a high standard for me in other endeavors. Somehow, I understood that there were lessons in life, lessons about being a good person, and lessons about humility that were as important as academic skills. I learned these on the athletic field, through body surfing, and through hard work along with the elders in Kuliouou like Aunty Abigail Ching, Aunty Rose Reeves, and Uncle Tommy Kaulukukui who always provided a safe haven and quiet guidance.

I also began to develop a dislike for people who misused their authority and threatened others. I previously related what I did to a newspaper circulation manager who was threatening my friend Wayne Ho. I also developed sort of a sixth sense that allowed me to anticipate what others were going to do. One night, Wayne Ho and I were outside of Kuliouou Park gigging fish at night. I saw a person next to the bath house where he was illuminated by the lights. He shone a flashlight towards us. I sensed that he was a fish and game warden. I convinced Wayne that all we should catch were eels, and we proceeded to do so. We had them in a rice bag and proceeded to come out of the water. The fish and game warden came up to us, shined his flashlight in our eyes and flashed his badge. He demanded to see what we had in the rice bag. I acted as if I were scared and said, "Yes, Sir!" while dropping the bag at his feet. Acting like he was a tough guy; he opened the bag and stuck his hand inside. The next thing Wayne and I knew he screamed and pulled his hand out of the bag. Wayne and I ran away laughing knowing that he was afraid that one of the moray eels would bite him!

In my senior year in high school, I was injured in a pre-season football game and lost my chance to be on the first team. Stupidly, I came up with a plan that I shared with an 'Iolani graduate who was the bus driver on my way home. His name was Ben Almadova, and he had been a multi-sport all-star at 'Iolani. I told him I planned on flunking so I could come back and play one more year. Ben squealed on me to Harold Han, who was an assistant coach under Uncle Tommy Kaulukukui who had become 'Iolani's football coach. Coach Han was a blocking back for the legendary All-American and All-Pro football player Frank Gifford at the University of Southern California and was a rugged guy. On the other hand, I knew he liked me along with another assistant, Moki Kealoha. Coach Han confronted me in the locker room one day before practice. He administered "wall locker counseling," i.e., throwing me against the wall lockers in the dressing room! He explained to me what the rules were and why flunking in school would not allow me to have an additional year. He got my attention! I did graduate, but the three years of goofing off academically did not help me. I scored very high on the National Merit Scholarship test and the Scholastic Aptitude Test, but my grades did not justify a scholarship.

That did not bother me as I had plans to either join the Air Force with Roy Tonaki, one of my classmates, or become a beach boy with my friend Wilfred "Mo" Keale who became a television actor and entertainer later in life. My parents pressured me into going to college. I knew I did not want to go to the University of Hawaii as there would be too many distractions hanging out with Mo and being a beach boy. I was scheduled to take the University of Hawaii admission examination and did not want to pass as I knew my parents would pressure me into attending that school. A bunch of us were shooting billiards at the Varsity Pool Hall near the university on the day of the admissions exam. We had been issued tickets to gain entrance to the examination. A few minutes before the exam, I took my ticket and stuck it in the pocket of Mel Tom and told him to take the test for me. Mel had been an all-star basketball player at Maryknoll High School and was not the smartest cookie in town. He was such a good friend that he didn't know how to say "no," so he went to take the exam for me. I knew he would flunk—as it turned out, he passed. Years later, I found out that it was another mutual friend, Clarence Scanlan, who had helped Mel cheat to pass the exam. Hilariously, when Mel took the test himself, he flunked. We had a good laugh over that a few years later when I was in the Army and ran into Mel in San Jose, California, where he was attending junior college. Mel became a professional football player for the Chicago Bears and Philadelphia Eagles, and his daughter became a multi-year Olympic volleyball player.

Well, I persuaded my parents to allow me to go to Lewis & Clark College, in Portland, Oregon. I can't remember what made me choose Lewis & Clark other than that I knew I had a job waiting that would pay two-thirds of my room and board. Ron Lee and "Bones" Siu were 'Iolani classmates who were also going to Lewis & Clark. The three of us stopped off in San Francisco to do some sightseeing. We got lost, but I took charge and told them I knew where we were. I kept circling until I did get my bearings and got us back to where we were staying.

At Lewis & Clark, freshmen were supposed to wear beanies as a minor form of harassment. I refused to do so with my dormitory roommate, Dave Pfaff, encouraging me to be defiant. Dave was in his senior year, and we got along well. The sophomores were supposed to challenge the freshmen who did not wear their beanies. The penalty was to get thrown into the reflecting pool at Lewis & Clark. One night Ron Lee and I were challenged by sophomores—we took up karate stances and shouted *kiai*, and the sophomores were afraid to take us on. I finally laughed and dove into the pool, but still refused to wear the beanie.

I settled into school and kept wondering what I should major in and why I had ever decided to go to college. Most of the classes were not very interesting or challenging to me. I also discovered that I needed to make more money to keep myself in school. So, I began to work additional hours for the college food service to get more money. I also discovered that Oregon got cold. I scraped up my money and went down to a military surplus store and stocked up with clothes to keep me warm. There were those who thought I was a military veteran, and I was invited to join the Veterans Club. I explained to them that I had never served and the reason

I had military items (without insignia) was that was all I could afford. The members of the club appreciated my honesty and many of them became good friends.

I found out what snow was all about when winter came around. There was a steep road bordering the school property, and on one snowy day, several of us came up with the idea of going sledding by taking some trays out of the cafeteria and sliding down the road. On my second slide I veered off course and ended up in a ditch with ice cold water. Brrrrr! Welcome to cold weather!

I started to make a lot of friends. The social life gave me a reprieve from working and I never put much effort into my studies as the professors and subjects were not very interesting to me. One of my close friends was Richard Rathbun from Palo Alto, California. He had a car and invited me to visit his family during Christmas and Easter vacations. The greatest thing about that friendship was that I was able to meet Professor Harry Rathbun, Richard's father. Professor Rathbun was a professor emeritus of the Stanford Law School. He had assisted William Hewlett and David Packard when they started the Hewlett and Packard company and received a substantial amount of money for his efforts. More importantly, Professor Rathbun was a very humble man who wanted to do things for other people. He started an effort known as Creative Initiative and wrote a book with that name. Professor Rathbun was concerned about how to get people to live up to their potential and to change the world for the betterment of humanity. His quiet demeanor and ability to see different issues with a calm mind made a significant impression on me. When it comes to *Intoku*, those qualities of calmness and reasonability are key ingredients to being able to do good without drawing attention to oneself.

Back at Lewis & Clark, I must admit that the social side of school was becoming more meaningful to me than academics. There were a number of fraternities that sought to have me join, but I thought their secret ceremonies and closed nature were not for me. Most of my friends were of the same mind and included basketball players like Bert Lundmark and Bob Brooks. Other rebels included Kilburn Roby and Gordon Alberti.

There were lounges on each floor of the dormitory that were allocated to the different fraternities to hold their meetings. One night my roommate Dave Pfaff talked me into playing a prank on the fraternity on the floor beneath our room. Dave had a tape recorder and carefully lowered a microphone so we could record their secret rites. After recording their rites, Dave turned the volume up on the recorder and began to play it back. We had a plan, so I stood in the doorway at the stairwell and shouted a loud *kiai* as the fraternity types came rushing up the stairs. That scared the daylights out of them, and they retreated. Dave made them negotiate to get the tape recording from him. He and I had a big laugh over that prank.

That same fraternity had painted a large boulder in front of the dormitory along with the Greek letters for their name. I had tried to reconstitute some powdered poi mix from Hawaii that did not turn out well. I took that lumpy, brownish paste and smeared it all over the boulder. The fraternity guys were afraid to touch it … they thought it was some sort of biological agent! After several weeks, the poi finally washed off the boulder, but the fraternity boys kept wondering about the "poison." Another good laugh on my part.

Another friend was a fellow named Larry Hanks. Larry was a hippie with long hair who sang folk songs while strumming his guitar. Like myself, he didn't have a lot of money but was a smoker. He and I went out and bought a cigarette-rolling device and would roll our own cigarettes. From time to time, we would wander down to Caramico's Pizza down the hill from Lewis & Clark. We befriended the waitresses and convinced them to give us the leftover pizza from customers who had not finished their meal.

One of the best things that happened to me during my freshman year was to meet Moon Yo Woo. Moon was from Korea, had previously attended Lewis & Clark, and was a graduate student at Oregon State. He was very proficient at Kong Su, a form of Shotokan Karate practiced in Korea, and would come up from Corvallis to teach Kong Su. I enrolled in his class and really enjoyed his teaching. At five feet four inches in height, he could jump and kick the bottom of a basketball hoop. Despite his slight stature, he had excellent board- and brick-breaking skills. I quickly became one of his better students and developed my martial arts skills under Moon.

I returned to Hawaii for the summer of 1960 with the desire to make more money than I had working in a pineapple cannery for the three previous summers. My buddy Billy Brash and I saw an advertisement for painter's helpers and we went for an interview. We were hired by a wonderful older man by the name of Gunichi Morioka. He was a kind person and a wonderful boss. We were helping him at an all-girls school, Sacred Hearts Academy. Our first job was to refinish the desk/chair sets in several classrooms by sanding them down and refinishing them. On one day I learned one of my first lessons on explosives. Mr Morioka had me take the sawdust from sanding the desks and chairs and dispose of it in an incinerator. I walked up to the incinerator with a large box of sawdust and threw it into the fire. The next thing I knew I was flat on my back after getting blown back. Years later I learned about how to enhance explosive effects using sawdust, powdery material, and other accelerants! Nothing like learning on your own!

Mr Morioka told us that our next job would be going up on scaffolding to paint a tower at the school. Billy Brash was afraid of heights and I had a residual problem with a weak ankle that left me very unstable on things like scaffolding. With great regret, we tried to explain that to Mr Morioka. Unfortunately, he didn't quite understand, and Billy and I regrettably had to leave his employment.

We saw an ad for a house mover and signed up with what turned out to be a tyrant. He was abusive, always yelling at us and nothing we did was good enough for him. He would make us work over 60 hours in one week and then less than 20 the next week so he did not have to pay us overtime. I had enough of his abuse and got Billy, along with a Samoan who had joined us, to simply not show up for work on a day when we knew he had a critical deadline to meet and would lose money if he was not able to move the house on that day.

I then found a great job working as an interior cleaner for Hawaiian Airlines. The bosses were great, the pay very good, and the other workers were all helpful to each other. I worked the swing shift. Because of the timing and the fact that I did not have a car, I was lucky in that my other Kuliouou friend, Billy Pascoe, worked the midnight shift. When I finished my shift, I would climb in the back of his car where he had removed the rear seat and put down a plywood floor and get my sleep. I don't know what I would have done if it weren't for Billy's kindness.

Returning to Lewis & Clark opened another chapter in my life. I still had no idea what I was going to do with a college degree. I was also still on the hook to pay a major portion of my school costs and started working even more hours in the cafeteria for ARA Company. I learned something else about myself, which was that in addition to bullies and those who misused authority, I did not care for egotistical persons. The embodiment of egotistical attitudes resided in the fraternities at Lewis & Clark. Intramural sports were a big thing, so I decided to start a spoof fraternity and named it the Yogi Bears. The intent was to compete against the fraternities and to crush their egos by winning the intramural sports competition. I also learned that I seemed to have a talent to recruit others and to have them join me in doing different things.

The Yogi Bears finished second in flag football, won two sections of the volleyball intramurals, and were posing a great threat particularly to the fraternity composed of varsity athletes. In basketball, there were again two divisions, and the Yogi Bears won the lesser division. For the higher division, I had recruited a former Marine who left the basketball team and was six feet eight inches tall (Bob Heflin), an All-Class B High School all-star in Oregon (Hall Thomas), Ron Kenagy, and two Black football players that the athletic fraternity shunned, Sam Macon, a former Army soldier, and Nate Jones, a former Air Force enlistee. Nate was later to become a National Football League referee. We were running over the opposition and the final game was against the athletic fraternity (Phi Coms). The Yogi Bears were well ahead in the first half. At half-time I noticed that a couple of the Phi Coms had a private conversation with the referee. In the second half, the referee (who was the Lewis & Clark track coach appropriately named Eldon Fix) called over 20 fouls on the Yogi Bears and none on the Phi Coms. At the end of the game, he also made a call that said the ball went out of bounds off Sam Macon, which was a bad call. He then did not check the ball in and allowed the Phi Coms to just toss the ball in and win by two points. I was livid.

Later in the year, two intramural sports competitions were conveniently "cancelled." I still believe the reason was that the Phi Coms put the pressure to cancel the events because they knew who I had recruited for the swimming and track competitions. That left a very bad taste in my mouth. Many of the athletes were still friends of mine, but one smart-ass chose to tease me one day about the basketball loss. I lost my temper, jumped on a cafeteria table at lunch, and was proceeding to beat him up. I was tackled by Wally Sparks, a 280-pound tackle and Dick Miller, a tight end on the football team. They took me to Dick's car and drove me off until I cooled off. The perpetrator avoided me thereafter as he knew one cross word from him and he would have ended up in the hospital.

There were other trials and tribulations my sophomore year. The athletic conference rule was that one had to play two sports to qualify for an athletic scholarship. I still had good baseball skills and was working out with one of the varsity pitchers, Gordon Alberti, who believed I could make the baseball team. I then thought I could go out for the wrestling team and qualify for a scholarship based on wrestling and baseball. A couple of friends who were on the wrestling team were teaching me the skills and I thought I was ready. On the first day of practice, I ended up fracturing my ankle. So much for plans! One of the memorable experiences was to still be in my cast during Easter break without anywhere to go. I convinced the cafeteria manager to allow me to clean the dining hall during the one-week break and was able to stay in the women's restroom where there was a cot to sleep in.

I was developing quite a reputation as a rebel and prankster. On one spring day, I talked Bert Lundmark, Bob Brooks, Kib Roby, and several others into opening the doors on a number of cars (no one locked their doors), putting the gear into neutral, and then coasting them down the hill that the dormitories were on to other locations on campus. All my buddies were called in and chastised, but somehow, I was never called in. I guess I learned the skill of covert operations called plausible deniability.

The real watershed event came about in the spring. I was called into the office of Karlin Kapper-Johnson, the international relations professor. He looked at me and said, "Young man, you're stupid." That got my blood boiling, but I sensed he was trying to tell me something, and indeed he was. He told me that my grade point average was too low. I remarked that I still had about a 2.5 average out of 4 which was more than passing. He countered by saying that was insufficient to get into graduate school. That shocked me as I had never considered graduate school. He felt that I had a future in international relations but knew I needed a graduate degree to do well in that field. As we talked through the reason I was not doing better academically, it came to light that I was working 60–80 hours a week to make enough money to put myself through school. He convinced me that the best thing I could do would be to transfer to a lower-cost school and concentrate more on my studies. He helped me develop a plan where I would transfer to Los Angeles State College in California.

CHAPTER 3

The Army Calls!

The summer of 1961 saw me again returning to Hawaii and benefiting from getting a job through a man named Mead who lived in Kuliouou. He brought me on as a driver's helper with HC&D, an affiliate of Allied Van Lines, and paired me with one of the tough guys from Kuliouou, nicknamed "Fat Ishii." I made very good wages and saved them to help me with the transfer to Los Angeles State College, where I had been accepted, while also securing a job with the same food service company that I had worked for at Lewis & Clark College. I also decided to live with my best friend, Darryl Aiwohi and four guys from Hawaii, who were attending school in Inglewood, California.

I was optimistic about a new start, but I would learn the value of better planning through a series of mistakes that would lead me to join the Army. The first mistake was to discover that the school was some 20 miles away from Inglewood. Then I found out that I had to pay my tuition up front rather than the arrangement I had at Lewis & Clark where my work agreement was sufficient to reduce the tuition. Accordingly, I could not register for classes until I had made full payment.

Oops! I had left my savings with my dad in Hawaii, and it would take about a week to get the funds transferred. Then I came up with a not-so-brilliant idea of staying out of school for a semester and earning enough money so I wouldn't have to work at all. I figured that my previous employment with Hawaiian Airlines and with the Allied Van Lines affiliate would make it easy for me to find a job at Los Angeles International Airport or with Allied Van Lines, which was headquartered in Inglewood. Wrong! I stood in line literally around a city block in Inglewood and was told that I might be able to get a job in three months!

My Kong Su teacher from Oregon, Moon Yo Woo, tried to help me out. He found a location in the Watts area of Los Angeles to open a martial arts school, and I helped him get it ready. His thought was that I could be one of the instructors and make money that way. I felt that I was imposing on Moon, and that bothered me because he was so kind, and I did not want to take advantage of anyone. So, I came up with another not-so-brilliant idea. I was going to make a ton of money betting on horse races at Hollywood Park in Inglewood. I thought I had a system down, so I was going to make it big and set out one day to make my fortune. Well, by the fourth race of the day, I had lost virtually all my savings.

I shrugged my shoulders and said to myself that I'm going to join the Marines because I knew my friends Bert Lundmark and Bob Brooks had signed up for the Marine Platoon Leaders program. I headed for the Marine recruiting station and found that the recruiter was not around. I shrugged my shoulders again and found the Air Force recruiting station thinking that they might still have that martial arts training program in Japan. As I proceeded up the stairs to the Air Force recruiter, I felt a tap on my shoulder, and it was an Army master sergeant. To cut a long story short, he sold me a bill of goods and lied, as I was to find out later. I made my apologies to Moon Yo Woo, Darryl, and the other guys in Inglewood, and got set to join the Army.

On the day of my enlistment, I was interviewed by an older infantry captain who checked my enlistment papers. He asked me if my recruiter had told me that the Airborne quotas were filled. I replied that he had not, and the captain told me that I did not have to enlist as my first choice could not be granted. I told him that I had a small handbag with a change of clothing, $40 in my pocket and that I was 2,500 miles away from home across the Pacific Ocean and that I had no choice.

He looked at my papers and shouted, "EUSA, son, do you know where that is?" I replied that I did not. He was visibly shaken and said, "That's Korea!" He had the Combat Infantryman's Badge and a Silver Star, and I assumed that he had a traumatic experience in Korea. I remarked that I had asked for an assignment to Japan and not Korea. He shook his head and again said that I did not have to enlist. I again repeated that I had no choice. So, I entered the Army as a regular Army unassigned enlistee.

Despite all these mistakes and setbacks, I was still optimistic. One of the lessons I had learned early in life was to never "cry in my soup," that bad things could happen and be overcome. I reminded myself that in surfing there were times when one got smashed by a wave, but that I had never given up. I boarded a train from Los Angeles to Fort Ord, California, to begin basic training still optimistic that everything would be all right.

I was assigned to a platoon with a mix of draftees and regular Army enlistees. The Platoon Drill Sergeant was Francisco Champaco. His boots were spit shined and his fatigues starched and creased. He gathered the platoon, whipped off his helmet liner, and said, "My name is Champaco, the Japanese missed killing me," while pointing to a jagged scar on his head. I was trying to hide my name tag! As it turned out, Sergeant Champaco took a liking to me as he saw I would go out of my way to help others in the platoon. During the first week of basic training, the company commander inspected our platoon. He was a first lieutenant named Pacheco who had gone to Saint Louis High School in Hawaii. He asked me if I wanted to transfer to another platoon in the company that was composed of soldiers from Hawaii. Because of my respect for Sergeant Champaco, I told Lieutenant Pacheco that I was satisfied staying where I was. He looked down at my pistol belt and saw that I had used a shoelace to repair it. He then took off his own pistol belt and gave it to me. The kind of leadership that Pacheco and Champaco showed impressed me greatly. They were all about taking care of soldiers, a lesson that I would never forget. I enjoyed basic training with my only disappointment coming when I again volunteered to go Airborne only to be told two days before basic training ended that there were no slots. That also meant that I received my orders for my first assignment outside of basic training at the last minute. The orders read, "Special Troops, Fort Monmouth, New Jersey." I asked Sergeant Champaco if he knew where that was. He had no idea and could not find anyone that had ever heard of it.

***

En route to Fort Monmouth, I went back to Los Angeles with the intention of finding the recruiter that lied to me and to beat him up. He was nowhere to be found! The Fort Ord Travel Office had booked a flight for me to Newark airport and gave me no other information on how to get to the post. The next adventure was about to start. I landed at Newark and could not find any military personnel in the terminal. I grabbed my duffel bag and went outside where I saw a sign that read, "Bus Operator." There was a phone under the sign, so I strolled over, picked it up, and a female answered. I told her that I was at Newark airport and was trying to find a bus to catch to Fort Monmouth. She answered by asking, "What bus?" After a few more futile tries, I finally said, "I don't know—a white bus, a yellow bus, a red bus" and hung up. After waiting outside in the cold for about 20 minutes, a bus showed up. I asked the driver if the bus went to Fort Monmouth. He gruffly answered, "Get in." He didn't ask me for any money, so I figured I had nothing to lose. After about an hour's drive, he says, "Hey kid, get off." I could see the gate of a military installation, so I did. That was my welcome to the cultural shock of being in the New Jersey/New York area. As I later learned the bus driver was actually being kind to me!

I walked up to the gate and asked the Military Police officer manning the gate if this was Fort Monmouth and how could I get to Special Troops. He proceeded to give me a hard time and gave me some bad directions. I walked for about 45 minutes and finally had someone point out where the Special Troops barracks was. In no way were Special Troops anything special—it was the Army's way of designating a catch-all support organization. The first week of my assignment I was given a battery of tests, and then I was informed that I would be assigned to the Military Police company as a clerk. That disappointed me greatly as I certainly did not join the Army to be a clerk! But Fort Monmouth was the Army's Signal Center and school and there were no combat units assigned. The MP company was in the same quadrangle as the Special Troops company and only about 200 meters away, and that made me question why the MP at the gate had given me bad directions.

Little did I know at the time but getting assigned to the Military Police company was the best thing that could have happened to me on a post like Fort Monmouth. The next year and a half was filled with learning experiences and being mentored by some great soldiers. I crossed the quadrangle on a cold January day and knocked on the door of the orderly room. The first sergeant sat there in wrinkled khakis and asked me why I was there. I told him I had orders to report to the MP company. He looked me up and down and then asked me, "How good are you?" I had no idea what he meant. He finally said, "With this," and held up his fist. I replied that I could take care of myself. He said, "Okay, here's where you sit," and pointed to a desk next to his. He then scribbled something on a piece of paper, handed it to me and said, "figure it out." It was someone's name. I put two and two together and got into a fight that night. I must have passed the test as First Sergeant Ken Dijulio was pleased the next morning. It was a different Army in 1961, one where there were informal means of taking care of disciplinary problems, so I was to be his enforcer on some occasions when he thought someone just needed to have their butt kicked rather than receive an Article 15 or court-martial. Dijulio was a tough guy but had a great heart and cared about the troops. He taught me a lot about how to read people.

I was also very fortunate to have a great company commander, Walter F. Junkins. Junkins had fought in both World War II and Korea, reached the rank of master sergeant, and then got commissioned. He knew how First Sergeant Dijulio was using me as an enforcer and just turned his head. Staff Sergeant Ed Holowienka taught me the ropes of how to be a company clerk, but at the same time, I was taken under the wing of several others. They included the supply sergeant, Sergeant First Class Nick Skoulas and the mess sergeant, Sergeant First Class Pappa. But the one I learned the most from was a Criminal Investigation Division Agent William Fitzpatrick. Bill, Holowienka, Dijulio, and Staff Sergeant Anderson figured that I needed to learn how to be an MP also. By day, I was the company clerk; by night, I would go out with Bill Fitzpatrick or Anderson to learn how to be an investigator and MP. They made me live up to my potential, and I am grateful for their guidance and what they taught me. The clear lesson I learned was the importance of mentors and champions.

Bill Fitzpatrick had enlisted in the Marine Corps during World War II and lied about his age. He came from a large family out of Kearney, New Jersey. His oldest brother, Frank, was a New York Port Authority policeman; his older sister was a Catholic nun; his two younger brothers were Tommy and Pete; and he had two younger sisters. The rest of the family were named O'Loughlin. Bill, always a rebel, did not particularly care for his father, so he changed his name to his mother's maiden name: Fitzpatrick. Bill would take me to the family home on occasion and they made me part of the family. His family told me the story of how Bill was confronted by the regimental sergeant major on Guadalcanal the day after he reached legal age (16), who proceeded to chew him out and then officially welcome him to the Marine Corps.

Bill did much of his work at night, so he would gather me up and make me accompany him on whatever it was that he was doing that night. I could fill another book with all the things he taught me and the adventures I had with him. Probably the three most memorable follow.

Bill had me respond with him to a disturbance call from the Women's Army Corps barracks. We walked in and found that there had been a lover's quarrel between two female soldiers, one Black and the other white. The Black soldier was brandishing a knife and screaming her head off. Bill told me to get a towel which I did only to be told by him, "Wet it down, dumbass." I did that and Bill took the towel, twirled it, and then snapped it in the face of the gal wielding the knife. The knife went one way and she went to the floor in pain. Then Bill tells me to handcuff this nude female! The real lesson learned was that one doesn't have to pull a gun all the time.

On another occasion, we were standing by the MP desk station when the bank alarm on the post went off. Bill shouts at me and we jump in his car and head for the bank. He hollers at me to go down this alley while he goes in another direction. I am running down the alley when it dawns on me that I don't have a weapon. I came to a screeching halt, looked around and picked up the lid on a garbage can so I would at least have something to throw at anyone I might encounter. I don't know what I learned from that incident other than to be afraid!

The last story I'll tell about Bill was the night that we got a call that the Nike missile battery radar site in New York that was linked to the headquarters at Sandy Hook, New Jersey, was not operative. Using his intuition, Bill figured out that someone had probably cut the cable leading from Sandy Hook to New York. He grabbed another CID agent and told me grab a heavy wooden box that held a Speed Graphic camera. We tracked the cable, and sure enough, Bill's intuition was correct. We found where the cable had been cut, probably by someone trying to steal copper wire from it. I had been lugging the heavy box for over a mile at that point. Bill had me open it, pulled out the camera, and found that there was no film in the box! He could have easily blamed me but knew that I had no idea of what to check for. He blamed himself and we had a good laugh over that mistake. It reinforced a lesson that not everything will go perfectly in life, and one needs to be resilient.

I was really enjoying being in the Army and being a soldier. Being the company clerk was not the most challenging of jobs, but I did learn a lot about administrative tasks. The job was easy for me, so I filled my time taking correspondence courses, working as an MP at night, and playing sports. The next 18 months saw me accomplish a lot. As I look back on that time, it was as intense a time as I've ever had. Everything I learned was through what the Army called on-the-job training or OJT. Captain Walt Junkins wanted me to apply for OCS, but I did not think I was qualified. But he, Ed Holowienka, DiJulio and others kept pushing me to improve myself. They made me compete for the Military Policeman of the Quarter and then the Post Soldier of the Month. Thanks to their mentorship and browbeating me, I won both awards.

It was a different Army in the early 1960s. Each company had a cell where they could lock someone up if needed and the way disciplinary problems were dealt with was almost totally different. As an example, one morning I went to the mess hall to get a cup of coffee and was accosted by one of the MPs who was on kitchen police duty that day. He started making racist remarks at me. Amazingly, this was one of the very few occasions that I had run into racial prejudice at Fort Monmouth. When he persisted after I told him to knock it off, I grabbed him and held his face under the coffee urn and asked him if he wanted hot coffee for his eyes or hot water for his dirty mouth. I made the mistake of letting him go. He charged at me, and I had my back against a wall when I turned around. I gave him a head butt that broke his nose, then I punched him into a wooden rack of metal trays that we used to eat out of. The rack fell over with all the trays on him and he had to be sent to the hospital. I thought I was in trouble, but Sergeant First Class Pappa, the mess sergeant, had seen what occurred and stood up for me. First Sergeant Dijulio just laughed about it. Captain Junkins looked at me and snorted, then said, "I heard you didn't knock him out!"

Our slow-pitch softball team won the Post Championship, and I was the all-star pitcher and threw a no-hitter in one game. But it was a breeze because of the quality of the players we had. John Lee was a Chicago Cubs farmhand and would hit at least one homer every game. Our catcher, Walt Carter, was a Baltimore Oriole minor leaguer, and Lieutenant Reese Boyd was an outfielder who was a track star at Morgan State University and could run under any ball hit close to him. I was on the detail that fired 50-gun salutes on holidays from a 75 mm pack howitzer. I started out as the loader and ended up leading the detail. With Staff Sergeant Anderson and a couple of others, we taught self-defense to police at the Monmouth and Freehold County academies and put on demonstrations for public groups.

In the fall of 1962, Andy formed a flag football team. We had a great team and played for the Post Championship on a frozen field. We lost the game, but Andy and the rest of the team voted me as the Most Valuable Player. After losing the championship game, Andy talked the NCO Club, which was now being run by Nick Skoulas, the former supply sergeant, into some free beer. Andy handed me a beer and the bottle slipped through my hand and broke as it hit the floor. What had happened was that I had broken both my hands on the frozen field. The next morning, I went to the Post Hospital where they put a cast on one hand and then started to do so on the other. I stopped them, and when they asked why, I simply said that I needed to be able to wipe myself after going to the toilet! They ended up putting a splint on the other hand. I got a reprieve from typing for a while. My roommate Freddie Meadows helped me out.

The MP company assigned one MP to provide coverage at Monmouth Park, a horseracing track, during the season. Sergeant Clarence Smithers had the details for two years. He would stay up all night analyzing the races and figuring out what horses to bet on. He would see me in the morning before heading out to the racetrack and run his picks by me. I saw that he was good at picking winners, so I then started to give him a few dollars to place some bets for me. Unlike my experience at Hollywood Park, which caused me to join the Army, I started to win a goodly sum. The following year (1963), I came out over $800 ahead. Remembering that a private's pay was $72 a month, that was quite a bit of cash.

First Sergeant Dijulio retired but stayed in the Fort Monmouth area. Before he retired, he asked me to loan him $40. I knew I would probably not see the money again, but with my winnings at the horse track, and for all that he had done for me, I willingly gave him what he asked for. About four months after he retired, I heard someone knocking on the window of the orderly room. It was Mrs Dijulio. She asked me to come out and asked me if her husband had borrowed money from me. I said no, and she cut me off, and said, "Don't lie to me." With tears in her eyes, she gave me $40. Like her husband, she was a great person. She cared for soldiers and proved it through her actions.

Frank Grey, a Black American, became the acting first sergeant after Ken Dijulio's retirement. Frank was a fine solder who had been working in the Operations Office of the Provost Marshal's Office. Frank had fought both in World War II and the Korean War. His combat patch was that of the 92nd Infantry Division, which was a segregated unit during World War II. I had read an historical account that said the 92nd Division had a mixed record. Because I respected Frank Grey, I asked him candidly why he wore the 92nd Division patch when he could have worn the patch of the unit he was in during the Korean War. He acknowledged that what I had read was correct concerning the mixed record of the division. He then went on to say that the reason he wore the 92nd Division patch was in honor of those who gave their lives and who were fine soldiers. It was a lesson I'll never forget.

First Sergeant Wilson came back from Germany where he was in the U.S. Army Europe Honor Guard. Frank Grey went back to the Provost Marshal's Office and retired not long thereafter. First Sergeant Wilson was a spit-and-polish soldier. Highly shined shoes, immaculately pressed khaki or tropical worsted wool uniforms. He was a different person totally from Ken Dijulio and Frank Grey, but was a fine soldier in his own right.

Walt Junkins was promoted to major and moved to the Provost Marshal's Office. Before he left, he urged me again to apply for Officer Candidate School. I stupidly persisted in thinking I was not officer material. He then urged me to apply for a program where enlisted soldiers were allowed to go to college and get their bachelor's degrees. I did so and that was to be a great move a few years later.

Walt was replaced by First Lieutenant Tom Cook, who was a lot younger than Junkins, but cared about doing a good job and the soldiers under his command. Another change came when Nick Skoulas left to run the NCO Club. His replacement was Master Sergeant Estanislao Quitoriano who had been a Filipino Scout during World War II. I became his friend as the only other Asian Pacific Islander in the company. "Stan," as he was called, asked me to teach him how to drive. Then he decided that he was going to buy a car. I helped select one for him and found a good deal in Pennsylvania for him. I had to go with him and drive the car back as he still did not have a license!

Another colorful person was Specialist Fifth Class Juan Diaz-Leon. Juan was a cook when I joined the MP company. I found out that he had a private investigator's license and was used by both law enforcement and the courts to translate Spanish. I also found out that he had been a Military Police officer. On patrol one night, he stopped a car that was weaving down the road. He approached the driver and asked, "Who are you?" Well, the driver was the Provost Marshal Emmit Cox. The next day, Juan was no longer an MP! The better story, however, as it pertains to leadership, is that Captain Junkins felt that Juan was a good man and did not deserve to be punished. So, he convinced Juan to become a cook and allowed him to stay in the company and not have to transfer. That helped Juan and his business and his family. Leadership is taking care of your people, and Walt Junkins was superb at doing that.

As another example of Walt Junkins's leadership skills, our company armorer won the Silver Star in Korea. He was known to have a drinking problem and was deemed unfit to handle regular Military Police duties. There were no programs to deal with alcohol abuse in those days, but Walt felt that he should care for the soldier. Unfortunately, at a shift change, the oncoming MPs went to the arms room to get their weapons and found it locked. The armorer had been drinking in the arms room and passed out drunk. The arms room door was broken into to allow the oncoming shift to get their weapons. Captain Junkins had no choice in this case and had to discipline and transfer the armorer.

In February or March of 1963, Lieutenant Cook and the first sergeant came to me and told me to find a separate room in the company barracks that would house three civilians and to help them get settled in when they arrived. I was also told not to ask any questions. I did as they directed, and about a week later the three civilians showed up. All I knew was that they were from Pennsylvania, and I had no idea who they were or what their jobs were. I helped them get settled in and took them around Fort Monmouth and the Eatontown, New Jersey, area so they could take care of themselves. The only other thing I knew was that every day they would go to the post stockade that the MP company operated. The mystery was to be solved in a few months.

I came to work one morning and saw folks running around the company, and the first sergeant very excited. I asked him what was going on and he quickly replied that there was an article in *The Saturday Evening Post* that revealed a former Mafia (organized crime) figure by the name of Joe Valachi was going to be the first Mafia figure to testify before Congress and that he was being held secretly at the post stockade on Fort Monmouth! *The Saturday Evening Post* was one of the major weekly magazines in the United States at the time, so the story had national exposure. It was causing a great deal of concern because there were known death threats against Valachi and there were significant Mafia families living not far from Fort Monmouth in the Asbury Park, New Jersey, area. As it turned out, Valachi had been moved secretly from a federal prison in Pennsylvania to protect his life when he had agreed to testify before Congress. The three civilians were federal prison guards who had been sent to provide additional protection.

Colonel Cox, the Provost Marshal, immediately directed that the entire MP company go on high alert. We put sand-bagged positions on top of the stockade roof with machine guns in a couple of locations. A sand-bagged sunbathing enclosure was built for Valachi. Other positions and guard posts were placed on likely routes leading to the stockade. Thanks to the work of Chief Warrant Officer O'Brien who headed the Criminal Investigative Division Office and Bill Fitzpatrick, two MPs were quickly identified as having leaked the information to *The Saturday Evening Post* for money. They were disciplined and sent to Korea. I was told to cancel all orders for anyone else as we needed to retain our manning while Valachi was being held at Fort Monmouth.

The normal MP duty weapon was a .45-caliber pistol. Because of the concern over a possible attempt to kill Valachi orders were given to issue rifles for use at some of the fixed outposts along with the machine guns that were placed on the stockade roof. The company had just received M-14 rifles to replace the older M-1 Garand rifle along with the M-60 machine gun that replaced the 1919A6 older machine guns. On one occasion, Colonel Cox felt that he should personally check the outposts to ensure that our MPs were ready to stop any attack. As he approached one outpost, he heard a round being chambered in a rifle then he was ordered to halt and he did. The sentry then gave him a code word and Cox responded with the correct countersign. Cox then approached the MP and congratulated him on doing a good job. He then said, "Sergeant Donahey, clear your weapon." He did not see Donahey doing anything, repeated his order, and then asked him what the problem was. Donahey responded that he did not know how to clear the M-14 rifle! You better believe that Donahey got some instant instructions on how to clear the M-14 rifle. Donahey was a sergeant E5 at the time and I was a specialist fourth class. Nine years later, I ran into Donahey. Whereas I had been promoted three times and was now a sergeant first class, Donahey had been promoted but one time and was a staff sergeant!

As I mentioned previously, no one in the MP company other than the two that were disciplined for selling information to the media were allowed to rotate out of the unit. However, Walt Junkins, Chief O'Brien, and Bill Fitzpatrick came to me one day and told me that I was going to be sent to become a criminal investigator. I knew that they had my best interests at heart, so I was prepared to leave the unit. After a week or so, they came back to me and told me that, unfortunately, I did not meet the age requirement to go to CID school, but Walt Junkins had figured out a way for me to become a counterintelligence agent. I did not argue with him as I admired him as a leader. Within days I had orders directing me to attend the Counterintelligence Agent Course at Fort Holabird, MD. I had mixed feelings only because no one else in the company was allowed to leave on orders, but Junkins and Fitzpatrick made it clear that I was to go! I bid a reluctant farewell to the many friends I had made in the MP company, packed my bags and was out the door on my next adventure in the U.S. Army.

CHAPTER 4

Learning the Craft of Intelligence and Leadership

My introduction to the craft of intelligence began in the summer of 1963 when I reported to Fort Holabird, Maryland, to attend the Counterintelligence Agent Course. The course was about six months long, and it was a great learning experience. There were fifty in the course, and it struck me that most of them had come straight from basic training. There were twelve in the course that had prior service including two Marine sergeants, two from the 82nd Airborne Division, one from the 101st Airborne Division and one from the Intelligence School. I immediately bonded with the Marines and the three that were Airborne. These three were William Franklin, Gerald Halbert, and David Smith.

The course was intense and embodied all the skills needed by a counterintelligence agent to include tactical human intelligence or agent handling skills. In addition, we were taught how to conduct offensive counterintelligence operations against an adversary, how to conduct investigations, how to interview subjects of an investigation and other sources of information, and surveillance/counter-surveillance skills. There was a great deal of practical work, which made the course even more enjoyable. As an example, downtown Baltimore, Maryland, was used for surveillance exercises to allow real experience in an urban area.

The best instructors were civilians. Being able to type was a mandatory subject as agents were required to type various reports in detail. The instructor was Mrs Klecka who had held the world record for speed typing when she was younger. Mrs Klecka was remarkable. She could be facing away from students and call out a student by name and tell them what they were doing wrong. She would say things like, "Stop looking at your keyboard" or "Keep your fingers on the keys!" Her hearing acuity was unparalleled. Through her efforts, I increased my typing speed to over 100 words a minute.

There were three professional actors used in various scenarios to help the students learn the art of interrogation, elicitation of information, and how to interview people providing information or those under investigation. One of them was a female and the other two males with all three of them being superb at acting out different roles.

One of the males drove many of the students up the wall because one of the roles he played was that of a homosexual. Many of the students had a challenging time dealing with him when he played that role.

One of the things that struck me as somewhat odd was that I cannot remember any of the instructors in uniform as exceptional. Most were adequate, and a few left something to be desired, but none of them came across as being truly exceptional instructors like the civilians were.

There were several instances where I wondered about the leadership skills of those in the intelligence field. On the day that President John F. Kennedy was assassinated, a major came into our classroom. He was crying, physically shaking, and announced that President Kennedy had been assassinated. I could not help but question why he was so distraught and how he might react on the battlefield in an intense firefight.

The following week was Thanksgiving. I was invited by my Lewis & Clark College friend, Bert Lundmark, and his wife, Liz (Marto), to have Thanksgiving dinner with them. Bert was in school at Quantico Marine Base, Virginia, and had been commissioned a second lieutenant. I wanted to buy them a gift and went shopping. In one store, I asked the sales clerk how much a vase cost. She sneered at me and said, "More than you can afford." I didn't know if her attitude was based on racism or my rank (I was in uniform). It angered me, and I responded with, "How much would it cost you if I dropped it on the floor and it broke?" Her eyes got really big and she was speechless. I just turned and walked out of the store not wanting to give them my business. I did find a gift for Bert and Liz and had a memorable Thanksgiving dinner with them.

There was one master sergeant in our class who was made the class leader. Then there were some other sergeants first class in the class also. It appeared that all of them had language skills and were transitioning from being interrogators to counterintelligence agents. They were nice enough persons but did not seem to have good leadership skills that I believed noncommissioned officers should have. I felt that my friends Franklin, Halbert, Smith, and the two Marines had much greater leadership skills than those who were formerly military intelligence noncommissioned officers.

The one instance where I really questioned the quality of the leadership came at the end of the course. I was supposed to be the honor graduate for the course. At the last minute, one of the major tests was dropped to allow a classmate who had been an administrative clerk in the Intelligence School to become the honor graduate. That was a clear disappointment to me and caused me to question the integrity of people who would do that sort of manipulation. I was reminded that for months the instructors had pounded the concept of LIDMC (pronounced Lid Mack) into the students. It stands for Loyalty, Integrity, Discretion, Morals, and Character. Those were the things you looked for to determine a person's suitability for a security clearance as well as the qualities you may want in a recruited agent. The school officials certainly did not demonstrate these qualities by manipulating the course results.

I did not dwell on my disappointment as I was excited when I received my orders to go to Korea. I saw the assignment as a chance to be in support of a tactical unit that was faced with the prospect of dealing with combat action on the Korean Peninsula. The last practical exercise in the counterintelligence course involved a tactical scenario that really resonated with me, and I felt that working in a tactical, battlefield environment was the one that suited me the best. It was a long trip to Korea; the first leg was on a C-121 Super Constellation propeller-driven airplane. We stopped at Tachikawa Air Base in Japan, transferred to another plane, and then flew to Kimpo Air Base outside Seoul, Korea. I reported to the 502nd Military Intelligence Battalion in Seoul and was very happy to learn that I was to be reassigned to the 191st Military Intelligence Detachment in support of the 1st Cavalry Division along the Demilitarized Zone (DMZ) in Korea. It was January of 1964 during a typical cold Korean winter, but that didn't bother me in the least because of my anticipation of being assigned to the 1st Cavalry Division.

Sergeant First Class Humberto Pineda, the 191st MI Detachment first sergeant, picked me up in Seoul. We drove over two hours from Seoul in an M38 Jeep over bumpy dirt roads. The 191st had its own compound located in Paju Ri, Chunae Myon (District), Paju Gun (County), Kyonggi Do (Province). The compound was on the lower slope of a hill mass known as Charlie Block, which was a commanding terrain feature. The detachment's back fence abutted the 1st Battalion, 5th Cavalry Regiment and was enclosed by a barbed-wire fence.

Upon reaching the compound after the drive from Seoul, I was greeted by the detachment commander, Major Tomomi Ando, and the executive officer, First Lieutenant Leonard Dacquisto. I had a very favorable impression of both, along with Sergeant First Class Pineda, and my instincts proved to be right. Major Ando interviewed me and asked if I had any problem with being the covering counterintelligence agent for the three infantry battalions located north of the Imjin River that were arrayed across a portion of the DMZ that had been established with the truce agreement in 1953. That suited me fine, as I knew those battalions would be the ones to bear the brunt of any North Korean incursion across the DMZ, and I was pleased to support them.

Len Dacquisto and Humberto Pineda took me around the compound and introduced me to the others in the detachment. Most of the buildings were Quonset huts with a few other wooden structures on the compound that had offices, a motor pool, and a few other functions. It was winter and I got my introduction to "space heaters." These were stoves fed by five-gallon military cans of diesel oil. They were indeed a fire hazard, but essential to keeping everyone warm. The trick was to ensure that you had a full five-gallon can before going to sleep so you wouldn't have to get up in the middle of the night to change the fuel can.

There were about 10 agents assigned to the detachment. Realizing that I had much to learn, I was interested in finding someone who could mentor me and make me a better agent. Of the agents that were there when I first reported to the unit, Chief Warrant Officer Frank Miccio was the one that best fit that mode, along with Bob Sloan. Paul Horrigan was another that I could learn from. Major Ando and Len Dacquisto were also mentors of mine. Shortly after I joined the unit, Robert E. Cross was assigned as an agent. Bob and I bonded and had similar outlooks on the military and trying to do the best we could. Bob was assigned to an area just south of the Imjin River to include the 1st Battalion, and the 12th Cavalry Regiment. Bob continues to be a friend to this day and lives in northern Virginia.

The unit also had several Korean civilians on its rolls. There were five interpreters who were each different but very competent in what they did. These were Chon Tong Sop (nicknamed "Louie"), Kim Chong Ho, Lee Ki Yol (nicknamed "Doc"), O Pyong Ki (nicknamed "Charlie O"), and Yu Taek Chin. I quickly learned that when it came to doing anything in a dangerous situation, the two I could most rely upon were Louie Chon and Doc Lee. That is not to take away from the others, but I felt I could trust Louie and Doc to accompany me on any combat-type mission. We also had a Korean mechanic and three superb cooks. There was also a squad of so-called Korean Augmentation to the U.S. Army (KATUSAs) assigned to us for security purposes. They manned the gate to the compound and patrolled the perimeter at night. They were led by a staff sergeant and only one (Corporal Cho Nam Chun) had fluency in English. We also had our own mess hall and two excellent cooks in Mr Om and Mr Paek.

The unit needed a photographer and Major Ando asked me if I was interested. As I was eager to learn any new skills, I answered that I was interested. I was then sent for an intensive one-week on-the-job training with the 502nd MI Battalion in Seoul. I learned how to use the Leica Rangefinder camera, which was issued to military intelligence units, and how to develop film, to print and enlarge photographs. Upon return to the 191st, I found that we had a rudimentary area set aside for a darkroom and photography. I had to self-learn how to get the chemicals to the right temperature to develop film and negatives, as there was no running hot water in the darkroom. I took up photography as a hobby and invested in a Pentax single-lens reflex camera for my personal use. I also bought a Yashica twin lens reflex which was like the Roleiflex camera but a lot less expensive. Photography became a hobby, along with being valuable for an intelligence operative.

My 13-month tour with the 191st MI Detachment, along with Major Ando's leadership, allowed me to engage in every aspect of what a human intelligence operative and counterintelligence agent is expected to do. I was able to recruit and handle sources, conduct investigations, do interrogations, and participate in counter-infiltration operations by North Korean operatives.

We had a so-called area intelligence case officer who lived on the compound with us but reported directly to the 502nd MI Battalion in Seoul. I would accompany him as he launched and recovered agents that were being sent into North Korea. The DMZ in those days was not the heavily fortified and fenced border that one sees today. It was rather easy to cross the DMZ and to dispatch agents across the border. The North Koreans also used that to their advantage by frequently inserting teams into South Korea.

There were three infantry battalions from the 1st Cavalry Division stationed across the Imjin River whose main mission was to patrol the DMZ and maintain observation posts. The DMZ was a large area, and the battalions were really pushed to maintain continual patrolling of the DMZ. The south bank of the Imjin River was known as the Civilian Control Line. Only civilians who possessed passes were allowed legally across the Imjin River, and there were but two bridges (the Freedom and Libby bridges) crossing the Imjin into the area controlled by the 1st Cavalry Division. Because the economy in South Korea was not very strong, there were civilians who would take the chance of crossing the Imjin River illegally and then enter the DMZ to retrieve expended cartridges from the Korean War. They were referred to as "brass pickers" because the cartridges contained brass that would be melted down and resold.

On one occasion, a night patrol from the division encountered three figures. The order was given for them to halt, but they ignored the order. The staff sergeant leading the patrol then fired three well-placed rounds into one of them with his M-14 rifle killing the intruder. His two companions were captured. It turned out that they were brass pickers. The staff sergeant was from Hawaii, I believe his name was Mahiai, and I had to do an investigation to clear him of wrongdoing. We brought the body of the intruder back to our compound and were able to identify who he was through the interrogation of his two partners. The village from where the deceased person came from refused to accept his body. One of my interpreters and I took the body to the village government office forcing them to do what was right by burying him properly. Government officials sometimes need to be put into situations where they must do the right thing for their citizens.

Major Ando asked me to take charge of what was called the Korean National Employee Screening Office or KNESO. The office was responsible for conducting background checks on Koreans seeking employment with the Army in the 1st Cavalry Division area. In addition, pre-marriage checks were made on soldiers who had applied to marry a Korean. I was reluctant to take charge but found that it was a nominal position with my primary responsibility being to ensure that our interpreters were assigned equitably to assist the three agents assigned to do these background checks. All that was required was to do a check with an applicant's neighbor, a records check with Korean National Police, and a health check for marriage applications. The assigned agents needed no supervision, so it was a nominal position. In addition, I was responsible for submitting status reports of the number of investigations conducted monthly and that was easy to do. The investigating agents prepared succinct reports and provided me with a status count. My reward was to get promoted twice in one year, first to sergeant and then to staff sergeant.

Here are some highlights of my time with the 191st MI Detachment. I received a call for help from the 1st Cavalry Division Criminal Investigation Division (CID) Office. They had picked up a young soldier who was suspected of dealing in drugs but also of selling communications instructions illegally. The CID Agents knew the soldier was guilty of drug dealing but could not get the evidence they wanted or a confession. They thought that I might be able to help. I picked the soldier up, handcuffed him and drove him in my jeep back to the 191st MI compound and locked him in a cell that we had. He was a big man and was screaming obscenities at me. I never said a word, left the hutch with the cell and returned with two five-gallon cans of fuel. It was chilly and a space heater was operating. I placed the cans right outside the cell and then opened the door to the space heater with the flames visible. The soldier was confused and asked me what I was doing. I never said a word, but then went back to the fuel cans and opened them up. His eyes opened wide, and he stopped shouting obscenities. He then started to mumble; you can't pour that fuel, I'll burn to death. Again, I never said a word but picked up a 2 × 4-inch board and proceeded to break it with a loud *kiai*. He was petrified at this point. I then spoke and told him that I was opening the cell and if he thought he was so tough I would take him on and see how tough he was. After seeing me break the board, he was afraid. I then opened the cell, told him to sit down on the floor and began interrogating him. It was clear that he had not sold the communications instructions which would have been a matter for counterintelligence to handle, but I got him to provide details on his drug dealing. I then handcuffed him and took him back to the CID Office and gave them the details of the soldier's drug dealing. This incident reinforced in me the power of psychological approaches to dealing with people. Never once did I mention pouring the fuel on the floor, but that is what he had in his mind. The loud *kiai* and board breaking also put him in a cooperative mood. It's all about getting into someone's mind!

One night I received a call that a soldier had been found huddled under one of the two bridges that crossed the Imjin River into the DMZ. It was pouring rain and the soldier was completely wet. He had a Bible in his hands. When I tried to talk to him, he would not respond and had the proverbial thousand-mile stare in his eyes. It was evident to me that he had suffered a mental breakdown. I then transported him to the Division Medical Battalion and had him admitted. The next day I talked to members of his unit and then went back to see if he was better. He was still in a catatonic state and would not talk or acknowledge that I was there. He was still clutching his Bible. I knew there was nothing to be gained by trying to interrogate him. I walked over to him, put my hand gently on his shoulder and said, "You'll be alright." Tears appeared in his eyes, but he still never said a word. I talked to the doctors and hoped that he would receive the care he needed. One must still maintain compassion for others.

Another interesting case was where two sergeants from the 1st Cavalry were pheasant hunting in the DMZ when their dog sensed the presence of Koreans in the area and started growling. The sergeants then went to see what the dog was growling at and immediately started receiving automatic weapons fire from a three-person North Korean infiltration team. The sergeants were armed with shotguns with bird shot and wisely took cover knowing they were outgunned. The North Koreans then left the area. A major effort was launched to locate them, but they had too much of a head start. This was the second time that I was called out on a so-called agent sweep—an attempt to track down and kill or capture infiltrators. The Division G2 (intelligence officer) criticized the sergeants for not attacking the North Koreans. I prepared a lengthy report supporting the sergeants and the G2 stopped his criticism. Little did I know that the thoroughness of my investigation and standing up for the sergeants would help me four years later in Vietnam.

One morning, I received a call from the 1st Battalion, 9th Cavalry Regiment patrolling the DMZ. They had picked up a Korean civilian in the DMZ. I picked the civilian up and returned to our compound to interrogate him. It was in the early fall and quite chilly outside. When he was found, he was only wearing boxer shorts, no shoes, and had a hair net on the top of his head. He wore glasses, was well-built, and appeared to be in his late 30s. My interrogation was not having any success. I was fighting a bad cold and broke it off to get some rest for myself. Several hours later I got up only to find that the individual had been transported to Seoul and the 502nd MI Battalion. I was never given a reason as to why that was done nor able to find out who the individual was. My speculation is that he was either one of our agents or a South Korean operative.

On another occasion, I assisted Bob Cross in investigating a charge made by a Korean civilian that he had been wrongfully attacked by a patrol dog in the 12th Cavalry Regimental area. Simply stated, the Korean had trespassed onto the compound and was attacked by a patrol dog. So, nothing came of his charges. The good thing that came about was that I was able to meet three NCOs from Hawaii, Sergeant Major Sammy C. S. Kealoha, Sergeant First Class Bob Bode, and Staff Sergeant Wilfred Aki. Sammy was nicknamed "Chicken Shit" for his middle initials and his strong leadership. Bob had grown up in Kapahulu in Hawaii where I had spent my early childhood. Aki was noted for being so strong that he could carry an 81 mm mortar with baseplate by himself. They became friends and I would pick them up periodically and bring them to the 191st compound to eat and drink. I cherished their friendship as it was a long time since I had any friends from Hawaii close by.

Bob Cross had a somewhat funny experience with the 12th Cavalry. On a rainy night, he was called to the 12th Cavalry to investigate a soldier who claimed to have been kidnapped by North Koreans wearing silver helmets and transported across the Imjin River where he escaped from them. Bob saw that the soldier's clothes were not wet despite him saying he swam back across the Imjin River. Bob's interrogation quickly determined that the soldier was lying and that he had missed curfew and was trying to come up with an excuse. Bob would later leave the Army and became a police officer with the Prince George's Country Department in Maryland.

Another hilarious incident was when I was called to investigate a field telephone line leading from the Division artillery compound outside the perimeter fence. I tracked the line down to a hutch in the village below the compound. Upon questioning the female occupant, she confessed that she was the girlfriend of a senior NCO in Division Artillery Headquarters. I called the NCO in and determined that he had emplaced the phone line so he could be alerted to quickly go back to the compound in the event of an emergency. I counseled the NCO on his actions but chose not to report it to his superiors, leaving any explanation up to him.

The stupidest thing I did in 1964 was to ask a North Korean defector to show me how he had crossed the DMZ and made it across the Imjin River without being detected. Along with Louie Chon, my interpreter, we took him to the location on the northern bank of the Imjin River where he claimed to have crossed the Imjin. I then asked him if he could trace his path from that point to where he crossed the DMZ. He willingly agreed to do so. Along the route, we entered an area marked as containing land mines. I asked the defector to halt; I didn't want to lose face and tied a rope around his waist and told him to proceed through the minefield. Fortunately, we did not encounter any mines. His route to the DMZ took us within two hundred meters of the Joint Security Area, which abutted the Panmunjom site where meetings were held between North Korea and the United Nations command. Outside of my stupidity, we learned that we never once encountered a friendly patrol along the route that he took and how porous the DMZ really was.

One day we received a call from the 1st Battalion, 9th Cavalry Regiment, saying that they had captured five Koreans just south of the DMZ. They had no identification and I asked that they be transported to the 191st compound. They refused to answer questions and were placed in a small building on the compound. I heard loud sounds coming from the building and knew they were trashing things inside the room. I went to the arms room, picked up a shotgun, opened the door and fired two rounds into the ceiling. The Koreans got really quiet at that point. Our Motor Sergeant was Cliff Tousignant, and he was about six feet five inches tall and hefty. I asked Cliff for his help to bring the Koreans to the employee screening office where we took their fingerprints and photographs. I then separated them again and started an interrogation. What with the firing of the shotgun and the intimidation because of Cliff's size, they became cooperative. It turned out that they were Korean intelligence operatives that had crossed into North Korea and kidnapped a North

Korean villager. I then notified the 502nd MI Battalion, prepared a report, and then transported the five to Seoul.

There were two incidents that I investigated concerning an Army Security Agency unit that was stationed south of the Imjin River. Their mission was signals intelligence. The first incident was when the Military Police picked up a sergeant first class who was running through one of the local villages yelling that Kim Il-Song, the North Korean dictator, was going to attack. On investigation, it was evident that the soldier had a nervous breakdown. He was relieved of duties and sent to Seoul. The other incident was on a Sunday and the ASA unit reported that they were in a firefight with intruders. On investigation, it turned out that there was a Korean family on their way to church service, walking down the road, when the ASA unit opened fire on them. Fortunately, no one was injured. The soldiers who had opened fire on the civilians were admonished but not punished. This was another case of how stress and hard duties can affect one's thinking.

In December 1964, I had severe abdominal pain and went to the aid station of the 1st Battalion, 5th Cavalry Regiment, which was located behind the 191st compound. The battalion surgeon made the determination that I had gastritis and attributed it to too much drinking. I had not had a drink for over a week. He did not provide any medication, so I returned to the 191st compound. A few days later, the pain had become unbearable. I asked Louie Chon to transport me to the Division Medical Battalion. When I walked in bent over, the same doctor I had first seen was the division medical duty officer. He realized that he had misdiagnosed me and that I probably had appendicitis. I was transported immediately on an older Army ambulance to the 43rd Mobile Army Surgical Hospital where they had better surgical capabilities. It was an extremely bumpy ride for over 15 miles.

I was administered morphine for the acute pain I was having but I was semiconscious and would drift in and out of being awake. I awoke at one point to see a person in a surgical gown and mask holding my penis and shaving down my groin area in preparation for surgery. He asked, "Do you remember me?" It turned out he was the first sergeant of the hospital. I had conducted a security inspection of the hospital a couple of months before and found that they were in terrible shape. Thanks to Bob Sloan, I learned that inspections were not meant to punish anyone but rather to get the organization to be able to better protect themselves from various threats. On the inspection, I saw that the first sergeant had little or no experience and training in security but appeared to genuinely want to do what was right. Instead of flunking them, I worked with the first sergeant and came back several times to help them improve their security. Was glad that I took that course of action, especially when he had a razor in one hand and my penis in the other!

I was taken into the operating room and noticed that the surgeon was an Oriental. I asked him where he was from and he replied, "Hawaii." Typical of Hawaiians, my next question was, "What high school did you go to?" In Hawaii, it was more important to know what high school one went to rather than their college! He replied, "'Iolani." That was where I had gone to high school! His name was Nathaniel Ching and he had graduated from 'Iolani several years ahead of me. When he operated on me, he found that my appendix had ruptured. I had to remain in the hospital for over a week to allow the wound to drain before they sutured me back together. I still have a six-inch scar from that operation.

Fortunately, I was in great physical shape from practicing Tae Kwon Do and recovered fairly quickly. Christmas 1964 was spent in the 43rd MASH. The entertainer Bob Hope and his troupe were coming to Korea, and I had fond hopes that I would get to meet him and the pretty women who accompanied him. That was not to be. But I did get to meet the renowned television actor named Raymond Burr who had acted in television series, like *Ironside* and *Perry Mason*. We spent about half an hour chatting and he did much to help my morale. I learned later that he was a homosexual, but the lesson for me was to avoid stereotyping people and to judge them on their character rather than their sexual proclivities.

One night as I was laying in my hospital bed, an older nurse came into my room with tears in her eyes. She was a major and why she chose to come to my side was beyond me. I held her hand and asked her what was wrong. She then went on to describe that she had just come from the operating room where a sergeant first class from the 9th Cavalry had passed away. He had been shot while attempting to calm down one of his men who, for no known reason, had started firing his M-60 machine gun. In trying to calm his soldier, the soldier swiveled the machine gun and shot the sergeant. I spent over an hour with the major getting her calmed down and relating how tough life was for the soldiers along the DMZ. I explained that they worked 12-hour shifts, and after their shift they would then have to spend cleaning their equipment and getting ready to go back out the following day. They were working at least 15 hours a day. I explained that workload placed a great deal of stress on the soldiers and that is what probably caused the young soldier to go berserk and start firing his machine gun. The major appreciated that I took the time to spend with her and to help her overcome her grief. I reminded myself that all leaders should have empathy.

The last of the interesting cases I investigated concerned Sergeant Charles Jenkins who was a squad leader with the 1st Cavalry Division stationed across the Imjin River along the Demilitarized Zone. He disappeared from his unit in January 1965 and the thought was that he might have defected to North Korea. Other American defectors prior to Jenkins appeared on propaganda leaflets within a few days of their defection showing them dressed in suits and smiling. This did not happen with Jenkins. However, North Korea did declare that an American soldier had defected.

In conducting the investigation, I found out that he was not well-educated and came from a rural area in North Carolina. His squad had little respect for him as he frequently bragged about different things that the squad members knew were not true. One night he declared that he was going to defect, and his squad members paid little attention to his statement and taunted him to prove himself. He disappeared that night with his M-14 rifle. My investigation concluded that there was a high probability that his defection was based on his feeling that he had lost face with his squad members.

In 2004, Jenkins was released by North Korea and allowed to go to Japan. During the time he was in North Korea, he had been made to marry a kidnapped Japanese woman and they had two children. The North Korean dictator, Kim Jong-Il, had admitted kidnapping Japanese citizens and had allowed Jenkins's wife to return to Japan in a spirit of detente. She was followed shortly by Jenkins and the two children. Jenkins reported to U.S. Army authorities at Camp Zama, Japan, and was court-martialed. He received a dishonorable discharge, a demotion in rank to private, but was released for good behavior. He became a Japanese citizen and passed away in 2017.

The Jenkins case was the last major one I did in Korea. It was one of the best 13 months I had in the Army. It was filled with the opportunity to learn, to help others, and to become a better soldier.

CHAPTER 5

Hawaii—Finding and Losing

Before leaving Korea, I had applied for an assignment to the 25th Infantry Division in Hawaii. On the one hand, I wanted to remain tactically oriented in the intelligence field. On the other hand, I knew that hostilities were picking up in South Vietnam and that the 25th Infantry would likely be one of the first units called up to fight in Vietnam. I was aghast when my orders directed me to the 116th Intelligence Corps Group in Washington, DC. I discovered that the 502nd MI Battalion in Korea had never forwarded my request for assignment to the 25th Infantry Division. I filed a complaint with the battalion inspector general, who refused to do anything and was accused of claiming racial prejudice—a claim that simply was not true. I failed to get any support from the person who had replaced Tomomi Ando as the 191st MI Detachment commander, so I reluctantly left Korea with a bad taste in my mouth.

I took a short leave in Hawaii. My dad knew Major General Fred Weyand, who commanded the 25th Infantry Division, and asked him for help in getting me assigned to the division. General Weyand put me in touch with his 25th Division lawyer or Staff Judge Advocate. We talked and he suggested that I put in for a compassionate reassignment. I responded that there was no compassionate reason, and I would swallow a bitter pill and go on to Washington, DC. While I was on leave, my Uncle Kenji Aihara offered to pay my way through college should I decide to leave the Army. That was tempting, but I did not want to take advantage of anyone.

The 116th was situated in World War II-era wooden buildings outside the wall surrounding Fort McNair. I reported in and was told by folks in the personnel directorate to report to the major. I was then made to go through an exercise to prove I could do background investigations. I thought that was rather odd because I was already experienced. I sailed through the exercise and more than proved my abilities. I also had to find a place to live on my own as there were no government quarters available, and the unit offered no help other than a young soldier in personnel named Inman, who was the only one to offer any assistance. I became friends with him and his wife and was grateful for their help.

During the initial few weeks in the unit, I was berated by the mail clerk for having a subscription to the Honolulu newspaper delivered to the mail room. He claimed that it was the commander's policy not to allow that. I asked to see the policy in writing, and he could not show it to me. The mail clerk concocted a story and said that I was insubordinate by questioning the colonel's policy. Without being allowed to give any explanation, I was chewed out by the major. That left a very bad taste in my mouth as I was a staff sergeant, and the mail clerk was not an NCO.

The major decided that he would make things hard for me by assigning me to take over a case backlog that had existed for two years from an older NCO agent who was a nice person, but not very competent. My area started at Fort Belvoir and extended all the way to Fredericksburg, Virginia; I inherited some 75 cases that required background investigations. I analyzed them and devised a plan to deal with the backlog. It was a simple matter to group the cases by the locations where I had to do interviews. For example, about 15 cases involved senior officers (lieutenant colonels and colonels), who were all assigned to the Defense Atomic Support Agency at 6801 Telegraph Road. They all knew each other, and most had worked together for almost 20 years. That made it easy to schedule interviews and to get character references for those requiring a new background investigation.

There were also some 25 cases in Prince William County, which was a rural area in those days and sparsely populated compared to the large suburban community it is today. In general, the soldiers being investigated had all gone to the same schools in the County and had grown up near each other. I called the County Sheriff to make an appointment as one of the requirements was to do a law enforcement check. The Sheriff asked that I meet him at his house rather than his office. I showed up for the appointment, and the Sheriff's wife had just come back from grocery shopping. I offered to help her carry the groceries into their house from her car after identifying myself. When the Sheriff showed up, his wife told him what a gentleman I was and how I had helped her. The Sheriff was impressed. I gave him the names of the soldiers I was checking on, and he was immensely helpful as he knew all of them. He provided and helped contact their neighbors, teachers, and friends. So, with three weeks of effort, I could clear out more than half of the backlogged investigations. Being courteous and being organized were the keys.

The major was determined to make life difficult for me. On one occasion, we were preparing for an annual inspector general inspection. I was assigned a civilian vehicle and took it to a car wash before the major's inspection as I was busy conducting my investigations, and had an hour's drive from where I had interviews that day. The major put his finger under the front bumper and found some dirt. He never did that with the other vehicles being inspected and ordered me to stay and clean my car thoroughly. He assigned a captain to ensure that I did my job. I was very angry but kept my temper. After thoroughly cleaning the car, I tore a small cloth and was taking my time, acting like I was polishing the car. The captain, who was not a bad person, kept telling me that I was good to go. I knew he wanted to go home as it was well past 7 PM, but I insisted that I wanted to do more. He finally pled with me to stop and admitted the major had it in for me.

Another show of poor leadership occurred in April 1965. There was to be a massive protest march in Washington, DC. Martin Luther King, Jr., led the march in protest over racial prejudice and seeking the passage of civil rights legislation in the United States Congress, and it involved some 250,000 people. The leaders (if one could call them that) of the 116th declared that agents would be posted along the route, we would be issued .38-caliber revolvers but no ammunition. I was stunned by that stupidity and asked if we could be issued radios rather than empty revolvers. All I got was the proverbial "thousand-mile stare." It made absolutely no sense as the primary contribution we could make would be to report on activities. In addition, this was a civilian protest, and the military had no jurisdiction to become involved unless the Insurrection Act was invoked, or Posse Comitatus waived. In the end, we were not deployed, but I still question the shoddy leadership of the 116th Intelligence Corps Group. In my 10-month assignment to that unit, I never once met nor saw the colonel commanding it nor his sergeant major.

Despite the harassment from the major, I cleared out the backlog of cases initially assigned to me within five months. In doing so, I had impressed three of the officers subordinate to the major. One of them asked me to take a team of three other agents and to help the Central Clearance Facility at Fort Meade, Maryland, with a backlog of investigations they had. When reporting to the Clearance Facility, I analyzed how work was being done and asked the officer in charge to allow my team to try an innovative approach. The approach was very simple: we would be allowed to open an investigation, conduct the checks necessary to grant or deny the security clearance, and then adjudicate and close the case. This approach would keep paperwork from going from inbox to outbox to inbox to another outbox and would save a lot of time. In about a month, the four of us had completed close to 1,500 cases. These were not full background investigations but consisted of records checks necessary to grant secret security clearances.

After completing the temporary assignment, I went back to doing background investigations. Some of the cases I was assigned required me to do interviews in the Pentagon rather than my previously assigned area because I had cleared the backlog. I had finished conducting an interview and was walking through the basement of the Pentagon, when I saw a door sign which read, "Enlisted College Training Program." That was the program Walt Junkins had urged me to apply for when I was a Military Police officer at Fort Monmouth. I had time, so I thought I would see if my paperwork was still in the system. I was greeted by the proverbial little old lady in tennis shoes. I introduced myself and she went to check on the status of my request, which had been made some three years earlier. She came out with my file, reviewed it, and asked me, "When do you want to go?" I was astounded, recovered my shock, and said, "As soon as possible!"

Thanks to that kind lady, I soon received orders to go to the University of Hawaii beginning in January 1966. I was elated and decided to reenlist for six years in the Army. I took my reenlistment bonus and went to Arlington,

Virginia, where I purchased with cash a 1965 Chevrolet Nova Super Sport. It had a 327-cubic-inch engine with a four-speed transmission and was a real sleeper when it came to racing.

Life was going well at this point. I was going to leave a lousy unit where I had never seen or met the commander in 10 months and had to deal with a prejudiced major. I could forget that because I was headed home, going to finish my bachelor's degree, had a spanking new car, and money left in my pocket from my reenlistment bonus! Perseverance, hard work, and never giving up along with some luck can do wonders.

I arrived in Hawaii in early January 1966. I saw my friend, Bob Bode, who was deploying to Vietnam with other members of the 25th Infantry Division. I felt remorseful because I had so much wanted to be assigned to the division after I completed my tour in Korea in 1965. I had committed to the Enlisted College Training Program, so I had to swallow my desires and concentrate on my schooling. In-processing was easy and made even easier as my cousin, Aileen Higa—by coincidence—was responsible for monitoring my assignment. She helped to ensure that I had no duties other than attending the University of Hawaii. However, I did limited undercover work for an intelligence organization in Honolulu. Unlike my years at Lewis & Clark, I did not have to work to pay my way through school and had plenty of time to see old friends, get back into bodysurfing, and pursue things that I had wanted to do previously.

My majors were in political science and Asian studies. Now that I didn't have to pay for my education, I could spend more time studying. Academics, for the most part, came easily to me; I had gained more self-discipline, knew how to research, and had developed my writing and thinking skills thanks to my Army experiences. I was able to make made the Dean's list and didn't have to work very hard on my studies except for my Japanese language classes. My college major required that I have three years of a language, and I decided to take my first two years of Japanese in an intense summer session. That decision turned out to be a bit of a mistake on my part.

Most of the students in the class were of Japanese descent and had gone to Japanese language school after their regular schooling as they grew up. They were already proficient in speaking and writing Japanese and were taking the class to get an easy "A," and boost their grade point. The instructors were catering to them as they didn't have to make much effort teaching. There was a Black American Air Force sergeant and me who had to really go all out in an effort to learn the language. We were made to sit in the back of the classroom!

Things got worse in the second month after beginning my Japanese studies.

My friend Bob Bode had deployed to Vietnam in April 1966. In June 1966, one of the Honolulu newspapers selected him as the Father of the Year for Father's Day. A few weeks later he was killed in action in Vietnam. He left seven children and his wife, who was in her early 30s. I helped her and the children by ensuring that she received survivor benefits and helped plan his funeral. Bob had served with the Merchant Marines during the Korean War and requested a burial at sea. On a bright sunny day, we boarded a Navy destroyer escort and sailed from Pearl Harbor to the Waianae coast of Oahu. A bugler played Taps, and a gun salute was fired. Then sailors tilted the palette with Bob's casket, and it plunged into the ocean. My heart felt like it stopped beating. I struggled not to shed a tear as I wanted to appear strong for the Bode family. I felt both guilt and anger, as I felt I should have been in Vietnam with the 25th Infantry Division, except for some clerk failing to process my request to be assigned to the 25th when I was in Korea. As I look back on that day, it triggered what is now known as Post-Traumatic Stress Disorder (PTSD). From that day in 1966 until 1982, I had tears come to my eyes but one time. I became a cold and sarcastic person.

Because I was spending time helping the Bode family, my Japanese language studies suffered. I had too much on my mind and the first month after Bob's death required a lot of effort. But I did what needed to be done without regret and out of respect for a great American, Hawaiian, and soldier. Bob Bode was the best of people with a wonderful family.

I had to find ways to get past Bob Bode's death. I started drinking heavily with my friends from the Lunalilo Home Road area. Jerry Lau and David Nalu were two big Hawaiians and close friends. We often wondered how much David Nalu weighed and one day, we found a way to trick him into getting weighed. Jerry bought a pig for a *luau* (a Hawaiian feast), and we had to weigh it. Jerry estimated the pig's weight and set the scale for 300 pounds above the weight that he thought the pig was. We talked David into dragging the pig onto the scale and Jerry quickly adjusted the weight with David on the scale with the pig. After David got off the scale and the pig was weighed alone, we found that David weighed some 440 pounds. One big Hawaiian! We spent the weekends playing music and drinking. I traded my Chevrolet for a Mustang Fastback as it could hold 24 cases of beer that I used to buy from the Pearl Harbor Class VI liquor store. There was lots of time to get back into bodysurfing and to be with friends.

I also bought a Kawasaki motorcycle that almost proved to be my undoing. I was headed to a Post Office to mail a letter when a car started playing games behind me. I slowed and pulled over to the side to allow him to pass, but he just kept following me. I twisted the throttle and sped away. I was zipping along when I stupidly said to myself that I need to mail the letter. At high speed I turned into the parking lot of the Post Office. I encountered gravel and straightened the motorcycle. But I was on a grass median, and hit a water sprinkler head, causing it to burst. I was desperately trying to slow down as I left the median and went into the parking lot. I spotted a space between several cars and aimed for it where I intended to lay my motorcycle on its side. A car reversed out of the adjacent parking space, hit my knee, I flew over the car, did an Aikido roll, and ended up on the pressure mat that opened the doors to Longs Drug Store! The motorcycle had a bent fork. I swore I would never ride a motorcycle again!

The one thing that helped me get my mind straight was to get more involved in the martial arts. I evaluated different schools and decided to learn from Sensei Masaichi Oshiro who taught Goju Ryu Karate. Sensei Oshiro had started his martial arts training with a unique person named Professor William Chow who was known for his toughness. He started what became known as Kaju Kenpo. Sensei Oshiro migrated away from that and spent time in Okinawa and Japan learning from Yagi Meitoku Sensei and Yamaguchi Gogen Sensei, who were two of the ranking practitioners of Goju Ryu. Sensei Oshiro taught his classes in the basement of the McCully Recreation Center. He was an excellent teacher, and the practices quite intense. We would finish our sessions with our *gi* (uniform) soaking wet from sweat. Thanks to my previous training I advanced very quickly and was promoted to Shodan (1st degree black belt) within a year. The senior students were great people, tough but with the desire to help the juniors. Some of the ones I best remember were Sal Ebanez and Tino Cerebano, who took Goju Ryu to Australia. Then there were fierce fighters like Howard Lau, Luther Yam, Arthur Lim, and Rodney Hu. In October 1966, Gogen Yamaguchi and his youngest son Goshi visited Hawaii and held a seminar and a demonstration. I was lucky enough to be invited to accompany Yamaguchi Sensei on a visit to Hawaii and was the photographer on the trip. I owe Oshiro Sensei for helping to develop my character and learn that one can be a fierce fighter and a kind person at the same time.

I had always been interested in learning Aikido so I enrolled at the Aiki Kai dojo in Kaimuki. My interest stemmed from high school when Larry Mehau was an assistant line coach and proficient in Aikido. It was rather strange as the beginner classes were led by students who did not have Dan (black belt) ranking. Nonetheless, I was learning the basics of Aikido. Unfortunately, that did not last for very long. At practice one night, one of the people leading the class was demonstrating a defense against a punch. He taunted me by calling me a name and daring me to punch harder. His attitude angered me, so I launched an attack using my karate skills and knocked him out. I decided that I could not learn from people like that and stopped my training at the dojo. However, I had a friend who was more advanced in Aikido who would give me lessons occasionally.

My two years in Hawaii went by quickly. Other than dealing with the tragic death of Bob Bode, 1966 and 1967 were wonderful years filled with good memories and reconnecting with old friends and family. I also received my bachelor's degree, became proficient in Goju Ryu Karate, and continued to evolve as an adult. As my tour started winding down, I had many opportunities for consequential assignments and was offered the chance to apply to become a commissioned officer. However, my mind was set on going to Vietnam. We were at war trying to preserve the freedom of the South Vietnamese. As a soldier, I very much wanted to be part of helping others.

CHAPTER 6

Vietnam and Resilience

My orders for Vietnam did not assign me to a specific unit and had me reporting to a Replacement Unit at Long Binh, Vietnam. Six young soldiers were also headed from Hawaii to Vietnam, and as a staff sergeant, I was placed in charge of looking after them and ensuring they were taken care of en route to Vietnam. We started from Hickam Air Force Base in Hawaii and flew to the Philippines for an overnight stay. This was the first time the six young soldiers had been overseas, and they were uncertain about what awaited them in Vietnam. I got them together, took them to Angeles City outside Clark Air Base for a good meal, and then carousing in the town. The next morning, we boarded a C-130 aircraft headed for Tan Son Nhut Air Base outside Saigon.

We arrived on February 12, 1968, which was President Abraham Lincoln's birthday. Even in Vietnam and shortly after the Tet Offensive in 1966, it was a holiday for most support personnel. When we disembarked the plane, there was no one to greet us and no idea where to go. The young soldiers were visibly nervous. I took them to a location under a huge hole in the airport roof where a rocket had come through previously. I told them to remain together and to stay under the hole, proclaiming that the chance of another rocket coming through that hole was over a million to one! I then set out to find how we could be transported to the Long Binh Replacement Unit. After some 15 minutes of wandering around, I finally found the person responsible for transporting us to Long Binh.

I honestly have no recollection of how we got to Long Binh—I was hungover from the previous night in Angeles City! Upon arrival at Long Binh, we were taken to a wooden barracks and told that we would be in-processed in the morning. We had arrived at dusk, and I got the young soldiers fed and then bunked down. I climbed onto my cot and went into a deep sleep. I found out the next morning that the base had received mortar fire, and those in the barracks had been taken to a bunker. I slept through it all.

Sometime in the early morning I awoke to hear someone breathing heavily and the springs on a cot squeaking. I thought that the person must have been masturbating.

But then I heard a voice crying, "Sarge, Sarge (for Sergeant)" and then another voice that said, "I'm not the Sarge, he's in the next bunk over." I then sensed something was wrong, so I got up and found a sergeant holding onto a cot with tears in his eyes. I went to him and calmed him down. In short, he was on his second tour in Vietnam and had a nervous breakdown. I then asked another soldier for help, and we took the sergeant to a medical aid station and explained what had happened and that he needed help. Just like taking care of the young soldier coming from Hawaii with me, all I was doing was living up to what I had been taught that leaders are supposed to do—take care of others.

The following day, I reported to the Replacement Unit and was told I would be assigned to the U.S. Army Vietnam (USARV) G2 or Intelligence Office. I asked to be reconsidered for assignment to a tactical or field organization rather than a rear headquarters and was informed I had no choice. I proceeded to the G2 Office and was greeted by someone who told me that I would be working for a specialist seventh class, but I had to be interviewed by a major. All of this did not sit well with me, even though I was one pay grade lower than the specialist, Army protocol was that NCOs do not work for specialists. My luck was soon to change. The major in charge walked out of his office. We looked at each other and immediately broke out into smiles. Unfortunately, I don't remember his name, but we had worked together in Korea when he was with the 1st Cavalry Division G2 Office and he had been impressed with my work, especially the case where I stood up for the two sergeants who were fired at by North Koreans in the DMZ.

He invited me into his office, and he asked me if I was ready to take on the job in USARV G2's Office. I replied that I was not happy to be working for a specialist and that I really wanted to be assigned to a tactical unit. With his understanding of my background, he smiled and said, "I'll release you on one condition." I asked him what that was, and he replied that if I spent the rest of the day catching up on old times, he would let me go. We talked about our assignments in Korea and what had happened since then. I was very thankful and happy for his friendship and leadership. This was another example of good leaders doing what was right for a soldier.

I returned to the Replacement Unit with a signed release from the major. I asked to be assigned specifically to the 5th Special Forces Group or the 25th Infantry Division. The personnel section would have to see what was available. I returned in a couple of days and found out that the personnel turkeys had put 5 and 25 together and that I was assigned to the 525th MI Brigade, and that I had no choice. I packed my duffel bag again and was transported to the headquarters of the 525th outside of Saigon, with a few others also assigned to that unit.

On arrival, we were taken to temporary barracks. Later in the day, a young buck sergeant came into the barracks and announced that if we came under attack, we should proceed to the perimeter fence surrounding the compound. I looked at him, and said "No way in hell." He looked at me incredulously but respecting that I outranked him, asked me what I intended to do. I told him that I would remain in the barracks until I saw someone with a weapon die. I also said that it was madness to head for the perimeter without a weapon and take cover behind empty 55-gallon barrels—that I had already checked out—and found that they were neither filled with water or dirt. The buck sergeant lowered his head and walked away, never to return. It reminded me of the ineptitude I encountered with the 116th Intelligence Corps Group, and the April 1965 March on Washington.

The following day I was told that I would be assigned to the 2nd Battalion of the 525th in Nha Trang, Vietnam. I packed my duffel again and boarded a C-130 for the flight to Nha Trang. At least this time a representative of the unit met me. I was interviewed by Major Smith, the battalion operations officer, and told that I would be assigned to the Counterintelligence Team Nha Trang. Major Smith was an infantry officer with a secondary specialty in intelligence. I asked him if there was any way I could be released for assignment to a tactical unit. I explained my desire and he listened to me. He then explained that he needed my help in improving the operations of the CI Team Nha Trang, and other than Chief Warrant Officer Bill Miller, who led the office, all the other agents were very inexperienced. Smith had noted by reviewing my records that I had human intelligence and offensive counterintelligence experience. He further explained that there were officers who outranked Bill Miller, but he had put Bill in charge because of his experience. He also stated that if I proved myself and helped Bill out, he would approve a reassignment after six months. I respected Major Smith's candor and his desire to improve the operations of the team under Bill Miller.

Once again, I packed my duffel bag and was picked up by Bill Miller and transported to the villa close to Nha Trang Beach where the CI Team was headquartered. Bill briefed me on the team and said that we had outlying offices with one agent in Phan Thiet, Cam Ranh Bay, and Tuy Hoa. All were on U.S. air bases at those locations. He also told me that we had responsibility for two other provinces where Dalat (home of the Vietnamese Military Academy) and Gia Nghia were located but we did not have any agents assigned to those provinces. Without criticizing the other agents assigned to the team, he told me that they were very inexperienced and I could be of value in helping to train and mentor the others. I instantly liked Bill Miller, and we became close friends over the next six months.

The mission of the CI Team Nha Trang was to conduct offensive counterintelligence operations against the Viet Cong and North Vietnamese and to establish tactical human intelligence networks. In reality, the only productive operation was the one at Tuy Hoa led by a young captain. During the height of the Vietnam War, one could be promoted to captain after only two years in the military. Although the captain was young, he was energetic and competent. Of the other agents in Nha Trang, only Dick Trebino was productive. The ensuing days and nights were filled with training and mentoring others. I recruited and began training a Vietnamese former Air Force officer as a human intelligence operative.

Two coincidental meetings that I had turned out to be great experiences for me. I met a Korean American who was well-connected politically. He was a close friend of a female journalist whose brother was the Korean Lieutenant General Chae Myung Shin, who commanded Korean military forces in South Vietnam. One weekend, my friend invited me to a party on Hon Tre Island off Nha Trang Bay. We boarded a Korean LST (Landing Ship Tank) and took a short trip to Hon Tre. Much to my surprise, I met Nguyen Cao Ky who had risen from being the head of the Vietnamese Air Force to Prime Minister and then Vice-President of South Vietnam. It was a memorable party and event.

The other coincidental meeting that undoubtedly helped me was meeting Chief Warrant Officer Clarence Kawahigashi. Clarence was assigned to the 5th Special Forces Group as their source control officer. He found out about my desire to be assigned to the 5th Special Forces and arranged for me to be interviewed. I informed Bill Miller of what was happening. He was totally supportive and understood my desire to get assigned to a combat unit. Bill knew about the promise that Major Smith of the 2nd Battalion, 525th MI, had made to me about being able to transfer after six months. With Bill's support and knowing that I had a job with the 5th Special Forces, I went to the 2nd Battalion Operations Office only to find that Major Smith had rotated, and a new operations officer was in place. I informed that officer of the promise that Major Smith had made to me, and that Bill Miller was fully knowledgeable and supportive. The new major looked at me and said I was crazy. I didn't think he was serious, but he was and ordered me to be psychiatrically evaluated. There was another officer in the room when this happened. He walked out with me and expressed his opinion that the major's actions were ridiculous.

Regardless, I had to follow orders and set up an appointment with a psychiatrist at the 5th Field Hospital in Nha Trang. I was interviewed and the psychiatrist not only gave me a clean bill of mental health but said that I should send the major over for an evaluation. I replied that it was impossible for me to do that, and he nodded his understanding of the situation. I returned to meet with the major and showed him the psychiatric report that said I was fine. He still insisted that I was crazy and that he would not release me. Once again, I was dismayed by the lack of leadership shown by a military intelligence officer. I tried to see the battalion commander, but he would not take the time to see me. I then placed an inspector general complaint with the group headquarters outside Saigon.

Bill Miller arranged for me to fly to Saigon where I was to meet the deputy commander of the 525th MI Group. His last name was Manken, as best as I can recall. I explained the promise made to me by Major Smith, what happened with Smith's replacement ordering me to get a psychiatric evaluation, and that I had the support of Bill Miller and a job waiting for me in the 5th SF Group. The colonel heard me out and then stated that he did not want to approve my transfer. I pled with him one more time, and he could see how much I wanted the transfer. He asked me for the name of the person in the 5th SF Group who had helped find me a position. I replied, "Chief Warrant Officer Clarence Kawahigashi." Manken asked me to repeat the name and I did. His eyes got misty, and he was silent for almost a minute. He then said, "Clarence Kawahigashi taught me all about being an intelligence officer when I was a brand-new lieutenant in the Korean War." He then said he would approve my reassignment only because Clarence Kawahigashi was involved. Was I ever relieved and happy with Manken's decision!

CHAPTER 7

5th Special Forces Group and Detachment B-57

I flew back to Nha Trang with orders in hand and told Bill Miller what had transpired. I out-processed from the 2nd Battalion and Bill drove me to the headquarters of the 5th Special Forces Group. My date of reporting was August 7, 1968, one of the happiest days of my life. I knew I would be assigned to Detachment B-57 and was collected from group headquarters for a short ride to the B-57 headquarters in Nha Trang. Sergeant Major John Voter, a rugged Special Forces veteran who was on his third tour in Vietnam, met me. John loved to chew tobacco and was a man of few words. But when he spoke, you listened! He introduced me to the detachment commander, Major Bob Thrasher; the operations officer, Captain Darlington Andrews; and others in the detachment. I would be attending a two-week-long indoctrination course conducted by the RECONDO School. I looked forward to attending that course with great anticipation. The following day I was taken by the detachment supply sergeant, Ross "Pete" Potter, to be issued with jungle fatigue uniforms and combat equipment.

The indoctrination course was taught by instructors who had genuine combat experience. They were there to ensure that everyone learned properly and did an outstanding job. The training was intense and ranged from learning or reviewing how to call for artillery fire support, weapons firing of various small arms and both the 60 mm and 81 mm mortar, grenade throwing, use of claymore mines, patrolling, and other subjects aimed at getting one prepared for combat in Vietnam. It culminated with an exercise on Hon Tre Island where we went through a live shooting lane and drills and then had to do a combat patrol.

Upon completion, Sergeant Major Voter told me I had done well and I would be sent to assess some potential sites to establish a B-57 operation at Southern III Corps in the Mekong Delta area. Before I was sent, I was given a comprehensive briefing on B-57 and its operations. I was told that the detachment was formed in 1967 and initially headquartered in Saigon in a villa that had been previously owned by a South Vietnamese general, nicknamed "Big Minh." B-57 was also known as Project Gamma. In the early days, there were two missions that the detachment was given. One was under Operation Blackbeard which consisted of recruiting indigenous personnel to perform agent missions inside Cambodia. The other was called Project Cherry, which recruited Cambodians to conduct reconnaissance missions inside Cambodia. Mike Eiland, who would later become a great friend, was one of the early leaders of Project Cherry. It was decided to close Project Cherry in 1967 and transfer its assets to the Military Assistance Command Vietnam Special Operations Group. In November 1967, after Cherry had been closed, Captain John McCarthy allegedly shot and killed an interpreter/principal agent involved in Project Cherry. He was court-martialed and convicted but his conviction was later overturned. That incident was at least partially responsible for B-57 being moved from Saigon to Nha Trang. In Nha Trang, the detachment was housed in wooden buildings adjacent to the B-55 Mike Force.

The detachment's mission was to collect intelligence on Viet Cong and North Vietnamese Army activity in Cambodia and operated under an Operations Plan known as Blackbeard. The collection of intelligence was done by recruiting and running indigenous personnel into Cambodia rather than American personnel being the collectors of information. In 1968, B-57 was operating out of 10 different Special Forces camps close to the Cambodian border in the II, III, and IV Corps areas of South Vietnam. Each of those stations had a three- or four-person B-57 team. Those teams typically consisted of one military intelligence agent, an intelligence-trained Special Forces officer or NCO, and a high-speed radio operator.

Once the field teams obtained information from their indigenous agents, they would prepare a report, encrypt it using a one-time pad encryption system, and then send the report to B-57 headquarters. On receipt, the message was decrypted and analyzed, and then a formal Intelligence Information Report would be prepared by personnel assigned to the Operations Section of B-57. In 1968, the Military Assistance Command Vietnam's intelligence officer (J-2) assessed that B-57 was providing 65–75% of the useful intelligence on enemy activity in Cambodia.

One of the things that greatly impressed me was to see the radio operators at work. They operated at a network speed of greater than 30 groups per minute using Morse code, whereas the graduation standard from the Special Forces communications course was 15–18 groups per minute. Many of the field radio operators used electronic keys to help them send their messages faster, but there were remarkable operators like Warren "Ed" Fisler who used manual keys. The radios used were Collins KWM 2-A single side-band high-frequency radios with an Army standard PRC-74 radio as backup.

I also learned two other interesting things before being sent to assess potential operating sites. First, I learned that one of our radio operators, Sergeant First Class Ken Hain, was undergoing a court-martial for using a false name. Ken had received either a bad conduct or dishonorable discharge at the end of World War II for assaulting an officer.

He was determined to continue serving America so he took the name of a high school friend and used that friend's identity and social security number to enlist in the Army. Because B-57 required Top Secret security clearances, Ken had to undergo a background investigation where it was discovered that there were two people contributing to the same social security account. Further investigation found that Ken was falsely using the name Pat Carter.

Ironically, on a previous tour in Vietnam, Ken's brother had been killed in action and Ken had escorted his body back to the States using his alias of Pat Carter. Ken survived the court-martial and was allowed to remain in the Army and retain his rank. He was a superb soldier and his Army achievements helped him survive the court-martial.

I also learned more about our operation at the Duc Lap A Camp. I met Captain Charles Yancey and Master Sergeant James "Pappy" Butler, who were assigned to Duc Lap. They were trying desperately to get back to Duc Lap as it was under a major attack. Two other members of their team were still at Duc Lap. As was learned later, Sergeant First Class Shigeo Uchino manned a .50-caliber machine-gun position for two days without relief and was wounded. The radio operator, Staff Sergeant Harold Kline, was said to have been operating the radios for Detachment A-239 at Duc Lap for two continuous days and nights in a bunker. He came out of the bunker to take a break and was killed by a rocket-propelled grenade. Yancey and Butler were unable to return to the camp before the battle ended, though they tried everything they could to get back. They were deeply despondent that they could not. I was really impressed by the likes of Yancey, Butler, and Ken Hain. Remarkable soldiers that I looked up to.

With the knowledge of where and how B-57 operated, and impressed with the quality of personnel assigned to it, I set out to assess three locations for possible B-57 expansion. All three locations were on the southern edge of III Corps in the Mekong Delta area. The camps I went to were the B Detachment at Duc Hoa and two of the A Detachments under that B Team, Duc Hue and Tra Cu. Succinctly, none of the three were suitable for expansion. For example, the A Detachment at Tra Cu was surrounded by water. The camp had to be resupplied by air boats or helicopters and there was no indigenous population in its vicinity from which to recruit agents. Access to indigenous persons, whether they were Vietnamese, Cambodian, or another ethnicity like Montagnards, was critical to success. They needed to be able to cross into Cambodia.

I returned to B-57 headquarters and rendered my assessment which was accepted. John Voter decided he wanted to send me to our operation in III Corps at the Bu Dop A-341 Detachment. I was pleasantly surprised and delighted as it would give me an opportunity to gain firsthand experience with a tactical operation. Sergeant Major Voter ensured that I had my equipment and personally took me to Trang Air Base where I was to fly in an Army De Havilland Beaver single-engine plane to Bu

Dop. In preparation for the flight, I had carefully done a map reconnaissance so I would have a general awareness of where we were if the plane ran into trouble. I really admired Sergeant Major Voter and knew that he had a tremendous reputation in Special Forces.

While waiting for the plane to show up, a Special Forces soldier named Luciano Brash came walking towards us. John Voter, in a loud voice, said, "Stop right there Brash, don't come any closer." Brash took a couple more steps towards us, and Sergeant Major Voter drew his .45 pistol and said, "I told you to stop!" Brash stopped and said something and Voter told him to get the hell out of there. Brash complied. I was shocked and amazed. Sergeant Major Voter told me that Brash was a dirt ball and never gave any other explanation. Some four years later I was to find out why John Voter felt that way.

The flight to Bu Dop was uneventful. The Bu Dop camp had a dirt airstrip adjacent to it. On landing, I was met by Sergeant First Class Francesco Zamarippa who was the A-341 weapons sergeant. He helped me unload a small safe that I had transported, and we got on a front-line M-151 ambulance and rode to the compound. Zamarippa took me into the underground bunker where the team lived and told me to relax, and he would find Master Sergeant John C. Anderson, who led the B-57 team. The bunker had a room equivalent to a day room in Army terms—an area to relax like a great room in today's terminology. There was a bar, a refrigerator, and some couches.

While waiting, I saw a U.S. Army Vietnam Field Force magazine lying on a table. I picked it up and the cover story read, "Phuoc Long Province, the Siberia of Vietnam." Bu Dop camp was in Bo Duc District, Phuoc Long Province, so the magazine immediately drew my attention. I picked it up and started reading the article with some trepidation. As I read the article, I calmed down as the main message was about how isolated the province was and that it was sparsely populated. It also described the unique animals that ran wild in Phuoc Long Province.

They included wild elephants, tigers, sun bears, giant lizards, venomous snakes, pythons, a miniature rhinoceros, monkeys, and a form of antelope the size of a deer. During my time at Bu Dop, I never saw the miniature rhinoceros and only saw the tracks of wild elephants and tigers, but I did get to see the other mentioned animals. I thought this was going to be an exciting time at Bu Dop!

Soon after I arrived, John Anderson came into the bunker and introduced himself. He showed me where I would have a cot to sleep and then introduced me to Jim Parris, the B-57 radio operator, and our interpreter/principal agent, Tho. John went by the nickname of "Andy," and he and Jim Parris would become lifelong friends. Andy had a unique background. He was born and raised in Latvia, joined the German Air Force Auxiliary during World War II, was captured by American troops, and then released at the end of the war. He did not want to return to Latvia as the Soviet Union had made Latvia one of its Socialist Republics. Andy found a job working in a coal mine in Belgium and told me that he and the other laborers were mistreated by the owners. The Lodge Act, which sought to recruit soldiers from Soviet-occupied countries, gave him the opportunity to join the U.S. Army in 1951 and to eventually gain his citizenship. He was sent from Germany to Fort Benning, Georgia, for airborne training and then was assigned to Special Forces. He spent most of his time with the 10th Special Forces Group in Bad Toelz, Germany, and was a skilled skier and mountaineer. He was on his third tour in Vietnam when I had the honor to meet him and work for him.

Jim Parris was from Oklahoma and had served previously in the Navy as a high-speed radio operator who was very skilled in sending Morse code at a high rate of speed. He was on his second tour in Vietnam and had been in the 1st Special Forces Group in Okinawa, where he married his first wife, Eiko. Tho was a lanky Vietnamese national who stood over six feet tall, making him unusual for a Vietnamese. He was a great person, a hard worker, and always had a smile on his face. Once again, I was very pleased to see the quality of the people I would be working with. We were attached to Detachment A-341 as Civil Affairs and Psychological Operations augmentation. That allowed us to work with the indigenous people outside the A Camp and to recruit agents for cross-border operations. We helped to organize and conduct medical civic action projects where we provided medical care mainly to the Montagnards in Bo Duc District and assisted them in improving their living conditions. On the psychological operations side, we helped to bring entertainers to Bo Duc and show movies that were very popular with the Montagnards and the indigenous personnel inside the A Camp. The goal was to get them to support the Vietnamese government.

I soon met the members of A-341. Typically, a Special Forces A Detachment consists of 12 soldiers, led by a captain with a lieutenant as the executive officer in those days (the lieutenant position is now filled by a warrant officer), a master sergeant to be the detachment sergeant and plan operations, an intelligence sergeant, two radio operators, two engineers/demolition sergeants, two medical sergeants, and two weapons sergeants. A-341 was woefully short of personnel with only eight on the team vice 12. The team leader was First Lieutenant Carter instead of a captain, and the executive officer was Paul Fager, who was on his first assignment out of Special Forces training. The team sergeant was Sergeant First Class Roger Dion instead of a master sergeant, there was only one weapons sergeant in Francesco Zamarippa, and only one medical sergeant in Julian Aguilar. Leonard was the engineer sergeant, Larry McKim served as the intelligence sergeant, and the two radio operators were Gil Aparis and Mike Parks.

I was told the reason was that the B-57 augmentation provided three soldiers and a medical team from the Walter Reed Army Institute of Research augmented the A Detachment. That team consisted of two captains who were medical doctors and one Special Forces master sergeant medical specialist. Their primary mission was to conduct research on malaria and elephantiasis. The six of us augmenting A-341 would also engage in field operations but on an infrequent basis compared to the eight who were assigned to A-341. Three interpreters were hired by the A Team. Another reason for not fully staffing the A Detachment was that enemy activity in Bo Duc District had significantly decreased after a battle in November 1967.

The role of the A Detachment was essentially to assist the Vietnamese Special Forces known as the Luc Luong Dac Biet (LLDB) in planning and running operations, together with helping to train indigenous personnel that were part of what was called the Civilian Irregular Defense Group (CIDG). At Bu Dop, these were mainly Cambodian and Montagnards assigned to company-size organizations. In today's parlance, they would be considered paramilitary forces. They were not in the Vietnamese Army and received their pay through the CIDG program. The Americans were also responsible for administering the CIDG program, including accounting for weapons and ammunition and paying the CIDG personnel. On combat operations, the Americans were also very much involved in calling in air strikes and heavy artillery from American forces remote from Bu Dop. Bu Dop was very fortunate to have an outstanding LLDB commander, Dai Uy (Captain) Nguyen Cong Trieu. He was intelligent, brave, and ethical. Thanks to Trieu's leadership, the Americans and Vietnamese worked very well together. We also had a battery of Vietnamese Army 105 mm howitzers located inside the camp. They proved themselves very competent artillerymen and could place accurate artillery fire within range of their guns within 10 to 15 minutes of being called to provide artillery support.

***

One of the oddities in being assigned to a Special Forces A Camp was that each soldier was authorized separate rations or a monthly stipend to pay for food. The problem in a camp like Bu Dop was that there were no restaurants and a limited ability to purchase food in the area. We pooled our money and would send someone to a place like Bien Hoa, where the C Detachment overseeing Special Forces operations in III Corps was located, or Saigon. It was also a way to give the guys a break to get some relaxation away from Bu Dop. They would scrounge or buy food and transport it back to Bu Dop. Viet Cong paraphernalia was sometimes used to trade for food. On the one hand, getting resupplied for weapons and ammunition was not a problem and there was a system in place to get those supplies, but it did not apply to food. Three Vietnamese females cooked and cleaned our living and work areas. On one occasion—that I'll describe later—we had enough food, but it certainly was not up to the standards that other units in Vietnam enjoyed. The other strange thing was that a system was in place to supply food for our CIDG and LLDB personnel, but not for the Americans in the A Camp.

The American advisors assigned to Bo Duc District had a system whereby they would periodically get supplied with fresh food. I was insanely jealous of that. Their food supplies were delivered by plane to the Bu Dop airstrip, and then we helped transport the food to Bo Duc District. I decided to steal some of their food on one occasion and sneaked some fresh eggs and steaks from them. I then helped to take the advisor who had flown in with the food to district headquarters. On my way back, the three-quarter-ton truck I was driving broke down. It was getting dark, and I radioed back to camp for help. I just knew God was punishing me for being a thief and that the Viet Cong would attack me! I took the radio out of the truck's cab and crawled under the truck with the radio and my M-16. Gil Aparis came out on a two-and-a-half-ton truck with a few strikers and towed the broken-down truck back to camp. I breathed a sigh of relief and promised myself never to steal food from the district advisors again!

The enemy situation in the area around Bu Dop was greatly reduced after the fierce battle in November 1967 when a portion of the camp was overrun by the People's Army of Vietnam (PAVN). The PAVN were Viet Cong who were organized into conventional units unlike smaller Viet Cong guerrilla operations. The U.S. 1st Infantry Division, 25th Infantry Division, and Special Forces Mobile Strike Teams known as Mike Force, helped to retake the camp, and inflict substantial casualties on the PAVN unit, which retreated into Cambodia. The intelligence that we and our LLDB counterparts collected said that the Viet Cong guerrilla operation around Bu Dop was tiny and consisted of an estimated 20 or so guerrillas. Bo Duc District was sparsely populated, with perhaps two thousand people living around the district headquarters, which was a few kilometers away from Detachment A-341. In addition, there were some small Montagnard settlements in the district and a French rubber plantation that was populated with about 200 people. That plantation had been a recreational area for other rubber plantation owners and had an Olympic-sized swimming pool and a large villa. However, the plantation was no longer active because of the war. The total number of people inside the A-341 compound was about 600, including family members.

Bo Duc District and Bu Dop were isolated from any major American or Vietnamese Army units. To the east was Cambodia, with no populated areas, but with two known North Vietnamese Army base areas that were large supply depots. There was no vehicular traffic from Bo Duc District into Cambodia. On the other hand, there were times at night when we could see vehicle lights moving along the Cambodian border and knew they had to be North Vietnamese Army vehicles. Gil Aparis, the A-341 senior communications sergeant, and I reflected one night as to what we would do if those lights started coming in our direction. Captain Trieu decided to take action, and led an ambush one night where he stood in the middle of a dirt road and opened fire with an M-60 machine gun on the first of four vehicles. It reinforced his bravery in my mind.

Over 60 kilometers to the south was Loc Ninh Special Forces camp and conventional U.S. Army combat units, but the road was not deemed safe to travel, and was considered interdicted. It was over 100 kilometers to the north to find any friendly forces, and that road was also interdicted. The closest location of major forces to the west was over 80 kilometers away in Song Be. Song Be was also the location of the A-341's higher headquarters, Detachment B-34. Again, the road network to and from Song Be was interdicted. A-341 was totally dependent on aerial resupply as there was no road traffic coming into the district. In essence, the area around Bu Dop was a "no man's land."

The small Viet Cong contingent in Bo Duc District never posed a threat of a direct attack against the A Detachment or district headquarters because of their small size. However, they would infrequently mortar both locations and place explosives along the road from the camp to Bo Duc District Headquarters. To counter their activities, A-341 conducted a sweep of the airstrip and the road to Bo Duc District every morning to look for mines or explosives that may have been implanted during the night. In general, one- to three-day-long patrolling operations were conducted to try locate the Viet Cong or to detect any movement from North Vietnamese forces across the Cambodian border. The longest operation conducted while I was at Bu Dop was a five-day operation where we flew a company of indigenous personnel to Loc Ninh and then proceeded north back to Bu Dop. The intent was to look for any North Vietnamese equipment caches. That operation did not detect anything of note but was somewhat hilarious as we put over 100 indigenous on a C-123 plane for the flight to Loc Ninh. They all had to stand to fit everyone on the plane.

John Anderson reluctantly agreed to allow me to go on one-day operations occasionally as our B-57 focus was to collect intelligence and build our network of agents. Our interpreter/principal agent, Tho, was an invaluable asset in that regard. He would accompany us on civic action visits to outlying Montagnard villages to spot, assess, and recruit agents. Montagnards were the only ones who would frequently cross the border into Cambodia and, consequently, were the source of all our agents out of Bu Dop. In general, we would dispatch them to report on activity around the two known North Vietnamese Army base areas and to scout for any noteworthy movement of North Vietnamese forces towards South Vietnam. Getting inside the base areas was impossible because of tight security and because Montagnards were being used as forced labor.

There was also a report that American prisoners of war were being held in Cambodia close to Bu Dop, so we would have the agents look for activity in planned areas, but they were never able to ascertain anything about a POW holding area. Upon return from a mission, the agents would be debriefed by Tho, who would then report to Andy or myself. A report would then be prepared in writing, transposed onto a cryptographic one-time pad and then sent using Morse code to B-57 headquarters in Nha Trang. I learned how to transcribe a report onto a one-time pad and assisted our radio operator, Jim Parris, in getting the information ready to send to Nha Trang. Candidly, the B-57 operation out of Bu Dop was moderately productive. Unfortunately, we could not collect any earth-shattering information because of the lack of activity on the part of the NVA during my time at Bu Dop.

The A Detachment operations likewise were not able to detect much North Vietnamese activity. Until I left in June 1969, there were only two firefights that I can remember. I mentioned seeing vehicle lights at night towards the Cambodian border. Captain Trieu planned an operation and was able to shoot up a four-truck movement one night. He led the assault by getting in the middle of the road with an M-60 machine gun. The other firefight came about when a Viet Cong female deserted and turned herself in at Bu Dop. She was young, attractive, and less than five feet tall. When she turned herself in, she was barefoot with numerous lacerations on her swollen feet.

We were not sure that she was a bona fide defector when she turned herself in, so we decided to use a "Mutt and Jeff" technique to begin the interrogation. The A Detachment had just received a replacement for Larry McKim, the intelligence sergeant for A-341. I talked to him and asked him if he knew what the Mutt and Jeff technique was, and he nodded his head. I said that I would begin by being the bad guy and then he could come in and act like the good guy: a typical Mutt and Jeff technique. I entered the room and started screaming and pointing my finger at the defector and then stormed out. The new intelligence sergeant just stood in the doorway frozen. Fortunately, Captain Sullivan, one of the Walter Reed doctors, played the nice guy, treating her feet and quietly talking to her. She was a wealth of information. It turned out that she had been with the Viet Cong element in Bo Duc District for about eight months. She was sexually abused and finally got tired of it and ran away.

Captain Trieu then drew up plans to act on the information provided by the defector. The first was to mount a company-size operation to look for the base camps in the jungle that the defector had helped to map out. We were able to sneak up on the VC and launch an assault. We killed two of the VC and saw several blood trails leading out of the camp. As we attacked the camp, one of our Montagnards was in front of me. We took fire and he immediately dove to the ground. It's amazing how some things can slow down in certain situations. I saw that he had landed on some punji stakes, and I saw one protruding through his thigh. I was going to the prone position when I saw that, and threw the butt of my rifle to break my fall. I was fortunate not to impale myself on a punji stake and only had one partially penetrate my right calf. Captain Bill Sylvester had become the A Detachment team leader and the other American besides myself on the operation was our medic, Julian Aguilar.

After cutting off the sharp point, Julian and I lifted the Montagnard off the punji stake. We then moved towards a cleared area on a map reconnaissance and called for medical evacuation. A UH-1 helicopter came in and I helped carry the Montagnard onto the helicopter. Jim Parris came in on the helicopter because he thought that I was the wounded person. He jumped out of the helicopter on the side away from which we were loading the wounded Montagnard. After the helicopter lifted off, I saw Jim standing there, and he explained that he thought I was the one injured. We had a good laugh over that. Jim now had to join us for the rest of the operation! The bonds we had for each other in Special Forces were very close—as witnessed by the likes of Jim Parris. He remained a close friend until his passing.

The female defector gave additional information about possible caches of supplies that the North Vietnamese had emplaced south of Bu Dop on the road to Loc Ninh. Captain Trieu planned an operation to see if those caches could be located. The operation called for a CIDG company to be airlifted to Loc Ninh and then proceed north back to Bu Dop. A C-123 twin-engine cargo aircraft was requested to transport the company to Loc Ninh. The C-123 is not a large airplane, but we managed to load over 120 men on board for the short flight to Loc Ninh. The movement from Loc Ninh back to Bu Dop took five days to accomplish. Unfortunately, no caches were found, but Gil Aparis told me that they had come across an area where the ground under his feet appeared hollow. He and several others jumped up and down and felt that there was something under them. They lacked digging equipment, and all we could do was record the grid coordinates for possible exploitation later.

The Viet Cong defector also told us that one of the females working for us in the camp was a Viet Cong agent. We had two females working for the American team who were cooks and helped to clean the living areas. Their nicknames were Co Map and Co Tuyet. Co Tuyet was known to have previously been a Viet Cong but had defected. Regardless, the Vietnamese LLDB began questioning both. Paul Fager was paranoid that our food might be poisoned and refused to eat for two days. I implored him to eat, but he refused. I had received a food package from Hawaii, and I finally got Paul to eat. I didn't get to eat any of my goodies. However, taking care of a teammate was worth more than my personal satisfaction! As it turned out, it was Co Map that was working for the Viet Cong. She was arrested and taken to prison.

On another operation, we were proceeding down a shallow river bed when I suddenly fell into a hole. My immediate thought was that I was going to get impaled on punji stakes and the only thing I thought of doing was to bring my rifle horizontally across my body and hopefully stop my fall. As it turned out, I hit the bottom of the hole and had water up to my chest. The interpreter on that operation laughed at me. He soon stepped into a hole himself, and because of his smaller height, he was totally immersed. I had the last laugh. Strangely, some years later, I was visiting my grandmother in Hawaii. She told me that she had saved my life and described how I was falling into a hole and her prayers stopped me from getting hurt. She described the month when it happened and showed me a picture of me in karate *gi* (uniform) kicking a *makiwara*. My face was obliterated as she told me she would pray and rub the picture in her hands. I was in awe and gained even more respect for my grandmother, and I still believe she had psychic powers.

***

The Viet Cong element in the district would sometimes lob mortar rounds into Camp Bu Dop. They weren't very accurate and did minimal damage, but they were still a threat. On one occasion, I was helping Gil Aparis rig a new antenna. He was high up on a slender steel tower when Captain Trieu ran through the area, shouting, "Mortars, mortars!" He had heard mortar rounds coming out of their tubes. Gil started scrambling down the tower and looked like a monkey. Foolishly, I was laughing so hard at the sight that I did not take cover. I felt a burning sensation in my arm after the mortar rounds hit and saw some blood. I felt fortunate not to have been hit more severely, but I still remember that attack from the humor of seeing Gil scramble down the tower. One must maintain a sense of humor even in war.

We were getting mortared enough that the Field Force Headquarters decided to experiment with a mortar detection radar and install it at Bu Dop. The engineers that came in built a massive tower structure and placed the radar on top of it. It proved not to be very effective—it was too slow to determine direction and distance. The joke was that our two monkey mascots, Clyde and Dip, were more accurate at locating the source of mortar fire and much quicker. When we would get mortared, Clyde would climb on an antenna tower and start gesturing. Jokingly, we said that he was pointing towards the direction of the mortar fire! The experiment was abandoned, and the radar was removed. It left us with this substantial structure. It was decided to place large water bladders on the structure which the sun would heat and give plenty of hot water for showers. Ingenuity always pays off! Nothing should go to waste.

In many cases, the location of the mortar fire was coming from the rubber plantation. We did several search operations of the plantation under the premise that there must be a hidden tunnel complex that the Viet Cong were using to hide their mortars and ammunition. We were never successful. On two occasions, we were mortared shortly after the French plantation owner visited the plantation. He would fly in on a single radial-engine airplane that looked very much like the Lockheed Vega that the noted American aviator Wiley Post had set records with in the 1930s. The French owner would also be accompanied by a dwarf. Years later, when the television series *Fantasy Island* was produced, I would always think about that airplane and the role played by Hervé Villachaize. Captain Trieu was convinced that there had to be a tunnel complex in the plantation. He coordinated with Bo Duc District Headquarters, and we mounted an operation to relocate all those living on the plantation and move them to Bo Duc. Then an airstrike was called in to demolish the plantation. Lo and behold, the tunnel entrance was found in the fireplace inside the plantation owner's house.

Strange things can happen in war. The North Vietnamese overran the Special Forces camp at Lang Vei in February 1968 using PT-76 tanks in their attack. At Bu Dop, we were concerned about the possible use of tanks to attack the camp. Over months, we had created a large crater on the dirt road coming from the Cambodian border towards Bu Dop from the north. The hole was made by taking bad lots of ammunition and detonating it which created a crater of at least 8 × 15 foot. One day coming back from a patrol along the Cambodian border, I was approached by a Montagnard who called out to me, "*Trung Si, Trung Si* [Sergeant]." He held up a cluster bomb unit in his hand. These were tennis-ball sized but very powerful bomblets that our Air Force had seeded along the Cambodian border to help deter enemy activity. Fortunately, we were at the crater, and I gestured to the Montagnard to toss the bomblet into the crater. He did as I asked, and it exploded—much to my relief as no one was injured.

On another occasion, I helped John Anderson take a large amount of bad ammunition to the crater for disposal. It included a 105 mm howitzer round from the Vietnamese Army artillery battery at Bu Dop. Andy placed the 105 mm round on the bottom of the crater, then stacked C4 explosives on top of it and the rest of the bad ammunition. He detonated the C4, and we drove back to camp to find that the 105 mm round had somehow inexplicably flown over 800 yards back into the camp and landed on the head of a Cambodian CIDG soldier as he was standing in line in their mess hall for lunch and killed him. Andy was distraught at what had happened and was concerned that the Cambodians would be very angry at him. Andy asked for my help in writing a report. With the perverse humor that one develops in stressful situations, I teased him by saying, "You know Asians can't write English." He looked at me and said, "Not funny, help me out," which I did. As it turned out, the Cambodians thought that what happened was an act of fate and were not angry at Andy.

I received a radio call from Dick Warren who told me to return to Nha Trang as quickly as possible as there was a promotion board meeting, and he wanted me to get promoted to sergeant first class. Bu Dop had no regularly scheduled aircraft coming to the camp, but luck was on my side. An Air Force C7 Caribou came to the camp to deliver some supplies, and they were glad to take me to Saigon. In Saigon I was again fortunate to be able to get on an Air America King Air plane that was headed to Nha Trang. The day was overcast with little visibility and the pilot told me that we might not be able to land in Nha Trang. I explained to the pilot that I had to get back for a promotion board. He was empathetic and told me to hold on. He found a hole in the clouds and dove through it and landed safely in Nha Trang. I went before the promotion board and had a mental blank and did not answer one of the questions properly. Dick Warren talked to me and got me back before the board the following day. My mental block had disappeared, and I was soon to be promoted. It would never have happened if it weren't for a leader like Dick Warren.

The perverse sense of humor extended to the pets we kept. In addition to the two monkeys, Clyde and Dip, we had a dog that was named George to mock the 5th SF Group command sergeant major whose name was George Odom. Odom was known to wear his sleeves down on his uniform and would have several Seiko watches on his arm that he would pressure newly assigned soldiers to the 5th SF Group to buy. We also had a cat that was an excellent rat killer down in the bunker. We decided that we would make the cat airborne qualified, built a small parachute for the cat and asked an Air Force forward air controller in a light plane to take the cat up and toss it out. When the cat was thrown out, the parachute did not fully open. Somehow the cat survived but ran off, never to be seen again.

The perversity extended to our monkey Clyde. A Montagnard village had given us a giant iguana-type lizard that he had found in the jungle. The lizard was a good three or four feet in length. We tied a cord around the lizard's neck and put him in a cage with Clyde. Clyde went berserk as he had never encountered a lizard before. We got a good laugh out of that. The following day, we checked on how Clyde and the lizard were getting along. We found the cage open and the lizard outside. We soon saw Clyde pulling the cord and the lizard towards the cage and then dropping it. Now we started betting on how long it would take for the lizard to perish! As I said, a perverse sense of humor develops in stressful situations. Some may view this as cruelty to animals, but that was not our intent. War does strange things to people's minds.

Andy purchased a sun bear that a Montagnard had captured in the jungle to replace the cat as a mascot. You would have thought that the bear was his child as he would cuddle and feed it with a bottle. Andy didn't take into consideration that this was still a wild animal. One day, the bear clawed him, and with the fear of rabies, Andy had to be subjected to a painful series of rabies shots in the event the bear was rabid. I found out after I left A-341 that all the pets were lost. The two monkeys died from eating C4 explosives as they could not find anything else to eat. George, the dog, was run over by a truck driven by a 1st Cavalry Division soldier who had come to reinforce the camp during a siege by the 9th NVA Division. The sun bear was traded to the A Company Sergeant Major Louis Brown, for food that the team never received.

I was on radio watch in the spring of 1969 and received a call that a VIP was on his way to Bu Dop. When the helicopter landed, I drove to the airstrip to greet the person. It turned out it was a brigadier general walking with a cane. He asked me to gather up the A Team and to provide him with a briefing on enemy activity in the area. Paul Fager started the briefing, and it was evident he was very nervous and probably had never briefed a general officer before; the general sensed his nervousness and gently asked that the team sergeant take over the briefing. I was impressed that the general was understanding of Special Forces organization and that he did not berate Paul Fager.

Roger Dion was the team sergeant at the time and took over the briefing. Upon completion of Roger's briefing, the general asked, "What would you say if I told you that the 9th NVA Division was planning to come across the Cambodian border towards this camp?" The general must have had signals intelligence or imagery intelligence that indicated the 9th NVA Division's plans. Those two sources of intelligence were not generally available to isolated Special Forces A Teams. We were incredulous and could not comment. The general then asked us to determine what would be needed to better defend the camp. He departed, the team immediately informed Captain Trieu, and planning for additional defenses began.

A conventional U.S. Army Engineer platoon was sent to Bu Dop. Their primary mission was to emplace a minefield within the barbed wire defenses that surrounded the camp. They worked hard and we enjoyed having them with us. Captain Trieu also requested that a few bunkers be built inside the minefield with marked lanes to get to the bunkers. This was very insightful as the manned bunkers helped stem a ground attack on the camp that occurred later. The engineers were also tasked with helping build some defenses in Bo Duc District. One of their young soldiers insisted on driving a forklift to District Headquarters one morning before our normal road-sweeping operation between Bu Dop and Bo Duc. We heard an explosion and immediately went to check it out. The soldier had detonated a roadside bomb that blew the forklift on its side. Fortunately, the soldier was not grievously wounded but was dazed and had cuts and bruises from being thrown off the forklift. We laughed when the first words out of his mouth were, "Do I get a Purple Heart?"

One morning we heard a loud explosion at the outer perimeter barbed wire fence surrounding the camp. John Anderson ran out to see what had happened and came across a Montagnard child who was severely burned. Andy saw the remains of a white phosphorous grenade. White phosphorous grenades have a small explosive charge, but they expel and ignite phosphorous that can continue burning as long as oxygen is available. Andy administered first aid and a medevac helicopter was called in. Unfortunately, the child was so severely burned that he died. The Montagnard tribal chief had seen what Andy attempted to do to save the child. The following day, he came to the camp gate and asked to see Andy. When Andy came out, the chief presented him with a large portion of water buffalo meat out of gratitude for what Andy did for the child. The meat was filled with maggots, but Andy graciously accepted it as he did not want to offend the tribal chief. Learning to be culturally sensitive is a crucial trait imbued in Special Forces soldiers.

Knowing that an attack from the 9th NVA Division was imminent, I practiced my ability to fire an 81mm mortar. These mortar rounds come with explosive charge bags attached. Some or all the bags would be removed depending on the range of the target. I had heard that in the 1967 attack on Bu Dop, one of the SF members was killed when charge bags ignited in the mortar pit. I dug a small trench outside of the mortar pit to toss unused bags outside of the pit itself. We all knew that it would be difficult to stop an attack, but we felt we were as prepared as we could be.

CHAPTER 8

The Green Beret Case

In May 1969, Sergeant Major Dick Warren informed me that he needed me to take over the duties as the S3 operations sergeant at B-57 Headquarters. I tried to protest as I didn't want to leave my comrades with a major attack on Bu Dop camp imminent. I also said that I was a junior sergeant first class (E-7) and that the operations sergeant should be a master sergeant (E-8) or sergeant major (E-9). Dick had replaced John Voter as the B-57 sergeant major, and he was as tough and dedicated a soldier as John Voter. Dick heard me out but insisted that he needed me more at the headquarters. He had consulted with John Voter along with two of Dick's Hawaiian friends, Master Sergeant David Kauhaahaa and Sergeant Major Julian Haleamau, with all three of them giving me strong recommendations.

I reluctantly bid farewell to my teammates and friends at Bu Dop and flew back to Nha Trang. On arrival at the headquarters, I found that there was a shortage of folks working in the S3 shop and that the operations officer, Captain Darlington Andrews, and the detachment commander, Major Bob Thrasher, were due to rotate back to the States in a month. Dick's concerns were that there was a backlog of reports that needed to be submitted and to ensure that there would be a good transition for the incoming S3 officer and commander.

I kept up with what was happening at Bu Dop. I was concerned for my friends' safety and wished that I was still there with them. It reminded me of my desire to be with the 25th Infantry Division when my friend Bob Bode was killed in action in 1966. Fortunately, the only friend who was wounded was junior communication sergeant, Mike Parks. Mike was a big, strapping guy born and raised in Midwest America. He was quiet and had a great sense of humor. He would also do odd things; one day I found him hammering on a Chinese stick grenade for no good reason. In months, he had never run into a firefight while on patrol. His luck changed one day when he ran into a significant element of the 9th NVA Division. From what I heard, a fierce firefight ensued. Mike called in for air support and AH-1 Cobra gunships responded. I was told that Mike was asked to mark his position with a smoke grenade but the wind blew the smoke back on his position. The responding helicopters were from the area around Loc Ninh, and one of them had the call sign Blue Max 67, Mother One. Mike was wounded both by the NVA and by our own gunship. Remarkably, after being medevaced for his wounds, he was back in the camp some two weeks later. One tough Midwesterner!

The heartbreaking tragedy that occurred during the siege of Bu Dop in 1969 was when an Air Force C-130 aircraft skidded off the dirt airstrip, plowed through the defensive wire, and into the barracks of a Cambodian company. Over 100 died, including the wives and children of some of the Cambodians. It proved again that war is unpredictable and that good people, including innocents, will be killed. As I learned once again, one is not always the master of his or her own destiny.

Shortly after I began as the operations sergeant, a decision was made to close our operation at Moc Hoa because it had been unproductive for close to a year. Staff Sergeant Alvin L. Smith, Jr., was the case officer at that location and was brought back to headquarters to work in the operations shop. I soon learned that Smith was lazy and had a weird personality and background. He was in his late 30s and I wondered why he was only a staff sergeant. I discovered that he had twice left the Army previously, only to return. On one occasion, he allegedly worked for the CIA, but no one knew what he did for the Agency. On the other occasion, he was a book salesman and then a shoe salesman. He had no explanation as to why he was not able to start an operation out of Moc Hoa, but it was evident that he wanted to find some alibi for his failure. He bonded with another Military Intelligence staff sergeant working in the S3. At night, they would be at one end of the detachment bar drinking martinis while everyone else was guzzling beer or whiskey. At work, I had to counsel him several times to increase his productivity.

To improve our operations, I took a short trip to Saigon and met with the Military Assistance Command Vietnam J2 (MACV J2), an intelligence organization. My purpose was to see how useful our reports were and how they might be improved. I was told that the J2 was very pleased with what B-57 was doing. I also had the opportunity to visit the Combined Intelligence Center Vietnam which was a subject of the MACV J2. I was impressed with what I saw in that they had printouts that showed enemy activity by grid coordinate and that they combined human intelligence with signals and imagery to produce their product. I asked that B-57 receive a monthly printout from them, and they were fully supportive. This was a way that we could analyze reports coming from our field stations to check that our agents were not fabricating information. Every month, I would send a limited number of grid coordinates to our field stations, without saying what intelligence said was at those map locations. The case officers in the field would then selectively ask their agents to reconnoiter the map locations and to report what they had seen. The very good news was that we never saw any deception on the part of our agents regarding what they said was at the sites they were asked to reconnoiter.

Being the operations sergeant gave me a tremendous opportunity to meet and know everyone assigned to B-57 and the field operations. Our two operations in the II Corps area were at Duc Lap (A-239) and Duc Co (A-253). The Duc Lap B-57 effort was led by Captain Charles Yancey with Master Sergeant Pappy Butler at his side. I had met them when I first reported to B-57 in August 1968. Duc Co was led by Master Sergeant Robert "Hook" Pronier. Hook was one of the early High Altitude, Low Opening (HALO) parachutists in Special Forces. All three of them were highly competent and their operations were quite productive in the amount and usefulness of the information reported.

The III Corps operations were at Bu Dop (A-341) which I had left, with Chris Griffin replacing me to assist John Anderson. This operation was moderately productive. Loc Ninh (A-331) was led by Captain Jeff Tom with Nelson Kieff and Benny Dunakoskie there also. Loc Ninh was our most productive operation. Jeff was from Hawaii, and we became very close friends. Our operation out of Tay Ninh East camp was in III Corps. This location was not assigned to any Special Forces camp and was unique. Tay Ninh was also a very productive operation. It was led by Captain Jim O'Hara with Frank Nolte. Their radio operator was Warren "Ed" Fisler, who was one of the most remarkable SF radio operators I ever met. Ed could send messages at 30 groups per minute using a manual telegraph key, rather than the electronic devices used by many to increase their speed. He would tap out a message using his right hand, flip the page on a one-time pad, switch the key to his left and then use his left hand to send out the next page. It was an amazing thing to watch.

B-57 operations in IV Corps were located at Thanh Tri (A-414), led by Captain Robert Marasco, who oversaw Alvin Smith's operation at Moc Hoa before it was closed. This operation was moderately productive. The Special Forces B Detachment at Chau Doc also housed a B-57 operation where Captain Budge Williams was assigned. It also had moderate productivity. The last operation in IV Corps was located at Ha Tien (A-405) where Captain Larry Reiman and Master Sergeant James "War Daddy" Newsome were located. This location also was moderately productive.

I would be remiss if I didn't mention the names of some of the superb radio operators that were in B-57. They clearly ran the fastest and most reliable continuous wave (Morse code) network in Vietnam. They were exceedingly well-respected within the Special Forces Communications community. These are some of the names I remember: Jack Harper, Ken Hain, Pappy Loggins, Clarence "Topsy" Counts, Jim Parris, Jim Trmier, Ted Smith, Jack McIntyre, Johnny Clark, Ed Fisler, Chuck Hiner, Glenn Forsythe, Basilici, and Carl Hargus. It was an honor and privilege for me to work with professionals of their character. There were other well-respected Special Forces NCOs also assigned to the B-57 headquarters. They included Jack Willis, Dick Cruse, and Willie Knoll. Willie had been a young soldier who was on board the USS *Missouri* when it sailed into Tokyo Bay and took the formal surrender from the Japanese at the end of World War II.

Going back to the Green Beret incident, I received a roll of film from Jeff Tom at our Loc Ninh operation. Although I had a photographer assigned to the S3, I sought to keep up my skills and went into the darkroom to help develop and print what we had received. As the prints were drying after being enlarged, Alvin Smith looked at one of the enlargements and excitedly said, "That's my man, that's Chuyen." I asked him what he was talking about, and he replied that Chuyen was his interpreter/principal agent at Moc Hoa. The picture Smith was looking at showed a Vietnamese civilian with either Viet Cong or North Vietnamese in uniform next to him.

Smith went immediately to Darlington Andrews, the B-57 operations officer, and stated that he recognized Thai Khac Chuyen in the picture. Smith further declared that Chuyen had to be a double agent and was the reason Smith could not get an operation started in Moc Hoa. Smith also insisted on talking to the B-57 commander, then-Major Robert Thrasher. While this was going on, I pulled out the dossier on Chuyen and compared his photo with that of the one received from Jeff Tom. I could not see any resemblance and stated that to Andrews and Thrasher. For whatever reason, they decided not to take any action. I don't know whether or not they believed Smith or whether it was because they were within weeks of finishing their tour in Vietnam and going back to the States.

Thrasher and Andrews were replaced by Major David Crew and Captain Budge Williams, respectively the B-57 commander and operations officer. Smith went to them and pleaded his conviction that Chuyen was a double agent and the primary reason why he had not succeeded in establishing an operation at Moc Hoa. I had no idea that Smith had done this. Otherwise, I would have submitted my analysis that I did not believe that it was Chuyen in the photograph with the VC or North Vietnamese. For reasons not known to me, Crew and Williams decided to conceal this matter. The only other B-57 people directly involved were Alvin Smith and Robert Marasco. Marasco had been Smith's boss at Thanh Tri and Moc Hoa. They also involved the 5th SF Group Counterintelligence unit with Captain Leland Brumley and Warrant Officer Ed Boyle. Ostensibly, they also went to Colonel Robert Rheault, who had just taken command of the 5th SF Group; the group executive officer, Ken Facey; and the S2 major, Thomas Middleton.

Other than Smith, none of the B-57 NCOs were brought into the plans for what should be done with Chuyen. That included Dick Warren, the B-57 sergeant major, and myself as the operations sergeant. Well after the incident ended, I heard that Crew had gone to the CIA in Saigon to seek advice. Why he did that is beyond me as the allegations against Chuyen were strictly a military matter and could have been handled without the CIA being involved. The CIA refused to take custody of Chuyen and isolate him where he could do no harm to B-57 operations or any other intelligence effort. Crew also sought guidance from Colonel Rheault who had many other higher-priority issues to handle because of the problems he had inherited from

Colonel Harold Aaron, the previous commander of the 5th SF Group. Rheault told Crew to figure out a course of action, essentially saying that Crew was responsible as a leader for developing a plan.

The plan developed was for Smith to go to Saigon and make contact with Chuyen, under the guise of offering Chuyen a new job. Smith would be accompanied by Warrant Officer Ed Boyle and a polygrapher. Smith lured Chuyen to come to Camp Goodman in Saigon, the headquarters for the 5th SF Group's Command Liaison Detachment. Chuyen was told that it was necessary to ask him a lot of questions and to use a polygraph machine. What ensued were several lengthy sessions ensued, and it became obvious to Chuyen that he was being interrogated, rather than interviewed. He was also injected with sodium pentothal, otherwise known as truth serum. Boyle and the polygrapher felt that Chuyen was lying with regard to contact with the Viet Cong and North Vietnamese Army. It was subsequently decided to bring Chuyen to Nha Trang for further interrogation. Chuyen was restrained, drugged, and then sent by plane to Nha Trang.

In Nha Trang, he was placed in a shipping or CONEX container without windows or air conditioning in the heat of summer. I had my suspicions about what was going on, as I would hear someone yelling and pounding the walls of the CONEX container, but kept my mouth shut. Chuyen was again injected with sodium pentothal and subjected to sleep deprivation and intense interrogation while wired to a polygraph machine. Reportedly, the polygrapher said that it was useless to continue using the polygraph as Chuyen was physically and mentally in no condition for the polygraph to register any meaningful results. Captain Brumley had also been brought in to interrogate Chuyen. More importantly, Chuyen never confessed to being an agent for any non-American intelligence service or having worked for the Viet Cong or North Vietnamese.

Crew visited the CIA Base station in Nha Trang and again asked for help with Chuyen. Once again, they told him that Chuyen was a military problem and that the CIA could not offer any support. There are some individuals who believe that the CIA should have offered to take Chuyen from B-57. However, I do not agree with them and believe that the CIA did what was right and proper. Crew was now in a dilemma regarding what to do with Chuyen. Consideration was given to releasing him, putting him on the American pay roll with no significant duties, turning him over to the South Vietnamese for action, and other scenarios. The one selected was to assassinate Chuyen. The counterintelligence office made arrangements to borrow a small boat with an outboard motor. The B-57 supply officer, Steve Wolf, and NCO, Ross Potter, were tasked with providing chains and mailbags but were not told what they would be used for.

Chuyen was drugged, taken from the CONEX container, and put on the boat with Brumley, Marasco, and Budge Williams. The boat proceeded out in the ocean past Nha Trang Bay. Chuyen was killed with a shot to his head from a suppressed

.22-caliber High Standard pistol, weighted with chains, and dumped overboard in shark-infested waters. The three officers proceeded back to shore, cleaned the boat, and then Marasco and Williams returned to B-57 headquarters. Budge Williams asked me to accompany him the following morning and to dress in a tiger stripe camouflage uniform, a non-standard uniform used by Special Forces in Vietnam, and to pack a rucksack. I felt uneasy when a few of us were asked to be on the lookout for Chuyen who was taken from the CONEX container to his fate. I wasn't quite sure what Williams had planned, and I took my Walther PPK/S .380-caliber pistol and taped it under my left armpit with a round in the chamber.

Early the next morning before the sun had risen, Williams woke me, and we proceeded by jeep to the 5th SF headquarters. I was sitting in the back of the jeep when Major Middleton came up, looked at me, and then inquired of Williams, "Is he one of us?" I just gave him a devastating stare and spat on the ground in front of his feet. We then proceeded to Nha Trang airfield and boarded an L-20 single-engine Beaver airplane with U.S. Army pilots. We took off and headed south from Nha Trang and overland. Williams nodded off to sleep, but I stayed awake to make damn sure that I had some inkling of where we might be. It was an overcast day, and into the flight, the pilot turned back to me and said, "We can't land at Cu Chi." I shrugged my shoulders and mumbled "No speak English," and gestured for him to write a note. He did so, passed it to me, and I shook Budge Williams awake. He then asked if we could land at Tay Ninh East and the pilots replied affirmatively. Williams then had them contact Captain Jim O'Hara who was the B-57 case officer at Tay Ninh East.

On arrival, we were met by Jim O'Hara, and taken to where he had a small compound and several buildings. We spent the rest of the day in idle chatter, had a nice meal, and went to sleep. During the night, Tay Ninh East received 122 mm rocket fire. I was sleeping above ground in a hutch with Frank Nolte, O'Hara's assistant. I got up when the rockets impacted, and then had a good laugh after Frank woke up and immediately dived off his bed onto the floor. I chided him by saying, "Frank, you're a little slow, aren't you?" The next morning, Budge Williams told me that we would go to Saigon and then back to Nha Trang. He never told me why we were supposed to go to Cu Chi, but I assumed that it was to pretend that I was Chuyen going on a mission. However, I never asked the question of Budge Williams.

The next morning, we worked our way back to Saigon and then on to Nha Trang. While in Saigon, we ran into Master Sergeant Marvin Compton who ran the 5th SF Group Mess Association. The Mess Association was widely believed to be conducting all sorts of illegal activities, with its officers pocketing money by charging a monthly fee to those assigned to 5th Group headquarters, and running the Air America Club in Nha Trang for personal profit. Marv kept warily eyeing me and I thought he must have been thinking that I was surveilling him. I played a mind game with him by not saying a word but looking at him with a steely stare.

It was back to work as usual. Smith was acting even weirder than before. After work, he would join us in the B-57 bar. He continued to do a lousy job in preparing intelligence information reports. It was like he wanted to write an academic essay instead of focusing on the facts that had been reported by our field teams. I had to counsel him several times, as he was also slow to prepare his reports. I told him I would kick his ass if he didn't shape up. Towards the end of June 1969, Smith asked for some time off to look for stereo equipment at the Air Force Exchange on Nha Trang airfield. I told him that the Air Force Exchange didn't have what he was looking for as I had just been there two days before. He still wanted to go, so I offered to give him a ride as I needed to go to the 525th MI Group to pick up some intelligence information report forms that we needed because we were running short of stock. Because we only had one jeep assigned to the headquarters, I had arranged with Dean Levay, our administrative and mail clerk, to combine the trip so Dean could pick up our mail.

We drove to the Air Force Exchange and Smith went in by himself. He came out and confirmed they didn't have what he was looking for. I nodded and said I had told him as much, but that there was another Army Exchange close to the 2nd Battalion of the 525th MI Group that we would gladly take him to so he could look for the stereo equipment there. We stopped at the 2nd Battalion headquarters, and I went inside to pick up the forms from an acquaintance from my time at the CI Team Nha Trang. I came out and did not see Smith in the jeep. I asked Levay, "Where's Smith?" He responded by saying that a jeep came out of the gate of the MI compound and that Smith jumped out of our jeep and ran to the other one and acted as if he had run into an old friend. I shrugged my shoulders, and Levay and I headed back to B-57, knowing that Smith could easily find a way back to B-57.

Smith had not returned to B-57 that evening. I called the 2nd Battalion, 525th MI, and spoke to my contact there. He denied knowing Smith's whereabouts. I could tell he was lying by the hesitancy and the trembling nature of his voice. I went to Budge Williams and told him what had happened with Smith that day, and that I suspected he may have turned sour and accused those in B-57 of misdoings. Budge nodded and asked that a few of us look at various bars and clubs in Nha Trang to see if we could find Smith. We did so and found no trace of Smith.

Smith was never reported as being Absent Without Leave. I never tracked that as I was busy with the Operations Section. Candidly, I didn't miss Smith at all because it was easier for me to pick up his workload and do it myself rather than review his shoddy work and counsel him on correcting it. Without direct knowledge of what happened to Thai Khac Chuyen, I still assumed that he had been killed and that Smith was blaming others for his disappearance or death. Smith had a propensity to always blame others for his faults. Less than a week after Smith's disappearance, I saw two people in civilian clothes in the B-57 barracks. They were highlighted in the hallway where we had our offices. I knew instinctively that they were investigators.

I stripped naked, grabbed my Randall knife, and snuck around behind them. I came charging down the hallway screaming and brandishing my Randall knife. The two were immobilized in shock and just stood there with their mouths open! I snuck back into our barracks and told Budge Williams that I believed we were being surveilled.

Within two days, I was summoned to be interviewed by Army Criminal Investigators, for no stated reason. Nonetheless, I again knew instinctively that it would be concerning either Smith or Chuyen. I walked into the room and saw two persons wearing civilian clothes. They showed me their badges and credentials and identified themselves as Frank Bourland and Robert Bidwell. Bourland was an older man and Bidwell looked like he was in his late 20s or early 30s.

Bidwell took the lead in questioning me. I was never read my Miranda rights and Bidwell began the questioning by saying that they were investigating the disappearance of an agent named Chuyen. He then stated that there were no charges against me, but that if I refused to cooperate, they would "throw the book" at me and accuse me of murder. He also threatened to subject me to a polygraph test, if I didn't cooperate. The last thing he said in opening the questioning was, "You see that phone, this case is so important that you can call General Creighton Abrams [the Commanding General of all U.S. forces in Vietnam] anytime you want to."

I quickly sized the situation up in my mind and thought what a bunch of rank amateurs these two are. I knew very well that they had not read my rights against self-incrimination and that they used threats, coercion, and possibly a false promise (about being able to call General Abrams anytime). I knew that because of these violations, any testimony I gave might not be admissible as evidence. Bidwell's questioning began by asking me what my duties were. I responded, "I type a lot." As I found out later, he stupidly and erroneously listed me as a clerk.

Throughout their questioning, I truthfully disavowed any direct knowledge of Chuyen being murdered or seeing him during May and June 1969. They asked me about the night that Chuyen was taken from the CONEX container. I stated that the only thing I knew was being asked to keep watch outside the offices of B-57 and to keep anyone away who was not in the unit. I also stated that someone was being locked up in a CONEX container and that I heard pounding and yelling from within the container but had no idea who was in it. The last thing I was asked about was the trip to Tay Ninh with Budge Williams. Again, I answered truthfully and said that I had no knowledge of why we went on the trip.

Bidwell and Bourland continued to interview others in B-57, including Dick Cruse, Bob Clegg, Pete Potter, Steve Wolf, Marasco, and Williams. A few days later, Dave Crew, Budge Williams, and Robert Marasco were taken into custody and sent to Long Binh and locked in cells. We soon learned that Colonel Rheault, Thomas Middleton, Leland Brumley, and Ed Boyle were also incarcerated. They were charged with the murder of Thai Khac Chuyen, and a court-martial was to ensue to determine their guilt or innocence. All of us in B-57 were concerned with the fate of the eight that were charged, but we had a job to do and continued with our collection and reporting duties. Ironically, the eighth person to be charged was Alvin L. Smith! Years later, Budge Williams told me that he was very despondent when he was locked in his cell. He heard someone sobbing and crying next to him and inquired what was wrong. The one crying identified himself as Alvin Smith, and Williams's morale went up as he felt strongly that Smith was the one who initiated the fate of Chuyen.

The military equivalent of a grand jury hearing is termed an Article 32 hearing. One was scheduled to be held in Long Binh. Dick Cruse, Pete Potter, Jim Parris, Steve Wolf and I were instructed to travel there; we would be called on to testify at the hearing. While we were waiting to testify, Bob Bidwell came to the room where we were waiting. He had a smile on his face and greeted us like he was a friend. I turned to Bidwell and said, "You remember that promise you made about being able to talk to General Abrams at any time? Well, I want to talk to him right now!" At first, Bidwell thought I was joking. I assured him in no uncertain terms that I was dead serious and demanded that he make it happen immediately. With a worried look on his face, he scurried off.

After Bidwell ran off, I went to the Staff Judge Advocate Office inside Long Binh jail and asked for a military lawyer. I was greeted by a specialist who identified himself as a lawyer, who had chosen to be drafted rather than join the Army as an officer and lawyer. He stated that he did not want to incur the additional service time had he taken a commission as an officer. He listened to my request and told me that, in all likelihood, a Major Kane would be sent to see me. He also warned that I should not trust Kane, as he was supposed to advise all the defense military lawyers and was doing so, but in reality, he was also reporting to those prosecuting the courts-martial. I thanked the Specialist Fourth Class and asked him for a favor. The favor was to take a note I scribbled about being threatened, coerced, and made false promises to secure my testimony to one of the defense lawyers. He grinned and said he would be most happy to do so.

Bidwell came back to the room where we were waiting. He had a worried look on his face and was sweating. He told me that General Abrams was not available, but would I be willing to talk to Major General Mabry, the MACV Chief of Staff. I looked at Bidwell and said, "Nope, and guess what—you made a false promise to gain testimony." He then left the room knowing that none of us in the room were friends of his.

I was summoned to testify and proceeded to the Long Binh jail chapel where the hearings were being held. As I walked into the entrance, I saw that the defendants were on my left and the prosecutors on my right. The person seated immediately to the left as I entered was Alvin Smith. I started trembling as my body was saying, "kick his ass." My mind was saying, "You can't do that, this is a formal military proceeding." I stared straight ahead and proceeded to the witness stand. I had been introduced as a witness for the prosecution for reasons not known to me. The defense lawyers began the questioning, led by Captain Steve Berry. Apparently, the specialist that I had spoken to previously had given my note to Captain Berry. Berry's line of questioning was whether I had been threatened, coerced, and made false promises by the CID investigators. I was only too happy to answer affirmatively. Berry stopped his questioning, fully knowing that any testimony I gave would be inadmissible. One of the prosecution lawyers jumped up and, in a rattled voice, said, "You knew your rights were being violated!" Then he said, "Oh, never mind," and sat down. He knew that despite my knowing my rights were being violated, it made no difference. I was dismissed and strode out of the chapel only to bump into Bob Bidwell. I gave him a dirty look and walked past him without acknowledging him.

As I later found out, Bidwell was raked over the coals by the defense lawyers for violating rights and getting testimony using illegal tactics. It turned out that Bidwell was accused of violating the rights of almost everyone that he and Bourland had questioned to make their case against the defendants. I later heard that the Article 32 hearing got very messy. The defense questioned the role of Major Kane by pointing out that he was supposed to lead the defense attorneys but then showed up with a prosecution witness. They also demanded certain information held by the CIA along with the appearance of CIA personnel as witnesses. This included the overall head of CIA operations in Vietnam, Ted Shackley, and the lead CIA base officer in Nha Trang. Reportedly, the CIA refused to testify at the Article 32 hearing except for one individual, named Chipman. The contention of the military defense lawyers was that the CIA had offered advice concerning the killing of Chuyen and that the CIA itself had committed acts of murder through the Phoenix program in Vietnam and elsewhere around the world, including the death of the Cuban Che Guevara in Bolivia. Chipman's testimony was marked by the defense lawyers being able to point out many inconsistencies and the strong probability that the CIA did in fact offer advice concerning the killing of Chuyen.

The defendants had also retained civilian attorneys. They included the well-known and respected trial lawyers, Edward Bennett Williams and Henry Rothblatt. Tom Middleton's civilian lawyer was a friend, George Gregory, from South Carolina. Gregory travelled to Vietnam and played a key role in defending Middleton. The key role Gregory played was not so much about his legal abilities but because he engendered great interest from the press. Henry Rothblatt also traveled to Vietnam and engaged in further hearings that were being held. As a skilled trial lawyer, he was able to call into question the admissibility of a wide range of testimonies that further weakened the prosecution's case against the eight defendants. He pointed out the lack of a corpse to prove factually that Chuyen had been killed. He was unaware that MACV had sent a U.S. Navy minesweeper to Nha Trang Bay to find Chuyen's body and the chains he had supposedly been weighed down with to sink his body. The Navy minesweeper failed to find any evidence.

Unbeknownst to us in B-57, there was a lot happening back in Washington, DC, concerning the case. The media was following events closely and reporting on the case, influential members of Congress were seeking information and asking questions related to appeals for help by the defendants and their families, and the Secretary of the Army and Secretary of Defense were interested. In mid-August 1969, Secretary of the Army Stanley Resor made a trip to Vietnam; a principal reason being the review of the Green Beret case with General Abrams. Shortly after his visit to Vietnam, the defendants were moved out of solitary confinement and grouped together with Colonel Rheault in a "house arrest" situation where they were still confined but could talk to each other and weren't in jail cells. Yet, the Army was still determined to seek prosecution, despite the lack of a corpse. The prosecution plan was to offer immunity to Ed Boyle and Alvin Smith but still pursue charges of murder against the other six.

The CIA decided that they would refuse to provide any additional testimony based on national security interests. The White House staff and President Nixon were believed to have become heavily involved. Back in Vietnam, there was talk about launching an operation to free Colonel Rheault and the others. Rocky Nesom, a former Green Beret who had gotten out and was flying for Air America, reportedly visited with Colonel Rheault at Long Binh. He told the colonel that he was prepared to fly in and take him to a safe site in Vietnam where he had Montagnards who would provide security. Colonel Rheault refused Rocky's offer.

I also did something foolish. I procured nine handguns, stowed them inside my field jacket and went to Saigon to see Colonel Rheault and the others. I went to the Command Liaison Detachment at Camp Goodman in Saigon, and they provided me with a jeep and a Nung (ethnic Chinese) driver. I asked the driver to take me to the Staff Judge Advocate Office in Long Binh and he did so. I walked in and asked for help in finding Colonel Rheault. All I got were questions about who I was and why I wanted to see him. I got pissed and stormed out of the office throwing two large safes to the floor. I got back to the jeep and the Nung driver said to me, "*Trung Si*, you look plenty pissed off!" I explained that the lawyers refused to tell me where Colonel Rheault was. The Nung looked at me and simply said, "Oh, I know where he stay." I felt stupid at that point. We drove to where Colonel Rheault and the others were under house arrest. I went up to Colonel Rheault and opened my field jacket so he could clearly see the weapons I had. I then proceeded to get the biggest ass-chewing of my life without being chastised. Colonel Rheault put his arm around my shoulders and steered me away from the others. Without once mentioning the weapons, he started talking about the greatness of America and its constitution that provided inalienable rights for all citizens. I limped off and flew back to Nha Trang. On reflection, had Rocky Nesom or I been successful, it would have been the death knell for Special Forces by showing a rogue nature and defying military discipline and law. I will never forget that for the rest of my life.

At the end of September 1969, Secretary of the Army Stanley Resor held a press conference in Washington, DC, and announced that all charges would be dropped against the eight defendants. Dave Crew and Budge Williams came back to B-57 to quickly pack their belongings. There was no time to talk, but I wished them farewell and good luck in the future. Alvin Smith did not return, and I imagine that he convinced MACV that he would be in danger if he did. They would be returned to America for reassignment without penalty. Colonel Rheault was offered another command, and he stated that he wanted to command the 5th Special Forces Group again. When the Army refused to allow that, he decided to retire. Marasco also decided to leave the Army. I am not sure what happened to Middleton, Brumley, Boyle or Smith. Budge Williams stayed on and would later retire as a lieutenant colonel. Dave Crew would get promoted twice and retire as a colonel some years later.

***

Colonel Rheault was replaced by Colonel Alexander Lemberes. He was a "leg" (non-airborne) and brought his personal masseur to the command. He decided that he wanted to become airborne qualified and went to the jump school run by Special Forces at Dong Ba Thin. He grievously injured himself while in jump training and had to be medevaced. He was then replaced by Colonel Mike Healy who was Special Forces qualified. At B-57, an interim commander was sent, Major Robert Richfield. Richfield was a signal intelligence officer without any human intelligence experience. He came in acting like he was God's gift to the world. One night at the B-57 bar, he loudly proclaimed that in five years there would no longer be Special Forces in the U.S. Army. Bob Pronier, who ran our Duc Co operation said, "Ish, tell him what you think!" I was drunk and pissed at what Richfield said. I jumped on the bar in front of Richfield, turned around, dropped my pants, and "mooned" him. I said, "You can kiss my ass, and if you don't like that then … " as I jumped around to face him, "… you can suck my dick." Richfield had this petrified look on his face and quickly left the bar. I was lucky not to get court-martialed for insubordination. I guess Richfield figured that no one in the room would verify what I had done! It's great to have teammates that will stand up and be counted!

Before Richfield relinquished command, he wrote an officer's efficiency report on Captain Larry Reiman. Richfield had never even met Larry but wrote a report that vilified Larry. It was totally unprofessional and uncalled for. Larry knew the report would end his military career if unchallenged. I wrote a long statement on Larry's behalf, and he believes that statement was taken into account and his career saved. Larry would retire years later as a colonel and head of the Army's foreign liaison program. We became lifelong friends after that and still see each other frequently.

Two quick stories about Larry. Larry led the B-57 operation in Ha Tien which was on the ocean adjacent to Cambodia. He made a trip to Cam Ranh Bay one day and was driving out the gate when he was stopped by a Military Police officer who questioned what he had in the back of the three-quarter-ton truck that Larry was driving. Larry acted very nervous and lifted the canvas covering in the back of the truck. The MP saw several cases of steaks and asked Larry to see the paperwork authorizing him to have the steaks. Larry acted really nervous and offered to give the MP a case of the steaks. The MP accepted the bribe, and Larry drove out the gate. In reality, he had "moonlight requisitioned" (i.e. stolen) a trailer, a boat, and two outboard motors that he later had transported to Ha Tien! One could say that he demonstrated his skills as either a con artist or his skills as an intelligence operative.

The other story was when Larry, Jack Harper, and me were headed out of our compound and going to enjoy a lobster and wine dinner at a noted restaurant called Francois. I was driving and was stopped at the gate by an MP who asked to see my "trip ticket." I showed it to him, and he said that it was improperly filled out (which it wasn't). I was angry and got out of the jeep and gave the MP an evil stare. His hand started moving for his pistol. I said in a loud voice, "If you put your hand on that gun you will have two seconds to live." That scared him and he backed off. Larry got out of the jeep and demanded that the MP call his superiors. A patrol soon came up and an MP sergeant pulled Larry and I to the side and asked, "What did that dumb shit do now?" We described what happened and the sergeant asked that we go to the MP station and file a report. We did and I guess that the punk MP was disciplined! Our meal at Francois's that night tasted especially good.

Despite all the turmoil, Detachment B-57 continued to collect and report intelligence on Cambodia. This was a tribute to the field teams and their dedication. We heard that B-57 would close in 1970, but never received official word or the date the detachment would close. The operations officer position was left vacant, and I had to assume that role. For a short period of time, we had an MI warrant officer assigned to be the operations officer. He had joined B-57 in August and was initially sent to Duc Co with Bob Pronier. Because of his age and because there weren't any warrant officers in Special Forces line organizations, he was placed undercover as a captain. Shortly after he got to Duc Co, he was shown around the camp by members of the A Detachment. He came across a 105 mm recoilless rifle and remarked that the recoilless rifle was an automatic mortar. He blew his cover with that stupid remark. Bob Pronier sent a message to headquarters that we needed to remove him from Duc Co, and Sergeant Major Dick Warren made that happen post haste. When the warrant officer came back to Nha Trang, we didn't know what to do with him, so we assigned him as the operations officer. It turned out that he had been an enlisted aircraft mechanic in the Air Force and took advantage of a program where Army Military Intelligence was offering warrant officer positions without much screening. How this idiot ever got through Intelligence School was beyond me, and once again, I started doubting the leadership in Army Intelligence.

One of the key duties of the operations officer was to review the finished intelligence information reports and approve them prior to sending them to MACV headquarters. It turned out the warrant officer was not only lazy but not very adept at reading and understanding intelligence reports. Yet he would make two trips every day to the Post Exchange. I tried to help him and urge him to review the reports as it was critical for those reports to be sent on a timely basis to MACV. After a few weeks, he literally had three piles of reports, each a foot high, on his desk. I lost my cool and went to Dick Warren and stated that I had all I could take and that I was going to seek a reassignment. Dick told me in no uncertain terms that I was not going to be reassigned and to get back to work. The following day the warrant officer was sent packing. No one missed him!

Even before I was brought from Bu Dop back to the headquarters, I had been planning to again extend my tour in Vietnam and to take extension leave to travel to Hawaii and participate in the National Goju Ryu Karate tournament that would be hosted by Sensei Masaichi Oshiro in Honolulu in November. I was practicing diligently in the early morning and late at night to prepare for the tournament. When I got to Honolulu, I stayed with my close friends, Billy and Tiny Brash. The morning after I arrived, I felt very ill, started throwing up, and had a high fever. Billy took me to Tripler Army Hospital where I was admitted. I either had malaria or dengue fever, but the doctors could not determine what it was and characterized it as a "fever of unknown origin." Despite being terribly ill, I was determined that I would fight in the tournament.

On the flight from Vietnam, I had brought back a war trophy; a Springfield '03 rifle. When we landed at Hickam Air Force Base, my rifle was missing. Fortunately, Pete Potter from B-57 was on the flight and would continue to Travis Air Force Base in California. Pete was able to find my rifle and arranged for the rifle to be sent to me in Honolulu. How it got to me at Tripler Army Hospital is still a mystery to me. The head nurse on the ward where I was recovering happened to be the mother of a high school friend's wife, Jean Otake. I pled with the head nurse to get me discharged. She knew I was in no shape to be discharged and kept scolding me. After receiving my rifle, I plotted in my mind how I would get discharged. Jean's mother came into the ward one day and saw me aiming the rifle out the window and working the bolt of the rifle. She asked me what I was doing, and I responded that I was going to shoot some anti-war protestor. She was aghast, but I again pled with her to help me be discharged, and she did so.

The day after I was discharged from the hospital, I went to practice at the home of Sensei Oshiro. I was weak, dehydrated, down to 145 pounds, and promptly broke two of my ribs when we were engaging in *Kumite* or free-fighting. The tournament was a week away. My string of bad luck continued when it was decided that the names of the entrants coming from the continental U.S. would be placed in a hat. The guys from Hawaii would reach in and pick out a piece of paper with a name and that would determine who would fight whom in the first round of the tournament. It was my luck that I picked out the name of Bill Reuter. Bill had turned down promotion to 4th Dan so he could fight in the tournament. He was originally from Hawaii and was six feet three inches tall and weighed around 225 pounds. Sensei Oshiro knew how weak and banged up I was after breaking my ribs.

He was amazed that I still wanted to fight. He saw that I took adhesive tape and bound my ribs to help alleviate the pain and then entered the tournament. I could see in Bill Reuter's eyes that he wanted to win badly. I also sensed that he was going to play a defensive and counterattack game. After we bowed to each other, I immediately launched an attack by trying to sweep his feet from under him. I hit him as hard as I could, and he didn't budge. I felt the pain shoot through my body! I tried to launch a couple other attacks but realized I was just too slow. As he blocked my attacks, I felt more pain. I was not about to quit and devised a plan in my mind. I dropped my hands to entice him to attack me. My plan was that I knew he would attack my head, that I would drop under his attack and then counterattack. The plan almost worked, but I didn't drop far enough, and he hit me on my right shoulder. He didn't score a point, but now I couldn't move my right arm! We fought to a zero-to-zero tie, and the referee correctly awarded Bill a referee's decision. Sensei Oshiro commended me on my courage and was the only one who knew what I had to do to even fight in the tournament.

***

I returned to Vietnam in December 1970 ready to start my third year in the country. Dick Warren asked me what the hell happened to me as I looked emaciated and was moving gingerly. When I told him what happened, we both had a good laugh. Then it was back to work and not worrying about when B-57 would be closed. Major Don Steiger arrived to take command of the unit. He was a decent person and helped to restore a sense of normalcy to B-57.

In March 1970, I was in the field when I was summoned back to Nha Trang. A helicopter was sent to pick me up, and on arrival in Nha Trang I saw a chaplain waiting for me. I walked up to him and said, "You're going to tell me that my mother passed away." He looked at me and asked, "Do you have a brother named Jerry Brighter?" I was stunned beyond belief. Jerry was the youngest son of my Uncle David and Aunty Ruth, who was my mother's younger sister. Jerry had been serving with the 101st Airborne Division in Vietnam.

Dick Warren pulled me aside along with Ed Coulter who was the B-57 S1. Dick told me that all my stuff was packed, and that Ed was trying to get me on a flight to Hawaii to attend the funeral. I went to my barracks room and found that everything was indeed packed into two-foot lockers. I asked Dick, "What the hell is going on?" He said that I was going home. I said that I was coming back, and he responded that I was not. He showed me the orders that had been issued sending me to Okinawa on an emergency permanent change of station. I started to argue with Dick, and then backed off. He was my sergeant major, he was my friend, and I now realized that he knew I would go off the deep end if I returned to Vietnam. Ed Coulter handed me some paperwork so that I could return my field equipment and check out with other places to be able to leave.

One of the places I had to stop and get a release signature was with the 5th Special Forces Group Sergeant Major Myron "Bac Si" Bowser. Bowser had taken over from George Odom when Colonel Rheault took command. Bac Si Bowser was a soldier's soldier, tall and lean, and a great leader. I sat outside his office waiting for him to return. He walked in and said, "Ish, what are you doing here? I already have a job lined up for you when B-57 closes. You're going to be a lifeguard on Nha Trang Beach." With great respect for Bac Si Bowser, I told him that I was not sure if I would have accepted a lifeguard job, but that was not the reason I was there to see him. He looked at me with a puzzled expression and I told him about Jerry Brighter's death and that change of station orders were out on me. Sergeant Major Bower profusely apologized and gave me his condolences. I told him not to worry. He then asked what he could do to help, and I responded by saying that Dick Warren and Ed Coulter were taking good care of me. We hugged and I went back to B-57.

Ed Coulter had been pulling all the strings he had to get me to Hawaii as quickly as possible. He had checked for flights out of Da Nang, Cam Ranh Bay, and Tan Son Nhut. He said that I had a chance of getting on a flight out of Tan Son Nhut but that we needed to hurry. He rushed me to the Nha Trang airfield, and I boarded a C-130 headed for Tan Son Nhut. On arrival, I went to the terminal only to find I had just missed the flight to Hawaii. The airman manning the desk checked and said there was a flight leaving from Bien Hoa. I asked him if there was any transportation for me to get there and he regretfully told me that there was none. I then hitchhiked my way to Bien Hoa, ran to the terminal and found that once again I had just missed a flight. The airman at the counter told me that there was a scheduled flight the next morning and that he would ensure I was on it. I asked him if there was a place where I could get a shower and sleep and he replied that there was not.

All I had were the fatigues I was wearing and my Browning 9 mm Hi-Power pistol. I went to sleep on the floor of the terminal, got mortared one last time, checked in the next morning and I was on the flight. When they called to board the aircraft, I went up to the Air Force security cop and asked him if he could use some 9 mm ammunition. He said that he certainly could. I then pulled out two magazines for my 9 mm, emptied them and passed him the rounds. His eyes got big, and I stated that I had the papers to legally carry the weapon out of Vietnam and showed him those papers. I was tired, dirty, and probably smelled bad from sweat after my whirlwind trip from Nha Trang to Tan Son Nhut to

Bien Hoa. I was one of the first to board the plane which was a United Airlines charter Boeing 707.

As I boarded the aircraft there was a male flight attendant. He asked me where I was from, and I replied "Hawaii." We chatted for a short time, and he told me to wait at the entrance. He came back a short time later and told me to follow him. He saw what a mess I looked like and had cleared three seats so I could prone out and get some sleep. We were able to talk more with each other, and I found out he grew up in Kapahulu on Duval Street. Duval was the street next to Catherine Street where I had lived until we moved to Kuliouou in 1950. We knew many of the same people. I never got his name. Years later I asked friends who were with United Airlines whether they could find him, as I wanted to profusely thank him for his kindness. But we had no luck in finding him. After getting fed, I lay down exhausted and slept until we landed in Hawaii.

I called my Uncle Kenji Aihara and his wife, Aunty Mitsue, and asked if I could stay with them. They came and picked me up and took me to their home in Aiea. I finally had a chance to take a shower. I went out to buy some civilian clothes, and had a great dinner that Aunty Mitsue cooked. We talked for a bit, and I found out about the funeral arrangements for Jerry. I went to sleep still very tired from jet lag and the long journey from Vietnam. Early the next morning, my aunt and uncle came running to the room where I was sleeping after hearing a loud thumping sound. They found me crouched, with a wide-eyed stare on my face, and my arms in front of me as if I was holding a rifle. It scared the hell out of them. What had happened was that I was awakened by a news helicopter that flew over their house. Somehow, I imagined I was in the field in Vietnam, and that I was under fire and had to get to the helicopter to be extracted. This was another encounter with what I would learn was Post-Traumatic Stress Disorder.

The following day, I headed for Fort Shafter to request that I be issued a dress uniform and leather boots to wear to Jerry's funeral. I was greeted by a punk private first class who started giving me a hard time by asking who I thought I was to request a uniform. I explained that I had just come out of Vietnam wearing my fatigue uniform and that I needed a dress uniform to attend Jerry's funeral. He gave me more lip, and I lost it. I jumped over the counter he was behind, yelled at him and grabbed him around his neck and threw him against a wall. His boss, a staff sergeant, heard the ruckus and came out of his office to find out what was going on. I was quickly given the uniform items and left for the Post Exchange and tailor shop to get my patches and rank sewn on. I had rented a car and, on the way back to my aunt and uncle's home, a car adjacent to me on the freeway had an engine backfire. I swerved across three lanes of highway thinking there was a bomb that went off and was fortunate that I did not get into an accident. Again, the specter of PTSD was with me. I knew I was not in the right frame of mind but didn't know what to do except try to calm myself down.

Jerry was buried at the Hawaiian Memorial Park on the windward side of Oahu near Kaneohe where his parents lived. On the day of the funeral, I rode with Uncle David and Aunty Ruth, Jerry's parents, and stoically stood there throughout the service. As we left the graveyard, I asked Uncle David to stop the car. I got out and started walking back to their home which was about two miles away. I don't know what was on my mind, but I just needed to be alone. I also hoped that I would come across some anti-war protestors so I could beat the living daylights out of them. I encountered several groups of people on my walk back. They all gave me a wide berth and were probably scared by the evil look I had in my eyes.

Although he was not able to make the funeral, Jerry's first sergeant came to Hawaii on rest and recuperation leave. He took the time to meet with the family and talk about Jerry. I was grateful and thought that he did what good leaders do—care about their troops and their families. He told me that the 101st Airborne was very short of personnel. Jerry, a young specialist, had been an acting platoon sergeant. Jerry, because of the lack of experience in his platoon, took the point (lead position) on a patrol and was killed with a shot to his head. I thanked the first sergeant and his wife for their concern and kindness. It made me sad that Jerry had passed on, as he was the youngest of four brothers who would never be able to accomplish the things in life that he wanted.

CHAPTER 9

Special Action Force Asia

With a great deal of sadness, I arranged to fly to Okinawa where my orders directed me to report to the headquarters of the U.S. Army Ryukyu Islands (USARYIS). I knew that Dick Warren had contacted Sergeant Major Julian "Corn Beef" Haleamau who was the sergeant major of A Company, 1st Special Forces Group. When I reported to USARYIS, I was told I would be assigned to a military intelligence unit based on Camp Kue. I called Corn Beef and he told me not to worry. He had worked the "good old boy" network. When I reported to the intelligence unit, their sergeant major said that orders would be issued reassigning me to the 1st Special Forces Group. Was I ever happy! I thought I was on my way to work for Corn Beef in A Company. When I signed in at 1st SF Group headquarters, the personnel folks told me to see the Group Command Sergeant Major Duane Vierk, and deputy commander, Lieutenant Colonel Dick Kim. They told me that there was a leadership problem with the 441st Military Intelligence Detachment which was part of the 1st SF Group. They said they wanted me to go there and straighten it out. I was perplexed and mentioned that there had to be NCOs there who were senior to me. I was told there were, but they still needed me to go there and straighten things out. They also implied that the commander was weak. Oh well, at least they told me that I would be assigned to A Company at a later date.

The 441st MID had an excellent record and history during World War II and the Korean War. At some point, it was transferred to be under the 1st Special Forces Group. The commander was Lieutenant Colonel Tajiri. He had a reputation as a nice person but not a strong commander or leader. The executive officer was a captain who struck me as someone taken with himself and also not a strong leader. There were two lieutenants who were fine officers. Both were graduates of Middlebury University. One was assigned to oversee the counterintelligence section of the 441st MID, and the other to look after agent collection operations. Their names were Brice Bailey and Jim Betz. A third lieutenant was wet behind the ears and did not receive any mentorship from Tajiri or the executive officer.

The unit had failed two annual inspector general inspections in a row. The senior NCO was a counterintelligence agent who masqueraded as the mail clerk and never did anything of note from a counterintelligence perspective. There were two sergeants first class who outranked me. One was the first sergeant for the detachment, and the other was an American of Japanese ancestry who was working at the 1st SF Group S2 section. Unfortunately, both E7s did their jobs but did nothing with respect to working with the rest of the soldiers assigned to the 441st MID. I quickly analyzed what was happening and found that none of the younger soldiers had any meaningful work other than the actual mail clerk, a Chinese American from Rochester, New York, named Lincoln Lew. All the soldiers were performing meaningless details such as mowing the grass in different 1st SF Group areas.

Because I was unmarried, I moved into the barracks where the 441st MID was located. The unit was on the western side of Okinawa, north of Torii Station and close to an Army firing range, nicknamed "Bolo Point." I rapidly found how low the morale was with the young soldiers. I asked the first sergeant and the other E7 what had been done to put the soldiers to useful work. All I got were blank stares. I thought that the morale of the young soldiers would greatly improve if they had worthwhile work in their intelligence specialties. It happened that a friend of mind, Master Sergeant George Banias, was the NCO in charge of the S2 section at 1st SF Group headquarters. I talked with George and determined that he could use help in producing analytical products to support 1st SF Group elements that were deploying all over Asia. I also discovered that the returning teams were not being debriefed on their return to Okinawa; they were a great source of information on key personnel in the military of the countries to which they had been deployed. George was eager to use 441st MID soldiers trained to obtain information—a perfect fit for interrogators. In short order, George put many of the 441st MID soldiers to gainful work and morale started to improve. Their self-esteem soared simply by having meaningful work rather than just being used for lowly details.

A few of the soldiers were content with the old ways where they didn't have to work very much, if at all. I suspected one individual of instigating the reluctance to work. I also had a feeling that he was using marijuana but could not prove it. One weekend I walked into the Orderly Room where the Charge of Quarters was supposed to conduct a watch over the compound. A party was being held, with liquor all over the room. I told the group that the Orderly Room was a place of business and that they could still have their party but needed to move it into another area. The troublemaker came at me with a baseball bat. The next thing he knew he was flat on his back with the bat aimed at his mouth. The party promptly broke up! I never found out if he was using, but it didn't matter.

Another inspector general inspection was scheduled, and little was being done to prepare for it. I asked the first sergeant for the results of the past two inspections where the unit had failed. It was easy to understand what needed to be corrected

My father, Paul Ishimoto, 2× AAU boxing champ, the 1930s.

Me as a young child.

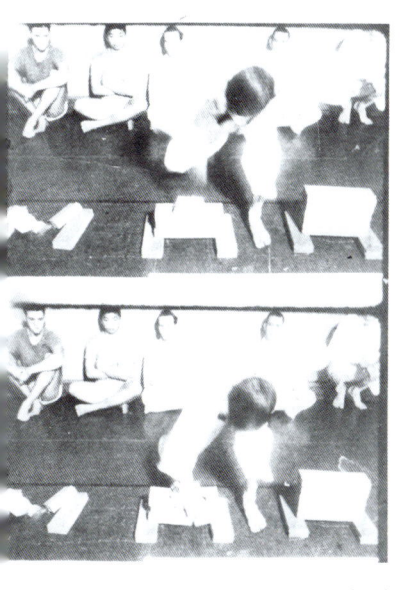

ong Su teacher Moon Yo Woo, Portland, Oregon, 1959.

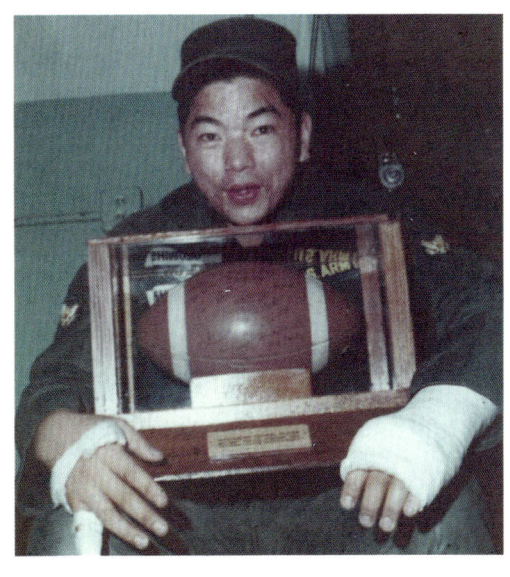

MVP Post Football Championship 1962. Fort Monmouth. I broke both hands on the frozen field.

Post Softball Championships, 1962, Fort Monmouth. I am third from the left in the front row.

191st MI Detachment, 1st Cavalry Division, 1964.

191st MI Detachment, Paju-Ri, Korea, 1964.

The burial at sea of friend Bob Bode, KIA in Vietnam in 1966.

Bodysurfing at China Walls, 1966.

Outside the Military Police Company, 1963.

CI Team, Nha Trang, with Bill Miller, 1968.

With Nguyen Cao Ky and sister of Chae Myung Shin, Hon Tre Island, 1968.

Bu Dop with John Anderson, 1968.

Bu Dop with Clyde and Dip, 1968.

Bu Dop, 1968.

Karate exhibition, Bu Dop, 1968.

Aerial view of Bu Dop, Detachment A-341.

Destroyed rubber plantation at Bu Dop—suspected Viet Cong location.

Project Gamma patch.

Medical civic action, Bu Dop.

Leaving B-57 with Sergeant Major Dick Warren, March 1970.

1st Battalion, 1st SFGA, 1972.

With Korean Special Forces Sergeant Major Chae, Exercise Foal Eagle, 1972.

SF School Instructor of the Year, 1974.

University of Santa Clara ROTC, 1976.

Hostages on November 4, 1979. (U.S. Army via Reuters)

Eagle Claw evasion map of Iran with Desert One location at bottom right.

Road Map of
iran
ایران
Caspian Sea
DASHT-E-KAVIR
KAVIR-E-LUT
Persian Gulf
خلیج فارس

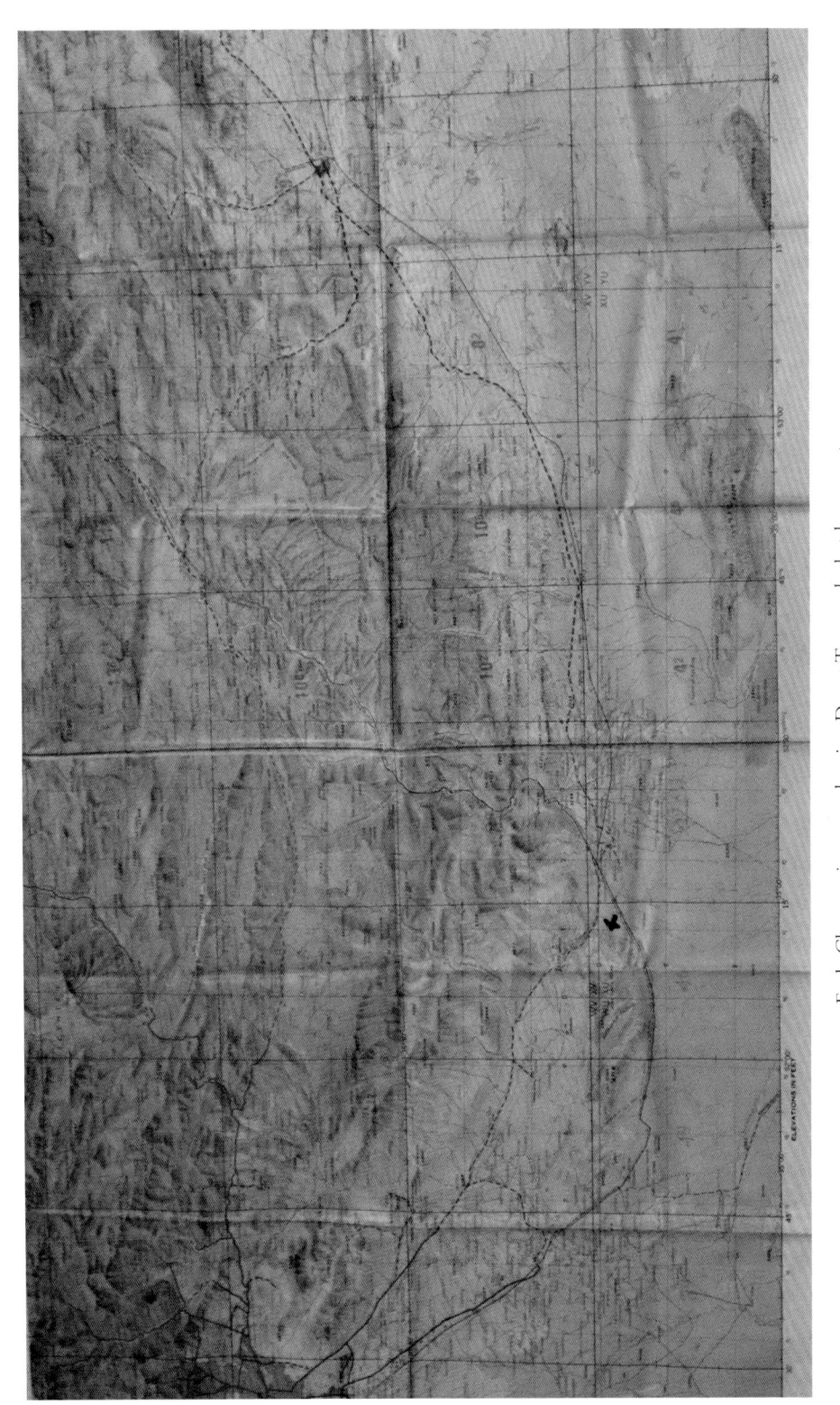

Eagle Claw evasion map showing Desert Two marked at lower center.

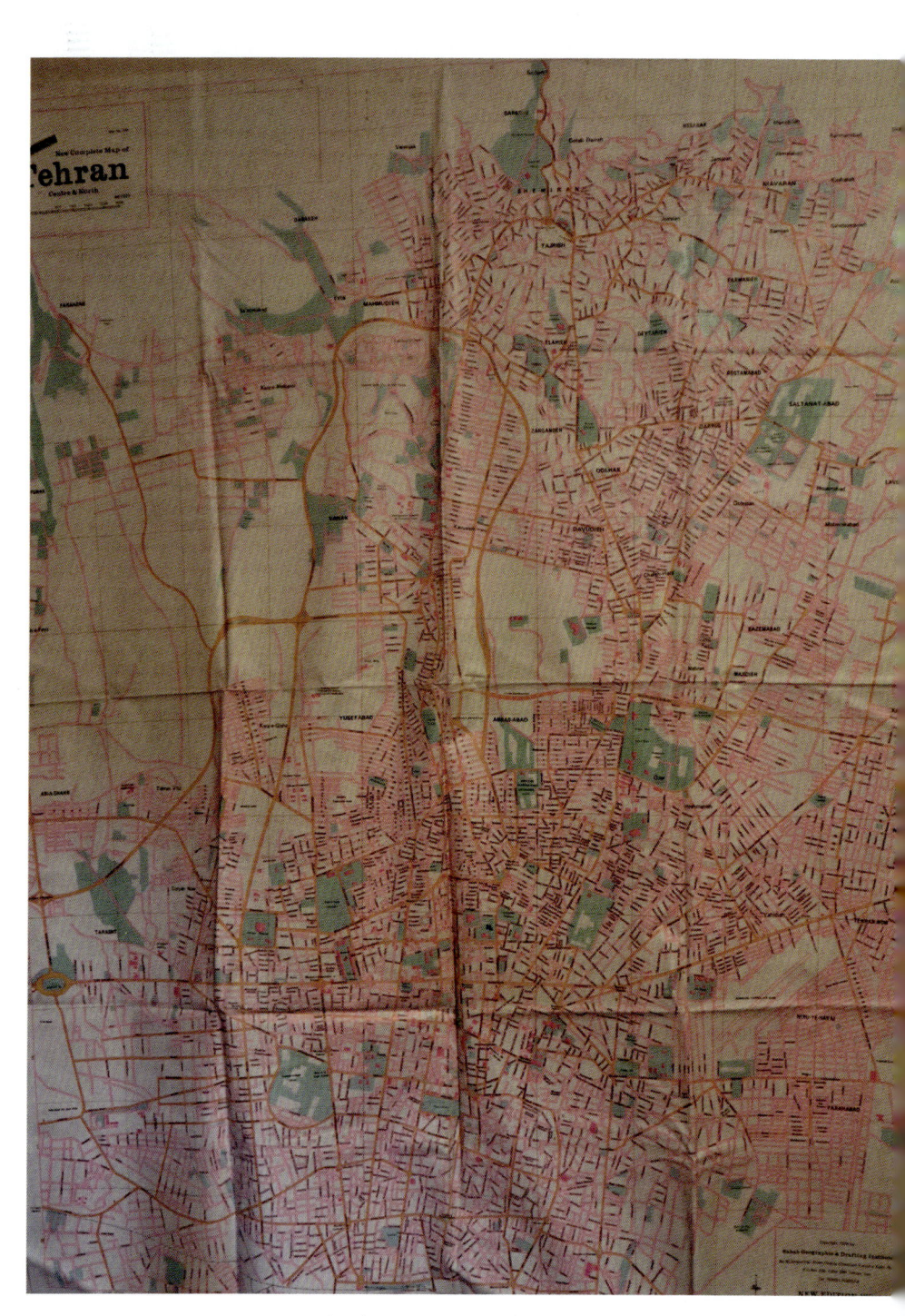

Eagle Claw evasion map of Tehran City.

Eagle Claw, June 23, 1980.

Eagle Claw blood chit.

Travel voucher for Fort Bragg to Egypt and back, Operation Eagle Claw, June 1980.

The truck destroyed at Desert One. (Wikimedia Commons)

Desert One crash. (*Stars and Stripes*)

The holster I carried into Desert One, now on display as part of the Eagle Claw Exhibit, National Museum of the U.S. Army.

Terrorist exercise with U.S. Secret Service acting as terrorists, 1980. Rick Race on far left and Paul Kelly on far right.

At the White House on the day President Reagan made his first trip after being shot, 1980.

Delta Intel: front row, John Stanley, Allyn McElrath; back row, Jim Coughlin, Lonnie Bristol, Gary Moston.

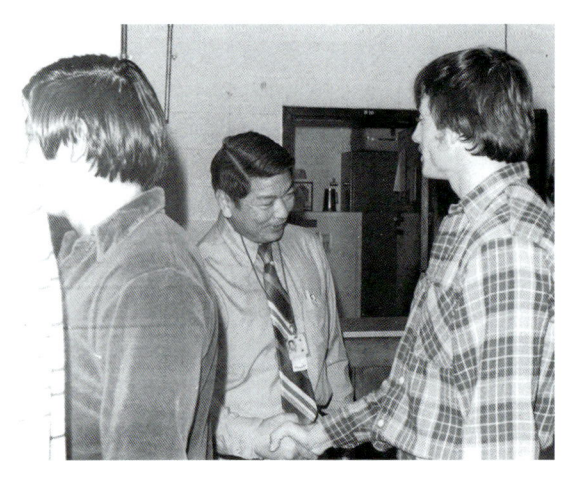

Delta farewell with Norm Taitano and Fred Lewis, 1981.

On retirement, 1981.

Eagle Claw ceremony at Arlington with Command Sergeant Major Chris Abel and the flag he hoped to raise in Tehran in 1980.

and I got the first sergeant to help assign different tasks to correct past deficiencies. Tajiri and the XO were nowhere to be seen. Nevertheless, the preparations continued for the inspection. One of the past deficiencies concerned the need to paint the buildings. Bruce Bailey and Jim Betz rolled up their sleeves and were working without regard to their rank. Jim and I were painting a building when the master sergeant roared up in his car dressed in a coat and tie. He smiled and acted like he was a good guy. I asked him where he had been, and he replied that he had just picked up the mail for the unit. Knowing that Lincoln Lew was a capable mail clerk and thinking the master sergeant was just avoiding doing any manual labor, I lost it. I took my paintbrush and left a swath of paint starting from the top of his head, across his face, and down his coat and tie. I threatened him that I would kick his ass if he didn't show up the next day ready to help prepare for the inspection.

The other lieutenant thought that his contribution to preparing for the inspection would be to go through the barracks and see if there was anything to improve. One of the young soldiers came to me and complained that the lieutenant accused him of having an illegal weapon above his bed and to get rid of it. The supposed weapon was an aluminum replica of a samurai sword. It was merely a decorative piece that would have bent and broken if used as a weapon. I found the lieutenant and explained this to him. He was reluctant to reverse his decision. I felt sorry for him because he was not getting any mentorship from anyone. I found a 2 × 4-inch piece of lumber and broke it using *shuto uchi* (knife-hand strike). I then told the lieutenant that he had now seen a real weapon, and I asked if he was going to ask me to remove my hand. He got the point and allowed the soldier to keep his toy sword on display.

Thanks to the hard work of the soldiers, along with Lieutenants Bailey and Betz, the unit passed the inspector general review. I felt a great deal of relief and pride in what the soldiers had done to pass. There was little left that I could do with the 441st MID, and I was eager to get reassigned to A Company of the 1st SF Group. Before that was to happen, I was summoned to 1st Group headquarters by Master Sergeant David Kauhaahaa, who was the noncommissioned officer in charge of the Group S3 section. I had met David in Vietnam, and we were friends and part of his extended family. David's nickname was "Bruddah K," and he was from Makawao, Maui. Bruddah K told me that he needed to send me to the Yaeyama Islands, south of Okinawa and closer to Taiwan than Okinawa. The mission would be to help the residents with a request for a civic action mission. He said that he was sending me because I spoke Japanese. I told him that I didn't speak Japanese except for some basics. He refused to believe me and told me I was going on the mission! I was given the names of a few folks in the government on Ishigaki Island. I flew on a C-12 King Air to a small airstrip and set out to meet the elders armed with my Japanese phrasebooks and dictionary!

I apologized to the elders for not being able to speak fluent Japanese. Fortunately, they spoke English well enough, and I knew enough Japanese to figure out most things. When details were needed, they arranged for a schoolteacher to help interpret.

They took me on a tour of Ishigaki. It was a very picturesque small island. One of the areas they showed me was a small sugar cane plantation, where the husband of Congresswoman Patsy Mink (from Hawaii) had helped install an irrigation system, and they were pleased to learn that I was from Hawaii and had many Okinawan friends. They helped me find a *ryokan* (Japanese hotel) and provided transportation for me. I found out that the project they needed help with was the construction of a school with a wall around it. We decided on a location for the school, and I set about getting information concerning the number of students that would attend, any special needs required, and taking measurements for the wall and the school buildings. All of this went well, and I was ready to head back to Okinawa with the information. The elders came to me the following morning and told me that the pumping station for an important well had broken down and that there was an acute water shortage.

In 1970, Okinawa and the Ryukyu Islands were under U.S. military control, a High Commissioner was appointed to govern the islands. I called Bruddah K, and he put me in touch with the High Commissioner's Office. I explained what had happened and requested that water be transported to Ishigaki along with engineers who could repair the pumping station. I provided the number of residents in Ishigaki to ascertain how much water should be sent. An Army lieutenant colonel who worked in the High Commissioner's Office flew down, and I briefed him on the situation. He also made a call to Okinawa and that no doubt helped expedite the delivery of water and the repair crew. The next day a landing ship with "water buffaloes"—Army 400-gallon water trailers—arrived at Ishigaki. The Ishigaki residents were clamoring to get water. I climbed on the top of one of the water trailers with a wooden *bokken* (sword), gave a loud *kiai*, and banged the *bokken* on the water trailer. That got everyone's attention. I then told them that the older people and children were to come to the front of the line to get water first. I guess I must have been an imposing figure as they complied! The lieutenant colonel was impressed. In talking with him and Bruddah K, I was thanked for what I had done and told I could return to Okinawa. The Ishigaki elders also thanked me, and I left with a good feeling about helping those on the island.

Upon returning to Okinawa and the 441st MID, I was in a dilemma on how to bring about my reassignment to A Company. Fate was on my side. The captain, who was the executive officer for the 441st MID, decided that he needed to get his mail one day. Lincoln Lew, the mail clerk, was on an errand to pick up the unit's mail. The captain decided that he could not wait. He got a crowbar and broke into the mail room shattering the door and leaving it unlocked and unattended. Lieutenant Colonel Tajiri did not know what to do. I jumped in my car and drove to 1st SF Group headquarters and to Dick Kim's office. I informed him of what the captain had done. I respectfully said to Lieutenant Colonel Kim that I had done my part to get the 441st MID straightened out, but things were now in his hands. I also put in a pitch to remind him of the promise to send me to A Company. Within a day, I was on my way to a former Nike missile site where A Company was in Ishikawa, Okinawa. Once again as happy as I could be! Call it fate, or call it God's will.

***

In 1970, Special Forces were organized differently from what is the case today. Subordinate to the Group Headquarters were three companies. The companies had B Detachments or Teams under them, and there were A Detachments subordinate to the B Detachments. The A Company that I reported to would become the 1st Battalion of the 1st SF Group in late 1972. Lieutenant Colonel Zachwieja commanded A Company and Corn Beef Haleamau was his sergeant major. Corn Beef was built like a fire plug, short and squat. During the Korean War, he had been severely wounded in action. While recovering from his wounds, he met and married Alene, who was one of his nurses. Alene and Corn Beef adopted me into their family, and I became an "uncle" to Karl, Keahi, Leslie, and Holly Ann. Corn Beef assigned me to the S2 section to assist Master Sergeant James Kenneth Wright, or "JK." JK was one of the originals when Special Forces was formed and had over 25 years of service.

Unfortunately, his physical condition was declining, and Corn Beef knew JK needed help. JK was not only known to many in Special Forces but also well-liked. He was invaluable to me in introducing me to folks and teaching me how a Special Forces company was run. What Corn Beef and JK did for me was to reinforce the importance of leaders mentoring others along with the value of networking associates.

During the winter of 1970–1971, A Company deployed to Korea to participate in Exercise Foal Eagle. This was, and continues to be, a major exercise involving U.S. and Korean forces. The Special Forces role was for A Teams to be inserted in remote areas of South Korea and to act as if they were North Korean infiltrators along with South Korean Special Forces teams. The South Korean regular military and police would then mount operations to locate the infiltrators. A Company's role was to help control the exercise and to monitor the Special Forces A Teams. We located our headquarters in what was called the 8th U.S. Army rear area bunkers. They were located in a hilly area close to Pyongtaek, Korea, near Camp Humphries. Knowing that I had served previously in Korea, Corn Beef Haleamau asked me if I knew anyone in the Exchange system. I responded by saying the Army Exchange area manager was a friend, named Kwon. Corn Beef then tasked me with getting a mobile canteen to service our needs with snacks and toiletries. He also tasked me with getting laundry service. The friendship I had developed in 1963–1965 with Mr Kwon helped immensely. He readily agreed to provide what we requested.

I jokingly said he should send a pretty woman with the mobile canteen or laundry service. Once again, God smiled on me. A pretty young lady named Mi Hye Choi was sent to operate the laundry service. One evening I walked into the building where she was located and found some Korean Special Forces soldiers giving her a hard time. She had a cup of hot tea in her hands and promptly threw the tea at them. I said to myself, wow, that's the kind of woman I want to marry! I scolded the Korean SF soldiers, and then introduced myself to Mi Hye. I was fortunate to be able to return to Korea several times from 1970 to 1972, and we were married in February 1972. In the interim, I had the pleasure and honor of meeting her mother, and we developed a strong respect for each other. She encouraged Mi Hye to marry me, for which I will always be profusely grateful.

There were four other guys from Hawaii assigned to A Company. John "Butch" Fernandez, who was an A Detachment sergeant who grew up in Kapahulu near where I had also lived; Clarence Young working in the S3 Section from Waiahole Valley on the island of Hawaii, who we nicknamed Taro Toes; George "Crab Man" Nakamoto, who was the A Company supply sergeant; and Julian J. J. Fernandez who was on an A Detachment.

During Foal Eagle, I became close friends with Clarence Young. He taught me a lot about Special Force operational concepts and methods. Foal Eagle was the first major training exercise I had been exposed to, and it was a great learning experience for me. I learned what went into preparing and conducting a major exercise, including what was required to make it realistic but to control it to achieve the desired outcomes. Another thing that I learned from this exercise was the tremendous strides Korea had made under President Park Chung Hee to modernize the country. When I left Korea in early 1965, I had an opportunity to watch the Second Han River Bridge being constructed. Laborers were literally passing large rocks hand-to-hand to build the pillars for the bridge and heavy machinery was scarce. In 1970, I saw the major freeway from Seoul to Pusan that President Park had directed. I also saw Shinjin automobiles now being produced in Korea—tremendous progress for the Korean people and nation.

There were two funny things that happened during the exercise. The first was after the exercise was finished. We could relax a bit and headed to the NCO Club on Camp Humphries. JK Wright, Taro Toes Young, and I were seated at a table when a young soldier came up to JK. He pointed at JK and kept saying, "I know you, I know you." Taro Toes told him to shut up and get the hell away from us. JK held up his hand to quieten Taro Toes. He then looked at the soldier and said, "Hi, my name is James Kenneth Wright, I am a master sergeant with the 1st Special Forces Group and grew up in South Carolina. Please tell me who you are." The soldier identified himself in a similar way to what JK had done. JK then said, "Unfortunately, I do not know you and have never seen you before." The soldier didn't know what to say and walked off. We wondered what the hell this was all about. JK nosed around and came back laughing with the true story.

The young soldier had a girlfriend and walked into her hooch only to find her engaged in intercourse with Bert Smith, an A Detachment team sergeant. Bert reportedly pulled a .38 revolver out and held the soldier at bay while he finished his "business." He then told the soldier to get the hell out of the hooch. The soldier ran off and could not make it back to Camp Humphries before curfew. He was either reprimanded or given an Article 15 (non-judicial punishment). He thought JK Wright was Bert Smith! We all wondered whether the soldier went back to his girlfriend after finding out she was cheating! I was reminded of a young man who worked in the motor pool of the 191st MID in 1964. On three occasions he came down with gonorrhea. After the first two times, we took steps to get him and his girlfriend cured. After the third time, I sat him down and told him that it was evident she was fooling around and was contracting a sexually transmitted disease from someone else. He looked at me and, in all seriousness, said, "Sarge, you don't know how good she is in bed!" I just shook my head and walked away.

The other funny thing that happened during Foal Eagle concerned a soldier who was attached to us from Camp Humphries. He was from a missionary family and had lived in Korea for many years. We used him as an interpreter with our Korean Special Forces counterparts as he was fluent in Korean. The Koreans would practice Tae Kwon Do every morning, and some of them saw the soldiers attached to us practicing martial arts also. The Koreans challenged him to a fight. Our American soldier humbly accepted. What the Koreans did not know was that our soldier had been practicing Hapkido for many years and was very adept. Tae Kwon Do in those days was what one would consider to be a very "linear" martial art, whereas Hapkido used Aikido techniques along with different ways of kicking and striking.

Korean Special Forces put forward their best fighter and the contest began. The Korean launched several attacks, which our soldier easily evaded. He suddenly launched a spinning leg sweep and the Korean fell heavily to the ground. Our man was on top of him in a flash and pulled a punch an inch from his opponent's face. The fight was over. To their credit, the Koreans engaged him in conversation and learned about Hapkido. They showed their admiration and respect and proved themselves to be good losers. One can't always win!

***

The year that followed the Foal Eagle Exercise was a great time for me. There was only one setback that occurred. Being single and not having much time to find a place to live, I was still in the A Company barracks. Jim Parris, my teammate in Vietnam, had returned to Okinawa. He and his first wife, Eiko, often had me over to their house for a meal. In the barracks, there was a phone in the hallway but not in the individual rooms. Jim called and called one day and never got an answer. He suspected that something might be wrong and drove from his home near Kadena Circle to Ishikawa. I had passed out on the floor of my room. When I came to, I was nauseous and running a high fever.

Jim immediately took me to Camp Kue Hospital. We sat there for over an hour waiting to be seen by a doctor. I thought for sure that I had a relapse of malaria or dengue fever, and was very dizzy. In front of us were three doctors chatting loudly about how their upcoming leave and plans to buy jewelry from India and Thailand. I looked at Jim, and said, "Watch this." I crawled over to the doctors, put my arms around the legs of the female doctor and proceeded to throw up. Geez, I promptly got medical attention! Sometimes one must do what one needs to do to gain attention!

My assignment to the 1st SF Group was the first time that I had been in a unit with so many soldiers from Hawaii. Being single at the time, I was always looking for a good meal! In the Hawaiian spirit of *hanai* (extended family), I was quickly adopted by many of them and became an uncle to their children. Corn Beef Haleamau and his wife Alene had four children: Karl, Keahi, Leslie, and Holly Ann. David Kauhaahaa and Rozelle had seven: Ronnie, Karlene, Marlene, Wendy, Anna, Arlette, and Jocelyn. Butch and Lei Fernandez had four: Bryson, Dawn (Dolly), PatLynn (Malia), and Letitia (Sukoshi). Clarence and Sakiko Young had two: Lynne and Claire. Pedro "Sonny": Abangan and Miyo had three: Alan, Arnold, and Audrey. Others from Hawaii, included Jason T. Woodworth, George Nakamoto, Gabriel Makalena, Wendell Enos, Angel Quisote, Jeff Tom, Mua'au Pau, and J. J. Fernandez. My high school classmate, Roy Adaniya, was also assigned as the 1st SF group surgeon. We were a tight-knit group and frequently had parties at their homes. There was another Hawaiian that I had looked up to growing up in Hawaii. His name was James "Jamma" Keanu. He was a half-brother of the noted waterman and surfer Rabbi Kekai. Jamma won the Makaha surfing contest in 1957. He was a mountain of a man, who was also proficient in karate and had been a contemporary of the well-known karate fighter, Mike Stone.

I was also privileged to be introduced to and become friends with many others in the 1st SF Group. I absorbed many valuable lessons from them and soaked up their knowledge like a sponge. I also learned that one should never rest on one's laurels and should always seek to improve oneself. On one occasion, I visited Chief Warrant Officer Cliff Eggers, who was in the S4 section of 1st SF Group; another time, I went to the home of Master Sergeant Richard Perkins. I found them both reading Army field manuals. When I questioned both why they were reading field manuals, they gently but firmly told me that I should never stop learning and striving to improve my knowledge. They made a big impression on me as they both had storied careers in Special Forces. Dick Perkins was someone I looked up to. He was about five feet four inches tall and tough as nails.

During the Korean War, he was a young soldier assigned to Task Force Smith, which was the first major American combat unit sent into battle. The task force was attacked by 34 North Korean tanks and infantry near Osan, Korea. Despite having limited firepower and outnumbered 10 to 1, Task Force Smith withstood the enemy attack. Dick became a skilled mountaineer and could free climb with the best. He also held an advanced degree in Uechi-Ryu Karate. There was a story of him taking on four Marines at the American Legion Club in Okinawa and beating all of them. He was also involved in a National Geographic expedition in Southeast Asia because of his tracking and skills in the jungle.

Dick Perkins was the real deal! In 1972 we were in Korea and Dick was the instructor demonstrating how to free climb. He was about forty feet up the wall of a cliff, turned around and said, "Should you fall, then extend your arms and feet like you are a cat." Suddenly it dawned on us that Dick was actually falling from that height. He did exactly what he described and broke his wrist!

In 1972 I was on an A Team with Jesse Simmons as the team sergeant. We were going to teach a class about tracking to eight Special Forces Reserve detachments coming from the continental U.S. to Okinawa. Jesse and I approached Dick Perkins and asked him for some tips regarding tracking. He told us to lie on the ground on our backs. Jesse and I thought he was pulling our legs and joking but we did what Perkins asked. He then told us to look at the grass leaves and other vegetation around us. It was remarkable—we could see where leaves had been trampled by someone walking over them! Fred Henry was on our team and told a story about how he came to join Special Forces. Fred was with the 173rd Airborne Brigade in Okinawa and was in a class being taught outdoors by Dick Perkins. Dick was facing the students with a large writing pad hanging on an easel behind him. A gust of wind blew the paper and easel over. Fred said that Perkins sensed what was happening, pulled out his knife, whirled around, and stuck the knife into the paper. That convinced Fred Henry he wanted to be like Dick Perkins, and he immediately signed up to transfer to Special Forces.

What I really learned from Dick Perkins was how to be an excellent instructor. He taught me how to prepare classes and how to get the right teaching points across to the students. He also taught me many ways to gain and keep the attention of students. Dick was one of the featured instructors for groups of Marines from the 3rd Marine Division who were headed to Vietnam. He would take the Marines on a terrain appreciation march along a route that Dick had carefully planned to be able to illustrate his teaching. He would stop the column, and then ask the Marines what kind of plant they saw growing in a field. Most of them had no idea. Dick would then tell them that it was tea and would pick a few leaves and stuff them into his canteen of water. Later in the march, he would stop the column and ask some Marines to taste the water in his canteen. They promptly would respond that it tasted like tea. What they didn't know was that Dick had put tea in his canteen in the first place.

But his aim was to help the Marines to identify different plants and foliage. Later in the march, he would halt the column and remark that he smelled a snake. Suddenly, a snake appeared across the trail they were on. Dick would then demonstrate how to capture a snake. The Marines were awed, but what they didn't know was that Dick had staged other Special Forces hiding behind the bushes with a snake in a bag that they released on Dick's cue! I never forgot the use of techniques to make one a better teacher that I learned from Dick Perkins.

To complete my transition to Special Forces, I requested a change of my military occupational specialty from being an intelligence agent with badge and credentials to being a 11F5S—a Special Forces Operations and Intelligence Sergeant. I was summoned to see the new commander of the 44 First MID who had replaced Lieutenant Colonel Tajiri. I explained why I had made the decision and that I felt that Special Forces was my true calling in the Army. It was evident that he was not listening, and he began to tell me I was making a stupid mistake and that military intelligence was far more valuable than Special Forces. I replied that I disagreed with his feelings and that I had thoroughly thought through my request to be reclassified into Special Forces. I don't know where he learned his supposed leadership, but he began talking down to me and challenging both my intellect and manliness. That thoroughly made me angry. I told him I was ready to go out into a field next to his unit with him and all his soldiers to fight. I also said that I might not win because of the odds, but that I knew he and many of his men would get hurt badly. That shut him up. Like a typical coward, in the letter he wrote approving my reclassification, he called me belligerent—but he never mentioned his lack of leadership or ineptitude. All I cared about was that my reclassification to Special Forces was approved. I learned that about six months later he died. My only emotion was to think, "Good riddance." Leaders need to listen and consider the desires of their men. They should be rational and factual rather than belittle a soldier.

The demands of being in the A Company S2 section were not great. I had plenty of time to start enjoying life. I found an apartment and moved out of the barracks. I went fishing with Clarence Young and Sonny Abangan on the weekends, frequented the Special Forces Club and the American Legion Club, and would show up to get free dinner from my Hawaiian extended family. I also started training with Goju Karate master Sekiichi Toguchi through his senior student in Okinawa, and Aikido with Roy Suenaka. I was having a lot of fun.

The fun extended to pulling pranks. Butch Fernandez, Woody Woodworth and Ben Dennis were in a typing class. They had me go to the instructor and ask if I could be admitted into the class even though it had been on for several weeks. I offered that I had some typing skills and would like to demonstrate them so that she would allow me into the class. She gave me a typing assignment. I completed it error-free at 105 words per minute. She knew she had been suckered in, but she had a great sense of humor. She, Butch, Woody, Ben, and I all had a good laugh.

Ben Dennis became a brother to me. Again, I was taken into his family. His wife, Iko, was half Korean and half Japanese, and would later become a great friend of my wife. I was, and continue to be, an uncle to their children Ben (Hideo) and Patricia (Patsy). Ben was in a Reserve Special Forces unit near Cleveland, Ohio, when the Vietnam War got hot and heavy. His entire A Detachment decided to volunteer for active duty. Ben was a rated skydiver and became one of the early High Altitude, Low Opening (HALO) instructors in Special Forces. In Vietnam, he had trained the first Special Forces team to use HALO to insert into North Vietnam and Laos. Ben really wanted me to become HALO qualified, and I wanted to also, but fate did not allow that to happen. Ben also loved to fish and, with his personality, was treated as if he was from Hawaii. Talking about fishing, one of my great fun times was to fish for ocean mullet with Clarence Young. Clarence had developed an innovative rig using a ping-pong ball. He would heat a paper clip, plunge it into the ball then seal it with Duco glue, and twist the paper clip to create eyelets on both sides. He would then tie a nylon leader and hook onto the eyelets. Clarence was adamant that we needed to use bread from Jiro Bakery in Futenma as it had an oily content that would attract the mullet. We would often hook two fish at the same time, and it was a lot of fun to then reel them in with a fight. They were also delicious to eat.

The story about my typing and writing skills spread and resulted in an opportunity. In 1964 the Special Forces Decade Association was started at Fort Bragg, North Carolina. Chapter II of the Association was formed in Okinawa with Harold Jacobson being one of the shakers and movers to start the chapter. The chapter produced a monthly newsletter called *The Rag*. The editor was a talented and colorful master sergeant named Mark Tocci. Mark was about to be reassigned to the States, and I was approached to take his place as the editor. I protested that I did not meet the requirement of having 10 years in Special Forces and could not be a member. The chapter officers told me to get to work editing *The Rag*. They requested a waiver for me, and I became Member 660 of the Decade Association. I was humbled by what they did and put my heart and soul into producing the monthly newsletter. It was a challenge because there were no personal computers and no copy machines, and I had to produce the newsletter on a mimeograph machine. Being the editor was a great learning experience for me, as I learned more about the men and their families in the 1st SF Group. The newsletter was a great morale booster, and I ensured that it would remain that way after the masterful job that Mark Tocci had done.

***

The one sad event that happened to me was that my uncle, David Brighter, passed away in Hawaii. I took a short leave and travelled by space-available military aircraft back to Hawaii for the funeral. He was a mountain of a man and played a powerful role in my upbringing. His passing was devasting to my Aunt Ruth (Shizu) as she had lost her son Jerry in Vietnam in 1970. Uncle David's oldest son, David Jr., was brought out of prison to be at the funeral. He was in leg irons with a chain around his waist and handcuffed to the chain. He would not be able to help carry his father's casket to the graveside. Uncle David's nephew, George Perry, interceded. George was believed to be the chief enforcer of organized crime in Hawaii. George was close to Governor George Ariyoshi. George called the governor who contacted the prison guard to take the handcuffs and leg irons off to allow Junior to help carry his dad's casket.

It was also sad for me as Junior had spent most of his adult life in jail or prison for dealing in drugs. Uncle David had asked me years before to try and intervene and help get Junior straightened out. I told my uncle that it wouldn't do any good as I was in the Army and not able to be with Junior all the time. Junior was soft-spoken and a talented mason, but he could not overcome his addiction to drugs. In those days, there weren't any good drug rehabilitation programs; it started me thinking about better ways to help those addicted.

My idyllic time soon came to an end. Corn Beef Haleamau volunteered me to help plan the Foal Eagle Exercise in Korea for 1972. Master Sergeant Roy Johnson was assigned as the principal operations planner, and I was the main intelligence planner for the exercise. The world of the 1970s was totally different from what one sees today. In today's world, it would take well over a year to plan an exercise like Foal Eagle. Probably there would be a field grade officer assigned to oversee the planning with a large staff of both military and contractors to do the planning. In the 1970s, much more faith was placed in the ability of noncommissioned officers, and one's knowledge and abilities were far more important than the rank of the planners. It's not bragging to say that Roy Johnson and I brought those qualities to bear.

It was a great opportunity for me as there were several temporary duty trips to Korea to plan the exercise. That gave me time to cement my relationship with Mi Hye. I proposed to her, and with the acceptance and support of her mother, we were married in February 1972. There was no formal wedding, we sat in a tea house as a facilitator took the paperwork to Seoul City Hall to get them signed. I still owe Mi Hye a honeymoon! For whatever reason, my mother-in-law took a great liking to me, and we would remain close until her passing 40 years later. A strong wife and a strong mother-in-law are great ingredients to ensure a military marriage works.

Most of the planning before the conduct of Foal Eagle was done in Seoul, Korea, at the Yongsan Army compound adjacent to today's Korean National Museum. Mi Hye left her job in Pyongtaek, and we rented a small apartment within walking distance of the Yongsan Compound and close to the Han River. My mother-in-law spoiled us by frequently cooking for us. Exercise headquarters was at Camp Walker in Taegu.

The objective of Foal Eagle at the time was to prepare Korea for infiltration by North Korean Special Forces. Our units out of Okinawa played the role of those infiltrators, and the Second Republic of Korea Army, along with the Korean National Police, were tested on their ability to find the infiltrators. Our teams were to infiltrate by parachute or come in from the sea. During the exercise, the headquarters personnel made an administrative jump near Yeongchon, Korea. The Korean Police were slow to respond, and we were well on our way back to Taegu and saw them streaming towards the drop zone.

The exercise went well, with only one hiccup. Lonnie Johnson's team found themselves in an active minefield. An administrative halt had to be called for that team to extract them from the minefield safely. Lonnie was astute enough to realize their predicament and radioed in their location. Lieutenant Colonel George "Speedy" Gaspard oversaw the headquarters and had also assumed command of A Company. I was dismayed by his ego. We had a great weapons sergeant of Filipino descent named Manny Coniconde. Manny was also a very skilled graphic artist. Gaspard had been a football player at Louisiana State University and brought clippings and other mementoes from his college days. He diverted Manny away from his duties on the Foal Eagle Exercise to put together a scrapbook on Gaspard's college exploits. His misuse of Manny severely disappointed me.

When we returned to Okinawa, we learned that the new concept of Special Forces organization was instituted. The former Special Forces Companies now became Battalions, and the former B Detachments became companies. A Company was redesignated as the 1st Battalion, 1st Special Forces Group. I was also thrilled to learn that I was being transferred from the battalion headquarters to an A Detachment. That A Detachment's Team Leader was Captain Tony Avgoulis, who had been an enlisted SF communicator and had gone to Officer Candidate School. Tony was a great team leader. The Detachment XO was a lieutenant that we nicknamed "Rock." Rock was both competent and had a great sense of humor. The team sergeant was Danny Dimingo, one of the smartest team sergeants that I ever knew. The two communications sergeants were friends, Dirty Dingus Magee and Jack McIntyre. Roy Needham was our medical sergeant. One of our weapons sergeants was Jean Paul "Frenchy" Castagna, who had just rotated back from serving in Vietnam.

***

In the year 1972 Okinawa was to revert from American control back to Japan. There were frequent anti-American demonstrations principally by Okinawan labor organizations. The only combat units on Okinawa were the Third Marine Division and Special Forces. Both organizations were called upon to provide security at different installations when demonstrations were scheduled. In two months, we were called upon twice to provide security. On one occasion we were deployed to the Machinato port area. There was little for us to do as the port already had adequate security. So, we just hung out and wasted our time. On that occasion, a young specialist came to where we were located and told us that we needed to start cleaning different facilities and grounds. Danny Dimingo took the young soldier aside and told him that we were all noncommissioned officers and were there to provide security rather than being a clean-up crew. Danny also told him that specialists do not give orders to noncommissioned officers and that if anyone was going to do a clean-up detail it would be him! The specialist walked off with his tail between his legs! Danny Dimingo gave him a lesson on military protocol and demonstrated his leadership. We all laughed when the specialist beat a hasty retreat.

On another riot control call-out, we were told to billet ourselves in a gymnasium where there was also a Marine unit sleeping. The Marines were young and were chatting loudly with themselves one night when suddenly there was a dead silence. We asked a Marine what was going on. His reply was, "The Gunny [Gunnery Sergeant] told us to shut up and go to sleep!" There's nothing like the influence a gunnery sergeant has over Marines!

On the second riot control call-out, our team was inexplicably divided. Dingus Magee and I were assigned to help secure a compound in Machinato that housed the Army Exchange headquarters and had a military-dependent school. The Okinawan demonstrators had a fixed routine, and we could predict when they were about to conduct a demonstration. You would hear bull horns shouting directions and the demonstrators forming into a queue. That signaled us to close the gate onto the compound and place concertina wire in front of the gate. The demonstrators were non-violent but would have entered the compound had the gate not been closed. We were issued batons but no other weaponry. That was because in 1970 there was a major demonstration that did turn violent. Demonstrators were trying to enter the U.S. Army Headquarters for the Ryukyu Islands command. Master Sergeant Courtney Silva from Hawaii was in charge of a group that fixed bayonets on their rifles and used standard riot control techniques to move the demonstrators away. Some of them were pushed against a fence, panicked, and moved forward to impale themselves on the bayonets. In negotiations with the Okinawan labor groups, it was agreed that weapons would not be used if the demonstrations were not violent.

Captain Travis Mills oversaw us at Machinato. He tasked me with pulling the concertina wire in front of the entrance gate as a demonstration was about to occur. Twice in one day, the gate was closed and chained. I was stranded outside the gate with no way to get back in. I raised hell with Travis Mills after the first demonstration. Nevertheless, he ordered the gate closed and locked the second time also. During the second demonstration, one of the demonstration leaders came up to me to mock me. I told him that anytime he was ready I would take him out. When the demonstration ended and I came through the opened gate, I again raised hell with Mills. He had no comment.

Dingus Magee talked, and the next day we got even with Mills. Dingus had some .30-caliber rounds for an M-1 carbine and brought them to Machinato the next day along with files. Mills came up to us and asked us what we were doing. I looked up to him and said, "We're making dum-dum bullets and Dingus has his carbine here." At which time Dingus spoke up and said, "Yeah, and I've also got grenades." He pulled out an inert grenade and showed it to Mills. Mills almost had a heart attack. I looked at him with an evil eye and stated that if he closed the gate on me again, I would throw grenades at the demonstrators, and Dingus would open fire. Guess what? The gate never closed again before I was through it. Sometimes it takes unconventional means to ensure things are done right!

***

I got great news after the second riot control call-out. Our team had been selected to go back to Korea and engage in joint training with the Korean Special Forces. We would link up with a Korean A Detachment equivalent and take them to the field to help them learn American techniques. We initially stopped in Seoul to coordinate with the Korean Resident Team, a 1st SF Group element stationed in Yongsan Compound. One of the key objectives of the training was to show communications techniques. Our team was to be inserted into a mountainous area west of Taejon called Sangju. East of Sangju was a tall mountain peak known as Songnisan. We were expected to make radio contact with the Korean Resident Team and all the way back to Okinawa, using Morse code and our ANGRC-109 radio. There were those on the Resident Team who stated it would be impossible for us to make reliable radio contact from the Sangju area. Dingus Magee and Jack McIntyre dismissed these skeptics and told them that they would prove it was possible. Magee and McIntyre later proved what they could do by making five-by-five (loud and clear) transmissions back to Seoul and Okinawa from the Sangju area. Their secret was simple—they knew how to tune their antenna. They also made modifications to the Resident Team's antenna array. One of the naysayers on the Resident Team was their team sergeant, Dick Henderson. He was embarrassed and resentful when Dingus and Jack proved him wrong.

We deployed to Sangju and linked up with the Korean Special Forces. Sangju was very remote with few modern amenities. The residents had not seen Americans since the Korean War, and many were seeing Americans for the first time in their lives. One of the elementary school teachers brought students to where we were encamped to allow them to see what Americans were like. The children looked at us in awe because of our height and build. They wanted to feel our uniforms, and we had a good time entertaining them.

There was good-natured competition for physical fitness between the Korean troops and our team. The first few days saw them outperforming us in moving over mountainous terrain, but after that we outdid them. The primary reason was that they were not getting the nourishment they needed. They had erected a tent with a kitchen and had cooks with them. However, they ate radish or turnip soup and rice at every meal and only infrequently had protein in the form of dried fish or meat. Our team had military rations, and we supplemented that by my going to the local market and purchasing food for us to cook. Good nutrition is essential to maintain one's physical abilities whether on military operations or in daily life!

One of the humorous things was that both the Korean Special Forces and our team were clearly outperformed on a climb to the top of Songnisan mountain. The peak was about 3,500 feet tall, but the approach was very steep. On a climb we made to the top of Songnisan, we were passed by older Korean men with heavy loads on an A-frame or *jjigae* built out of wood branches. They frequently made the climb and were not psychologically deterred as they knew their route thoroughly! Nothing beats experience!

After about a week in Sangju, we moved back to Seoul to deliver a report to the Resident Team and rest for a few days. The team was billeted in the Hamilton Hotel in Itaewon close to the Yongsan Compound, and I was allowed to stay with Mi Hye at the apartment we had rented. On two occasions, Frenchy Castagna was assaulted by U.S. Army soldiers assigned to the Eighth U.S. Army in Yongsan. Frenchy was still recovering from wounds he suffered in Vietnam and could not use his fists very well. He resorted to the strongest muscles in the human body—the jaw—and bit the ear off one of his assailants and the nose of another! In both cases, Frenchy did not start the trouble. I was standing in line with Mi Hye to attend a movie at the Yongsan Compound theater when I saw Dick Hendrickson walking into the Military Police Station. I knew intuitively that he intended to say something bad about our team and Frenchy. I was ready to kick his ass, but Mi Hye pled with me to calm down.

On our return to Okinawa, we were greeted by a surly Sergeant Major Ed Kuligowski who told us that we better be at morning formation the following day. We did so and were told that our team was going to be disbanded and that Frenchy Castagna had committed an act of cannibalism. Neither Gaspard, the battalion commander, nor Kuligowski gave us a chance to tell our side of the story. From that point forward, none of us had any respect for Gaspard or Kuligowski. We also learned that indeed, Dick Hendrickson and the Korean Resident Team commander, Major Reed Myrick, had provided inflammatory information back to Okinawa. Any respect we had for those two also went out the window. Tony Avgoulis took it particularly hard as he had strong moral and ethical values and was a fine leader. He was never accorded the privilege of providing contradictory information.

***

Good fortune and the blessing of the Lord were with me again. I was reassigned to another A Detachment whose team sergeant was Jesse Simmons. Jesse was one of the originals when the 1st SF Group was established. Jesse was from the

Lumberton, North Carolina, area along with his brother Lonnie who was also in Special Forces. Jesse's wife was from the Kagoshima area of Japan. The team leader was Captain Richard Schultze and the executive officer a young lieutenant who had no Special Forces training. I was to replace Fred Henry on the team, a friend of mine. Our team medic when I joined the team was Joe Halligan who became one of the first Army physicians assistants. Others on the team included Jay Massey, Paul Harrison, John Cli, and Ben Butler. The team was designated as the 1st Battalion's Rough Terrain Parachute Team and as a Special Atomic Demolition Munition (SADM) team.

On the day I reported to Jesse's team, they were going to make a rough terrain parachute jump into the Northern Training Area of Okinawa. That area was heavily forested making it eminently suitable for rough terrain parachuting. That form of parachuting was based on civilian smoke jumpers that would parachute into an area to fight forest fires. Our team was issued heavy canvas overalls used by smoke jumpers to help protect them should they fall through trees on insertion. We had the optional use of civilian helmets with metal faceguards to provide additional protection. The last item of special gear was either a rope or a nylon tape lowering line to help you descend, should you be suspended in a tree above the ground. The 1st SF Group had a rough terrain parachuting school in Taiwan, west of Kaosiung City in a mountainous area on the southern part of Taiwan.

I had never been to that school. Jesse told me that we were going to make a rough terrain jump that day and inquired as to whether I had any questions. I looked at the special gear and was convinced there was only one way to put the protective suit on. The only question I had was how to attach the lowering line! Jesse gave me a quick lesson. We suited up, and I did my first rough terrain jump. We had transitioned to the MC-1-1 parachute which was a modification of the civilian Para-commander parachute that provided a great deal of maneuverability. Ben Dennis had given me lessons on how to get the most out of that parachute, and I was confident in my abilities. I spotted a clearing and maneuvered to land on the ground rather than in a tree. As I found out later, that was the preferred outcome rather than landing in a tree! I later had the opportunity to practice how to use the lowering line. That was a scary experience. Should you become hung up in a tree, you would take the lowering line with a carabiner attached to it, place it through the risers of the parachute, and toss the lowering line towards the ground. Next, you were to take up a rappelling position—with one hand behind your back in a braking position—and release one Capewell device that would free you from one of your risers. You would then immediately list to one side.

After that, you would reach up and release the other Capewell attachment, freeing you from both parachute risers. You would also hope that you were securely hung up in the tree so that you would not immediately fall to the ground. Once free of the risers, you could rappel to the ground.

Jesse also designated Paul Harrison and me to be the designated jumpers for the Special Atomic Demolition Device (SADM). The SADM was a small nuclear weapon based on the W54 warhead with a yield of 18 tons of TNT. It was placed in a cylindrical packing container for airborne operations and with the container weighed over 85 pounds. The SADM would be used mainly as an engineering device to create avalanches and block roads but could also be used against troops. There were strict protocols on how to handle and prepare the SADM. Paul and I were sent on lessons to learn all the intricacies of those protocols. We were also subject to an annual inspection called a Technical Tactical Proficiency Inspection (TTPI) conducted by the Defense Nuclear Agency. One of the requirements to pass the inspection was to ensure that a precise number of twists were made on a safety wire. They were called Western Electric twists because they were developed by Sandia National Laboratories when they were an affiliate of the Western Electric Corporation, later AT&T. Paul and I aced the inspection. Jumping with the SADM was, at the very least, an exciting experience. The packing container was cylindrical and that made it challenging to jump out of an aircraft and get away from the body of the airplane. To say the least, it was a cumbersome container. Because of the device's weight, one had to release it from the attachment to the parachute harness before landing. It could be a shocking and painful experience if you did not cinch up the straps around your crotch!

Our team was designated as one of the A Detachments to help the Korean Special Forces integrate three Ranger companies and make them Special Forces qualified. I had the task of preparing intelligence lesson plans along with some operational planning lessons. All of us worked hard as we were required to finish our lesson plans and get them translated into Korean. The lesson plans were then mimeographed, and copies left with the Korean Special Forces. While we were preparing to go to Korea, I got a big surprise. I heard a knock on my apartment door. I opened it and found my wife, Mi Hye, with Dawn Fernandez. I was shocked and asked, "What are you doing here?" That did not go over well with Mi Hye! I explained to her that our team was headed for Korea very shortly. I had no idea that she was coming to Okinawa. In her fierce independent spirit, she decided to get a plane ticket and come to Okinawa. She landed at Naha Airport without speaking Japanese or knowing where my apartment was located. With God's blessing, the cab driver took her to the home of Butch and Lei Fernandez. Dawn, the oldest daughter, knew where I lived and brought Mi Hye to the apartment. What a way to start her time in Okinawa! She did not know how to drive, had no knowledge of Okinawa, and yet she showed her spunk by being able to fend for herself with the help of the Fernandez family while I deployed back to Korea.

The Korean Special Forces had moved into a new location near what was K16 Air Base south of Seoul in Seongnam, where we conducted their training. The days were long, but it was gratifying to see the attitudes of the Korean soldiers and their leadership. Jesse Simmons believed in keeping physically fit, so our day would start out by having to scramble to the top of the Namhansan peak, situated behind the Seongnam Special Forces Compound. There was no road and no defined trail. Jesse tasked me with finding a way to the top of the peak and to come down. Psychologically, it was tough going for a couple of days to get to the top and back down. But we soon gained confidence and greatly improved the time required to get up the peak and back down.

Teaching the Korean soldiers required an interpreter, and my experience in using an interpreter, which I gained in my previous intelligence assignments, helped me immensely. I knew how to look at the students rather than the interpreter to keep the students' attention; knew how to pause to make teaching points and not overwhelm the interpreter; and other techniques of instruction. It was much like using an interpreter to conduct an interrogation or interview, and I learned that I had almost a natural ability to instruct. Before the deployment, I had studied the Army's field manual on how to conduct instruction, which proved to be very useful. The lesson that Cliff Eggers and Dick Perkins taught me regarding always seeking to improve oneself never left me. I was pleased that I was doing well, as one of the tenets of Special Forces is to act as a force multiplier. In other words, a small group of Special Forces should be able to organize and lead a much larger indigenous force by teaching them different tactics, techniques, and procedures.

The Korean Special Forces leadership was old school and hard as nails. The students would have to run five miles every morning carrying a rucksack and their weapon. At their jump school, I observed an officer berating some students. He had a big stick in his hand and would act as if he was going to hit the student. One of them flinched, and the officer proceeded to hit him. I asked why he did that, and his response was that the student flinched! I just shook my head knowing that no matter what I said, he would not change his ways.

There were some humorous incidents. I heard some Korean officers calling me an "*Ilbon saraam*" (Japanese). I then asked them in Korean whether they were "*Ibuk saraam*" (North Korean). At first, they were shocked that I spoke Korean, and then got angry and asked me why I called them North Koreans. I replied that just because I had a Japanese surname didn't mean I was Japanese, just as having a Korean surname, like people in North Korea, didn't mean they were North Koreans. We had a good chuckle and became friends.

During this deployment, I had my first parachute malfunction. We were doing an administrative jump out of a UH-1 helicopter. My main parachute did not deploy, and I activated my reserve parachute. My main parachute then gained a full canopy, and I pulled my reserve parachute between my legs before landing. I had heard the old wives' tale that if you have a malfunction, get back up and do another jump. So, I did. Well, on the second jump, I had what is called a Mae West where my main parachute was not going to open. Once again, I deployed my reserve and came down hard in a quarry, landing about 10 feet away from a bulldozer. I decided that two in one day was enough for me! As it turned out, the suspected reason for the malfunctions was that the helicopter was not going fast enough to allow proper deployment of the main parachute.

***

Our team deployed back to Okinawa, and we had a chance to spend time with our families. Mi Hye and I moved from the apartment to a house on a bluff overlooking the Futenma Marine Corps Air Station. She had her first experience on how to survive a hurricane: filling the bathtub with water to ensure we would have fresh water, putting shutters on the windows to keep them from breaking, and stocking up on food supplies. She responded like a champion, but I could tell that she was a bit concerned about our safety. There was a stray dog that would come by her house. She was awfully skinny, and we took pity on her. At first, she shied away from our attempts to pet her. Mi Hye and I would put food out for the dog, which finally won her over and allowed us to pet her. Our neighbor was a Marine gunnery sergeant working as a supply sergeant. He had a Japanese wife, and both were very helpful in taking care of Mi Hye whenever I deployed. Nothing beats the military with respect to taking care of each other.

As mentioned previously, Jesse Simmons was a stickler for physical fitness. Our daily physical training included a five- to ten-mile run in boots over hilly terrain. We would also do rucksack marches in the hills surrounding the Ishikawa Compound. One day, Jesse had something to do, and he put me in charge of the team for a rucksack march. Dick Shultze, the team leader, was highly competitive and never wanted to be outshone by the NCOs. However, we knew that he was putting an inflated air mattress in his rucksack rather than carrying the weight that the rest of them were packing. We were climbing up a steep hill when I put my head down and sped past Schultze. He couldn't stand that, so he picked up speed and passed me with the executive officer closely following him. The executive officer also had an inflated air mattress in his rucksack. I had timed what I did with malicious forethought. Schultze and the lieutenant kept pushing themselves and went around a bend. I stopped the rest of the team, and we went back to our team room and broke out beer. An hour later, Schultze and the lieutenant showed up. They knew they had been taken for a ride. But we all laughed.

We weren't going to spend much time at home in Okinawa. In September 1972, the Palestinian Black September Organization killed 11 Israeli athletes at the Munich Olympics. Black September also threatened that they were going to get their hands on an American nuclear weapon and detonate it. The 1st SF Group was tasked to help improve security at nuclear weapons sites in Korea. I was sent on an advance party to help plan how we would perform that mission. Three A Detachments, including our team, were sent to Korea. Our team was assigned two Nike air defense missile sites and the large ammunition depot located in Taejon. Our first stop was in Gimje, Korea, where there was a Nike missile site.

I was excited because I knew Gimje was the birthplace of Masutatsu Oyama, an ethnic Korean who had migrated to Japan and was the head of the Kyokushin Kai style of karate. Gimje was located southeast of Kunsan Air Base in a very rural area. There were no paved roads, and the Nike site was a hilly area outside the village. Jesse sent me to meet with the Nike battery first sergeant to see where we could sleep on the compound. The first sergeant took me to what was no more than a 10 × 10-foot room with a large space heater in the middle of it.

I informed him that we had 12 people (including three officers, with the others being noncommissioned officers) and the room was unacceptable. He gave me a blank look and professed that was the only space available. I knew damn well that he was lying. Rather than argue, I found the Korean Special Forces lieutenant who was attached to our team and asked him to find someplace in Gimje Village where we could stay. Jesse was pissed at the first sergeant when I told him what had been offered. Because the first sergeant barred us from eating in their mess hall, for dinner the team went to a local restaurant that our Korean lieutenant found.

We also learned that a few days before we got to the Nike battery, about twenty of the soldiers had brought a prostitute from the village to their club. They proceeded to gang rape her, stuck beer bottles in her orifices and then threw her unconscious into the snow. Apparently, a few of the despicable bastards who had raped the woman thought that we were coming to their unit to clean it up. They stupidly thought that they could handle us in a fistfight. They soon learned how wrong they were as we pummeled them into the ground.

The next morning, our team went to the battery headquarters. We saw a helicopter landing and saw the first sergeant and battery commander getting on board with a captain and master sergeant getting off. The first sergeant and battery commander had been relieved for incompetence. Our team went about looking at the battery's plan for defending the site and made suggestions on improving those defenses. However, it was clear that the new battery commander and first sergeant had to resolve morale and disciplinary problems before anything of substance could be achieved. This was a rude awakening for our team with respect to the state of the conventional army.

From Gimje, we proceeded north to Taejon for our next site visit. In Taejon was a large ammunition depot operated by an ordnance battalion. The depot was in what might have been a former crater. It was in an area shaped like a bowl with high ground surrounding it. Bunkers to store the ammunition were dug into the hillside. A Military Police company was assigned to the ordnance battalion to provide security. Security was far superior to what we had encountered at Gimje. We learned that there had been a security event where a soldier locked himself inside an ammunition bunker. The MPs were able to talk him out before he did any destructive harm.

Once more, we witnessed what was happening in the conventional army. One of the ordnance battalion soldiers had died of a drug overdose shortly before our team arrived. The following morning, the battalion commander had a formation for all his soldiers. I thought he did a good job of talking to his soldiers, explaining the consequences of drugs, that it was illegal, and that each soldier had a responsibility to report and stop the use of drugs.

I had an unexpected experience. I ran into Donahue, who had been in the MP company at Fort Monmouth, New Jersey, with me. He was the guard on duty when the Mafia figure, Joe Valachi, was held in the Fort Monmouth stockade. Donahue was the one that the provost marshal found who could not clear his M-14 rifle. In 1973, Donahue was an E5, and I was an E4. He was now an E6, and I was an E7. I teased him about what happened at Fort Monmouth. He just shook his head over the memory of that incident.

From Taejon, our team moved north to a Nike battery located in Inchon, Korea. Although not as large as the Inchon of today, the soldiers at the Nike site could enjoy the amenities that Inchon provided. This was unlike the isolation that the soldiers in Gimje were faced with. Morale appeared to be better at this site. On the other hand, we found problems with drug usage by the soldiers. Inside the restricted area, which is supposed to be the most secure area on a Nike site, I spotted used syringes on the ground. I asked the battery commander what that was all about. He responded by saying that some of his soldiers thought they could get a high from injecting themselves with atropine syrettes, which were part of the kit issued to deal with chemical attacks. I shook my head in wonderment. Outer security for the site was assigned to an infantry platoon. Their leader was a West Point lieutenant named Miller, who had been a starting basketball player under the legendary coach, Bobby Knight. The lieutenant was squared away, and a fine soldier. The plans he created were good, and the men under him were good soldiers.

After Inchon, our team returned to Okinawa. We were met by Sergeant Major Kuligowski who berated us for wearing jungle boots instead of leather ones. We never said a word, but again wondered about his leadership. He also told us that we were to report in the morning for a race relations class. Race relations had become a hot topic in the Army, and required four hours of mandatory instruction. The next morning, we reported to a classroom at our Ishikawa compound where we were greeted by a lieutenant, a master sergeant, and a staff sergeant. They told us that they were graduates of a race relations school. It became evident that they were following a script dictated by someone else. It was also evident that their teaching skills were poor. They were "legs" (non-airborne) and had no appreciation for Special Forces and how diverse we were. The methods they used were designed to assume that all of us were racially biased, to berate us, and get us to prove that we were racists. A young soldier in the class, who was not Special Forces, proclaimed he was there because he had missed his class in his unit. He kept jumping up and expressing how he had been discriminated against.

It was evident that the soldier was a plant and put in the class to be a provocateur. About the third hour into the class, Ben Butler had all he could take of this soldier. Ben jumped up and said that we knew he was a "plant" deliberately placed in the class to provoke feelings. Ben told him to shut up and sit down. The soldier took one look at the anger in Ben's face and shut up. The lieutenant then tried to say this showed that we were racists. I came unglued and berated the lieutenant and the other two instructors. I called them out for not wearing their uniforms properly, for not knowing how to instruct, and for the despicable tactic of placing a provocateur in the class. The master sergeant slunk out of the classroom, not to be seen again. The lieutenant lost it and started calling me a racist and other names. He yelled that he was wasting his time and would not continue the class. That was fine with all of us and we left the classroom.

I headed directly to Sergeant Major Fred Robinson who was the A Company sergeant major. Fred, a fine SF soldier of African descent, heard what I said happened. He told me to get in his car, and we drove to the 1st SF Group headquarters. Robby walked into the S3 section and raised holy hell for the shoddy class and the demeanor of the lieutenant. I had always thought highly of Fred Robinson, but what he did made me want to put him on a pedestal! He showed his leadership by standing up for those under him and was not afraid to challenge something he thought was wrong. That's what leaders are supposed to do, and Fred Robinson did that in spades!

After the race relations class fiasco, our team was told that we were to take over a Special Forces training area called Camp Hardy. Camp Hardy was named after Captain Herbert Hardy who had won the Distinguished Service Cross in Vietnam and was killed in action in 1964. Jesse Simmons was elated that our team was chosen. The camp had been used for A Detachment training and to help Marines prior to deployment to Vietnam with instruction from Special Forces. It had classrooms, barracks, a mess hall, a shooting range, access to the ocean for small boat training, and a unique obstacle course. Much of the obstacle course had been built under the leadership of Lieutenant Colonel Newlin Happersett, a colorful figure in the 1st Special Forces Group who retired in 1970. The obstacle course included a jungle trail where one had to run over a large water pipe with a board on top of it. When it rained it was treacherous to cross. Happersett also made the training realistic by setting off quarter-pound TNT charges. There was an occasion when two Marines were killed when they jumped into a crater where the charges were located. The Marine Corps never complained as they believed those were the kinds of risks that had to be taken to better prepare their troops for combat in Vietnam. Another feature of the obstacle course was a slide for life consisting of a cable from a bluff that terminated in a rock outcropping in the ocean. If one did not release from the slide at the right moment, they could be severely injured by colliding with outcropping or landing on the coral reef.

We were also informed that our team was to host and train eight Special Forces Reserve teams who were coming from various locations in the States. The teams were coming from Hawaii; Portland, Oregon; Washington State; San Francisco, California; San Diego, California; Tulsa, Oklahoma; Chicago, Illinois; and Arkansas. The purpose of the training was to refresh their skills in unconventional warfare and to provide additional skills for the team members. In preparation for their arrival, Jesse had us tidy the camp and ensure that everything we would use in the training worked well or was otherwise ready for use. We also used the Sukiran jump school location and the Yomitan drop zone to either refresh or provide new training on the MC-1-1 parachute that some of the Reservists had not had the opportunity to use previously.

We reviewed the gamut of Special Forces skills including operations and intelligence, demolitions, small arms, radio techniques, and medical techniques. We also provided them with small boat training where they used inflatable rubber boats in the ocean off Camp Hardy. During the small boat training, I was a safety swimmer and encountered a large school of stinging jellyfish. I got stung and saw that I was surrounded by the jellyfish and that my only way out was to dive and swim underwater to get away from them. I was badly stung and signaled for Ben Butler, who was operating a motorboat, to pick me up. Our medic, Joe Halligan, injected me with Demerol to deal with the pain. That afternoon I delivered a four-hour class on intelligence and agent handling. I could not even remember giving the class as I was affected by the Demerol shot! When I asked for feedback from the trainees and my team, they all said I did well. I still wonder if I could have done better, as "well" was not good enough in my mind. Overall, the Reserve teams enjoyed the training, and our team felt good that we could add value to their skills. We also made lifelong friends with some of the Reservists.

After training the Reservists, we had some stand down time and used that for our own team training. We invited a SEAL platoon stationed at White Beach, Okinawa, to do some joint training with us. We had a great time and the training culminated with firing different small arms at the Camp Hardy range. Some weeks before the training, Jesse had told a young engineer—leaving for temporary duty— who was attached to our team to remove a vehicle that he intended leaving at Camp Hardy. The young man failed to do so, and we rolled the car to the range and had a blast shooting it up. The SEALs used a sawed-off M-60 machine gun, and we saw that reducing the size of the barrel did not help with accuracy. We also used grenades against the car and demolished it. Later, when the young engineer returned from his temporary duty, he just shrugged his shoulders when he saw his demolished car. He knew he had not done what Jesse Simmons had instructed and took what happened in his stride. I found his attitude to be remarkable and commended him for it.

New Year's Eve of 1972 brought about a radical change in my life. I was a heavy smoker and also drinking quite a bit. I knew that Mi Hye was not happy with me doing either of those. I didn't think that I could quit both those vices at the same time. Upon reflection, I recalled that there was an instance when I drove back from Jim Parris's house (some 20 miles), without remembering how I had gotten back to my apartment. Maybe I should have quit smoking, but my poor rationale was that I was running 5–10 miles a day without any strain. So, I decided I would quit drinking. My last drink was at a New Year's Eve party in 1972.

Because the team had some downtime and because there was an opportunity to go to Jumpmaster School, Jesse had Jay Massey and me go to the course. Jay and I were both senior E7s and had not had the opportunity to go to Jumpmaster School beforehand. The Jumpmaster course was run by the 2nd Battalion, 1st SF Group. Two of the main instructors were my friends Ben Dennis and Ken Loring. Ben had already taught me how to be a jumpmaster, and I was not concerned about being able to pass the course. On the other hand—and typical of the perverse humor in Special Forces—I knew that Ben and Ken would try and make life miserable for me by nit-picking everything I did! That did not bother me because I knew their real intent was to get me to be the best I could be. I was more than up for the challenge. The first week in Jumpmaster School is spent learning the jumpmaster commands, how to spot a release point on the ground for parachutists to exit from an airplane, and how to conduct a jumpmaster inspection. Thanks to Ben's tutelage before, I was well-versed in all these aspects. However, as I mentioned previously, Ben and Kenny would give me extra scrutiny every day, and I had to be perfect to pass their inspections. At the end of the week, I was far ahead of the rest of the class despite the extra attention on inspections. Over the weekend, Ben, Kenny, and I had a good chuckle over what they had done and how I had responded.

The second week was jump week, and I was paired with my teammate and friend Jay Massey. We did not know who would be selected as the jumpmaster until the cadre had completed their first inspection. Knowing that Ben Dennis and Kenny Loring would be looking for anything to nit-pick me on, I decided not to wrap masking tape in the middle of my equipment lowering line as the jumpmaster manual did not specify that procedure.

On the first jump, Jay was selected as the jumpmaster and I would be the jumper that he would inspect, give the jumpmaster orders to and then send me out the door of the aircraft. Jay was always a perfectionist, and he was a bit nervous. As we approached Yomitan Drop Zone, I was standing in the door of the C-130 airplane. Jay leaned way out the door under me as he was unsure of the landmarks to look for as we approached the drop zone. I tried to tell him to look for the military working dog kennel, which was a good landmark. I don't think he heard me. He then pulled himself back into the airplane and looked left for the "T" marking on the ground. This marking, set up with signal panels, indicated the release point.

He told me, "Go," and I exited the aircraft. To play games with Ben and Ken, my plan was to do a standing landing on the "T" marking and flip my middle finger towards Ben and Ken.

As I was steering my parachute towards the "T," I felt a strange resistance around my neck. I looked towards my left and saw my equipment lowering line dangling below my shoulder. I realized something was wrong. I released my toggles that are used to maneuver the parachute, traced the lowering line, and found that it had two wraps around my neck. I untangled the lowering line, but the time it took to untangle it meant that I would not be able to land on the "T." I noticed that I had drifted over the concrete runway of Yomitan, and that I was at an altitude where I should release my rucksack. I did so and noticed that I was being blown backwards. The MC-1 parachute has a forward speed of 9.5 miles per hour, so I knew the wind must be blowing strongly for me to be blown backwards. I was prepared for a hard landing. I looked over my left shoulder and saw that my line of drift was headed straight for a truck that was parked on the runway. I thought that if I hit the truck, I'll be banged up but okay.

On the other hand, if I clear the truck and my rucksack snagged on it, then there would be a good chance that I could land on my head. I pulled down on my left toggle to avoid the truck. That meant I hit the runway while oscillating and landed on my left heel. I instantly heard my bones breaking. I did a judo breakfall by slapping my left hand on the concrete. I hit the ground so hard that my watchband snapped. The wind was dragging me down the runway, so I released my canopy to stop being dragged.

An Okinawan farmer came over to check on me. I saw a young man picking up my watch and hollered at him. The farmer went over to the youngster, scolded him, and retrieved my watch. Shortly thereafter, Steve Hoffman, who I would later serve with in the Delta Force, came up to me and saw that my leg was broken. He pulled out an air splint, affixed it and said they would get an ambulance for me. I was looking up at the next jumpers coming into the drop zone and saw two of them collide in mid-air. I told Steve that he better hold the ambulance for them!

Ben Dennis also came to where I was lying on the runway. He told me that when I landed, he had clocked me on the anemometer (a wind measuring device) as landing in a gust of 28 miles per hour. He was pissed at the drop zone safety officer, as training jumps should have been aborted because the winds exceeded the safety limits. I was taken to Camp Kue Hospital in an automobile. X-rays confirmed that I had severely fractured my left tibia and fibula. An Army doctor proceeded to set my bones manually and without anesthesia, then put a full leg cast on my left leg. The next morning, more X-rays were taken, and the clown that masqueraded as a doctor came back, ordered a wedge cut in the cast, and then reset my leg again without anesthesia! Why he didn't insert pins into my leg is beyond me. In the civilian world, I would have sued him for malpractice, but that was not allowed in the military. The net result is that I was left with a

14-degree bend in my left leg. That doctor's incompetence changed my life forever in a negative way.

While in the hospital, I learned that there were three persons arrested for drug trafficking who were associated with Special Forces. Master Sergeant Luciano Brash, the first sergeant of the 1st SF Group Signal Company, was arrested for smuggling marijuana in the hollow panels of signal trucks going to Korea. Brash was the same one that Sergeant Major John Voter had pulled his .45 pistol on in Vietnam as I was on the way to Bu Dop. The other two, Doc Koethe and Tim Kephart, were arrested for selling heroin. Koethe was a former 1st SF Group surgeon who had left the Army and was working as a contract doctor at Camp Kue Hospital. Tim Kephart was the manager of the Veterans of Foreign Wars Club in Okinawa. Kephart had won the Silver Star while assigned to B50 in Vietnam. On his second tour, he was assigned as a liaison NCO at Cam Ranh Bay Air Base to facilitate 5th SF Group personnel going on rest and recuperation leave or otherwise coming in and out of Vietnam. On that tour, Tim was court-martialed when his Vietnamese girlfriend was caught masquerading as an Army nurse; she'd been heading for Hong Kong on a supposed leave. Tim had forged her documents as well as documents for himself. He was reduced in rank, got promoted back to sergeant, and then left the Army to become the VFW Club manager. He and Koethe had an elaborate scheme. Kephart would travel to Thailand and bring back raw heroin in his golf clubs. Koethe would then cut the heroin. An extensive elaborate distribution system was being used with hiding places in the red-light district of Okinawa. I wasn't shocked by Brash as John Voter had warned me about him before. But the arrest of Koethe and Kephart was a real surprise.

After a few days in the hospital, I was discharged to go home. I was on crutches with a full leg cast. Mi Hye was very worried as she had never encountered anyone with very bad injuries before. Of course, my buddies gave me no mercy. Butch Fernandez teased me about not being able to drive. I had a manual gear shift in a Datsun Sunny car. I set out to prove to Butch and others that I could drive even with a full leg cast. Sadly, I had to be relieved from Jesse Simmons's team. I would still go into work and do light duty in the S2 and S3 sections of A Company. After a couple of months, my full leg cast was removed and replaced with a PTB or patellar-tendon-bearing cast. That PTB cast was a real relief as I could move about without crutches. The cast covered my lower leg and ended at the knee with a dimple in it where my kneecap helped with stability. I was unable to run, but I could do exercises to try and keep in physical shape. I also thought that I would try to get assigned to the Korean Resident Team after I was able to run and jump again.

Fred Robinson had been replaced by Sergeant Major Charles "Bull" McGuire. Bull had designed the McGuire rig in Vietnam to enhance the extraction of reconnaissance personnel without the helicopter having to land. Bull McGuire was a legend and tough as nails. I went into work one day, and he called me into his office and said, "Ish, you've got to go back to the States." When I asked him why, he stated that the Department of Army had issued instructions that anyone with over four consecutive years overseas had to return for stateside duty. I looked at him and said, "Sergeant major, that doesn't apply to me." He looked at me quizzically but said nothing. The next day, he called me into his office again. He started out with, "Ish, you lied to me." He had checked my records and found that I was on my eighth consecutive year overseas! I responded that I would never lie to him, and that he had said four years! He pounded his desk and then we both broke out laughing. I was very disappointed. I had my heart set on going to Korea, and I also regretted leaving the many friends and mentors that I had in Okinawa with the 1st SF Group. Sergeant Major Dick Perkins was also told that he would have to return to the States. We were both going to be assigned to Fort Bragg, and I was relieved that I would have one close friend there.

One night before leaving Okinawa, I received a call from Larry Dickinson, a close friend and Special Forces medical sergeant. Larry had a great sense of humor. He once swallowed a 10-dollar bill to see how long it would take to pass through his system. It took over 24 hours and the bill came out bleached! The call I received was not humorous. He asked me to come to the house of JK Wright. JK was passed out on the floor, reeking of alcohol. Larry and I picked him up and took him to the Camp Kue Hospital. JK had been warned that his liver was failing from alcohol abuse. Larry and I sternly talked to him after he was revived. Larry and I convinced JK that he needed to stop drinking and that if he continued to drink, he would be dead in months. Fortunately, he listened to us. He moved back to the States, remarried, and passed away in 1998. It was gratifying to help JK as he had taken me under his wing when I was first assigned to A Company, 1st SF Group.

Mi Hye was somewhat excited to be going to mainland America, but also a bit nervous as she had no knowledge of where North Carolina was. We prepared to move, and I sold my car for a song to David Kauhaahaa's brother, Hosea. Hosea was a Marine and had been using my car when I was on the frequent temporary duty trips that I had off Okinawa. One of the sad things was that the stray dog we had adopted knew we were leaving. She came around to say a last goodbye and licked our hands. We wondered what would befall her after we left. We said our farewells to our many friends in the 1st Special Forces Group and boarded a plane for the next assignment.

CHAPTER 10

New Challenges and Opportunities

Mi Hye and I planned to take leave and stop in Hawaii so she could meet my family. In Hawaii, she enjoyed seeing Oahu and meeting my family. My grandmother and she took an instant liking to each other. My grandmother told us that she had saved my life in Vietnam, pulling out the photo of me that she had prayed over every day. Before leaving Hawaii, I went to Tripler Army Hospital and requested that they remove the cast from my leg. The doctor told me that I should leave it on until I got to Fort Bragg, but I insisted he cut it off. That was dumb on my part! With the PTB cast, I could walk okay and carry things. Once the cast was off, I found out how much muscle I had lost, and I had to use crutches again.

From Hawaii, we traveled to San Bruno, California, and spent a few days with my Aunt Marjorie (Kyomi) and Uncle John Rose. We then took a bus to Medford, Oregon, where I had ordered a new car to be picked up. Mi Hye struggled with our suitcases as we walked to the bus station. Shortly after leaving San Francisco, it began to rain. The rain never stopped all the way to Oregon and then back to California. Mi Hye swore that she did not want to ever live in Oregon! Our trip to Fort Bragg was uneventful. We had little chance to do any sightseeing along the way, but Mi Hye did get an appreciation for how large the United States is.

When we arrived at Fort Bragg, I was told to report to Sergeant Major Henry Czerniak, who was at the John F. Kennedy Center for Special Warfare. I had no idea what my actual assignment would be, and I told Sergeant Major Czerniak that I was not sure if I would every run or jump again. He looked at me and said, "I didn't hire you for your looks, I hired you for your brain!" He then told me that I would be assigned to the Special Forces School Operations and Intelligence (O&I) Committee. I was greatly relieved to hear that I could remain in Special Forces and thanked him for the opportunity. I got a pleasant surprise when I reported to the O&I Committee. The officer in charge was Lieutenant Colonel Robert Joczik, who had been my commander on Okinawa with A Company, 1st SF Group before A Company became a battalion. Even more importantly, the NCO in charge of the committee was Forrest K. Foreman. Forrest had an excellent reputation in Special

Forces. Forrest was glad to have me join the committee as the committee lacked real experience regarding intelligence subjects.

All instructors had to be certified through attendance at an instructor training course that was two weeks long. Thanks to the mentorship of Dick Perkins on Okinawa, I had thoroughly studied the Army's field manual on how to present instruction and knew how to prepare lesson plans and teach. I did learn new techniques as the Army had adopted a systems engineering approach. The tasks to be taught, along with the conditions of performing those tasks, and the standards to demonstrate the ability to execute the tasks, were important. One of my classmates was Eulis Presley whom I had met briefly beforehand. Eulis was ready to quit the course as he was having a bit of trouble academically. I took Eulis aside and gently counseled him while also offering to help him. I reminded him that he had to teach Montagnards and Nung indigenous soldiers in Vietnam when he was with MACV SOG, and he could use those skills to pass the course. That gave him the confidence to continue, and it also resulted in us becoming the best of friends. At the end of the course, my desire to excel and to master the systems engineering approach resulted in my selection as the honor graduate. I was pleasantly surprised and silently thanked those in Okinawa who had taught me how to instruct.

Forrest Foreman was determined to raise the quality of instruction in the O&I course. Shortly after I joined the committee, Forrest was able to get Art Hutchins transferred from another section of the SF schools. My teammate from Okinawa, Jay Massey, also came on board. We were all sergeants first class, and Forrest wondered why we had not been promoted. The Army had gone to a centralized promotion system for senior NCOs a few years before, and promotions were based more on centralized records held at the Army's Military Personnel Center than on local promotion boards. Forrest said that we should go to the Military Personnel Center which was in Alexandria, Virginia, to check our records file. With Art Hutchins driving his Ford Torino like a NASCAR driver, he, Jay, and I took off one morning to check our files. I was shocked to see only four pieces of paper in my central files. My Department of the Army Form 2-1, Personnel Qualification Record, was not in my file. Three papers were meaningless, including one order authorizing me separate rations (money for food when a dining facility is not available). The fourth piece of paper was my selection for the Army's first Advanced Noncommissioned Officer course. I did not even know I had been selected and received no notification of my selection in Okinawa. The lack of a completion certificate told me that was the reason I had not been promoted. I had the opportunity to talk with Ron Matysek, who was the Special Forces NCO assigned to the Military Personnel Center. He was shocked to see the paucity of my records and set out to also rectify my attendance at the Advanced NCO Course at Fort Benning, Georgia.

Attendance at the Advanced NCO Course gave me an opportunity to see old friends from Okinawa, including Fred Henry, Roland Nuqui, and Tom Johnson. The course was not challenging for most of the Special Forces soldiers. Fred Henry and I engaged in shenanigans to keep ourselves amused. Part of the course was to replicate the use of armored personnel carriers. To save money, we maneuvered on all-terrain vehicles rather than M-113 armored vehicles. Fred and I bought water guns and would soak some of our classmates just to have fun. On most of the weekends, there were four of us who would head back to Fort Bragg to be with our families. The trip normally took over seven and a half hours, but we mapped out back roads and speed traps and would do it in under six hours. Teamwork paid off, as we had a radar detector to avoid getting speeding tickets. As for the course, I spent much of my time mentoring and tutoring others regardless of whether or not they were in Special Forces. My only challenge was to pass the run in the physical fitness test as I was still recovering from my shattered leg. It was painful for me to run in boots, but I could pass the running test by removing my boots, draping them around my neck and running barefoot. The cadre scratched their heads, but I insisted that I was wearing boots—albeit they were around my neck instead of my feet! Once more, the innovation I learned in Special Forces came to the fore!

The two years I spent on the Operations and Intelligence Committee were filled with many challenges and memories. I was astounded to find that Lieutenant Colonel Joczik was using one of the instructors as a personal assistant. The individual was not a good instructor but was a likeable person. Joczik was using him to walk his dogs, paint his house, and do menial personal chores. I was unsure of what to do as this was clearly a misuse of a soldier. My dilemma was solved when Joczik announced his retirement. He was replaced by Budge Williams who had faced court-martial charges in Vietnam over the killing of Thai Khac Chuyen. Budge was laid back and never got in the way of the instructors.

After Colonel Charlie Beckwith took command of the Special Forces Schools, Budge was fired and replaced by Chuck Odorizzi. Forrest Foreman was the pillar that kept the committee moving in the right direction and providing quality instruction. He proved the value of noncommissioned officer leadership not only in Special Forces but also in the U.S. Army. The quality of our NCO corps makes our military stand out when compared to most other nations.

There was an occasion when our committee was asked to support the Robin Sage exercise, which is the culminating exercise before graduating from the Special Forces Qualification Course. Forrest assigned Art Hutchins and me to provide the support. Art had come from the committee that ran the Robin Sage exercise and was totally familiar with the rural area where it was conducted, as well as what the exercise consisted of. Art took me to remote areas like Star and Biscoe, North Carolina, to meet some of the civilians who supported the exercise and played roles to test the students. The exercise was conducted where there were active members of the Ku Klux Klan. Art took me by one farm barn where the owner had a half-track armored vehicle with working .50-caliber machine guns. Did my eyes ever open wide! I asked Art if I was in danger because of being a minority, and he assured me that was not the case. We spent a week living out of his camper trailer and became fast friends forever.

Much of the Operations and Intelligence Course was spent on intense practical exercises that demanded the creation of plans and the processing of intelligence. Thanks to my mentors, I understood that the desired outcome was to make the students capable of demonstrating their skills in Special Forces operations and intelligence rather than flunking students. There were times when we had to do the latter, but that would only happen after we attempted to tutor them. Hugh Hubbard, a friend from Okinawa and a great medical sergeant, came during the course. He came to me one day and said he was going to quit and that he couldn't do the planning. We sat down and had a heart-to-heart conversation. I reminded Hugh he had been sent to Micronesia independently to organize a medical civic action program during his time in the 1st SF Group. I convinced him that he knew how to plan and organize an effort and he had proven so on that mission to Micronesia. I convinced him that he had the skills to succeed in the course. I was happy to see Hugh continue and graduate.

Part of the Operations and Intelligence Course was conducted at Fort Huachuca, Arizona, by the U.S. Army Intelligence School. Forrest and I sensed that our students were not getting the proper training at Fort Huachuca. Accordingly, he sent me on a short trip to find out what was being taught and how well. What I found was quite disconcerting. Special Forces intelligence sergeants are expected to have a broad spectrum of skills that include agent handling, order of battle analysis, intelligence collection and reporting, intelligence planning, and elicitation and interrogation. I discovered that the Intelligence School was concentrating mainly on interrogation techniques. No wonder the students would show up at Fort Bragg with very little intelligence skills. I returned to Fort Bragg and submitted a report requesting that the Intelligence School revamp their curricula for our Special Forces students. Sadly, the Intelligence School could never fully adapt to Special Forces requirements. Over the years, Special Forces intelligence training has been conducted at Fort Bragg with much more success. There is a Special Forces Intelligence Sergeants Course and three levels of Advanced Special Operations Techniques, with the third level providing a solid grounding in conducting agent operations.

On the home front, our time at Fort Bragg was a most interesting time for Mi Hye. We moved from a temporary apartment to the Humphrey Plaza location on Fort Bragg. The homes were former officer quarters built in the 1930s. They were of stucco construction with tile roofs and were very sturdy. Mi Hye discovered that North Carolina was a great place to buy quality furniture. Art Hutchins introduced us to the Cagle Furniture Company in Spout Springs, North Carolina, and Mi Hye promptly upped her taste in quality furniture! She took a job working as a cashier in the Post Exchange to help contribute towards the furniture expenses. The Cagle family took a liking to us and always gave us great prices.

Mi Hye also wanted to learn how to drive a car. I tried to teach her, but I failed! She enrolled in a course taught by a Korean instructor and got her license. She was rightfully proud of that accomplishment. Wigs were a fashionable item in the early 1970s, and Mi Hye found several wig shops on Hay Street in Fayetteville. Following her visit I had to explain to her why some of the other customers she met were buying wigs—she had never before met anyone who was transgender. We had great neighbors who would check on Mi Hye when I was on travel.

The daughter of one of our neighbors was walking in the woods one day and came across a decapitated head. That was a traumatic experience for her, and I spent time talking with her to alleviate her stress. The head belonged to the sister of Willie Welsch, who would end up working for me five years later. It was strongly suspected that her husband had killed her, but evidence was inadvertently destroyed, and he was never convicted.

One of my challenges was to recover from my shattered leg and get back into peak physical shape and on-jump status. I bought a set of free weights and a bench and worked hard at it. Within three months of getting back to Fort Bragg, I started jumping again. Ben Dennis was worried about me and gave me an old pair of skydiving boots with thick cushioning soles. The boots helped me initially, but after a few months, I no longer needed to use them. Every day I forced myself to run a course known as the Military Assistance Training Advisor (MATA) mile. It had been established to prepare military advisors for assignment to Vietnam. It was tough going at first, but I was determined to regain my running proficiency. After some 10 months, I achieved the maximum points for the two-mile run on the Army's physical fitness test.

Mi Hye and I were settling into a routine and life was good. My workload on the Operations and Intelligence Committee kept increasing, but I enjoyed that as it gave me more opportunities to work with the students and improve their Special Operations skills. Forrest Foreman also had me participate in a study looking at the future of Special Forces and a changing world picture and operational environment. I also prepared a study seeking a change in how Survival, Evasion, Escape, and Resistance (SERE) training was being conducted. I guess I was ahead of my time as it was not adopted. Some years later, Colonel Nick Rowe, who had escaped from being a prisoner of war in Vietnam, was able to introduce significant changes in SERE training.

Unexpectedly, my name appeared on the promotion list to master sergeant. That was great news, and I hoped to become a team sergeant in A Detachment. I was shocked to find out from the Army's Military Personnel Center (MILPERCEN) that there were no Special Forces assignments available for me. I got a rude awakening to learn that Special Forces had diminished in size from a high of roughly 12,000 during the height of Vietnam to less than 4,000 in 1975. Liz Alexander, who had replaced the legendary Billy Alexander at MILPERCEN, went out of her way to try and find me a Special Forces assignment. She thought she had one in Thailand with the Special Forces 46th Company, but that was an assignment for an E7 rather than an E8. The choices available came down to an assignment in Ethiopia, becoming a Reserve or National Guard advisor, or being assigned to an Army Reserve Officer Training Corps (ROTC) assignment. I went to the Post Exchange where Mi Hye worked and asked her what she thought about Ethiopia. She yelled, "Ethiopia!"—and I knew she was not happy about that. I did the proverbial low crawl out of the Post Exchange and called Liz Alexander. She told me that the Reserve Component Advisor's position was in Corvallis, Oregon, and that the ROTC position was at the University of Santa Clara. When Mi Hye got home from work, I told her what the choices were. All she remembered about Oregon was the trip we had made in the rain to pick up our car in 1973. Okay, so I opted for the University of Santa Clara.

Liz Alexander told me that the person I was replacing had been in the assignment for six years. She also told me there was a chance that I would not be moved as the Army was instituting a policy of reducing the number of permanent changes of station moves for the foreseeable future. She was realistic and stated there was a good chance of my staying there until I would have over 20 years of service and could retire. With that in mind, I sadly went around Fort Bragg to say goodbye to my friends. When I saw Dick Perkins, he wanted to give me two baby rattlesnakes that he had caught under the building where he was teaching. I politely declined his offer.

One of my last stops was to see Sergeant Major Arif Zaky. Arif accepted a direct commission to become a captain while we were serving in Vietnam. I was also offered a direct commission and Zaky had implored me to take it, but I declined. After Vietnam, Arif was caught in a reduction-in-force and reverted to becoming a sergeant major again. When I went to say goodbye to Arif, I intended to tease him with my perverse sense of humor. I asked him, "Why did you lower yourself to take that direct commission?" He looked at me and said, "700." I couldn't figure out what he was talking about and asked him what he meant. He called me a dumbass for not taking the direct commission and said it was $700 a month pay difference. I was stunned and muttered something about if the opportunity ever came again that I would take it. Arif then told me that there was a Reserve Commission Board in session, and he could get me before the board, provided I had the necessary paperwork ready by the next day. I couldn't turn down this opportunity and hustled home to prepare the papers. Arif lived up to his promise and got me before the board the following day. I was told I had passed the board with flying colors and that I would receive a reserve commission as a captain. Because of my intelligence background, they would recommend that I be branched as a military intelligence officer. I convinced them that I should be commissioned in the infantry, and they did so.

***

Mi Hye and I departed Fort Bragg in the summer of 1975. We did not have the opportunity to do much research on the area we were moving to. In 1975 there was no public internet or personal computers. Accordingly, trying to find information on anything was a much more protracted process. However, I knew the area from the times I had spent in Palo Alto with my friend Richard Rathbun while we were at Lewis & Clark College. I also knew my aunt and uncle in San Bruno, California. After a hurried but uneventful trip to California, we stayed with my aunt and uncle for a few days. I found an apartment in Sunnyvale, California, not far from the Santa Clara University campus and we established a temporary residence there. Sergeant Major John Slabbers greeted me when I reported for duty. He gave me an overview of the ROTC program and introduced me to the officers in the detachment. Slabbers also told me no military housing was available, and that we would have to live on the economy. Luckily, Mi Hye and I found a great real estate agent named Bill Anderson. Bill was a retired Naval aviator and still cared for those in uniform. We considered renting a house, but the prices favored us buying a home. Bill found a former model home at a great price. The two-car garage had been the sales office and was carpeted and paneled, giving us about 1,900 square feet of living area.

We had to use almost all our savings to make the down payment. Mi Hye did her part by applying and getting a job at the Navy Exchange at Moffett Field. We needed two cars and did not have much cash left, so I found a beat-up clunker that had obviously been in a bad accident, but I got it for $150. I worked on getting the engine to run decently and used it to get to work while Mi Hye used our newer car to drive the 14 miles to Moffett Field. The house was in good shape, but the yard needed work. Over the next two years I installed a lawn sprinkler system and planted a hedge in the front yard. The backyard sloped down from the roadway towards the house. I realized that would be troublesome during heavy rains as water would flow towards the house from the roadway. With a pick and shovel, I took down about two feet of the backyard and leveled it off. To do so, I built a sled out of heavy lumber, tied a rope to the sled, put my barbell weights on top and had Mi Hye stand on it as I dragged the sled to level the ground! This effort was undertaken with the belief that we would be in the house for a long time.

The Santa Clara ROTC detachment consisted of three NCOs—Sergeant Major Slabbers, me, and a supply sergeant—and five officers. The Professor of Military Science was Lieutenant Colonel Jerome Rogers, a military intelligence officer who had served in Finland with my friend, Special Forces Colonel Charles Norton.

Two majors and two captains were assigned. There were about fifty ROTC cadets for whom we were responsible for training and advising. I soon learned that my predecessor did not appear to do much of anything during his six years assigned to Santa Clara. My cousin Joe Peterson, who had graduated from Santa Clara in 1972, apprised me that my predecessor had a side job; generally, his only contact with the cadets was when he wanted them to work for him at a low pay rate.

One of the first things I did was to review the planned events for the year and get involved in planning those activities, which the operations officer appreciated. I also saw the need for a reference library for the cadets. I ordered the necessary field and technical manuals along with professional reading material and set up a library with a way to account for the materials that would be loaned to the cadets or available for research. I was fortunate because the university paid for two student helpers. Meg Sullivan was especially helpful with the library.

The detachment had some low-cost .22 rifles built by the Savage Corporation, intended to be used by a rifle team. Since there was no rifle range at Santa Clara, I arranged with a National Guard Armory in San Jose to use their indoor range. I also contacted my friend Clarence Young. Clarence was assigned to the Fort Ord marksmanship unit after he left the 1st SF Group. I asked Clarence for help, and he dispatched one of his NCOs to conduct a clinic for the cadets at Santa Clara. I also arranged to take the cadets to Fort Ord where they received further coaching and training. Unfortunately, I was not able to get better rifles for the team. Nonetheless, they were good enough marksmen not to finish last in their competitions.

It was crucial for me to build a rapport with the cadets and also important to show that I could be a trusted source of advice, without lecturing them. The only officer who fit that role was Major Carl Gentine. The cadets needed the opportunity to ask personal questions and express their views, with the confidence that they would not be criticized. Human nature being what it is, I realized that not all the cadets would take advantage of the opportunity. I also understood that some had joined ROTC to receive financial help with their education and were not going to be career officers. During my first year, there were two who took advantage of my mentoring. They were Rita Tamayo, who was an American of Filipino ancestry, the Corps of Cadets commander and the first female to achieve that status, and Florian Rothbrust. Rita's father was a retired Army master sergeant who lived in the Fort Ord, California, area. She would be commissioned as a Military Police officer. Florian's parents had emigrated from Germany. Florian had to learn to speak English and became a naturalized American citizen. His parents owned a bakery in San Jose and were wonderful people. He would receive a commission as an infantry officer. I remained in contact with them when they went on active duty. Rita died a tragic death due to an aneurysm. Florian retired as a colonel.

One of the great things that happened to me was meeting a Jesuit priest who was on the Santa Clara faculty. We struck up a conversation after finishing a workout in the gymnasium, and I found out that during the summers he was a visiting priest for the Holy Trinity Church in Kuliouou. He knew most of my former neighbors, and we talked at length. He did some homework on me, and the next time I saw him he said he arranged for me to be a Faculty Club member and that I could teach courses for credit. I was honored to have him go out of his way for me. I approached Lieutenant Colonel Rogers and obtained his approval for me to teach courses for credit. The following semester I began teaching a military leadership course and a military history course.

Other activities were to take the cadets to Fort Ord to introduce them to patrolling techniques and how to live in the field. I also assisted in mapping out a course in one of the State parks for orienteering. Orienteering is a competition which stresses physical fitness and the ability to read a map and plan a route. We also took the cadets on tours for so-called adventure training and for military history. That included a trip to Yellowstone National Park. I also offered to teach the cadets karate, but there was only one taker—who was only interested in finding out what karate was—so I did not continue after he had satisfied his curiosity. On a personal level, I attempted to train with Yamaguchi Sensei in San Francisco; unfortunately, the length of time it took to commute and the two-hour class took too much out of me.

The summer of my first year at Santa Clara, I was sent to the ROTC Summer Camp at Fort Lewis, Washington. The summer camp was for those in their third year of ROTC and would determine whether they passed the field activities and qualified for a commission. Butch Fernandez was also slated to go to the camp, and he was the sergeant major at the University of California Davis. I collected Butch in my old clunker and we headed north. We stopped in Oregon and spent the night with Malina Kaulukukui, who was like a younger sister to me.

At Fort Lewis, I was disappointed to find that I would be assigned to the headquarters as the senior NCO rather than being with the cadets. The former Professor of Military Science at Santa Clara had been reassigned to the ROTC Regional Headquarters. He had heard about my planning and organizational abilities and thought I would best serve the command by being the senior NCO at the headquarters. The work was relatively easy, which allowed me to keep track of the Santa Clara cadets who were scattered through different companies. Corn Beef Haleamau was also at the camp from the University of Hawaii. Butch and I found out he was playing golf when we first got to Fort Lewis, and we figured out where he would be on the golf course, and set up an ambush. Corn Beef hit a ball on the green. I walked up to the ball, put a marker down, and then picked his ball up and threw it into the woods. Butch and I were disguised, and Corn Beef couldn't see who had done that. He started yelling and cursing at us and we flipped him the bird! Corn Beef came storming up to the green—angry as all hell. When he saw that it was Butch and I, he started shaking his head. We all had a good laugh, and I showed him the marker where his ball had landed on the green.

The one good thing about being in the headquarters was that I had lots of time to work on my car. I found an auto shop on Fort Lewis, fixed the body of its many dents, and repainted the car. After painting it, I had it parked in a graveled parking lot adjacent to the headquarters. A colonel from the 4th Infantry Division, whose brigade was supporting the ROTC camp, came speeding into the parking lot flinging gravel towards my car. I approached the colonel and told him that the next time he did that, he would find himself flat on the ground. He apologized.

Another thing of note that summer was when one of the 4th Infantry Division soldiers assigned to the headquarters was reportedly stealing supplies from the headquarters. I checked it out and found that the thief was putting supplies into a laundry bag, and then lowering the bag out a back window to pick it up later. I went outside, retrieved all the supplies, and substituted some rocks to make it appear that what he had stolen was still in the bag. I also attached a note about what happens to thieves. The next morning, he showed up for work, beckoned at me to come to where he was standing, and instructed me to "Come here." I literally had two phone calls simultaneously and did not appreciate his demeanor. When I ended the calls, I walked up to him, and he swore at me. I was angry and slapped him so hard that it knocked him to the floor. He got up and pointed towards a female major in the headquarters and said, "Ma'am, you saw that. He hit me!" The major looked at the soldier and said, "I didn't see anything!" I then told the soldier to get the hell out of the headquarters and return to his unit. I called his unit to let his first sergeant know what happened and never saw him again. The major and I talked, and I thanked her profusely for supporting me. I was glad I had treated her respectfully beforehand and had won her support as a competent NCO. She was also competent at her job—she was an officer and a fine soldier. That is what counted.

The civilian aide to the Secretary of the Army for the San Francisco Bay area was a multi-millionaire named Benjamin Swig. He owned the Fairmont Hotel in San Francisco, and he and his son also owned the professional hockey team in San Francisco. I was asked to be Mr Swig's escort during his visit to the summer camp because he had been a super donor to the University of Santa Clara. Over a four-year period, he had donated some $75 million to Santa Clara. I had heard a story that he had offered to make a significant donation to the University of San Francisco, another Jesuit school. The story goes that the University declined his donation, implying that they weren't interested in Jewish money. Mr Swig then went down the peninsula to Santa Clara and was greeted with open arms. Despite his riches, he was a humble man and flew in economy class. I had a female soldier who was his driver while he was at Fort Lewis. When we took him to the airport, he gave a gratuity to thank her for the work she had done. She did not want to accept the money, but I gave her a nod to tell her to take it. I later explained to her that he would have been offended had she not taken the gift. I was impressed with her attitude and wanting to do what was right.

My second year at Santa Clara saw me pretty much on "cruise control." I continued mentoring and advising the cadets, teaching classes, and planning field trips. On one of the field trips, a female cadet, Kit Wong, was chosen to carry an M-60 machine gun—she was five feet one inch tall and of Chinese ancestry. She was up to the task. On the return, I changed the roster and made the cadet leader carry the machine gun. He regretted picking on Kit! He struggled to carry the weight of the machine gun and I just smirked at him.

There were only a few things of note during my second year. One involved an officer who was recently divorced. While assigned to the ROTC detachment, he developed a relationship with a Santa Clara University employee. He came to me for advice when he found out that she was also having an affair with another officer. My advice to him was to break off the relationship as he could never trust the woman. He did so and later found and married a fine woman. One of the captains was a West Point graduate who genuinely wanted to do a good job and tried his best to develop good relations with the cadets. Unfortunately, the cadets thought he was weird. He was an engineer and very smart. We were doing an ROTC display on the campus to attract more cadets and had to erect a so-called General Purpose Large tent. To erect the tent typically took a squad of soldiers. The captain convinced me that the two of us could do the job. He was brilliant in the way that he proved to me that we could do it.

The detachment was under pressure to recruit more cadets as the expected norm was to commission at least 15 cadets annually. There were only two other four-year universities in the area. San Jose State had its own Army ROTC detachment, where my friend Ed Morales was assigned, and Stanford University. During the height of anti-war sentiment over Vietnam, Stanford ceased their ROTC program. I went to Stanford's Law School Professor Emeritus Harry Rathbun, the father of my friend Richard Rathbun, and asked him for his opinion about trying to get ROTC back at Stanford. Professor Rathbun didn't believe it was possible to get back on campus full-time but helped me convince the university to allow Santa Clara to recruit Stanford students. I successfully got one student that year to enroll in the Santa Clara program. The lesson learned was the proverbial, where there is a will there is a way.

However, I was not successful in convincing any of the cadets that they should go into Special Forces. I was amazed with the class of 1977, as there were six cadets who were to be commissioned in the Judge Advocate General Corps—as lawyers! They were all fine young men, but I felt I had failed. One of the cadets that sought a commission in the combat arms was a favorite of mine. His name was Eldon Regua and he went on to retire as a major general. Another personal favorite was Natalie Eblacas from Waianae, Hawaii. I still stay in touch with both.

During the second semester of the 1976–1977 school year, I was approached by the same Jesuit priest who had gotten me into the Faculty Club and permission to teach classes for college credit. He asked why I was not taking advantage of seeking an advanced degree. With the thought in mind of the six cadets who would be Army lawyers, and believing I was as intelligent as they were, I asked the priest if that included admission into the Santa Clara Law School. He assured me that it would not be a problem. I then started planning my enrollment in law school the following semester. Everything was looking great. Things got even better when Mi Hye became a naturalized American citizen with a ceremony in San Francisco. She was rightfully proud of that accomplishment. She changed her first name to Bobbi based on the advice of a *mudang* (Korean shaman).

Those plans went out the window when I got a call from Ben Dennis. Ben started out the conversation by saying, "Congratulations." I asked him what the heck he was congratulating me for, and he replied that I had been selected to attend the Army's Sergeants Major Academy. This came as a big shock to me as I was planning to finish law school at Santa Clara and retire. Ben told me that I had no choice and that the academy would be a permanent change of station assignment for some 10 months. By the time we finished talking, I was standing on our kitchen counter in denial. I remained in denial until I received the orders a couple of weeks later that would require me to report to Fort Bliss, Texas, in July 1977. Things got worse when I was informed that I would have to attend the ROTC Summer Camp at Fort Lewis in June and July. It was now May of 1977 without much time to sell our home and to prepare to move. I asked to be relieved of going to Fort Lewis because I needed time to prepare for the move. I was sorely disappointed when I failed to get support. I was put in touch with a colonel who tried to talk down to me. I tried to use logic, and that failed. So, I stood my ground and told him that I was authorized 30 days leave before a change of station, which meant I could be at Fort Lewis for no more than five days. The colonel didn't know what to say to that, but I was finally taken off the orders to go to Summer Camp.

We contacted our realtor, Bill Anderson, and he advised that it would take at least a few months to sell our house. We thought about renting the house, but when I did my calculations based on our income if we could not rent the house for two months straight, the answer showed that we would be in danger of losing it. So, we decided that Mi Hye would stay in California until we could sell the house. I had predicted that our property tax would rise and that would affect our monthly payment. Little did I know that the following year Proposition 13 would pass the California legislature, which effectively lowered the property taxes tremendously. We bought our house for $46,000 and when it finally sold in early 1978, it went for $78,000. That same house today is worth over $1,800,000. Oh well! I packed what I would need for the Sergeants Major Academy, and Mi Hye accompanied me in my clunker of a car to Fort Bliss and then flew back to California.

The first day I reported to the academy, I was met by my friend and former boss on the Special Forces School Operations and Intelligence Committee, Sergeant Major Forrest K. Foreman. I asked Forrest what the hell he was doing at the academy as he was already a sergeant major. He just shrugged his shoulders and never answered my question. He then told me, "Call Colonel Beckwith." I asked him why, and he responded, "Just do it." He gave me Beckwith's telephone number at Fort Bragg. I called Colonel Beckwith and his first words were, "Are you ready, boy?" I asked him, "Ready for what?" He replied, "You know, you're the intel puke." I had no idea what he was talking about, and Forrest hadn't given me any information. I quickly thought through what I would say. I knew there was no guarantee that I would get an assignment in Special Forces after completing the academy. I also knew that right, wrong, or indifferent, Charlie Beckwith would always be where the action was. I thought this would be my way back into the Special Forces fold. With those thoughts racing through my mind, I replied to Colonel Beckwith and said, "I have one question for you, Sir." He asked me what the question was, and I asked, "Are you going to trick fuck me again?" He laughed and said, "I guess that means you're coming on board!" I replied, "Yes Sir," and we ended the conversation.

I then found Forrest Foreman and asked him what the hell was going on. Forrest only told me was that Beckwith was forming a new unit and that it would have a new mission to perform within Special Forces. He also said that he was going to be part of the new unit. That's all I needed to know—it was a Special Forces assignment and my friend Forrest Foreman would be part of it. I trusted Forrest implicitly and looked forward to the opportunity to work with him once again.

I then set about becoming a student. The sergeants major course was to run from July until the following May or June of 1978. I joked with the cadre about allowing me to take a pre-test so I could leave early and join whatever unit Charlie Beckwith was creating. The cadre thought I was crazy. The course of instruction was not very challenging to me. I had left my wife in California as she was working at the Naval Air Station Moffett Field in the Navy Exchange. When I left for the Sergeants Major Academy, we decided to hold on to our house as there was no telling where I would be next assigned. I knew the separation would be hard and frequently called her to find out if she was doing okay. Fortunately, everything was all right with our home, and she did not have to worry about that. I once again felt very fortunate to have married a wonderful person with a strong personality.

Class 10 of the Sergeants Major Academy had over 35 Special Forces soldiers as students. For many, the academics were quite challenging, and they needed help in their studies. Accordingly, I set out to help mentor and tutor many of my classmates. The lessons I had learned in life about helping others and the spirit of *Intoku* once again came to the fore. Several members of the academy faculty saw how I was helping others, that would pay off shortly.

In late September 1977, Forrest and I were told that the new unit was well on its way to being formed and that Colonel Beckwith wanted us back at Fort Bragg as soon as possible. Forrest was already a sergeant major and was not challenged academically. So, for him, it was a no-brainer to leave the academy early without graduating. In my case, there was a good chance that I might not be promoted to sergeant major if I did not graduate from the course. I didn't care, as the opportunity to be part of what appeared to be an exciting assignment and get back into Special Forces was all that counted. A plan was formed back at Fort Bragg to have Forrest and I leave in November, six months before the graduation date.

Official orders were issued, and Forrest left in early November 1977. I was supposed to follow two weeks later. The Commandant of the Academy was Colonel James Crow. He learned that Forrest had left and that I would follow shortly. He became very upset and proclaimed that there was no more important assignment than being a student at the academy. I lost any respect for Colonel Crow when I heard that ridiculous statement. Here's where *Intoku* and the help I had been giving others came to the forefront. Major Dick Broder and Sergeant Major Louis Laul were two of the cadre that knew of the help I was giving others.

Dick Broder called me to his office and explained that Colonel Crow was furious and was determined to stop me from leaving. Dick asked me what I wanted to do and if I had any ideas. I knew that there were two significant sections of the course to complete prior to graduation. I asked Dick what he thought about allowing me to take the final examinations for those two sections. Dick looked at me incredulously and asked if I was serious. I reminded him of my joke about giving me the pre-tests when I first arrived. He then asked if I was sure, and I responded affirmatively and that I would take it "fair and square" (not cheating). Dick told me to come to his office in the morning and he would administer the two final examinations.

I took the examinations the following morning. Dick graded them and was astounded but not surprised that I passed with flying colors. He then told me what he was going to do. He would go to Colonel Crow and proclaim that I had conned him into giving me the two final examinations, that I had passed them with almost perfect marks, and that I also had a baccalaureate degree in international relations that constituted the last major section of the academy's curriculum. We both chuckled, and understood this was really an unconventional warfare technique used by Special Forces! Dick fulfilled his promise and came back to me laughing about how Crow had gone through the roof and how Crow had berated him for getting suckered. Crow forced me to Fort Bragg on temporary duty rather than on the permanent transfer that was supposed to happen. His actions would cost me, but I was happy to get to Fort Bragg.

CHAPTER 11

The Beginning of the Delta Force

The idea for what would become America's first dedicated counterterrorist force began in 1962 when then-Captain Charlie A. Beckwith served on an exchange assignment with the British 22nd Special Air Service (SAS) Regiment. Charlie succeeded in passing their rigorous selection course. While with the regiment in Malaysia, he contracted leptospirosis which can be fatal for many, but Charlie survived. He was highly impressed by the quality of soldiers in the SAS and had a burning desire to create a similar unit in the United States Army Special Forces structure. His opportunity to bring that about came to fruition in 1976/1977. It was more than simple luck on Charlie's part.

The stars were aligned for Charlie Beckwith during those years. The power of networking would soon be evident and show the importance of building trust. The commanding general of the U.S. Army John F. Kennedy Center for Special Warfare and the Institute for Military Assistance was Major General Robert C. Kingston. Charlie had been a team leader for General Kingston in 1978 when the Joint Casualty Resolution Center was established to recover Americans who were missing in action during the Vietnam War. In late 1976, Charlie relinquished command as the head of the Special Forces School at Fort Bragg under General Kingston's command. He asked for permission to conduct a study and write a paper to create an SAS-type organization within Special Forces and was granted permission by General Kingston. Beckwith and Kingston were impressed by the Israeli commando raid in July 1976 that had rescued 106 hostages held by the Popular Front for the Liberation of Palestine in Entebbe, Uganda.

Kingston liked Beckwith's paper and asked him to present the concept at an annual conference of the U.S. Army Training and Doctrine Command. General Kingston also assigned Colonel Tom Henry to help rewrite the paper to include terms that conventional Army officers could understand. Beckwith and Henry presented the paper at the conference and received rave reviews.

By coincidence, and luckily for Beckwith, in March 1976 a splinter group from the Nation of Islam seized three buildings in downtown Washington, DC. They were known as the Hanafi Muslims and were led by Hamaas Abdul Khaalis. In 1973, seven members of Khaalis's family had been murdered by Nation of Islam members who had been convicted and were in prison. Khaalis sought revenge by having 12 of his followers seize the B'nai B'rith building, the Islamic Center of Washington, and the John A. Wilson building, which was the headquarters of the District of Columbia City Council. The Hanafi's held 149 hostages. Law enforcement agencies like the Federal Bureau of Investigation and the Washington Metropolitan Police Department were unprepared to deal with this type of incident. A call was made to General Kingston at Fort Bragg, and he was asked if he could send Special Forces to Washington, DC, to resolve the incident. General Kingston, who had done an exchange tour in Britain, knew the difference between a surgical capability and a frontal assault. He bluntly responded by saying, "Only if you are willing to put the lives of all the hostages at risk."

Consequently, no Special Forces were sent to Washington. As a visionary, General Kingston saw the need to create a dedicated counterterrorist force and tasked Charlie Beckwith with modifying his SAS approach and concentrating on counterterrorism. Kingston then began to use his fellow general officer contacts to garner approval to create such a unit. The most influential of Kingston's friends was Lieutenant General Edward "Shy" Meyer, the Army's Deputy Chief of Staff for Operations and Plans, and a classmate of General Kingston's at the Army Command and General Staff College. Beckwith assembled a small team to begin serious planning to create what he called the 1st Special Forces Operational Detachment-Delta. That small group consisted of Lieutenant Colonel Curtis Hurst, Major Charles Odorizzi, Major Lewis Burruss, and Sergeant Major William "Country" Grimes. I understand they located themselves in a metal building behind the gas station on Smoke Bomb Hill close to the corner of Gruber and Reilly Roads.

By July 1977, they had developed their initial organizational plans and knew that they would be given permission to start 1st Special Forces Operational Detachment (SFOD-D). I knew that to be fact as it was in July at the Sergeants Major Academy when I was told to contact Colonel Beckwith, and I agreed to join his effort. Beckwith and the four others began planning the organizational structure for Delta. The assessment and selection course that Beckwith insisted on was a key part of ensuring the right people would be assigned to Delta, and to also recruit those Beckwith believed would form the initial staff and support elements for the unit. They soon added Captain Mike Smith, who would become the first S1 or personnel officer to start working with the Department of Army to get people assigned. I was fortunate to be one of those whom Beckwith had faith in to do a good job.

I flew in from El Paso for the Sergeants Major Academy and arrived in mid-November 1977. I made my way to the two buildings Delta was operating from; the former Operations and Intelligence Committee World War II wooden barracks, where I had worked in just two years before, and the former High Altitude,

Low Opening (HALO) classroom on Smoke Bomb Hill. I was warmly greeted by Major Wayne Long, who was the first intelligence officer, and Staff Sergeant John Stanley. Wayne was a Special Forces officer who had left the Army once to work for the CIA and decided to return into the Army. He had been assigned to the 519th Military Intelligence Battalion when Beckwith sought him out to become the intelligence officer. John Stanley was also in the 519th and had won the respect of Wayne Long, who convinced John to join him in Delta. Everything in Delta was in a nascent stage in November, and there were tons of items to be attended to before the unit and intelligence section would be up and running. John Stanley worked his tail off establishing security accounts, security clearance procedures, and handling classified information. I learned that the 1st SFOD-D mission was to concentrate on counterterrorism.

I quickly learnt other interesting information about the start of Delta. General Kingston was fully behind the creation of Delta with Charlie Beckwith in charge. Charlie had Kingston's approval to take two years to achieve full operational capability. Charlie believed he needed two years to establish a selection and assessment course, recruit the right cut of cloth for the unit, and establish an operator's training course to adequately prepare the unit for actual employment on surgical counterterrorism missions. Beckwith also envisioned that the unit would likely operate in a semi-permissive environment in which any overseas employment would be with the knowledge and permission of the host nation. He did not rule out employment domestically within the United States but understood that there were legal constraints and that the lead agency would be the FBI.

In March 1977, Major General Jack Singlaub, a Special Forces icon, was relieved of his duties as the Chief of Staff for the U.S. Forces Korea. He had openly challenged President Carter's desire to reduce the number of American troops in Korea. The Army decided to send Bob Kingston to replace Singlaub in Korea. Kingston relinquished command at Fort Bragg in June or July 1977 and was replaced by Major General Jack V. Mackmull. Mackmull did not have Special Operations experience prior to taking command of the JFK Special Warfare Center. However, he was a noted Army aviator who had done much to develop helicopter tactics and procedures. He was a big man who had played football at the United States Military Academy from where he graduated in 1950. Despite his size, he had a gentle personality and cared for his soldiers.

I was told that after taking command of the Special Warfare Center, Mackmull was briefed on Delta by Bob Kingston. Reportedly Mackmull was approached by General Jack Hennessey, the Commander of the United States Readiness Command. He informed Mackmull that he would be held personally responsible if something happened prior to Delta achieving its full operational capability. Additionally, if an incident occurred, a counterterrorism Army unit would have to respond within the two-year period that Beckwith had requested to achieve operational capability.

Mackmull then decided to form an interim capability that became known as "Blue Light." He designated Colonel Robert Montel, the commander of the 5th Special Forces Group at Fort Bragg, to form Blue Light. Mackmull undertook the formation of Blue Light on his own recognizance and without fully briefing the Army Staff in the Pentagon.

Montel went to his seasoned senior noncommissioned officers to develop that interim capability. They rapidly assembled a group of people, the majority of whom were combat veterans, and set out to establish a counterterrorism capability. They were eager to pave the way for new ground to defeat terrorists and to create new capabilities in Special Forces. Using their experience along with the high degree of innovation, ingenuity, and resourcefulness that Special Forces is known for, they developed unique tactics and procedures. Whereas Delta was receiving funding from the Army Staff, Blue Light used operations and maintenance funding allocated to the Special Warfare Center and not earmarked to develop a counterterrorism capability. Unfortunately, they were also led to believe that they had an opportunity to be designated as the Army's counterterrorist force, which would cause many hard feelings the following year. Regardless, they had my respect and, in my mind, did a tremendous job in establishing a counterterrorism capability.

Another interesting tidbit that I learned was that Colonel Beckwith, perchance, happened to be in the Pentagon briefing General Edward Meyer on October 18, 1977. Early that morning the German counterterrorism unit Grenschutz Gruppe Neun (GSG-9) stormed a hijacked airliner in Mogadishu, Somalia, and successfully overcame the hijackers and freed their hostages. GSG-9 was assisted by the British 22nd Special Air Service Regiment. News reports stated that "flash bangs" were used in the rescue. Reportedly, President Carter asked the Pentagon what flash bangs were and whether our military had a similar capability to GSG-9. Charlie Beckwith was able to describe what a flash bang was—a non-fragmentary grenade used to distract the enemy with a loud blast and a blinding flash of light created by the explosion. General Meyer briefed General Bernard Rogers, the Army's Chief of Staff, that the U.S. Army did not have a counterterrorist capability but that the Delta Force was being organized at Fort Bragg. That clearly helped to gain General Rogers's support for the formation of Delta. Being in the right place at the right time certainly can pay huge dividends, and this was another day when the stars were aligned for Charlie Beckwith.

Within a week of arriving, a lieutenant colonel showed up at the unit. We were told that he would replace Wayne Long as the intelligence officer. The lieutenant colonel literally sat in the background for a day and watched the rest of us scurrying around to get things done. He left the following day, never to return. So, Wayne Long became the third intelligence officer for the unit. As I will describe later, Wayne would also be the fifth and seventh intelligence officer! Charlie wanted a lieutenant colonel in the position but could never find anyone better than Major Wayne Long!

In November, the first deputy commander of the unit, Lieutenant Colonel Richard W. Potter, Jr., came charging into the headquarters full of energy and eager to roll up his sleeves and get involved. Dick was coming from an assignment at Fort Benning, Georgia. His wife, Annie, drove one car and Dick drove the other car. Somehow, they got separated, but both arrived safely at Fort Bragg. To this day, I continue to tease Dick Potter about abandoning Annie and two of the children and to praise Annie for her resourcefulness. The importance of having a wonderful wife and family in the military can never be overstated.

On the first day on the job, Dick came up to Forrest Foreman with a pair of boots and asked Forrest to get new heels put on the boots. Forrest and I looked at each other and wondered what kind of a person we were getting in Dick Potter! My concerns were soon shed. I received a call from the Fort Bragg Military Police that Dick Potter had punched a noncommissioned officer in Fayetteville's Cross Creek Mall. As it turned out, Dick was shopping with his family when someone who had known him previously came up to him and his family and started swearing at them. Dick tried to ignore it, but the NCO persisted and shoved Dick. Then Dick proceeded to floor him! I said to myself, "Well, hooray for Dick Potter. I like his style!" Delta was fortunate to have Dick Potter as its deputy commander. He kept the staff honest and provided the necessary oversight to ensure we were doing things legally.

In early December 1977, we were elated when we received the formal orders from the Department of Army establishing the 1st Special Forces Operational Detachment-Delta. The orders were dated November 19, 1977. That gave us the assurance that the Army Staff approved of Delta's formation. Dick Potter sought to determine what funding would be available for Delta and found out that the Army Staff was allocating $4 million to Delta for the first year of operation. That was sufficient to get us started; nevertheless, the unit needed to be cost-conscious and innovative to preserve funds. These funds would be required to pay for temporary duty and travel costs for the applicants coming to the assessment and selection course. Additionally, we needed to find a different location for the unit, as the two buildings we occupied were insufficient to house the entire unit and to provide an indoor firing range.

Some of the more pressing challenges for the intelligence section were to plan for personnel assigned to Delta to be placed on the Department of Army Special Roster. This was to protect the identities of Delta personnel to ensure they were safe from being targeted by terrorists and/or hostile intelligence. Wayne secured agreements from the Army's Intelligence and Security Command to implement this. The Intelligence and Security Command assigned two warrant officers, Rick Stevenson, and Pat Patterson, to be the liaison with Delta.

Another challenge was to determine how we could get intelligence reports and products from the intelligence community sent directly to Delta, rather than relying on the Special Warfare Center S2 for the specialized information required to support Delta's unique needs. To that end, Wayne Long talked with the Defense Intelligence Agency. He was given assurances from the Deputy Director, Lieutenant General Harold Aaron who had commanded the 5th Special Forces Group in Vietnam, that Delta would have its own account. As we found out later, that was not true. Only months later did we discover that we were made a sub-set of the United States Readiness Command headquartered in Tampa, Florida. It took years before that was rectified. Delta eventually got a direct account to request and receive intelligence from the national community.

There were other significant intelligence challenges to address. The initial table of organization allocated only eight positions to the intelligence section as Charlie Beckwith wanted to keep everything lean and mean. Wayne Long, John Stanley, and I planned how many analysts we would need and where we might recruit them. We also had to plan the equipment needed in the intelligence section to conduct analysis and to get a modicum of technology to assist with the collection of information. Another challenge was determining how we would gain access to sensitive compartmented information coming from signals intelligence and imagery. We had to rely on the XVIII Airborne Corps Special Security Office to provide access to that level of intelligence. Wayne also had discussions with the CIA liaison officer assigned to the Special Warfare Center to have access to CIA reporting. The final hurdle to overcome in November and December was to develop operations security plans and procedures for the unit.

A young counterintelligence agent, Willie Welsch, was assigned to support us in this regard. Early in 1978, we got Willie assigned to Delta. In addition, the 902nd Military Intelligence Brigade was tasked with sending Bob Nugent to Fort Bragg primarily to support Delta. Bob was given a letter from General Edward Meyer that clearly stated his priority in supporting the unit. Willie and Bob proved themselves to be invaluable assets.

The S3 or Operations Section of Delta was also lean and mean. Lieutenant Colonel Curt Hurst, Forrest Foreman, and one other were the only ones assigned. One of the critical efforts that the S3 had to work on was to plan how Delta would deploy in a crisis. To that end, Curt Hurst developed a flow chart on butcher paper, lining the walls of the headquarters, to plot how a deployment could occur and the best courses of action. Among many considerations, they examined the use of commercial aircraft versus Air Force or other government planes. In conjunction with the Air Force, they learned the difficulty and high cost of having a dedicated aircraft and crew available on an around-the-clock, seven-days-a-week basis, and that the better course of action was to have the Joint Staff issue an immediate directive to the Air Force to provide transport. Wayne Long and I assisted the S3 section in the planning for deployment by providing information on obtaining State Department and Combatant Command approvals and how to work with host nation intelligence and security forces.

Those days in November and December 1977 were long. I went to the Fort Bragg Housing Office and asked for temporary quarters. I was assigned to a World War II barracks, with a room the size of a large closet, and where I had to walk down the hallway to get to a restroom and shower. One night I thought that this was a hell of a way to treat a senior NCO. But I let that roll off my shoulders and put my thoughts into the formation of Delta.

My orders for a permanent change of station assignment to Delta were issued with a reporting date of January 1, 1978. Due to the actions of the Sergeants Major Academy commandant, I had to fly back to Fort Bliss, Texas. There I discovered that Colonel Crow made it mandatory that I pass a physical fitness test to graduate. I didn't have time to waste, jumped in my jalopy, drove non-stop to San Jose, California, spent two days with my wife, and then started the trek back to Fort Bliss and then Fort Bragg. When I got back to Fort Bliss, I had developed a severe cold, if not pneumonia. Rich Reilly, a Special Forces friend, was assigned to administer the fitness test to me. While at the Sergeants Major Academy, I had always achieved maximum points on the test. I started out well but was wheezing and coughing with a high fever. It was evident that I would not be able to make the run in the allotted time, as I was ready to collapse. It would have taken me days to get well and pass the fitness test, and I needed to get going to Fort Bragg. Rich fully understood that, and took into account my past fitness test results, and penciled in a time for the run and I was on my way to Fort Bragg.

Once again, I was pushing to the maximum and wanted to drive non-stop from Fort Bliss to Atlanta, Georgia. A cold front was going through the South at the time, and my car heater stopped working but I kept pressing on. Shortly before getting to the Mississippi State line my engine started acting up, and the car was lurching down the road. I pulled into a small town in Mississippi and was fortunate enough to find a small garage. The mechanic sized things up and got me back on the road. When I arrived in Atlanta, I was physically beat. I found a motel and knew there would be freezing weather and I should take my wife's plants into the room to save them from the frost. I just did not have the energy to do so. When I got up the next morning, I found that several of the plants had succumbed to the frost. I felt very annoyed at Colonel Crow for his petulance in requiring me to go on temporary duty—and then having to go back to Fort Bliss for the physical fitness test. Leaders need to always consider the impact of what they do on individual soldiers and the Army.

I pushed on to Fort Bragg and struggled to get what I had loaded in my car into my "closet room." I got a good night's sleep and, despite still being ill, the next day I hit the ground running. Delta had a bit of luck and we would be moving into the compound on Butner Road that had been the Fort Bragg confinement facility or stockade. It was a large jail that was housing fewer than eight prisoners at the time. It was concluded that it would be more cost-effective to move the prisoners to the Fayetteville, North Carolina, civilian jail and pay the expenses for their confinement rather than build a new facility for Delta. The Delta staff reconnoitered the facility and made plans concerning what elements would be located throughout the former jail. Delta's S4, or supply section, with Andy Almueti as the ranking sergeant, had its hands full figuring out how to get the move accomplished and to provide furniture for the unit.

***

January also saw the first significant assessment and selection course run in Pisgah National Forest. It was a cold winter, and those who made it through really had to prove their mettle. Among those who made it through the course included the colorful Sergeant Major Walter Shumate, a great friend from Okinawa; Major Logan Fitch, who would take command of B Squadron; and Captains Peter Schoomaker and William "Jerry" Boykin. Other notables also made it through, and I regret that I have forgotten exactly who they were as I was too engrossed in what the intelligence section had to do.

The move to the old stockade occurred in February 1978. The front portion held the offices of Colonel Beckwith, Dick Potter, and Country Grimes. To the right of the entrance was a large room that was declared a briefing and planning room. The administrative section (S1) was also in that wing. The former control center for the stockade, which had previously been where the centrally controlled cell doors had been operated from, was allocated as the S2 and S3 main offices. Behind that on a wing was the former medium-holding cell area, which we would convert into office space for our analysts, and a secure compartmented information facility to store special intelligence. Another wing towards the front of the stockade was designated for the communications section. Subsequent wings in the stockade were allocated to the operational squadrons. The S4 section was located in an adjacent building to the stockade and would also house our motor pool and the parachute rigger section. One of the nice things that came with the stockade was a mess hall with cooking facilities. A mess was brought on board together with Army cooks. The mess sergeant was a Black American who earned the nickname "White Water Willie," after he nearly drowned supporting a selection and assessment course in West Virginia. He moonlighted as a chef for a Mexican restaurant in Fayetteville and did a super job running the mess hall.

Plans were developed to build an indoor firing range behind the former stockade. Construction was started almost immediately as it was considered essential to have an indoor firing range where room entry could be practiced. A lot of work needed to be done to convert the stockade into a facility suitable for Delta. For example, the former control room had large consoles that previously housed the electronic controls to operate the cell doors. All of that had to be removed with attention given to electrical safety. The cots, commodes, and sinks in the cells had to be removed. The cots were welded to the floor and sunk into concrete. Andy Almueti procured several welding torches we used to cut the legs of the cots and to get rid of the plumbing fixtures. This was hard work that had to be done in addition to our regular duties. I never heard a single complaint as we were only too happy to have our own facility.

February, March, and April 1978 were spent on converting the former stockade into a workspace, starting the first Operator Training Course for those that had just completed the selection and assessment process, and filling out the ranks of our support organizations. In the S1 section, Master Sergeant Ron Matysek joined the unit after being with the Army's Military Personnel Center in Washington, DC. Ron was instrumental in helping me get back on track for promotions by bringing me into the Advanced NCO Educational System class after finding out I had been selected for the first class. I was never notified as I was in Okinawa. Two others of note to join the S1 section were Russ Vona and Angela Whitaker. In the S2, we brought on Alyn McElrath and had Major Hermann Adler assigned to the section. We also started the process to have Willie Welsch assigned as our counterintelligence support. Dick Meadows was brought on as a special assistant along with Captain Billy Anthony to give him support. Dick had won the Distinguished Service Cross in Vietnam and was also one of the leaders on the Son Tay prison raid into North Vietnam. The S3 section added two NCOs to assist Curt Hurst and Forrest Foreman. In addition, Penny Floyd was assigned as a civilian secretary. Penny was the original Delta secretary, but Charlie Beckwith wanted a more mature person and selected Marian Thomas to replace Penny. Penny just shrugged her petite shoulders and dove into the work that needed to be done. She was so dedicated that she was at work when her waters broke and she had to be transported to the hospital to give birth.

Roger Ahrens, Willie Maes, and Charlene Glass were brought in to lead the Finance section. Jim Turner was the first psychologist assigned to the unit. He was nicknamed "Pear Bod" as he was short and chubby but had a mind like a steel trap. The communications section had Jorge Torres-Cartagena assigned as the officer in charge. He had a captain as his deputy who was reassigned after he accidentally discharged his .45-caliber pistol while he was the duty officer. He was replaced by a lieutenant. Warrant Officer Paul Zeisman was also assigned and was one of the pillars of the communications section. Years later, he did marvelous things for the Joint Special Operations Command. Angel Candelaria, Steve Mozian, Herman Adams, Mike Kalua, Bernie Kaita, Jim Schwitters, and other skillful communicators were brought in. Buzz Blizzard and Andy Almueti in the S4 section were joined by a warrant officer to maintain the property records, three parachute riggers, and others.

Shortly after we had moved into the stockade, I got a call from our civilian gate guard saying an officer was trying to get into the compound. I went out to the gate to see who it was. I was greeted by a major who showed me his badge and credentials and said, "Hi, I'm Major Bob Bidwell, the head of the Fort Bragg

Criminal Investigation Division Office, and I'd like to visit your unit." I looked at him and said, "You don't have a good memory. Do you know the last time I saw you?" He looked at me with a blank expression. I told him, "It was at Long Binh jail in 1969 when I unmasked you for using coercion, threats and false promises to get testimony against those charged in the Green Beret affair." He paled, and I said, "You are not getting in this compound unless you have authorization in writing from the Army Chief of Staff!" He put his badge and credentials in his pocket and hurried off; he never got inside the compound.

March 1978 was a watershed month for Delta. We learned that there would be a meeting involving Lieutenant General "Shy" Meyer, Lieutenant General Volney Warner, who headed the XVIII Airborne Corps, and Major General Jack Mackmull. The rumor was that Delta's existence was on the line. The generals and a few of their staff assembled in Delta's briefing room. The Delta staff briefed them on what was happening in the unit. General Meyer thanked us and then told the Delta staff to leave the room except for Colonel Beckwith. I was the last one out, and as I slowly closed the door, I heard what I believed was General Meyer asking, "What the hell is Blue Light?"

The Delta staff gathered in the foyer of the former stockade. Mike Smith found his guitar and we began quietly singing. I'm sure many of us thought that this was going to be the last day for Delta. We could hear loud voices coming from the briefing room but could not make out what was being said. I can't remember how long the meeting went on, but the door to the briefing room opened and the participants walked out. Volney Warner, Jack Mackmull, and Charlie Beckwith were all red-faced. I kept thinking this is not good. After the VIPs left, Beckwith then informed us that Delta would continue with the chain of command going to General Mackmull and then directly to the Army staff. This put us out of the chain of command to XVIII Airborne Corps and the U.S. Army Forces Command. We all breathed a sigh of relief! Charlie also stated that Blue Light was to be closed.

It was back to work as there was much to be done. By the end of April, three selection courses had been completed, and there were roughly 40 operators who had passed. One of the wise things that Charlie Beckwith had done was to task Chuck Odorizzi and the Assessment and Selection Section to address the individual and team skills required in Delta. Those tasks were to be recorded in what Charlie deemed a "Black Book." Each task was accompanied by the conditions under which they were to be performed along with acceptable standards required to ensure the task was well executed. The Operator Training Course began and we sometimes had to use ourselves as instructors. John Stanley developed a briefing on terrorism and terrorist groups, and I taught the rudiments of information gathering and reporting, along with photography and hostage handling. Forrest Foreman and I gave lessons in some unarmed combat skills.

During the March meeting led by General Meyer, he had made it clear that all units in the Army would be told to allow soldiers who wanted to try out for Delta to be allowed to do so. General Mackmull had the unenviable task of telling the Blue Light personnel that their efforts would be stood down. He also directed Colonel Montel to make the Blue Light personnel available for a briefing on Delta. Most of the Blue Light personnel believed they had a bona fide chance of being designated as the Army's counterterrorist unit and were sorely disappointed when they had to cease their efforts. Unfortunately, many believe that Charlie Beckwith did not do well when the Blue Light personnel came for a briefing. They questioned why they needed to go through Delta's assessment and selection as most of them were combat veterans and had proven themselves capable of conducting those kinds of operations to counter terrorists. Most of them did not like the way Charlie Beckwith responded and left the briefing very angry. I had friends on Blue Light who would never talk to me again. I believe out of all those briefed that day, only three decided to try out for Delta, and they all succeeded. The Blue Light efforts were not in vain. The facility they had modified at Mott Lake became an advanced training area. The work they had done to learn better shooting techniques and other tactics became embodied in regular Special Forces training. Many believe that the Blue Light efforts were the forerunner of today's Special Forces Advanced Reconnaissance, Target Analysis, and Exploitation Course.

***

The next surprise we received was to learn that we would have to undergo an evaluation of the unit in July. Colonel Beckwith had always asked for two years to achieve full operational capability, and now we were to be evaluated even before a year had passed. The evaluation was to be led by Lieutenant General Volney Warner and Major General Guy Meloy III, with the main planner being Lieutenant Colonel Redmond and evaluators coming from JFK Center and other units. Beckwith was able to insist that the "Black Book" of tasks, conditions, and standards be used as the primary evaluation document. There were supposedly only three Black Books: one maintained by Delta's Assessment and Selection, another by Colonel Beckwith, and the third by General Meyer. Chuck Odorizzi was the head of Assessment and Selection, and he insisted that the Black Book was still a work in progress and not ready to turn over to the evaluators. Charlie Beckwith insisted that it still needed to be done. Chuck Odorizzi stood his ground and either resigned or was fired by Charlie. Although the Black Books needed refinement, they were instrumental in helping Delta to pass the evaluation, as the evaluators did not have a clear idea of how to evaluate the unit and its personnel.

As best as I can recall, the evaluation occurred in July during the heat of a typical Fort Bragg, NC, summer. It began with individual skills. Delta did not do well on the shooting skills. Delta's shooting skills were based on the British system of close-quarter battle inside rooms. The 22nd Special Air Service had sent one of their operators, code-name "Ginger," who spent about a year with Delta. He taught instinctive shooting where getting an aimed shot is not necessary and was a technique particularly suited to close encounters. The evaluators made the Delta operators shoot at longer ranges at different targets and did not use the close-range skills specified in the Black Book. On every other individual aspect, Delta's operators did extremely well. It helped that we were allowed to choose the specific person to be evaluated on a particular skill. For example, Fast Eddie Westfall, a horse of a man, was selected to demonstrate the use of a sledgehammer to break through a concrete hollow tile wall. With his strength, Fast Eddie demolished the wall without much effort. In the unarmed combat evaluation, a lean and mean Fred Lewis was selected to demonstrate a response to someone holding a pistol at his back. The evaluator was Sergeant First Class Willie Chong who presented himself as a karate teacher. He insisted that Fred should go full bore and not hold anything back. Fred did as he was told, Willie ended up on the ground with a broken arm! No more unarmed combat evaluation! Willie Chong was overconfident—and when you are overconfident, it won't always turn out the way you wanted!

The evaluation exercise culminated with a requirement to conduct a simultaneous rescue of hostages on an airplane and in a building. I was in the headquarters and connected with Sergeant Major Country Grimes via a PRC-74 radio with a telegraph key device. With an evaluator looking over my shoulder, I started sending "CQ, CQ" (Dah-di-dah-di-dah-dah-di-dah in Morse code) followed by a bunch of gibberish. I knew the evaluator had no idea what Morse code was about! On the other end, Country would also send me back a bunch of nonsense. The evaluator was impressed! If you're going to evaluate something, you better know what you are evaluating! The aircraft assault went off flawlessly. The building assault also went well. One of the amusing events at the building was when the squadron decided to make entry through windows. A window was broken out, and Ron Franklin was literally thrown out the window. By chance he landed on several of the terrorist actors! Colonel Beckwith was pleased that we passed the evaluation and so was General Meyer.

With the evaluation behind us, the rest of 1978 was a flurry of activity. More assessment and selection courses were run along with operator training courses. The number of operators and support personnel grew. An indoor shooting house was built in the former stockade compound; a dedicated outdoor range became available in Fort Bragg; selection and assessment were moved to West Virginia from where it had previously been conducted in Pisgah National Forest. The training was intense and there were some memorable events. The operators were training near Simmons Army Airfield when someone reported strange activity in the area. The Military Police responded and drew their .45-caliber pistols when they came across the operators. Fortunately, common sense prevailed, and no one was shot.

THE BEGINNING OF THE DELTA FORCE • 139

At the outdoor range, Billy Zumwalt attempted to shoot a bird on an overhead wire. Billy hit the wire and took out the high-speed data connection to all of Fort Bragg. Mark Gentry was practicing a fast draw and managed to shoot himself in the leg! An exercise was conducted in the Smoke Bomb Hill area of Fort Bragg to practice a hostage recovery onboard a bus. Flash bangs of stun grenades and blank ammunition were used, and suspicious activity was reported to the Military Police. To the great credit of our operators, the exercise was speedily concluded. By the time the MPs responded, there was nothing for them to see. Our S4 arranged to get vehicles from a rental car company on Fort Bragg to learn advanced driving skills. The rental company did not know the abuse their cars were being put through but were very happy with their profit! Luck was with us as there was an occasion when the car that Angel Macias was driving flipped over. Our S4 appeased the rental car company by paying for the vehicle. Angel was severely injured and almost lost his hand. He was able to completely recover. These events are but a small snapshot of the many stories that could be told about 1978.

One of the more exciting requests came from the U.S. Pacific Command. They asked that Delta send a small contingent to help them evaluate their counterterrorist options. With the approval of General Meyer, Wayne Long, Logan Fitch, and I were sent to Hawaii to observe an exercise. The exercise had two locations. One was on the beach near Kahuku, Oahu, and the other was at a former Nike missile site in a mountainous area in the vicinity of Kahuku. The Pacific Command had assembled three different units to be evaluated. One was a standard Marine rifle company assigned the notional rescue attempt on the beach. A second unit was an intelligence and reconnaissance platoon from the 25th Infantry Division that was not given a specific target but was to support the third unit in reconnoitering the former missile site. The third unit was a Marine Force reconnaissance platoon that would attempt the notional rescue at the former missile site.

Wayne Long was assigned to observe the beach site. He later reported that the Marine rifle company basically got in formation and did a frontal assault on the target. It was very unsophisticated and would have resulted in the death or injury of the hostages. Logan Fitch and I were to observe the former missile site event. An Army officer who was portraying a terrorist came up to me and started chatting. Behind him, on a ridgeline overlooking the site, I observed three of the 25th Infantry soldiers who were clearly visible on the ridge. At the same time, I observed a Marine Force recon member not more than 20 feet from us who had frozen his movement to prevent detection. The terrorist actor never saw the Marine. The Force recon unit did a credible job of sneaking up on the location of the hostages and then successfully launching an attack to rescue them. Our report to an Army brigadier general on the Pacific Command staff stated that the Force recon unit provided a capability but that they could use additional training to make them a surgical hostage rescue force and that would detract from their primary mission. We reported one other notable accomplishment. In the aftermath of the exercise, an Army CH-47 Chinook helicopter was sent to transport Logan and me back to the beach location. The winds were gusting over 20 miles per hour, and rain was pouring down. The pilot maneuvered where he was hovering at a hilltop, lowered his ramp without setting the helicopter down, and remained steady as Logan and I boarded the helicopter. That was an impressive performance.

***

Apart from operations, it was critical that Delta develop relationships with interagency organizations, both the support operations and the support preparations necessary for a successful mission. Delta's S1 section developed excellent relations with the Army's Military Personnel Command and Recruiting Command. These relationships were vital to motivating soldiers to try out for Delta, bringing them in on temporary duty and quickly reassigning them when they passed selection and assessment. The S3 section worked closely with the Army and Joint Staff to ensure rapid deployment should the unit be needed either domestically or overseas. One of their primary efforts was directed to the Director of Military Support (DOMS) organization in the Pentagon. DOMS was a joint organization with the Army as the Executive Agent to coordinate deployment matters for the military. The Air Force Military Airlift Command was another essential organization with which the S3 section developed relationships. One of the key lessons was that Delta was given priority on aircraft. That included redirecting aircraft in flight.

A great partnership was established with the U.S. Secret Service. Charlie Beckwith was convinced they had an excellent sniper program and wanted our operators to learn from them. We were assisted by agents Tom Quinn and Rick Race, who were assigned to the Secret Service training organization at Beltsville, Maryland. In that partnership, Delta helped the Secret Service develop their Counter Assault Teams, and Mark Gentry played a key role in that effort. Continuing liaison was established with the Federal Bureau of Investigation (FBI) mainly through what was known as Division Six at the time. Division Six was responsible for running the FBI Academy. Charlie Beckwith met Assistant Director Ken Joseph while he headed the SF schools and was also introduced to Assistant Director Jim McKenzie who replaced Joseph. Our main liaison was with the Special Operations and Research Unit headed by Conrad Hassel who assigned John Simeone as the principal liaison agent for Delta. We further understood that the jurisdiction for terrorism events inside the United States rested with the FBI, and we worked to understand how Delta would have to operate domestically should the unit be called upon. The bottom line was that in almost all circumstances Delta would operate under the command of the

FBI domestically. The FBI granted Delta permission to observe any domestic terrorist event under their jurisdiction and that would prove to be very useful.

The ground rules established for Delta to observe a domestic terrorist event paid close attention to not violating the Posse Comitatus law that forbids the use of the military to engage in law enforcement unless there is a declaration of martial law or under the auspices of the Insurrection Act. Five rules were established:

1. The observers would report to the FBI Special Agent in Charge of the incident
2. They would wear civilian clothing
3. They would not be armed
4. No advice was to be given
5. The observers would not participate in any operations

The first opportunity to allow Delta to observe was in August 1978 when two Croatian citizens took six hostages in the German Consulate located in Chicago, Illinois. Wayne Long and Logan Fitch, the B Squadron commander, were sent to observe the incident. This incident was the first test of a streamlined process to gain approval. Delta would initiate a request to the Director of Military Support (DOMS) organization in the Pentagon. DOMS was a joint organization with the Army as the Executive Agent responsible for coordinating and obtaining approval for the deployment of military forces within the United States and its territories, whether for acts of terrorism, natural disasters, or other emergencies. For terrorist events, DOMS would then contact the Department of Justice and the FBI to gain approval and the name of the FBI special agent in charge. The August 1978 event showed that the process worked smoothly and very rapidly.

The next opportunity to observe a domestic event happened in June 1979. I was returning from a recruiting trip to Arizona. I had taken a "red eye" (late night) flight out of Phoenix and landed at O'Hare airport in Chicago, Illinois, in the morning. I had an eight-hour wait before I could make my connecting flight to Fayetteville, North Carolina. I walked past a newsstand and saw the headlines proclaiming that there was an aircraft hijack in progress. I was tired and didn't pay attention to it. Then I saw a news broadcast announcing that the hijack was at O'Hare Airport and was ongoing. I bought a newspaper and saw that it was true. I just wanted to get home, but my conscience bothered me. I waited until I had 15 minutes before boarding my flight to Fayetteville, and called the unit. I asked Wayne Long if he wanted to find out if I could observe the event. He said that I absolutely should do so. I mentioned I had only 15 minutes and that I was calling from a pay telephone. I was sure there would be no way to gain the approvals in 15 minutes or less. Was I ever wrong! Twelve minutes later the phone rang, and Wayne told me to report to Special Agent in Charge John Otto. The bad news was that I was now committed—the good news was that the process had proven to be super-fast!

I found the FBI's command center established in O'Hare Airport. I identified myself and found they had received word I was on my way. I asked where John Otto was, and they took me to the runway and a remote parking area from where they were negotiating with a Serbian citizen, Nikola Kavaja, who had taken control of American Airlines Flight 293. Kavaja claimed to have dynamite on board (Kavaja had attempted to assassinate President Tito of Yugoslavia four times without success). During this hijacking, he sought to have a Serbian separatist partner released from prison. Kavaja had allowed the passengers to deplane, but kept the pilot, co-pilot, and flight engineer.

I observed was that there was an FBI agent who spoke Serbian and had interviewed Kavaja previously. This agent would have made an ideal negotiator. But unfortunately, the FBI had somehow been talked into using Kavaja's lawyer to negotiate. The lawyer would board the plane, come to the entrance, down some miniature bottles of liquor, then come down to tell the FBI what he had learned or what Kavaja had requested. The lawyer was inebriated and could not give a clear description of the supposed explosive device that Kavaja threatened to detonate. John Otto, the Chicago Field Office special agent in charge, was in a dilemma as he didn't know what to do. He asked me for advice, and I told him that I was not allowed to offer any advice. Mr Otto kept asking me for advice. I confirmed that although I could not offer advice, I could relate that in a training exercise, it was critical to identify an explosive device; if it could not be identified, then it should be assumed to be real. Mr Otto took this into account in his decision to allow the plane to take off for Ireland.

When the plane landed in Ireland, Kavaja was arrested and extradited back to America to face trial. It was past midnight when the plane took off for Ireland. The FBI tried to find me a hotel and weren't able to do so, and I spent the night sleeping on an examination table in the FBI's office, where there was a nursing station. In 1993, Department of Defense lawyers determined that giving advice was legal and stood the test with the Branch Davidian incident in Waco, Texas. In that incident, the 3rd Special Forces Group provided training to Bureau of Alcohol, Tobacco, and Firearms agents prior to the raid. After the FBI took jurisdiction, two former Delta commanders reviewed the FBI's plans. All these actions met the legal test of not violating Posse Comitatus.

The next incident that Delta was allowed to observe happened on December 21, 1978. A 17-year-old female named Robin Oswald hijacked TWA Flight 541 which was forced to land at the Williamson Country Regional Airport in Marion, Illinois. She demanded the release of Garrett Trapnell, an inmate at Marion Federal Penitentiary. Earlier that year, Trapnell had convinced Oswald's mother, Barbara Ann Oswald, to hijack a helicopter and have it flown into the prison to rescue Trapnell. The helicopter pilot managed to wrestle the gun that Barbara Oswald was carrying off her, and killed her. Her daughter, Robin, claimed to have dynamite on her body. Jack Clemens and I were selected to observe the incident.

The Military Airlift Command literally ordered a T-39 Sabreliner to divert and land at Pope Air Force Base to transport Jack and me to Marion, Illinois. There were several colonels on board the T-39 when it landed at Pope. They were grumbling and looked at Jack and me wondering who the hell we were. The DOMS mechanism and the Military Airlift Command proved they could deliver the goods when needed. When Jack and I got to Marion, we saw that the FBI and local law enforcement had established a security perimeter around the hijacked airplane, but the media had also surrounded the plane with video cameras and live reporting. That made it difficult for the FBI SWAT team to operate. Somewhat by coincidence, things worked out well.

The special agent in charge called a press conference, and the media immediately left their positions around the plane to attend the briefing. At the same time, the flight attendants on board the aircraft convinced Robin Oswald to allow them to feed the passengers. Oswald was seated towards the rear of the aircraft. The flight attendants blocked her view with their carts and got the passengers to get off the aircraft. The FBI SWAT team was able to enter the aircraft, and subdued Oswald. It turned out she had road flares, not dynamite.

Jack and I thanked the FBI for allowing us to observe and then found a hotel. We were unable to book any flights back to Fayetteville as it was very close to Christmas. Dick Potter, the Delta deputy commander, found out that we could not get home until after Christmas. Dick somehow was able to arrange for an Army U8D Sentinel plane to fly out to Marion and take Jack and I back to Bragg so we could be home for Christmas. That was just one of the many times that Dick Potter showed his leadership and care for those serving with him.

With so few personnel in Delta and so much to do, the workload and hours were very long. I can remember going home only once during the first seven months of Delta's start while the sun was still shining. My work hours were typically 6:30 AM to 8:30 PM. I did have one short break when I took leave to go back to California and finalize the sale of our house, and then travel cross-country back to Fort Bragg. It was a hurried trip, but I could take Mi Hye to see Yellowstone National Park. At Fort Bragg, we moved into a house at 100 Gatley Circle. The house was smaller than the one we'd had during the previous tour at Fort Bragg, but adequate for our needs. Even though Mi Hye was not happy moving back to the heat and humidity of North Carolina, she at least had friends like Iko Dennis, something she had lacked in California.

Much of 1978 was spent developing interagency relationships to help Delta perform its counterterrorist mission. In addition to the FBI and Secret Service mentioned previously, we spent a great deal of time with the Federal Aviation Administration, the Department of State, the Central Intelligence Agency, and the Department of Energy. In late 1978, we also began working with the Defense Advanced Research Projects Agency.

When it came to intelligence support, Wayne Long and I were hugely disappointed to discover a scarcity of analysts studying terrorism daily in the intelligence community. The Defense Intelligence Agency had no dedicated analysts, and their purported action arm for terrorism resided within an organization known as RSS-1. That organization was responsible for security inspections of defense attaché facilities worldwide.

Concerning terrorism, they had contracted with Rand Corporation, which produced what was touted to be a database of terrorist incidents. We found that to just be a compilation of events without any real analysis or the ability to gain detailed information on various terrorist groups. The Army's Intelligence and Security Command (INSCOM) also lacked any full-time analysts on terrorism. However, INSCOM did provide support by providing cover and with the Intelligence Materiel Development Support Office. The latter assisted us with technical intelligence and tradecraft including clandestine methods of entry. Warrant Officers Rick Stevenson and Pat Patterson were designated as the liaisons from INSCOM to Delta to assist with undercover support. Bob Nugent was assigned as the 902nd MI Group Resident Agent to Fort Bragg with specific instructions from General Meyer to support Delta. John Stanley established relations with XVIII Airborne Corps and its map depot, along with the Defense Mapping Agency to ensure that we would have priority on getting maps for any operation that Delta would be called upon to support. Liaison was also established with the National Security Agency, and they assisted with gaining certification for a secure compartmented information facility in the stockade. We also established relations with the Air Force Office of Special Investigations because they had full-time analysts working on terrorism, including a young captain named Les Duffin who would later become a Senior Intelligence Service official.

It was essential to work with the Federal Aviation Administration (FAA) for several reasons. By law, the FAA had jurisdiction over aircraft piracy or hijackings while in the air. They had established a hotline for interagency use when an aircraft was hijacked, and they allowed Delta to be part of that hotline. Secondly, the FAA was responsible for the security of airports in those days before the creation of the Department of Homeland Security and their Transportation Security Agency. The security section in FAA headquarters was small, but they were doing cutting-edge work on security matters, including developing a program to profile possible hijackers. The FAA headquarters security department helped us establish relationships with the Air Line Pilots Association and various airlines. The latter was highly beneficial in using commercial aircraft to practice hostage rescue. They also assisted us with developing procedures to ship weaponry on commercial aircraft should we use commercial aircraft to deploy. In a remarkable show of support, within weeks of asking the FAA, they agreed to fly a Boeing 727 aircraft they used for safety inspections to land at the Camp Mackall airstrip at night with Air Force combat controllers guiding them in. Their aircraft was then used for a training exercise. Another example of the tremendous support received from the FAA was during an exercise where our operators would have to travel undercover through a major U.S. airport, purchase their tickets, and then fly to the destination where the exercise was to occur. I asked for and received the support of Chuck Middleton, who was an FAA regional director of security, to alert his airport agents and to see if they could identify any of the Delta members flying out of that airport. It was a fine credit to the Delta operators that, at best, only two were deemed to be Delta operators!

Relationships with the Department of State were also crucial to Delta's ability to operate overseas. In the absence of a full declaration of war, any overseas military operation required coordination and support from the State Department. In any country of operation, it was essential to inform and coordinate with the ambassador and the country team to facilitate operations. In 1976, the State Department created an ambassadorial-level position, known as the State Department Coordinator for Counterterrorism. Upon being briefed on Delta, his support was critical to getting the word out to our embassies and helping coordinate activities.

We encountered an unexpected bonus in establishing a liaison with the State Department. We had expected to find the Bureau of Intelligence and Research fully engaged in terrorism analysis. That was not so, but their products were still helpful in understanding the environment in a given country. The bonus came when we met Sid Telford. Sid was a former Marine and regional security officer who headed the State Diplomatic Security analytical organization. He had five or six dedicated analysts working on terrorism. They were all top-notch analysts and were providing in-depth information on various terrorist incidents worldwide. They generally had maps and diagrams showing how a terrorist operation evolved, along with their weaponry and tactics. All of Sid Telford's analysts were superb, but two stood out: Beth Renwick, whose husband was the head of Secret Service Intelligence; and Lou Mizelle, who was a Diplomatic Security agent. John Stanley was assigned to be the principal liaison with Telford's folks, and the products we received from them were highly useful in preparing Delta's operators for operations against various terrorist groups. Because of the impression that Delta's staff and operators made on the State Department, we were soon asked to send individuals to help with embassy security in high-threat countries. The first shots fired in an actual situation were by Billy Zumwalt, who was responsible for stopping an ambush from happening. What he did was circulated widely in the State Department and solidified Delta's relationships.

The Central Intelligence Agency (CIA) was a vital partner for Delta. Their reporting on terrorism around the world helped shape our training and provided valuable insights into various terrorist organizations and the support they might be receiving from other nations. In addition, the help that could be received through their stations and bases worldwide was critical to operational planning and execution.

Charlie Beckwith had the foresight to keep pushing for a full-time liaison officer assigned to Delta rather than depending upon the CIA liaison officer assigned to the JFK Center.

In 1978, we were fortunate to have Burr Smith assigned from the CIA. He came from the CIA's paramilitary Ground Branch and had excellent contacts throughout the CIA. The CIA Air Branch also offered some support. One disappointment was that we had hoped to gain a specific analysis of terrorist groups through finished products. However, their raw reporting made up for the lack of finished products. Delta's analysts were put on distribution for CIA reports marked Originator Controlled or ORCON. This was a privilege that was not granted to many other military organizations. Delta would see the full extent of CIA support in 1979 with the Iranian hostage crisis.

The threat of either domestic or foreign terrorists conducting an act of nuclear terrorism became of increasing concern in the late 1970s. There were three hoax threats to detonate a nuclear device in Boston, Massachusetts; Spokane, Washington; and Los Angeles, California. In 1974, President Gerald Ford signed an order creating the Nuclear Emergency Search Team (NEST) under the Atomic Energy Commission. In 1977, that Commission became a cabinet-level department called the Department of Energy under President Jimmy Carter. The NEST program was overseen by the Nevada Field Office of the DOE. The NEST mission was to help locate a nuclear bomb or radioactive dispersal device used by a terrorist group and then to potentially disarm the device. To accomplish the latter (disarming), NEST had established agreements with the Army Explosive Ordnance Disposal community that had been in existence mainly to deal with the disarming of a U.S. nuclear weapon that had been in an accident. NEST and DOE also worked closely with the Defense Nuclear Agency (DNA) concerning command and control procedures. NEST was not limited to a domestic mission and knew they needed to have better security overseas along with the potential to take armed action to secure a nuclear device.

Somehow the NEST leadership found out about the formation of Delta, and they were granted approval to visit Delta in early 1978. They were led by Troy Wade, the Deputy Director of the Nevada Field Office. Jack Doyle from EG&G and Ernie Campbell from DOE accompanied Troy on the first visit. This was the start of what would become a great partnership. They freely shared their information on ways to deploy a large force, their advanced communications, and procedures. They also offered the use of the aircraft under contract to EG&G that had responsibility for the maintenance of radioactive search tools and the communications for NEST. DOE also offered the use of the Nevada Test Site, a 1630-square-mile location northwest of Las Vegas, Nevada, for training.

In late 1978, Delta's Intelligence Section was introduced to Dr Judith Daly, a program manager with the Defense Advanced Research Projects Agency (DARPA). One of Dr Daly's projects was known as TRAP/TARGIT. The project constituted building a true database on terrorism groups and events, along with a second portion to do predictive analysis. She had approached different intelligence community organizations who were not interested in that project. We immediately saw the potential for the project as we had been dismayed by the lack of a verifiable database on terrorism. The original idea was developed by a young engineer with the CACI Corporation. He had left CACI, and Jim Stinson had taken over the project. Jim had served in Special Forces in Vietnam, left the Army, became a police officer, and was last associated with the California Department of Justice and the California Advanced Training Institute.

Our belief was that a true database would be exceedingly valuable in analyzing the capabilities and modus operandi of a terrorist group. For example, we hoped that we could type in the name of a group and the word "weapons." With a well-structured database, a report listing the group's weaponry and information about their tactics would instantly be available. On the predictive analysis side, Jim had a few bright computer engineers who were committed and determined to use artificial intelligence to help with predictability. In 1978, the personal computer (PC) had yet to be developed. To help develop the program, DARPA supplied us with a forerunner of a PC with a cassette tape for memory and very little computing power. Nevertheless, we saw the promise ahead and put a lot of effort into designing the database. Our additional hope was that the development of TRAP/TARGIT would lead other intelligence organizations to have a standard way of entering data into a common database.

Another exciting project that Dr Daly introduced us to was called surrogate travel. In short, it was the predecessor of today's ability to take a virtual tour of a house or building—to enter a room and be able to manipulate the software to take in details from the floor to the ceiling. Again, this was a cutting-edge effort before the development of computing power that allows today's virtual tours to occur. The technique in 1978 required a 35 mm movie camera with a frame taken with every step! It was a start of something very valuable.

The initial efforts to establish partnerships and relationships with the FBI, CIA, FAA, Secret Service, Army INSCOM, DOE, and DARPA proved to be beneficial as Delta developed into a mature organization. Charlie Beckwith always believed that there was more than one answer to a given question, and he was always open to learning from others. Those organizations weren't the only ones that Delta engaged with in the early days. I will mention some of the others later.

One of the best things about Delta was seeing the attitudes of most of those assigned to the unit and the innovation they brought to bear to solve problems and create new ways of doing things. Regarding communications, there was a need to find portable radios for operational use. The standard military radios were too bulky and could not be used by individuals. The communications section found a small radio called the BXR-5 manufactured by Audio Intelligence Devices in Fort

Lauderdale, Florida. Jorge Torres-Cartagena wanted to demonstrate the radio to Charlie Beckwith and get his feedback. During the demonstration, Charlie asked how rugged the radio was. He then picked it up and slammed it onto the concrete floor. Jorge picked it up and the radio was still working! Charlie left the briefing without comment. Eventually, another radio used by law enforcement was selected as the primary radio for team use.

Through working with the DOE NEST people, they learned that DOE was using a commercial satellite system called INMARSAT. The radio did not offer encryption, but nonetheless was useful for certain situations. Standard Army military radios were kept in the inventory, and the Delta communicators showed their ability to use them under non-standard conditions. Steve Mozian used an issued military High Frequency (HF) radio to communicate from a hotel room in Italy back to Fort Bragg using a Slinky toy as his antenna. The Delta communications section also worked closely with the private sector to take a prototype backpack radio and were able to field it during the Iran hostage crisis. They collaborated with the CIA to develop a portable antenna that was used for the Iran rescue operation. One of the humorous things that occurred when Delta was in isolation at a CIA facility was when Randy Hofferth and Paul Zeisman were attempting to pick up a satellite to make communications. They were trying to figure out the correct orientation of the antenna to lock onto a satellite and weren't having much success. I tossed them my Silva compass and that helped them to pick up the satellite.

One of the issues where I was overridden on was the use of "handles" or nicknames as call signs. Standard communications security practices called for the changing of call signs on a regular basis to keep units and personnel from being identified. Charlie Beckwith allowed the operators to pick their nicknames over my objections. There were some interesting results. Pete Schoomaker was on the University of Wyoming Sugar Bowl football team and wanted the handle of Cowboy. He was outranked by Logan Fitch, who chose Cowboy as his handle. Pete then chose Coyote as his call sign. A couple of the operators wanted to rub it in when I was overridden. They came to me and taunted me by asking, "What's your call sign?" I replied, "DILLIGAF." They gave me blank looks and asked what the hell DILLIGAF stood for. I then replied, "Do I Look Like I Give A Fuck—DILLIGAF." We all had a good laugh over that.

***

Delta was organized into squadrons following the British SAS model. The squadron personnel were known as operators, and they showed great energy, innovation, and willingness to learn and try different techniques and procedures. The 22nd SAS was very helpful in sending the operator code-named Ginger to impart close-quarter battle techniques and instinctive shooting. Charlie Beckwith was sold on the .45-caliber as a bullet of choice. Accordingly, the operators were initially armed with M-1911 .45-caliber pistols and the M3 sub-machine gun. Delta hired an armorer/gunsmith named Ron Waananen who worked diligently on building custom .45 pistols for the operators. Ron was also an excellent marksman. I had purchased different parts for him to assemble for me, and he proved how well he could shoot as well as the accuracy of the pistol he built by placing two shots through the same hole at 10 yards. The M3 sub-machine gun was an accurate World War II stamped metal design, with a rate of fire that was slow enough to maintain excellent control. Beckwith wanted to design a safety for the M3. The Intelligence Material Support Office came up with a design, but one of the operators designed something even better and adopted it for use. The operators were always looking for better ways to conduct a hostage rescue and were constantly trying different ways to enter a building or room, an airplane, a train, or a bus. They developed both mechanical and explosive techniques to breach a structure, to use non-lethal weapons, including stun grenades and riot control agents, and to conduct reconnaissance and surveillance of a target.

The snipers experimented with different weapons and cartridges, including reloading of ammunition, to meet their desires. The snipers were also interested in learning more about high-angle shooting and the effects of different bullets on things like aircraft tires and window glass. What was most impressive was their ability to maintain humility along with a great sense of humor. As an example of humor, Charlie Beckwith insisted that they engage in exercises where they would use bricks in both hands to build better strength to fire their weapons. The operators knew there were better ways to build muscular strength, but they humored Charlie by doing what he prescribed.

Charlie Beckwith saw the need for Explosive Ordnance Disposal (EOD) personnel to be assigned to Delta. He thought that EOD capabilities could be used in a hostage rescue, not only to disarm boobytraps or terrorist explosive devices, but also to assist in explosive breaching. A recruiting effort was launched to find EOD personnel who were interested in joining Delta; five or six signed up. They were required to go through Delta's assessment and selection course. The three that I remember who made it were Irv Banta, Mike Vining, and Dennis Wolfe. Another one of the EOD recruits was named Sledge. Sledge went home over a weekend and did not show up for duty the following Monday. Logan Fitch and I were shooting the breeze when Sledge suddenly appeared. Logan asked him what had happened. Sledge went on to tell a tale of an argument he had with his wife that resulted in his arrest. He told us that his intentions were to "palletize" his wife—he meant "pacify." Logan and I burst out laughing after Sledge left the room. We then chuckled over how Charlie Beckwith would often mispronounce different words. Charlie pronounced Managua, Nicaragua, came out as Mana-goo-ah, Nick-car-goo-ah. He also called our communications officer, Jorge Torres-Cartagena, Jor-Gus. But make no mistake, Charlie was intelligent, and his cursive handwriting was immaculate.

There were lots of other innovative efforts during the early days of Delta. We bought a Wang word processor that Penny Floyd in the S3 section mastered. We were fortunate to hire Pat Kapp as our Intelligence Section secretary and she also mastered the Wang machine. Penny and Pat had a great sense of humor. One day I heard them giggling and asked them what was going on. They pointed towards Jerry Boykin who had come out of a shower in our SCIF wearing his baggy underwear. Penny and Pat pointed at him and said, "Look at that booty!" For intelligence, we saw the value of open-source reporting and obtained a NEXIS/LEXIS terminal along with ticker-tape subscriptions to UPI and Reuters news services. Charlie insisted that a psychologist be assigned to Delta. Dr Jim Turner, who was used for more than assessment and selection, was assigned. He proved himself to be a skilled negotiator. He also tried to introduce innovative mind control techniques to help the operators deal with stress and to perform better physically. He was met with a lot of skepticism which was unfortunate. As an example, he attempted to show ways to reduce one's heart rate and to raise or lower one's body temperature. He used me as a guinea pig because of my martial arts training. I demonstrated that I could raise my temperature by as much as 10 degrees Fahrenheit and lower it by six degrees. For whatever reason, the operators were not interested.

One of the heart-warming things Charlie Beckwith did was to invite retired Colonel Arthur D. "Bull" Simons to visit Delta and to stay for about a week. Bull Simons had been the ground commander on the fateful attempt to rescue American POWs in North Vietnam. Simons requested that Charlie send someone to watch his pigs while he was gone. Charlie knew that John Stanley was from Florida where Simons had retired and tasked Wayne Long and me to send John to watch Bull's pigs. John had a great experience. When he returned, he told me that Bull Simons had a name for each of his pigs and that John had to remember them all! Simons had a great time at Delta. He showed the operators how he reloaded ammunition and had many chats with the operators—a great experience for everyone.

After passing the assessment in July 1978, we planned our first field exercise away from Fort Bragg. It was conducted at the McGregor Range in New Mexico, near Fort Bliss, Texas. There was a haystack-shaped hill with abandoned buildings on top of it, close to the entrance to McGregor Range. Dick Meadows, Willie Welsch, and I went on the advance party to set up the exercise. The three of us had to clean the buildings to make them usable for terrorist actors to simulate a hostage-taking event. The buildings were filthy and littered with loose asbestos. We busted our butts to clean the buildings and were covered with dust and asbestos. Years later, I wondered if all that exposure to asbestos had anything to do with Dick Meadows contracting leukemia and dying from it. The scenario required the operators to move clandestinely by vehicle and then dismount and move stealthily up the slope of the hill to conduct their assault. One of the hilarious things that occurred was when one of the terrorist actors came out and emptied his bladder on Don Briere and Bruno Urbaniak. Don and Bruno kept their silence and were not detected. Better to be pissed on than detected! The mock hostage rescue was completed successfully, but the highlight was clearly what Don and Bruno had been subjected to.

Thanks to the support and relationship built with the DOE and its NEST organization, the second significant exercise away from Fort Bragg occurred a few months later. Before the exercise, a small group of snipers had the opportunity to experiment with high-angle sniper fire. They used the BREN tower on the Nevada Test Site which was over 1,500 feet tall and gave the opportunity to fire at different heights and angles against a variety of targets. Two of the Secret Service personnel who went along to also profit from the experiments were Bob Lutz, the noted armorer for the Secret Service, and Aranzo Milbourne. Aranzo was a uniformed division officer who held multiple National Rifle Association and other prestigious marksmanship records. He was an outstanding marksman with both a rifle and a revolver. We flew from Fort Bragg to Dyess Air Force Base in Abilene, Texas, and spent the night there.

The following morning, I decided to inject some fun into the situation. I summoned the three Secret Service guys from outside the barracks where we had slept the previous night. I informed them that their bosses confirmed that they were all airborne qualified and I intended to give them a jump refresher. This was necessary as we would have to parachute into the Nevada Test Site at night. They didn't know what to say and had worried looks as I barked out the jump commands: Get Ready, Stand Up, Hook Up, Check Equipment, Sound Off for Equipment Check, Stand in the Door! Bob Lutz dared to raise his hand and when I recognized him, he stated that they were not airborne qualified. I burst out laughing and told them I was pulling their legs. They weren't quite sure if I was crazy or not. We took off on a C-130 aircraft in the late afternoon. The plan was for a special Air Force Combat Control Team led by Major John Carney to do a High-Altitude, Low Opening (HALO) jump on the Mercury airstrip at the Nevada Test Site. They would then mark the runway and guide the C-130 to a landing.

The special combat control team had been specially assembled to support counterterrorist missions. Carney's team had worked with Blue Light and Delta. This was the forerunner of what today is a much-expanded capability in the Air Force Special Operations Command known as Special Tactics Squadrons. The folks on John's team that I can remember were Pappy Correle, Mitch Bryan, Rex Wolmann, Mike Lampe, John Koren, Bud Gonzalez, and Dick West. They bonded well with Delta. John had been an All-American linebacker at the University of Arizona and later was an assistant football coach under the renowned Ben Martin at the U.S. Air Force Academy. He thought his career was going nowhere when he was given the opportunity to stand up for his special combat control team. Their mission was to be able to infiltrate into a banned area using High Altitude, Low Opening (HALO) parachuting or swimming underwater using Scuba gear to set up and mark a landing zone, and then to guide aircraft into a safe landing.

The Secret Service guys were seated next to me on the C-130. As we approached the Nevada Test Site, the combat controllers got ready, including donning their oxygen masks as the jump altitude would be at 12,000 feet or greater, requiring oxygen. Bob Lutz had this wide-eyed stare as he saw them getting ready. When the rear ramp of the C-130 lowered, he really had a worried look on his face. I reached over, had him tighten his seat belt and told him there was nothing to worry about! The runway at Mercury had been blacked out. Carney's team showed their abilities and quickly set up the airstrip to bring in the C-130 after parachuting onto the runway. Bob Lutz was relieved when we landed. It was a fantastic experience for him.

After a few days of the high-altitude shooting experiments, one of Delta's squadrons flew in and the training exercise commenced. The FBI's Las Vegas Field Division provided the mock terrorists, and the DOE provided the hostages. The initial scenario had the mock terrorists and hostages located in the Engine Maintenance, Assembly, and Disassembly or E-MAD building on the test site. This was an eight-story, 100,000-square-foot structure that had been used by the DOE and the National Aeronautics and Space Administration to build and test a nuclear power plant for space flight. The building was abandoned after the conclusion of the tests. The scenario called for the terrorists to demand safe passage with an airplane flying out of the Mercury airstrip. They would further demand that a few of them with hostages would move from the E-MAD building to the airstrip followed by a second group also with hostages. This would require the Delta operators to plan a coordinated assault on the airplane and the bus carrying the second group from E-MAD to the airstrip. It was a very challenging exercise and the operators showed outstanding skills in performing the mission successfully.

Aside from the rescue, there were two interesting things that happened during the exercise. The first was using Delta's psychologist, Jim Turner, as the negotiator. The terrorist actors made an unreasonable demand on one occasion. Jim told them we would not comply and hung up the negotiating phone. Everyone was shocked by Jim's actions and believed that was not the proper thing to do. About thirty minutes later, the mock terrorist called Jim back, apologized and revised their demands for food. The other interesting event was that one of the DOE hostage actors was a psychologist by the name of Joe Krofchek. He wrote a lengthy paper about his experience after the exercise was over. I read it in great detail and was amazed at his misinterpretation of different events. However, it was a good reminder of how a stressful situation can alter how one thinks and remembers things.

The exercise was a great test for the operators and communicators as the distance between the E-MAD building and the airstrip was vast and the terrain was not conducive to line-of-sight communications. The operators and the communications section overcame those difficulties and executed a well-planned operation to free the notional hostages.

Bob Nugent, the 902nd MI Group Resident Agent at Fort Bragg, came to Wayne Long and me to ask for help. He had been approached by a Special Forces retiree who reported that he was suspicious of an operation in Libya providing training to Muamar Qaddafi's forces, including explosive techniques. Five Special Forces retirees had been recruited by Frank Terpil and Edwin Wilson under the guise that they were conducting a CIA-approved mission in Libya. They were: Billy Waugh, Felipe Ahumada, Chuck Hiner, Henry Corvera, and Luke Thompson. By chance, I had served with each one previously, either in Vietnam or on Okinawa, and shared what I knew with Bob Nugent. Bob prepared a report after a thorough investigation and then was told not to pursue the matter further ostensibly because INSCOM headquarters believed that it was genuinely a CIA mission. The five retirees returned from Libya, and I got a call from Henry Corvera saying that he wanted to talk. I mistakenly thought that he was going to reveal information about his time in Libya. I arranged to meet him at a remote location at one of the drop zones in Fort Bragg. Henry asked me for a job! So much for gaining information on the Libyan operation. Sometime later, it was revealed that Terpil and Wilson were not working for the CIA and they were acting on their own behalf. Bob Nugent was reassigned to recruiting duty and was on the road headed for his new assignment when he got a frantic call from INSCOM to return to Fort Bragg and provide INSCOM with the results of his previous investigation.

The first time that Delta thought it would be called on to conduct an overseas hostage rescue was in February 1979 when Ambassador Spike Dubs was kidnapped in Afghanistan. On February 14, before we could get off the ground, Ambassador Dubs was killed. On that same day, Iranian militants took over the U.S. Embassy compound in Tehran. Order was restored and the embassy returned to American control. Ken Kraus, a Marine security guard, was kept hostage for a few days and finally released. We requested authorization to go to Tehran and assess the embassy compound and surrounding areas on the assumption that the embassy would probably be taken over again due to the anti-American fervor in Iran. The militants were demanding the return of the Shah to Iran. The State Department was willing to issue country clearance to allow the assessment, but the European Command denied theater clearance. This denial left us bereft of inside knowledge of the embassy later in 1979.

***

A special relationship was formed in 1979 with the Los Angeles Sheriff's Department Special Enforcement Bureau (SEB) and the Los Angeles Police Department Special Weapons and Tactics (SWAT) unit. Jim Stinson made the introductions, and an initial visit was made to Fort Bragg by Captain John Kolman, the head of the SEB;

Lieutenant Jeff Rogers, head of the LAPD SWAT; and Sergeant Mike Hillman, the lead sergeant on LAPD's SWAT. Joint training and exchanges occurred to the benefit of Delta, SEB, and LAPD SWAT. SEB and SWAT were very accommodating in arranging different training venues in buildings that offered insights to the Delta operators. One of the most constructive techniques learned was how to operate in elevator shafts.

The operators were also able to refine their aircraft boarding techniques. The FAA helped by introducing Delta to airlines that made their aircraft available for training. Additionally, an aircraft renovation site was found, and permission was granted to train on aircraft at that location. It was particularly valuable because studies could be done of aircraft that were being either torn down or rebuilt with the opportunity to learn specific details of the aircraft structure and possible methods of entry. The FAA security folks were also very forthcoming in sharing their intelligence, a profiling system they had developed to identify potential skyjackers and to make introductions to the Air Line Pilots Association.

An interesting exercise was conducted in 1979 during which the operators were put into isolation at Dobbins AFB and denied permission to leave their quarters to do physical training. By chance, Vice President Walter Mondale was passing through Dobbins AFB with his Secret Service detail, and the operators were told that the detail would report any suspicious persons they saw. This gave us an excuse to isolate the operators. It was a challenge for some of the operators, and they learned a good lesson on how to handle periods of isolation. Some had no problem with isolation. Mike Moore was one of them. Mike was a sniper, into Dungeons and Dragons, and a vociferous reader. He just chilled out and read books! This was the exercise that required the operators to pass through Hartsfield International Airport in Atlanta, purchase their tickets and continue to the exercise location without being detected by FAA security. Thanks to the folks at FAA headquarters, I could contact Charles Middleton, the FAA regional security director in Atlanta, for support. He arrayed his agents throughout the airport to report anyone that might look like a military counterterrorist operator. To make it fair, we did not instruct the agents to focus on flights headed to Key West, Florida. For operations security, Delta operators were dressed in civilian clothes, and told not to acknowledge others going on the same flight with them. It was a sterling tribute to the operators that the FAA reported only two suspicious persons.

The 1st Ranger Battalion out of Fort Stewart, South Carolina, led by then-Lieutenant Colonel Joe Stringham, was incorporated into the exercise to establish a security cordon around the target facility and provide additional security during the assault. The Rangers were transported on military aircraft. On the way to the exercise, Charlie Beckwith fired the fourth Delta intelligence officer mainly because he had been bugging Charlie about starting a maritime effort using kayaks. Charlie told him his job was intelligence and not operations.

With the firing, Wayne Long once again took charge and was now the fifth Delta intelligence officer. The exercise went well—one of the comical things that happened was that two of the terrorist actors were having sex—they were lucky that the assault didn't occur while they were deeply engaged in their lovemaking!

This exercise was one requiring the operators to be resourceful. Charlie Beckwith, Chuck Odorizzi, and Bucky Burruss wanted to incorporate resourcefulness whenever possible. An exercise was conducted in Germany near the city of Dahn. The location was a youth camp with an immense tunnel complex constructed by the German Army during World War II. After the exercise, the operators were taken, in small groups, to different locations around Dahn. Each of them was given different instructions on a rendezvous point that they had to get to by using their resourcefulness. I took a small group to a small town and stopped in the middle of it. The operators knew they had to get to the Hauptbahnhof or main railroad station. They asked me why I had stopped, and I replied that I didn't know where to take them. John Yancey, who later would die in a tragic training accident, cussed me out and told me to take them to the central railroad station. I shrugged my shoulders and, lying, told them I didn't know where it was.

John and the others jumped out of the VW van, engaged local citizens using sign language and sketches, and came back to tell me where to drive. Once more, they showed resourcefulness. They were never told where their final destination would be and had to go to a series of different rendezvous locations before reaching their final destination—the United Kingdom. Everyone made it on time. Herman Adler from the Intelligence Section was a key planner for this and other resourcefulness exercises. Herman was born in Munich, Germany, became an American citizen and gained an officer's commission. He used to be teased and called the Kraut as he still had a German accent, and his personal vehicle was a Volkswagen Kubelwagen that looked like a German World War II military vehicle.

A secretive exercise was formulated to see how the operators would perform in an ostensibly real-world situation. A troop-sized element would be called in after duty hours, given a quick briefing and told to mount out with their equipment and live ammunition. They were flown for hours and told they were going to a foreign country. They would surveil the target, which had live actors inside, and plan a rescue. Shortly before the rescue attempt, the controllers would inform the actors, who would move realistic mannequins into place and then take shelter underground for safety. After the assault, a critique would ensue to determine how accurately the operators had fired on the targets and to discuss other lessons learned.

***

In preparation for the 1979 Pan American Games to be held in Puerto Rico, Colonel Beckwith, Logan Fitch, and I were sent to evaluate the situation if Delta was called upon to deal with a terrorist event. The Machetero terrorist movement was active in Puerto Rico and was cause for concern. On the way to San Juan, Charlie asked me how I would feel if I were brought on active duty in my reserve rank of captain. I knew that Dick Potter had been working at the Army's Military Personnel Center and General Max Thurman to bring me on active duty. Dick told me that the two liaison warrant officers from the Army's Intelligence and Security Command, Rick Stevenson and Pat Patterson, had asked Beckwith who I was after one of their visits. When Beckwith asked them why, they replied that although they knew Wayne Long was a major, this other guy seemed to be the brains—they were referring to me. Because I wore no rank insignia, they didn't know what my rank was. Charlie found out I had a reserve commission and tasked Dick Potter to bring me on active duty. In answer to Charlie's question, I responded with, "It's a pay raise."

I remembered clearly what my friend Arif Zaky had said when he got before a Reserve Commissioning board in 1975! I told Charlie that nothing would change and that I would still do what I was doing. One of the interesting things that happened on that trip was that the FBI special agent in charge was later found to be having an affair with his secretary and she was a member of the Macheteros!

General Edward "Shy" Meyer, who was the key advocate on the Army Staff for the formation of Delta, was promoted to four-star general in 1979 and became the Army's Chief of Staff, the Army's ranking general officer. He had the foresight to call for an international validation. Should Delta pass the validation, it would be the only organization in America to be accredited through a high-level validation. The evaluators were to include Brigadier Johnny Watts, the head of the United Kingdom's Special Forces and a former commander of the 22nd Special Air Service Regiment; Ulrich Wegner, the commander of the German Grenshutz Gruppe Neun (GSG-9) Counterterrorist force created after the 1972 Munich Olympics; and Christian Prouteau, the head of the French Gendarmerie's Groupe d'intervention de la Gendarmerie Nationale (GIGN). Other evaluators were senior U.S. government officials from the CIA, DIA, FBI, Secret Service, and FAA. The validation exercise was scheduled for the end of October 1979 and would run until the first few days of November 1979.

Mi Hye wanted to visit her mother in Korea since she had last seen her six years earlier. We decided that October and November would be an opportue time for her to go as I knew I would be engrossed in preparing for and participating in the validation exercise. I was brought on active duty as a captain, and we also knew we would be moving before long. So, it was great timing for her to visit to Korea. After she left, getting ready for the validation was another flurry of activity.

The validation exercise was conducted at Hunter Army Airfield and Fort Stewart, Georgia. The scenario called for a simultaneous assault to rescue hostages from both an airplane and a building separated by a long distance. The Delta operators again showed their proficiency and the validation exercise concluded early on the morning of November 4, 1979. Everyone in Delta was pleased that we had passed with flying colors and went to sleep. Around 6:30 AM, Randy Hoeffer, one of our communicators, woke me up and told me that the U.S. Embassy had been overrun that morning. I woke Wayne Long and Colonel Beckwith. We intuitively knew that Delta would be called upon to deal with the situation. Beckwith grabbed Bucky Burruss and told him to get a rental car and they proceeded to head back to Fort Bragg. Dick Potter pulled another magic trick and got the Air Force to send a C-130 to get the rest of us to Fort Bragg. When the aircraft landed, it had a flat tire. The Air Force, knowing the urgency, quickly replaced the tire, and we took off for Fort Bragg, with many of us having to stand as the plane was packed to capacity. Ironically, we beat Beckwith and Burruss back to Fort Bragg!

A few days after our return, Charlie Beckwith dispatched Bucky Burruss and Dick Meadows to the Pentagon in the belief that Delta would undoubtedly be called upon to participate in planning a response to the hostage situation in Tehran. They reported a surge of activity within the Pentagon focusing on various military strategies to manage the crisis. One of the options under consideration was a Special Operations attempt to rescue the hostages.

CHAPTER 12

Rice Bowl—Initial Preparations

The Pentagon formed a Joint Task Force within a week of November 4, 1979. It was designated as JTF 1-79, and its role was to focus on using Special Operations to conduct a hostage rescue. Security was a paramount consideration, and tight compartmentation of the effort was maintained from the start. The task force was kept very small with a total of fewer than 75 personnel assigned to it throughout the planning. In the military, an Operations Plan is used during the planning phases and an Operations Order used during the execution of the plan. During the planning phase, we chose the name Rice Bowl, as it was an innocuous term that would not reveal any intentions related to Iran. The name Eagle Claw was selected for the operation should it be implemented, and a mission launched.

Army Major General James Vaught was appointed as the task force commander. He had been responsible for regional operations on the Army Staff, working under the leadership of General Edward Meyer. Vaught had no appreciable Special Operations experience but had knowledge of the Delta Force and was trusted by General Meyer to lead the effort. Air Force Major General Phillip Gast was nominally appointed as the deputy to General Vaught. He was selected because he had been on a previous assignment in Iran where he was responsible for security assistance to the Iranian government under the Shah. Many of the remaining staff for the task force came from the Joint Chiefs of Staff J3 Special Operations Division, with selected experts brought in from around the country.

Colonel Jerry King, a Special Forces officer, was one of those. Jerry played various roles on the task force; he basically functioned as the deputy commander as General Gast was principally used as an advisor on Iran, rather than as the deputy commander. Jerry was also the Chief of Staff and the operations officer (J3). Jerry's first Special Forces assignment after completing the qualification course was as a first lieutenant with the 1st Special Forces Group on Okinawa. He served in Vietnam and returned to the 1st Special Forces Group as a battalion commander, which is where I first met him and gained tremendous respect for him. In 1973, he led a Special Forces contingent that greeted the prisoners of war who were released from

North Vietnam. After Okinawa, he was assigned as the inspector general for the 82nd Airborne Division at Fort Bragg, North Carolina. We would occasionally see each other during that assignment and reminisce about our time in Okinawa. General Vaught was fortunate to have Jerry King on his task force.

The J2 or intelligence officer for the task force was Air Force Lieutenant Colonel Rod Lenahan. Rod also came from the J3 Special Operations Division. In his previous assignment at the U.S. Readiness Command, he worked on terrorism matters and visited Wayne Long and me at Fort Bragg. Rod only had three others assisting him with intelligence; Army Major Dick Fredel, Marine Major Bob Mattingly, and Army Captain Tim Casey. Tim was a Special Forces officer and I had the pleasure of instructing him when he was going through the SF qualification course. He later became one of the members of Blue Light. Like Jerry King, Tim Casey was a real workhorse on the J2 staff and did super work. People often question how such a small number of people could produce the intelligence required to plan and execute the mission. The answer is that they knew what organizations to task for different products rather than trying to produce everything themselves.

There were three other super performers on the task force: Navy Chief Petty Officer Bill Collins was in charge of administrative support, and assisted in security functions for the task force; Air Force Colonel Jim Kyle fresh from an assignment at Kirtland Air Force Base in Albuquerque, New Mexico, to be the lead fixed-wing planner for the mission. Jim had combat experience as an AC-130 gunship pilot in Vietnam. He was instructed to report immediately and dress in civilian clothes. He brought one blazer with him, and it literally fell apart after a couple of months in the Pentagon. The joke was that he was being too frugal as his wife, Eunice (née Tom), who was of Chinese ethnicity from the Kaimuki area of Hawaii, wouldn't allow him to have much in his wardrobe! The other superstar was Marine Major Jim Magee. Jim was sent as a liaison officer from the U.S. European Command, where he worked in the Special Operations Task Force Europe. Jim was sent to the task force because the European Command had responsibility for Iran in the 1970s and 1980s. He went way beyond just being a liaison officer and was engaged in all aspects of the operational planning, including overseeing the use of two members of Special Forces Detachment A, out of Berlin, who had been sent to Iran twice before the actual execution of Operation Eagle Claw.

It was clear from the outset of planning that Air Force Special Operations assets would likely be required. The only extant Air Force Special Operations unit at the time was the 1st Special Operations Wing headquartered at Hurlburt Field, Florida, near Eglin Air Force Base in the Florida Panhandle. The total number of aircraft they possessed was 20. That number included AC-130 gunships, MC-130 Combat Talons, and EC-130s. That is in stark contrast to today's Air Force Special Operations Command which has several wings and over 30 AC-130 gunships in its inventory. Scuttlebutt said that the Air Force was not funding the 1st SOW robustly

RICE BOWL—INITIAL PREPARATIONS • 161

and that their aircraft maintenance budget was not robust. However, we believed in the quality of the 1st SOW pilots and maintenance personnel, as many of us in Delta had worked with them before. One of the challenges the 1st SOW faced was to learn how to fly with first-generation night vision goggles. Flying with night vision goggles affected the helicopter crews who also had to learn to use them. In late November 1979, four AC-130 gunships took off from Hurlburt Field, Florida, and flew non-stop to Guam with four mid-air refuelings during their flight. The reason they did that was to see if their crews and the aircraft could fly some 7,000 miles. That was the approximate distance that they would have to fly from Hurlburt Field to Iran.

As mission planning evolved, it was determined that additional Air Force assets in the form of C-141 passenger/cargo aircraft would be used to bring the rescue force out of Iran. Additionally, KC-135 tanker aircraft would also be required. These assets came from the Military Airlift Command, known today as the Air Force Air Mobility Command. We were told in Delta that there would not be any close air support over Tehran provided by jet aircraft. The reason given was the difficulty with the range of operation and the distance from either Turkey or the USS *Nimitz*. So, our only close air support would be provided by four AC-130 gunships armed with a 105 mm cannon, 40 mm guns, and 7.62 mm Gatling guns. The AC-130s would be no match against an Iranian Air Force flying F-14 Tomcats, F4 Phantoms, and F-5 fighters that had been provided to Iran under the Shah. The AC-130s would have to rely on stealth and avoid Iranian radar to succeed.

If the helicopters were needed to perform a rescue mission, the Joint Staff directed that six additional RH-53D model minesweeping helicopters be placed on board the USS *Kitty Hawk*. The *Kitty Hawk* carrier battle group was directed to steam towards the Persian Gulf for possible use against Iran. Delta was told that the RH-53D helicopter was selected because it had longer range than other comparable helicopters and it could be on the hangar deck of the aircraft carrier out of sight of overhead sea surveillance. The RH-53D was not air refuelable but had folding rotor blades and a folding tail boom to take up less space on the aircraft carrier. Army and Air Force helicopters lacked the folding rotor blades and tail boom feature. In addition, the number of Air Force helicopters that had been successfully used in Vietnam for search and rescue and on the Son Tay Prison raid into North Vietnam had been reduced in number in the aftermath of Vietnam. The Air Force was developing the MH-53 helicopter that was capable of being refueled in the air, but they were only due to come off the production line in late 1979, and were not fully operationally certified. Because the RH-53D was a Navy helicopter, Navy pilots from a minesweeping squadron were initially assigned to be the pilots on any rescue operation.

The 1st SFOD-D was selected to be the principal ground rescue force should there be a rescue attempt. As planning evolved, it was determined that additional ground forces would be required. The 1st Ranger Battalion was brought into planning along with the Special Forces Detachment A, out of Berlin. Other additions were to be made to augment the ground force as planning developed.

On the day of the embassy takeover, there had been no advanced warning that such an attempt might occur. JTF 1-79 was faced with a monumental task. In Iran, there were no stay-behind intelligence agents or undercover assets. The entire CIA station personnel were hostages along with the defense attachés. Intelligence on the hostage-takers and the theocratic government of Iran that the Ayatollah Khomeini had introduced in February 1979 was lacking. Unfortunately, American intelligence efforts in Iran, when the Shah was falling from grace, concentrated on the communist Tudeh Party in Iran because of the feeling that the Soviet Union might choose to invade Iran. The other concentration of effort was finding members of the Iranian military who might stage a coup and restore the military or secular government in Iran. With the latter, the problem was that many of the senior military officers fled Iran with the departure of the Shah and the ascendency of Ayatollah Khomeini as the supreme leader of Iran. Clearly, there was no noteworthy opposition against the Ayatollah that could be used to create a coup, collect intelligence, or create diversions for a rescue attempt.

JTF 1-79 also found that there were no contingency plans dealing with a possible hostage rescue attempt either on the Joint Staff or in the U.S. European Command, which had responsibility for Iran. Accordingly, the task force had to look at different options. It took until mid-December 1979 before a final concept was decided upon. A tremendous amount of time and effort went into looking at different options. Those that were discarded included using High Altitude, Low Opening insertion of the rescue force into the embassy compound—discarded because we could not jump out with the hostages! Airborne insertion using standard parachute techniques was also discarded because the rescuers would have to either walk or commandeer vehicles to get to the embassy, and could not be expected to jump out! The seizure of one of two outlying Iranian Air Force bases was considered—the bases would have to be held for at least two days and that was not deemed feasible—the Iranian military would quickly suspect that the base had been taken over. Consideration was also given to infiltrating the rescue force in commercial trucks coming out of Turkey with facades built in the cargo compartments to hide the rescue force. This was also discarded as too high risk for detection and the inability to drive out of Iran after a rescue was conducted. Another concept that was discarded was to airland at either Tehran International Airport (Mehrabad) or the Iranian Air Force Headquarters base and then drive with armored vehicles to rescue the hostages, and return to the airfield for departure. This made little sense as the Iranians would undoubtedly come out in force, including civilians, to block the roads. The final plan that came about in mid-December will be discussed later.

Another complicating factor was it took almost a week to determine the number of hostages in Tehran and their identities. It was determined after a week that there were initially some 100 hostages taken with 66 being Americans. It was learned that there were six Americans who had avoided capture and were being hidden by the Canadian Embassy in Tehran. These six were brought out in January 1980 in a CIA operation depicted in the film *Argo*. Among the initial 100 hostages were Japanese and Koreans who were visiting the U.S. Embassy on November 4, 1979. They were released quickly. In mid-November 1979, the Ayatollah declared that 13 of the 66 hostages would be released. Five of them were women and the others were Americans of African ancestry. The Ayatollah proclaimed that they were released because of anti-female and racist tendencies in America but not in Iran. Of the 53 remaining hostages, one African American, Charles Jones, and two females were kept hostage in the mistaken belief that they were CIA operatives.

After the formation of JTF 1-79, Delta was alerted that we would go into isolation at a CIA facility. Plans were quickly made to relocate the operators and a small number of support personnel to the CIA facility. Operations security was tightly maintained and only a few knew where the facility was located. Ron Franklin, one of the original operators and a great friend of mine from Vietnam and Okinawa, and I were dispatched to a motel about an hour's drive from the CIA facility. The operators were told they would leave Fort Bragg in small groups and go to the motel where they would receive further instructions. Ron and I had no idea when operators would arrive for their destination instructions. On the night we got to the motel, Ron wanted to go and work out, I insisted we should go out and get a good meal instead. He reluctantly agreed. It was the last good meal he would have for several days. The first night we were at the motel, I received a call telling me to pack up and that I would go to the CIA facility, leaving Ron alone. Later, I teased him unmercifully about what the hotel maids must have thought about all the guys coming to his room!

At the CIA facility, we were warmly greeted by Ed Mitchell, the station chief. Ed escorted us to our new headquarters in a retreat facility used by the intelligence community for meetings. There were bedrooms designated for the leaders of the intelligence community. I was assigned to the room reserved for the Director of the National Security Agency. Charlie Beckwith and Bucky Burruss were shown where our operators would be billeted during isolation along with a briefing on training areas available. We were introduced to five CIA personnel who would remain with us throughout the mission. Two were from the CIA Office of Imagery Analysis and were top-notch imagery interpreters. Two others were operatives who had previously spent tours in Iran. Jim Sterling (pseudonym) had been responsible for the security of former CIA Director Richard Helms when Helms became the U.S. Ambassador to Iran. Jim was also the agent handler for a former Savak and Iranian Special Forces officer nicknamed "Al" who would remain with us throughout the mission.

The third was Big Bill Dickey (pseudonym) who had worked in both security and signals intelligence in Iran. These five were invaluable assets to Delta.

Lieutenant Commander Rod Davis, a Navy helicopter pilot, arrived and was sent to the CIA facility, unsure of his intended destination or its purpose. Jerry Boykin and Pete Schoomaker told me that they had found him sitting outside the headquarters on a curb with his head in his hands. Jerry and Pete approached him and asked him who he was and whether he was all right. He informed them about his name and rank and that the day before he had been told to pack civilian clothes and to head to the motel where Ron Franklin was left by himself. He was then transported to the CIA facility but had absolutely no clue where he was or why he was there. He then recounted that a few minutes before, a big guy had come out of the headquarters and urinated over his shoulder (the big guy was Charlie Beckwith)! Davis was one of the only Navy pilots to continue with the ad hoc helicopter squadron that was formed.

Within two days of our arrival, Major General Vaught visited us at the CIA facility. In a raspy voice, he began by saying he was responsible for saving a million Chinese. I whispered to Forrest Foreman, "Does he mean during the Boxer Rebellion or at the end of World War II?" Forrest had to choke himself to keep from laughing out loud. General Vaught had a weathered face, and with his pronouncement about rescuing the Chinese, I nicknamed him the "Neanderthal Man." Vaught, a capable leader, then proceeded to brief us on the status of planning which was still not very advanced. He did talk about the potential for the use of helicopters. After his briefing, Charlie Beckwith approached Vaught and asked to have command or operational control over the helicopters. Vaught vehemently denied permission but did not give Beckwith an explanation. This greatly disappointed Charlie as the night before a Navy pilot had shown his inability to land at night using night vision goggles. Charlie clearly understood the need for unity of command and a coordinated effort.

Before leaving Fort Bragg for isolation, we had been told to break all contact with State Department intelligence. That included not having contact with the Diplomatic Security Watch Center analysts who were so helpful to us. The reason given was that Cyrus Vance, the Secretary of State, and his Deputy, Warren Christopher, were adamantly opposed to any military operation. That was a bitter pill for John Stanley to swallow after all his efforts to build relations with that organization. As I previously mentioned, intelligence to plan the operation was a tremendous challenge, and losing a reliable source of information was difficult to overcome.

Charlie only brought Wayne Long and myself to the CIA facility from the Intelligence Section. I became the only person doing analysis as Wayne was given other duties to perform, like going to Germany and sitting in on the debriefing of the 13 released hostages in mid-November. I ended up working 18 to 20 hours every day. The two CIA imagery analysts were a saving grace. Wayne Long and I asked repeatedly to get Charlie to allow me to bring John Stanley and one other analyst to isolation but we were turned down continually for some unknown reason. Charlie finally relented in mid-December and authorized Lieutenant Colonel Max Spears who had come from the Army's Intelligence and Security Command to be Delta's sixth intelligence officer (once again replacing Wayne Long as the head). Max Spears was a fine infantry officer but lacked experience in analysis or strategic intelligence planning. Max, unfortunately, did not know how to add value to planning. The second night he was at the isolation facility, and after a few drinks, he told Charlie Beckwith that he would do anything to go on the mission. Charlie asked him if he could fire a machine gun, and Max replied affirmatively. At that point Charlie fired him, making Wayne the seventh Delta intelligence officer. Charlie had been testing whether Max knew what his job was, Max failed the test. Charlie also disallowed communications to go back to the intelligence section at Delta's headquarters. Fortunately, Gary Moston, Delta's special security officer and imagery interpreter, was allowed to travel to the JTF 1-79 location in the Pentagon. I could communicate with Gary on a limited basis, and he ensured that I received imagery from sources other than the CIA.

Gary's ingenuity and knowledge of security procedures came in handy when I was approached by the CIA facility security chief who accused me of violating security rules. I asked him what he meant, and he stated that I was passing Top Secret Sensitive Compartmented Information (TS/SCI) to people who did not have those clearances. I was flabbergasted. My first response was to ask him whether he knew that we were preparing to send our folks into a dangerous situation where their lives might depend on receiving intelligence. He responded that it didn't matter. I then told him all our personnel had, at a minimum, secret clearances which was sufficient to grant interim TS/SCI clearances. He argued that was not sufficient. I asked him to mention his specific concerns, and he stated that there were imagery products that were TS/SCI. I took him to where I had two imagery products laid out and asked him if he could tell me the difference. He stared at them and then admitted that he could not. I told him that both were from a particular satellite and that the images were only secret. He didn't know what to say. What he didn't know was that both came from a Top Secret satellite—Gary Moston, following appropriate procedures, had cut off the markings that designated them TS/SCI! The security puke then wandered off. I reached out to Jim Sterling and Bill Dickey, who both outranked the security officer, and they proceeded to read him the proverbial riot act and tell him not to butt in. Ironically, the image most used by Delta operators to plan their mission was not classified at all. I had been sent to the Pentagon for a meeting with Task Force 1-79, and I had come across a copy of *Life* magazine with a great picture of the embassy compound and surrounding area. I sent that to Gary Moston and he enlarged the picture for our operators.

One of the key ingredients for the success of a ground rescue attempt would be detailed knowledge of the embassy compound and the Ministry of Foreign Affairs.

The task force headquarters and the CIA asked the State Department for blueprints and building plans; they could only obtain outdated and unreliable documents. Thanks to the efforts of the CIA's Office of Imagery Analysis (OIA), a call was sent out to anyone in the CIA or National Security Agency and to defense attachés who had been recently posted in Iran to send in any information they had about the buildings and grounds. Within a month, they constructed a huge scale model (15 feet by 15 feet) of the embassy compound. The chancery building was the biggest on a 27-acre compound with 14 major buildings inside the compound. The chancery building model was about two feet wide. One could lift the roof and see the floor plan for the second floor, all the way to the basement. It was a remarkable product. They also built a scale model of the Ministry of Foreign Affairs, but due to the lack of interior design information, it could only show the exterior of the Ministry and its surroundings. Other information, such as the height and width and composition of a 12-foot-high wall on the side of the embassy compound, along with the structure of doors in various buildings, became available due to OIA's efforts. Another helpful person was Air Force Major Harry Johnson who had left Iran a few weeks before the takeover. He was attached to Delta and provided information on the buildings inside the compound. His household goods were still inside the compound, and we would joke with him about seeing them moved. He didn't find the humor in that!

The location of the hostages was critical to conducting a surgical hostage rescue. Without that knowledge, the rescue force would have to use brute force to locate the hostages, increasing the likelihood that their captors would kill them in the process. Their exact locations remained problematic even up to the day the rescue mission was launched. We knew that three of the hostages were in the Ministry of Foreign Affairs and in which room they were being held. This was because the Iranian government allowed them telephonic access to the State Department. The three were Bruce Laingen, the chargé d'affaires and ranking American diplomat in Iran; Michael Howland; and Victor Tomseth. Precise locations for the other 50 hostages were impossible despite several attempts. The Japanese and Korean governments provided information on where their businessmen were inside the embassy, but because they were quickly released, that information was not very helpful. Wayne Long observed the debriefing of the State Department hostages released in mid-November 1979, but that information was also not very helpful other than to learn that they were moved around the embassy. Ron Franklin and I spent a few hours with the Marine security guards who had been released in mid-November with the same results. An attempt was considered to get a former employee of a prominent American billionaire to infiltrate the embassy, but it was deemed too high risk and his cover would be blown within a short time. In the end, after analysis, it was believed that the hostages inside the embassy would be found in no more than four buildings.

Another critical factor for success was understanding who was guarding the hostages along with their weaponry, numbers, and tactics or routines. We learned that inside the compound, security was being handled by the student militants who were responsible for the initial takeover of the embassy. However, there was little other information known about them. A CIA psychiatrist, Bob Bloomingdale (pseudonym), was attached to the State Department as the negotiator with those militants, who were very guarded about revealing their identities and any details about their operations and hostage locations. At best, Bob could provide what their attitudes were, along with their demands. Similarly, State Department negotiations with the Ayatollah's government provided no useful information regarding hostage locations nor treatment. The main Iranian negotiator was Abolhassan Banisadr, the Minister of Foreign Affairs, a confidant of the Ayatollah. Later in February 1980, he would be elected President of Iran in a rigged election. The strongest demand was to return the Shah to Iran to face punishment. There were reports from foreign media that Palestinians had been brought in to assist the militants with training, but there was never any verification that they remained as guards for the hostages.

On the outside perimeter of the embassy, there were Pasdaran (paramilitary personnel) guarding the area around the embassy. At times there would also be Iranian police. Notably absent was any military presence. The standard armament for the Pasdaran was a FN/FAL G3 rifle with at least one 20-round magazine of bullets. There was no information on who was guarding the hostages at the Ministry of Foreign Affairs. Until the CIA inserted Bob Plan close to Christmas 1979, we relied on reporting from our allies on the security around the embassy. In particular, the Canadians and the British were great reporters. Beckwith was also approached by the German GSG-9 commander, Ulrike Wegener, who was willing to send some of his men to collect intelligence. The picture of security around the embassy was created by Tim Casey who tirelessly examined television broadcasts and the printed media for information about the security at the embassy. The analytical picture put together estimated that at night there would be about 24 militants guarding the hostages and 12–18 Pasdaran on the outside of the embassy.

There were myriad other details necessary to plan the mission. There were occasions when time and effort were wasted on stupidity rather than trying to address the other requirements. For example, Howard Hart, the CIA liaison to the task force, came to the CIA facility where we were in isolation. He pointed to a tourist map of Tehran and asked Al, the former Savak agent, "We can land planes here, right?" Hart was pointing to an area of development known as New Tehran. Al was not a pilot, but when the leading question was asked of him, his only answer was that planes could land there. Hart went back to the task force and insisted that landing zones be looked for in the New Tehran area—time and effort wasted because that area was hilly with no possible landing sites. Hart should have known better than to ask leading questions.

Regarding maps, the Defense Mapping Agency had no reliable large-scale maps of Tehran that could be used for mission planning. Maps were also necessary to support any potential evasion and escape should the mission go sour. In the end, the maps used for planning and evasion/escape consisted of two tourist maps Al had brought out of Iran when he escaped; a 1:250,000 scale map showing Tehran and its outskirts; and two small-scale charts covering the entire country. Of the two maps Al brought out, one was a tourist map of Tehran, and the other was a tourist map of the entire country in Farsi and English. All these maps were reproduced on a special plastic to make them waterproof. I was told that the entire U.S. inventory of that special plastic was depleted to print the maps.

It was crucial to know all the road routes and security checkpoints in and out of Tehran. The bulk of that would be left to Bob Plan and an advance party to be inserted into Tehran a week before the mission. Weather patterns and information were needed, and the Air Force Weather Service did excellent work in providing that information. The Air Force and National Security Agency successfully mapped any gaps in Iranian military and commercial radar coverage. Information on Iran's military and combat police capability was needed. America had provided the Shah with state-of-the-art weaponry, including F-14 Tomcat fighters, F4 Phantom jets, and F5 jets. We had provided them with our most modern tank, the M-60; improved Hawk Air Defense Missile systems; modern radars; and two robust aerial surveillance aircraft. Succinctly, it was determined that although the military was capable, they were not as good a force as under the Shah because their senior leadership had either fled Iran, were imprisoned, or watched very carefully. This was because of the potential for the military to lead a coup against the Ayatollah's government. Nonetheless, knowing where those units were located and their response times to the embassy was needed.

The intelligence required to answer all the requirements was particularly difficult to obtain because of our lack of human intelligence. In 1979, CIA Director Stansfield Turner had eliminated about 400 case officers from the CIA's clandestine service. After a week in isolation, Beckwith heard me commenting on the lack of useful intelligence. He reported that to General Vaught who then complained to Howard Hart. Hart then informed Howard Bane, the CIA chief of what was known as Terrorist Group. Bane took great umbrage with that and made a trip to the isolation facility. He stormed in and confronted me by saying the CIA had provided some 600 reports over the past week and a half. I looked Bane in the eye and asked him if he would like to see the results of all that reporting. I opened a binder which had about five pages of helpful intelligence. Bane was shaken. I patiently explained that we didn't need to know the cost of food in Shiraz, taxi fares in Isfahan, or what was happening to the Persian rug industry; these were all elements of the reports we were receiving. I then proceeded to tell him the kinds of details we needed that were lacking. Bane calmed down and walked away quietly.

Delta's operators were kept busy figuring out how they would conduct the actual hostage rescue including entering the embassy compound, dealing with the guards surrounding the embassy and guarding the hostages, accounting for the hostages, and then evacuating them. The scale model prepared by the CIA Office of Imagery Analysis was scrutinized repeatedly to develop their plans. It was also determined that different weapons would be required rather than relying on the handguns and sub-machine guns that were the standard issue. Charlie Beckwith was reluctant to get weapons through normal military channels, to keep operational security tight. The CIA came forth and offered to provide M-16 and CAR-15 rifles out of stocks they held to supply indigenous personnel. Much time was spent on the range checking out the weapons and becoming proficient with them.

We spent a quiet Thanksgiving at the CIA facility. Ed Mitchell, the station chief, helped arrange for a decent meal. We didn't have fresh turkey, but everyone understood and just enjoyed a break and the camaraderie from being with each other. Shortly after Thanksgiving, we were alerted there would be a rehearsal to be conducted at Yuma Proving Grounds in Arizona in early December. We spent time packing our gear and getting ready for the rehearsal without knowing what Delta would be asked to rehearse.

We flew into Yuma Marine Corps Air Station and then trucked out to a remote site where there was a large hangar-type structure adjacent to a dirt runway. That was to be our home for a week. We slept on the concrete slab inside the structure and were packed into it sleeping head to foot. One of my concerns was that colds or the flu could spread easily. Fortunately, that did not happen. Portable toilets were delivered, but there were no other amenities. Country Grimes, Delta's Command Sergeant Major, used his ingenuity. He ordered immersion heaters that were placed in clean trash cans to heat water. Grimes also requested and received office trash cans and spigots. He punched the spigots through the sides of the trash cans and then sealed them. The trash cans were then filled with hot water and placed on the tailgate of two half-ton trucks to allow us to take hot showers. One evening a major from the task force drove his rental car to our location. He was full of bluster, acted like he was in charge, and questioned what we were doing with the trash cans on the truck tailgates. I confronted him and told him to buzz off or he would be picking my toenails out of his rectum.

On one occasion, Country Grimes asked me to go to the Post Exchange to pick up some things he needed. As I parked the truck I drove in, I walked past a Visiting Officers Quarters and heard loud voices arguing about how they would accomplish the Iran mission. I walked into their location and proceeded to chew them out, reminding them of operations security, and to get their act together. As I discovered, these were the helicopter crews. In early December, they were still mainly U.S. Navy pilots and crews and had their hands full trying to learn those skills to fly overland at night using night vision goggles.

The December iteration was far from being a rehearsal. For example, on one night, the helicopters were going to be asked to fly to a designated point in the desert to link up with the ground force. I drove a two-and-a-half-ton truck for two hours through the desert to get to the rendezvous point. The helicopters never showed up, and it was a frustrating two-hour drive to get back to where we were billeted. We were never given a reason why the helicopters did not show up at the rendezvous point. On the C-130 side, an experiment was conducted where fuel bladders were dropped from the tail ramp, potentially for the purpose of refueling the helicopters. That turned out to be a very bad idea. The operational plans were subsequently changed to call for C-130s to land with fuel bladders on board with pumping equipment to transfer fuel to the helicopters. For Delta, it was a massive waste of time. There were no ranges to keep up their marksmanship, and no mockups to rehearse actions inside the embassy compound. To keep occupied, several operators explored the Colorado River that ran through the Yuma Proving Grounds. They found old license plates and other artefacts.

After about five days, Delta packed its bags and prepared to be airlifted back to the CIA facility where we had first gone in November. The only eventful thing that happened on the way back was that someone had shipped barrels of CS gas (a riot control agent) out to Yuma. A young Marine forklift driver saw the danger markings and refused to load the palettes of CS gas onto a C-141. I calmly told the young Marine to check with his supervisors. He came back very angry but proceeded to load the CS gas onto the aircraft.

Upon arrival back at the CIA facility, Colonel Beckwith told me to meet with a CIA agent who was going to be dispatched to Iran. I was given the name of Bob Plan and a room number in the Wolf Trap Motel in Falls Church, Virginia, to meet with Bob. Beckwith wanted my opinion on whether I thought Bob Plan had the right qualities for a mission into Iran. Jim Sterling and Big Bill Dickey took me aside and gave me some basic information on Bob Plan. They told me that he was a great American and CIA operative who had served with the OSS during World War II in Yugoslavia. He was brought out of retirement and asked to undertake the Iran mission. At the appointed time, I knocked on the door of Bob's room and heard a deep voice telling me to enter.

As I entered the room, I saw an older gentleman with deeply tanned skin, sitting in a chair. I introduced myself, and Bob stood up and shook my hand with a firm grip. My immediate reaction was that I liked him and felt I could trust and depend on him. As we chatted, I ascertained he had indeed served in Yugoslavia with the OSS and had a long career with the CIA. I asked him where he was retired, and he told me it was in the Mediterranean. The hair on the back of my head stood up. He was a fitting image of the actor Anthony Quinn. My mind conjured up thoughts of the movie *The Guns of Navarone*, where Anthony Quinn played the role of a guerrilla who infiltrated German-held territory to collect intelligence and destroy German coastal artillery. I thought to myself, this is going to work out great and Bob Plan is the right person to go into Iran. After our meeting, I briefed Charlie

Beckwith on my feelings, and he was pleased to hear that Bob Plan was someone we could depend upon. Bob was sent to Tehran with one Iranian business asset just before Christmas 1979. He went in and out of Tehran on several occasions between December 1979 and April 1980. He was given innumerable tasks—far more than any single person could accomplish. Nonetheless, Bob did superbly. He collected intelligence, reconnoitered different locations, made discreet contact with U.S. Embassy employees who were not hostages, and procured vehicles for use on the rescue attempt along with a warehouse and fuel for them. Bob did his work quietly with a great deal of professionalism and humility. Bob Plan's character is a model for all intelligence operatives.

When Delta returned to the CIA facility from Yuma, everyone went back to their preparations for the hostage rescue. To give the operators some relief, some of them were allowed to go deer hunting. Otherwise, it was back to maintaining weapons proficiency and rehearsing and planning how the rescue attempt would occur. Everyone wondered whether we would be spending Christmas and New Year in isolation. Charlie Beckwith had insisted that operations security be strictly adhered to with no contact allowed with the families. There was a comical event that happened when a Special Forces officer who was a student at the CIA facility inadvertently ran into Delta personnel that he knew. He was promptly pulled out of his course and put into isolation with the rest of us to avoid any discussion of Delta being on the premises.

The restrictions on contacting family members had a demoralizing effect on my wife. As I mentioned previously, she had gone to Korea to visit her family in October. In November she kept calling our house phone without any answer. There was no voicemail in those days and no cell phones (not that we could use them anyway because of security). She was beside herself not knowing what to do and what may have happened to me. My dear mother-in-law contributed to Mi Hye's anxiety by questioning her about what she did to me and suggesting that I might have run away! Out of desperation, she sought help from our great friend, Ben Dennis, the noncommissioned officer in charge of the Special Forces Korean Detachment. Ben called Delta, got the run-around but put two and two together and told Mi Hye that I was away on a mission where I was not able to use the telephone. What Ben told her helped a little, but not that much. Mi Hye returned to our house in Fort Bragg in early December. The house was empty, there was no indication as to my whereabouts. Unfortunately, I believe this caused her years-long struggle with anxiety and depression. One of the big lessons Delta learned was the need to build a means of taking care of the families without needing to give them classified information but to ensure they received any assistance they might need.

After the dismal supposed rehearsal at Yuma, the final plan started to be formed. Delta continued to have concerns about the helicopter crews. At the task force, the matter was addressed, and the decision was made to turn to the Marine Corps to take over from most of the Navy pilots that were initially assigned. The rationale was that the Marines would have more experience in flying long-range overland missions. When Colonel Beckwith questioned the decision not to use Air Force pilots or Army pilots, he was again informed that he would not be involved in that decision. In the task force, Marine Colonel Charles Pitman was assigned to coordinate the helicopter options. He was a qualified CH-53 pilot and was one of the military assistants to General David Jones, the Chairman of the Joint Chiefs. He traveled to the CIA facility and took it upon himself to review what Delta was doing. That made me angry as we never had the same opportunity to review what the helicopter crews were doing. After the meeting, several of us, including Pitman and me, were to fly back on a CIA plane to Washington, DC. I played a mind game with him. I sensed that he wanted to seat himself in the co-pilot's seat. I let everyone else get on board except for Pitman. He kept looking at me, and I just gave him a blank look. He finally asked me, "Are you a pilot?" I looked him in the eye, and said, "Of course, I flew 50 kamikaze missions in World War II. That's why they call me Chicken Teriyaki." Pitman didn't know what to say. I laughed and said, "I guess you want to get in the co-pilot's seat." He replied affirmatively, and I told him that this one time I would give him the chance to do so. He learned never to screw with Wade Ishimoto!

CHAPTER 13

Eagle Claw—The Final Plan

By mid-December 1979, the key elements of the Eagle Claw plan were in place. During the planning phase, the term Rice Bowl was used, because it was thought to have no connection to a rescue attempt in Iran. Once the operations plan became an operations order, it would be known as Operation Eagle Claw. Although details remained to be worked out, the essence of the plan was:

- Prior to the launch of the mission force, preparatory events were to happen inside Iran. This included reconnaissance of the Ministry of Foreign Affairs where three hostages were located; additional attempts to collect intelligence on hostage locations; and the procurement of vehicles, along with a place to store them and fuel. In addition, a reconnaissance of a desert refueling station would have to occur. We would send a four-person advance party into Tehran about a week before the mission launch.
- An intermediate staging base would be established in Wadi Qena, Egypt, at a former MIG-21 air base built by the Soviet Union for Egypt. Two forward staging bases would be established, one on Masirah Island off the coast of Oman, and the other on board the USS *Nimitz*, from where the helicopters would fly.
- On day one and night one of the mission, the ground force would fly out of Wadi Qena to Masirah Island and then transfer onto MC-130 and EC-130 aircraft to fly into Iran to a desert refueling site. One MC-130 would depart Masirah at the same time the helicopters were launching from the *Nimitz*, and an hour ahead of the other MC and EC-130s. The flight from Masirah to the refueling site would take about four hours and 30 minutes on the MC-130. Should that first MC-30 crash land due to the surface's inability to support the weight of the aircraft, the mission would be aborted. If the landing was successful, roadblock security would be established. An hour later, two MC-130s with the ground force would land, along with three EC-130s with fuel bladders and pumps on board. The helicopters were also expected to land at that time.

- The ground force would board the helicopters and fly for about two hours and 30 minutes to Garmsar, a semi-remote location about 80 kilometers southeast of Tehran. They would be met by the advance party. The ground force would disembark from the helicopters and proceed to camouflage themselves. Then the helicopters would fly into the surrounding mountainous area and conceal themselves.
- On night two the advance party would return to the Garmsar area. They would meet drivers provided by the CIA, as well as U.S. personnel who spoke Farsi, who were called driver monitors. They would then take them to the warehouse to pick up the vehicles. The vehicles would subsequently return to Garmsar, pick up the ground force, and transport them to the embassy and Ministry of Foreign Affairs.
- Also on night two, a company of Rangers would embark on two MC-130s from Wadi Qena towards a hard-surfaced landing strip used by the Iranian Air Force, located adjacent to a bombing range. The Manzariyeh airstrip had no facilities and was believed to be unmanned. If obstacles were seen on the runway or if there were personnel on the ground, the Rangers would parachute in, remove the obstacles and deal with the personnel. If not, an air landing would take place. Also flying out of Wadi Qena would be four AC-130 Spectre gunships continuing to Tehran to provide close air support. Air refueling would be carried out over Saudi Arabia. Two C-141 jet transports would fly out of Dharan, Saudi Arabia, and land at Manzariyeh. They would be used to evacuate the hostages and rescue forces from Iran.
- The hostages would be recovered at the embassy and taken across a six-lane street into a soccer stadium. The helicopters would be called in to transport everyone to Manzariyeh. At the Ministry of Foreign Affairs, the hostages and rescue force would relocate to one of two nearby parks and call for helicopters to transport them to Manzariyeh. It was hoped that the ground operations would take around 30 minutes to carry out.
- At Manzariyeh, the helicopters would be destroyed, and everyone flown out on the two MC-130s and two C-141 planes. The need for medical care would determine where they would first land.

Clearly, this was a complex plan with many things that could go wrong. The complexity was based on two significant factors: the first was the lack of close-in launch bases from where helicopters could accomplish the mission in one night without refueling. The second was the scarcity of air-refuelable helicopters in our military inventory. As previously mentioned, other concepts had been explored and the one selected was the only feasible option. I will question that choice for as long as I live.

From the time the general plan was created until the following April when the mission was launched, myriad details had to be attended to for the plan to succeed.

Geologists and imagery interpreters set out to find an appropriate unimproved landing zone in the Dasht-e-kavir, the great salt desert of Iran. For reasons not known to me, they selected a site along a dirt road that was a major route through the desert. The CIA supplied native Iranians to be used as drivers, and Delta proceeded to train them and assess their character. All of them passed the Delta operators' scrutiny. The driver monitors also had to be trained. There were few Farsi speakers available, and it was difficult for the task force to find them. One of those selected was Navy Captain John Butterfield. John was a Naval aviator and a professor at the U.S. Naval Academy in Annapolis, Maryland. He was taken from his instructional duties and impressed as a driver monitor. He didn't feel qualified to do the job but he put his heart and soul into it, and I knew he would be capable.

The decision to move the hostages from the embassy compound across the then Roosevelt Avenue (a six-lane street) to the Amjadiyeh Soccer Stadium was based on speculation that two large fields inside the embassy compound were mined or booby-trapped. Intelligence indicated that poles had been erected on these fields possibly as anti-helicopter obstacles. However, intelligence also showed that the poles were being knocked down and not replaced. Vehicles were being moved in and out of those fields daily, which gave credence to the thought that the fields were not mined or booby-trapped. Two helicopters could land in the embassy fields at one time while only one could land in the soccer stadium, which would add to the time required to evacuate the hostages and rescue force, thereby prolonging the evacuation. When the plan was hatched to go to the soccer stadium, I told Colonel Beckwith that the only difference between that and the Alamo was that Davy Crockett didn't have to fight his way into the Alamo. I was referring to the battle in 1836 when a vastly superior Mexican force annihilated those defending the Alamo mission in a fight for Texas independence from Mexico. Beckwith promptly fired me! I shrugged my shoulders and went back to work. Getting fired by Charlie was a common occurrence. I knew that if he were serious, he would soon follow up and insist that I leave. He never did!

I began to work on an evasion and escape plan. As I assessed the situation, the chances of successfully evading and escaping out of Iran were remote. Regardless, I had to give it a try. I asked Al, the former Savak operative, to prepare a pointee-talkee (Farsi phrases followed by an English translation). A request for maps was placed. The CIA began to assemble money packets of both U.S. dollars and Iranian rials. The quest to find friendly Iranians to hide and smuggle out evaders was futile. The other constraint was the distance from friendly territory from which combat search and rescue missions could be launched. It was a bleak picture.

With the core plan in place, Colonel Beckwith weighed whether Delta should remain at the CIA facility or return to Fort Bragg for morale purposes and because of the ability to conduct more detailed training. He wisely decided to return to Fort Bragg. Delta was moved back in increments to maintain operations security. Andy Almueti, our S4 noncommissioned officer in charge, and I were the last to leave. We took off on a C-130 loaded with ammunition, explosives, and weapons. There was no place to sit. We once again flew out at night at a low level to preserve operations security.

I arrived home to meet a very distraught Mi Hye. I had a lot of explaining to do, but she was happy I was home, and so was I. There was additional stress placed on both of us when I found out that I was to be evicted from enlisted housing because I had been brought on active duty as an officer. No company-grade officer houses were available, which meant that we would have to look for a place to rent or buy. Fortunately, I could link up with Nick Goresh, who had been an officer in the 1st Special Forces Group on Okinawa when I was there. Nick had left the Army and was a real estate agent. He did a tremendous job, and we submitted an offer on a house in the Kinwood area of Fayetteville adjacent to Methodist University, which was accepted. It was a nice house but needed attention because the previous owners had divorced and not maintained the house.

Reunited with the intelligence team, I no longer had to work the 20 hours a day I had during isolation. The hours were still long, but I would rush home to clean the house we were buying after closing, painting it, and doing some repairs. We moved into the house in February but still had not finished unpacking. At the end of February, I had just finished eating lunch in the Delta mess hall when I was informed that Logan Fitch and I were to be sent to Bogota, Colombia. Our mission was to respond to a hostage event where the M-19 Communist Organization had seized the Dominican Republic Embassy. Diplomats from some 19 countries, including Diego Asencio, the U.S. Ambassador, were held hostage.

This time I could call home and let Mi Hye know that I was departing on an emergency trip. Logan and I were instructed to get to Miami International Airport where we would transfer onto a CIA plane going to Bogota. My guys checked and saw there was no way we could get commercial flights in time to meet the CIA plane. They contacted a private company at Grannis Field in Fayetteville and arranged for a charter flight to Miami. Logan and I grabbed our flyaway bags with civilian clothes and headed for the airport. Roger Ahrens, Delta's finance officer, had given me $10,000 in cash. When Logan and I got to the airport, the owner of the plane asked me how I would pay, and I said, "In cash." His eyes got big, and I think he thought Logan and I were criminals. He asked his friend to accompany us on the flight, and I noticed that he had a .44 magnum revolver in a shoulder holster!

The plane was a single-engine Beechcraft Bonanza, and it would take over three hours to get to Miami. The flight was uneventful until we got close to Miami. The pilot informed us that his transponder was not working and that he could not land at Miami International Airport. He said he could land at Opa-Locka Airport, some 10 miles away. Logan asked the pilot to call a taxicab to meet us. Upon landing, we grabbed our bags and boarded the taxi. Logan offered a $50 tip for the driver if he could get us to Miami post haste. The driver tried, but we missed the CIA plane.

I then bought tickets on an Avianca Airlines flight leaving the next morning and informed Delta headquarters what had happened. The next morning, we boarded a Boeing 747 that was also carrying chickens and livestock! We landed at El Dorado International Airport in Bogota where we were met by the Defense Attaché's Office, and taken to the U.S. Embassy where we linked up with Burr Smith, Delta's CIA liaison who had flown to Bogota on the CIA plane we had missed, and Marty Hawkins, the CIA Chief of Station.

Our mission was to see if the Colombian government would accept Delta attempting a rescue of the hostages; if not, then to render whatever assistance they might ask for. This weighed heavily on Logan as he commanded Delta's B Squadron, and we knew things were heating up regarding a rescue attempt in Tehran. After a few days, it was evident that the Colombian government did not want to ask the U.S. to attempt a hostage rescue. Burr, Logan, and I had been playing a numbers game to see who would buy the next meal. We made the decision that two of us could return to the States. So, we played one more game of numbers to see who would stay. I had won every other time, but now I lost. It was not until the end of March 1980 that I received permission to leave.

To maintain a low profile, the CIA arranged for me to live in a "house of ill repute." It was noisy at night with the "business" being conducted. Every day, I would walk to the embassy to review intelligence coming in and provide analysis to the Colombians. The CIA also sent an American of Japanese ancestry to assist with technical collection. He was of more value than me. Anyway, I was able to make some contributions. One of the big helps was the media. They infiltrated Colombian security and were taking photographs of the Dominican Republic Embassy and often would have shots of people inside. The media was also bringing out voice recordings. On one occasion, Marty Hawkins's people were puzzled by what they heard from a media recording. I put two and two together and determined that two of the terrorists were having sex! I guess my ears were attuned from the time staying at my lodgings! As it turned out months later, two of the men were jealous of each other and had a duel after they had received safe passage out of Colombia.

There were two other interesting things during my time in Bogota. The first was that the U.S. Southern Command was somewhat peeved when they discovered that a lowly captain was representing the U.S. Military. They then sent a lieutenant colonel to be their representative. What they didn't know was that the lieutenant colonel and I struck up a great friendship. He was in Special Forces, and we bonded well. The other interesting thing was that Ambassador Asencio was trying to give orders to those in the embassy. He was allowed frequent phone calls to the embassy, but the embassy patiently explained that he could not be in charge as he was a hostage. The Department of State resolved the issue by sending a special envoy to Bogota who—very nicely—informed Ambassador Asencio that he was in charge. Towards the end of March, I learned that President Carter had decided to mount the hostage rescue attempt in Iran. Without revealing the details, but with Marty Hawkins's help, the special envoy allowed me to return home. The Dominican Embassy hostage event did not end until the end of April when a ransom was paid, giving the terrorists safe passage to Cuba.

I got home to a very distressed Mi Hye who had been left to unpack and get things in the house organized in the month that I was gone. I learned that a day or so after I left for Colombia, there was a snowstorm in Fayetteville. Mi Hye needed to get some groceries and the only thing she could find to clear the driveway of snow was a broom and dustpan. She didn't have a support group of friends to help her, and she again showed her indomitable spirit and strength. The house we had moved into was the tenth place that she had lived in our eight years of marriage. I could not have married a better woman. For all military units, but particularly for those engaged in quick reaction and covert operations, it is essential to have family support measures as part of a unit's obligation to care for its men, women and families.

Upon my return to work, my guys quickly briefed me on the developments concerning the Eagle Claw mission. They told me that Colonel Beckwith had been summoned to the White House with General Vaught to brief President Carter. The President was concerned that diplomatic initiatives to release the hostages were at a standstill and that there was a chance of some of the hostages would be executed. Beckwith clearly stated that the mission was a high-risk one. Nonetheless, President Carter gave his approval to conduct a reconnaissance of the Desert One refueling site and to send two Detachment A personnel to reconnoiter the Ministry of Foreign Affairs because of the lack of information on the location where three hostages were being held. I learned there was a bit of humor when Vice President Mondale was curious about how flex-cuffs (plastic ties used to restrain people) worked. His hands were bound in a pair of flex-cuffs. No one had the tools to cut them open! The Secret Service detail promptly found a tool and cut the Vice President loose.

Clem Lemke and Scotty McEwan from Detachment A were launched into Tehran to garner intelligence on the Ministry of Foreign Affairs. They were overseen by Major Jim Magee, the European Command liaison to the task force. Jim gave Clem and Scotty explicit instruction that they would not attempt to go inside the Ministry of Foreign Affairs nor contact any Iranians guarding it. Clem and Scotty had experience at crossing into Soviet bloc countries undercover. They used that experience to determine that they would disobey Jim Magee. Accordingly, they came back from Tehran with close-up pictures of the Ministry with details of the structure in the background of the photographs and their arms draped around Iranian guards! What they did greatly assisted Detachment A in their planning to rescue the three hostages. Clem and Scotty displayed the courage and ingenuity that sets Special Forces apart from the conventional military.

The reconnaissance of the Desert One refueling site was also conducted at the end of March. The CIA launched a De Havilland twin-engine plane from a Persian Gulf nation with a four-part mission. Firstly, were the gaps in Iranian radar confirmed? Secondly, could a twin-engine plane land successfully on the desert floor? Thirdly, take soil samples to ascertain that the surface could bear up to the weight of C-130 aircraft. Lastly, emplace remotely triggered landing lights supplied by the CIA. Major John Carney had the mission to take soil samples and array the landing lights. The plane's pilot was Jim Rhyne, a legendary figure who had lost one leg while flying for Air America in Laos during the Vietnam conflict. The co-pilot was Bud McBroom. Bud had been both enlisted and an officer in Special Forces during Vietnam and had suffered from a reduction in force but became an Army warrant officer aviator. After retirement, he was hired by the CIA.

The Desert One reconnaissance was a huge success. A car radar detector was used to confirm the accuracy of the gaps in Iranian air traffic and military air defense radars. The car radar detector could pick up the radar bands used for air control. The landing was successful, and John Carney set out on a mini motorbike to emplace the landing lights. He was looking for a bend in the dirt road and could not find it. He returned to the airplane and Bud McBroom informed John that they had landed on the opposite side of the road to where John thought they had landed. He quickly set out again and set the landing lights in a planned pattern. He also took the soil samples. While they were at Desert One, they saw several vehicles passing by. Bud McBroom quietly started singing the song Chattanooga Choo-Choo. Bud showed the typical humor under stressful situations that many Special Forces soldiers display.

With the successful conduct of the two reconnaissance missions, everything was now in place to conduct the Eagle Claw mission. Although there was not an abundance of intelligence, the feeling was that there was adequate intelligence to be able to succeed with the mission. All involved knew that it was a high-risk mission but were determined to try our best. No matter what we might have personally thought about President Carter, he had the courage to authorize the rescue mission. The date was set for the nights of April 24 and 25, 1980.

CHAPTER 14

Conducting the Rescue Attempt

With the dates now set, last-minute preparations were underway. On the intelligence side, daily briefings continued but little change happened to affect the mission. The intelligence section assembled the evasion and escape packets that would be issued to each operator. The packets consisted of five maps printed on special plastic, a money package with both U.S. dollars and Iranian rials, signal panels, and a pointee-talkee with English and Farsi. Instructions were also given on a safe area for evasion and how to set out signal panels for observation from the air. Some operators asked me to obtain aviation FLIP booklets (Flight Information Packets). I intuitively knew they might attempt to find a light plane and fly it out. Typical of Delta operators, many had a Plan B in mind. A few approached me and asked me for my opinion on taking refuge in the British Embassy. I pointed out that was not a good idea as the Iranians would undoubtedly enter that embassy, especially after knowing how the Canadians had hidden six Americans after the initial hostage takeover. They then said that they would proceed to the Soviet Embassy instead. I also advised that was not a good idea because the Soviets were not friendly towards America and might turn them over to the Iranians or that the Iranians would also invade the Soviet Embassy. They then looked at me and asked what the hell I was going to do. I took my fingertips, moved them to the corner of my eyelids and raised them to create a very slanted eye picture. I then, in broken English, said, "I go Japan, or the Korean Embassy!" I was fortunate not to have my butt kicked!

While the unit was waiting to deploy, a burglar broke into the home of one of the operators, named Hobson. Hobson shot him fatally. Charlie Beckwith commented that he knew for sure that he had at least one guy who wouldn't be afraid to kill a bad guy. A final rehearsal was scheduled at the Nevada Test Site with the EMAD building used to replicate the U.S. Embassy. This building was the site of Delta's first exercise using the Nevada Test Site in 1978. In the early morning of April 18, my pager went off with a coded message to report immediately to the unit. Mi Hye woke up and asked me where I was going. I couldn't lie to her and said, "Iran." She shrugged her shoulders in disbelief, but was probably wondering, "What next?"

When I got to the unit, Dick Potter, Delta's deputy commander, told me that I would accompany him along with Willie Welsch and Joe Sumakeris to be the advance party at the Intermediate Staging Base at Wadi Qena, Egypt. We flew to Washington, DC, the next morning and checked into a Marriott Hotel near Boundary Channel Drive within walking distance of the Pentagon. That motel no longer exists. At the Pentagon, I was tasked to prepare Fred Arooji to go in on the four-person DOD advance party. I caught a taxi to go to the CIA facility in downtown Washington, DC, where they had their Cover Documentation Office and picked up Fred's papers. The documents were handed to me by Tony Mendes, who had gone into Iran in January to help bring out the six Americans that the Canadian Embassy had hidden. I was dismayed to find that all the documents were brand new, including a vinyl wallet. On the way back to the Pentagon, I rubbed some of the documents in my hands and with my feet to make them seem older. In the Pentagon parking lot, I put the vinyl wallet on the asphalt and scuffed it with my shoes.

I sat down with Fred Arooji and had him inspect the documents to see if he believed they were adequate for his cover. He did so and was only concerned about one piece of information. I wet my thumb and index finger and gently rubbed over that piece of information, causing it to be smudged. That satisfied Fred and he was ready to be launched into Iran to join Clem Lemke, Scotty McEwan, and Dick Meadows as the four-person advance party. I asked Fred if he had any questions or concerns. He quietly asked me if I would care for his family if he did not return. I solemnly promised him that I would do so. I then told him a lie. I told him he would be protected by my *mana*. I described scuffing the vinyl wallet in the parking lot but then lied and said that I pissed on it, so he had my *mana* with him. I never cracked a smile, so he did not know if I was serious or not. Nonetheless, he left satisfied that his family would be cared for. I then saw him to a taxi to take a commercial flight into Iran.

Early in the morning of April 19, we gathered in the Pentagon parking lot and took a bus to Andrews Air Force Base, boarded a C-141 that flew to Ramstein, Germany, and then on to Wadi Qena. I was instructed to proceed to the task force headquarters, which was at the far end of the Wadi Qena runway, in a facility that was air-conditioned and with secure communications for the task force. Dick Potter, Willie Welsch, and Joe Sumakeris proceeded to the other end of the runway where three former MIG-21 hangars were set aside to house Delta and the Rangers. The three of them found that the hangars were being used as latrines. There was human excrement on the floor and on the walls. Dick immediately went to the U.S. Air Force detachment responsible for Wadi Qena and demanded a fire truck and disinfectant. I was told that the Air Force major whom Dick approached for help was not willing to do so. I later heard that Dick promptly did some talking with his fists. The fire truck and disinfectant arrived post haste! When the rest of

At FBI Headquarters with Jimmy Adams, John Simeone, John Otto, Ulrich Wegener, Charlie Beckwith, and Jim Mackenzie, 1982.

John Kolman and I present a statue in memory of the ATF agents killed at Waco, TX, to ATF Director John Magaw, 1993.

On the Downing Task Force for the Khobar Towers bombing, 1996.

The aftermath of the Khobar Towers bombing in 1996 (Department of Defense)

Receiving the National Defense Industrial Association Rylander Award with Fred Raines and Admiral Ed Giambastiani, 2005.

Visiting the Sir David Stirling statue with 22 SAS, 2006.

Visit to the Japan Self-Defense Force with the Vice Chief of Staff, 2007.

With Lieutenant General Mochida J3 on the Japan Self-Defense Force visit, 2007.

Visit to Special Operations group, Japanese Ground Defense Force, at Camp Narashino, Japan, in 2006.

Gift exchange with Special Boat Unit, 2006.

PASOC conference with Japanese, Korean, and PRC attendees, 2007.

Movement in Iraq, 2007, in an armored vehicle.

Sitting In Saddam Hussein's chair, Iraq, 2007.

With Louis Zeisman, Water Palace, Iraq, November 9, 2005.

Iraq with Lieutenant Trooper Smith and Sergeant Flores of security detail, 2007.

With my personal security detail, Iraq, 2007.

Qatar visit with USAF Med Team supporting Special Ops, 2007

Kuwait with nephew Ben Dennis, 2007.

With Larry Reiman at the gravesite of mentor General Robert Kingston.

Pacific Area Special Operations Conference Hawaii, 2010.

Shinbudo Aikido seminar group, 2013.

Aikido 6th Dan.

Induction as a Distinguished Member of the SF Regiment, 2014.

Instructing Slovakian Special Operations in 2014.

Grupa Reagowania Operacyjno-Manewrowego, which translates to "Group for Operational Maneuvering Response," Poland's premier Special Operations unit.

SOCPAC visit with Paul Zeisman, Bryan Fenton, Gervin Miyamoto, Ed Bugarin, JC Cruz, and Jim Kyle, 2016.

Special Forces augmentation to the Defense Prisoner of War/Missing in Action Accounting Agency, Hawaii, 2016.

DPAA Hawaii with JC Cruz, Lynn Mariano Bob Silva Craig Chamberlain, and Brigadier General Spindler, 2016.

Halekulani Hotel with Gervin Miyamoto and Chandi Duke Heffner.

Pat and Malina, Mi Hye and me, Joyce and Tom Kaulukukui.

At SOC Africa with Rear Admiral Brian and Ivy Losey and their son, 2018.

With Dave Gibbs, Brian and Ivy Losey, and Blake Edwards in Stuttgart.

Induction into the USSOCOM Commando Hall of Honor, with General Tony Thomas and Command Sergeant Major Pat McCaulay.

At William & Mary College with Major General Joe Caravalho, Karen Conlin, and Kay Wakatake, 2018.

With Lieutenant General Mike Nagata.

With Colonel Magne Rohdahl in Norway, 2018.

With Major General Ed Reeder.

With Lieutenant General John Mulholland and General Mark Milley, 2022.

With Generals Joe Votel and Tony Thomas, 2023.

Peter Schoomaker, Army Chief of Staff.    Assistant Secretary of Defense Tom O'Connell.

With my Santa Clara University generals—Eldon Requa, Joe Peterson, and Garrett Yee.

the task force arrived a day and a half later, and thanks to Dick, Willie, and Joe, they had a clean place to bed down.

I was standing with Tim Casey, the Special Forces captain, who had done yeoman's work for Task Force J2, when Charlie Beckwith came up to me and told me to go in with the Ranger Roadblock Security Team. Although Beckwith never said it, I knew he had little faith in Major Jesse Johnson, who was supposed to be in charge of the Roadblock Team, and who was seen sunbathing at the task force headquarters while everyone else was gainfully involved in preparations. Tim would later remark that he was astonished to see how calmly I reacted, and continued with my intelligence duties. I then quickly walked to my sleeping area to gather my pistol and rifle, and the indigenous backpack that I had carried in Vietnam, including on the day that I was to masquerade as the supposed double agent Chuyen going on his last mission. Tim also urged me to take his camera in with me. However, I declined, explaining that I had too much else to take in. Hindsight is always good, I would have been able to take historical pictures had I taken Tim's camera with me.

We learned that the four-person advance party had all safely arrived in Tehran and had linked up with each other. They saw no changes in the situation around the embassy and Ministry of Foreign Affairs that would alter the mission. On the night of April 23, last-minute briefings, along with a rehearsal by the Roadblock Team, were held. I went out for the rehearsal and observed Jesse Johnson not saying a word to the Rangers. It was clear to me that he was not in charge and not leading the team. After the rehearsal, I returned to the task force headquarters and checked with Tim Casey to see if there were any new developments of interest. There were none, so I left to get a good night's sleep.

I awoke the next morning and learned that Howard Bane had awoken Charlie Beckwith in the middle of the night and told him there was a breakthrough in intelligence. He related that the Pakistani cook in the U.S. Embassy was leaving Tehran and coincidentally sat next to a CIA operative. As they chatted, the cook stated that all the hostages were inside the Chancery building on the embassy grounds. My immediate thought was this had to be a fabrication and that it was unbelievable that the cook and the agent would sit next to each other. I sought out Jim Sterling and Big Bill Dickey and asked them for the truth. They told me that the story about the cook and the operative sitting next to each other was a lie. However, they also told me that the true source was the cook's wife and the information she provided was based on her involvement in food preparation and delivery to the hostages. Her contention that all the hostages were inside the Chancery Building could not be confirmed.

I was now faced with a dilemma. Should I go to Colonel Beckwith and tell him that the story told by Bane was concocted? I knew that if I did, it would place doubt in the minds of those going on the mission. Instead, I decided to see if the operations plan had been changed. There was little change, the priority remained that of searching for the hostages inside the compound, including the three locations where we suspected that they might be held. That convinced me not to say a word to avoid doubt in the minds of the operators. I returned to the task force headquarters to change and prepare to leave. I saw Howard Bane looking disoriented and asked him what the matter was. He told me he couldn't find a shirt. Disgusted, but hiding my feelings, I took the shirt off my back and gave it to him and put on another shirt. I never got my shirt back!

I then returned to the far end of the runway and the hangar, where the ground force was preparing to leave. Charlie Beckwith stood on a platform in the hangar and gave a pep talk to everyone. After that, Jerry Boykin led us in prayer. Jerry was then followed by Bucky Burruss who would be the deputy to Charlie on the mission as Dick Potter was designated to be the rear area commander. It was a somber moment as we boarded the C-141 Starlifters that would take us from Wadi Qena to the forward staging base on Masirah Island. I noted that there was no frivolity, but a calm and determined look in the eyes of the operators.

The shortest route from Wadi Qena to Masirah would have been to fly over Saudi Arabia. For operations security, we flew down the Red Sea and up the Indian Ocean to get to Masirah. It was about a six-and-a-half-hour flight. The U.S. Air Force took great care of us. We sat on the equivalent of business class seats that were wider to help accommodate the equipment being carried in, and we had steak for dinner. The flight was uneventful, and we landed at Masirah mid-afternoon on April 24. Trucks were awaiting us, and we were transported to where tent canopies had been erected. There were cots and lots of water to allow everyone to get some additional rest and to keep out of the broiling sun as it was well over 100 degrees Fahrenheit.

Sticking to the operations plan, about 40 of us gathered to get on the first MC-130 that would leave Masirah an hour ahead of the other planes and simultaneously the helicopters would launch from the USS *Nimitz*. I waited for Jesse Johnson to gather the Rangers for last-minute instructions. He was nowhere to be seen. So, I gathered the Rangers and slightly modified how they would load the aircraft with the motorcycles and jeep. I also briefed them on evasion and escape. The last modification I made was to plan the actions upon landing at Desert One. I instructed Staff Sergeant Littlejohn that he should move to the rear of the aircraft when we were close to landing. Then, upon landing, and on my signal, he and I would depart the aircraft with Littlejohn moving forward of the plane to establish initial security, while I would move to the rear to do the same.

Johnson sauntered over after I had finished the final planning with the Rangers and asked me what was going on. It was all I could do from lashing out at him, but I calmly told him what the plan was upon landing. Shortly before takeoff, Sergeant First Class Glen Nickel offered Dramamine tablets to everyone as he knew the flight would be rough. Glen was an operator who had been a Special Forces medic before joining Delta. He had made sergeant first class in seven years and was an outstanding person. I didn't think that Glen had been in actual combat beforehand, but I looked at his eyes, saw his calm demeanor, and knew that I could count on him and he would do well in combat.

We boarded the MC-130 sometime after 4 PM. I checked to see where the Rangers were seated and proceeded to the rear of the airplane. I knew it would be about a four-and-a-half-hour flight to get to Desert One, the refueling site, and that we would be flying at low level and likely to be filled with turbulence. I took the Dramamine pill that Glen Nickel had given me and promptly went to sleep. At the same time that we took off, eight helicopters were lifting off the USS *Nimitz*. The captain of the *Nimitz* had developed a plan to get away from the Soviet trawler that was surveilling the *Nimitz* battle group. As soon as they were out of visual range of the trawler, the helicopters took off.

In Tehran, a sticky situation developed that we only learned about weeks later. On the morning of April 24, Fred Arooji and Dick Meadows went to the warehouse storing the vehicles that were to be used on night two of the operation to check on them. They saw a huge ditch dug across the warehouse driveway and knew that it would be impossible to drive the vehicles across the ditch. Fred saw an old man squatting by the roadside and quickly concocted a cover story. He approached the man and acted like he was in a panic. He told the man that his family would go bankrupt if he couldn't get the perishable produce inside the warehouse to market and pleaded for help to get the ditch filled in. The old man kindly offered to help, gathered his family, and filled in the ditch so that the trucks could be driven out.

On board the MC-130, the pilots reported that we had overflown the helicopters and that they were flying in formation. All appeared well at that time. I had set my biological clock and woke up about 30 minutes out of Desert One. I sought out Staff Sergeant Littlejohn and reminded him to come to the rear of the plane per the plan I had made before leaving Masirah. I found out later that as we approached Desert One, the crew had seen a vehicle passing through the landing zone. They did a so-called racetrack—an oval turn that allowed the vehicle to proceed through the landing zone—so that we could land undetected. I was standing on the rear ramp as we landed and swore it was a smooth landing. Perhaps it was the adrenaline flowing through me. Chief Warrant Officer Paul Zeisman, Delta's senior communications warrant officer, told me later that it was a very rough landing, and that a radio and other equipment were tossed onto the aircraft floor upon landing. The plane taxied on the desert floor for a short bit. The clamshell doors at the rear opened, and based on what I had worked out with the crew chief, he signaled when we were about to stop. I then signaled Littlejohn and he and I exited the plane. As planned, Littlejohn moved forward of the plane to establish initial security and I moved to the rear to do the same.

***

What happened next is described in the preface—the bus emerged through the blowing dust, Littlejohn fired a 40 mm grenade round that impacted in front of the bus and caused it to stop, and Rubio and I took off down the dirt road to get to our position. That was followed by encountering a 3,000-gallon fuel truck, stopping it with small arms fire and a light antitank weapon, and then seeing another truck approaching. As I related at the beginning of this book, it took over a minute to start the motorcycle and Rubio's night vision goggles weren't working. On my direction he tried to catch the second truck, returning when he wasn't able to do so. While waiting, I picked up the expended cartridges I had fired at the truck and checked my M-16 magazine. I would have sworn that I fired six rounds at the truck—I had fired 17 rounds.

Mike McGirr and Curt Massey joined Robert and me and we were soon reinforced by seven others. Mike McGirr asked me if I had anything to eat with me. He had thrown up on the ride into Desert One and was hungry! All I had was a small box of raisins which Mike devoured instantly. I deployed everyone in an ambush position and was thinking what else could go wrong. I reached into my backpack to grab one of the four radios I had and found that one was missing. Mike Lampe, one of the combat controllers, brought the radio that Carl Savory found (it had managed to bounce out of my backpack) as Rubio and I set off down the road. While waiting for the helicopters to arrive, I had a strong urge to defecate. I walked off into the desert, dug a cat hole, did my business, and made sure the tracks leading to the cat hole were visible. I perversely hoped that some Iranian would discover the cat hole and think it held something important! What a surprise they would get when they uncovered the hole!

Back at the bus, the passengers were panicky. I learned later that there were over 40 passengers on board. They were calmed down by the Farsi speakers we had on the mission. We decided they could not be left at Desert One. A plan was quickly formulated which called for the passengers to be flown out of Desert One back to Wadi Qena. On the second night of the mission, the passengers would be flown back into Iran and left at the Manzariyeh departure airstrip. They would be left far from their intended destination when the bus was stopped. However, they would be alive, safe, and would have the opportunity to ride different airplanes!

The truck continued burning for over two hours. Unfortunately, the location was close to where John Carney had placed the landing lights, so the flames made the landing lights almost useless. On the bright side, there was over 50% illumination that night and the truck fire still gave a good view of the landing zone. About an hour after the first C-130 had landed, the other six C-130s came in right on schedule. The three EC-130s with fuel bladders and pumps arrayed themselves to receive and refuel the helicopters with the combat control team ready to guide them to an appropriate EC-130. Two of the MC-130s, including the first one into Desert One, flew out and back to Wadi Qena. All of us on the ground were wondering where the helicopters were. Strict radio silence was being practiced and we had no idea where they might be.

As I recall, about 57 minutes after the second flight of C-130s had landed, a lone helicopter approached Desert One. It was piloted by Major Jim Schaeffer. Jim was the lead trainer for all the helicopter crews and was a very capable pilot. Jim gave a briefing to Colonels Beckwith and Kyle. He said that the launch from the *Nimitz* went fine, and spirits were high. They gathered in formation and followed their planned flight path into Iran. Shortly after crossing the coastline of Iran, one of the helicopters showed a blade imminent failure light that was an indicator of a significant safety problem, which might cause the helicopter to crash. Following safety procedures, they landed in a remote area where another helicopter landed and picked up the crew. That left seven of the original eight helicopters.

The helicopters regathered in formation and entered an area of suspended dust. The plan called for them to communicate using flashing light signals, but there was zero visibility in the suspended dust making communication using lights impossible. For safety reasons, the formation was broken. They came out of the suspended dust and once more gathered in formation only to enter a much larger area of suspended dust. Jim Schaeffer had no idea where the others were as strict radio silence was being practiced. Within 20 minutes, five other helicopters landed at Desert One. No one knew what happened to the seventh helicopter. As we discovered later, #5 had turned back during the second area of suspended dust and flew back to the USS *Nimitz*. They were about 30 minutes away from Desert One when they did so. They claimed they had navigational problems. The question I continue to ask is if they had navigational issues, then how could they locate the USS *Nimitz* in the Indian Ocean and fly back to it?

Regardless of where the seventh helicopter was, there were still six available. Six helicopters were the minimum required to continue the mission from Desert One. Planning had established this requirement for several reasons, including the potential for mechanical failure, the number of hostages and rescue force personnel to be lifted out of two locations, and the time constraints involved in leaving Tehran and reaching the Manzariyeh airstrip on the second night. The six helicopters were refueled, and the ground force boarded them in preparation to leave for the Garmsar hide site. The seven reinforcements I had received for the roadblock were needed, and I began to shuttle them on the back of the motorcycles.

I later learned that Lieutenant Colonel (USMC) Ed Seiffert, who commanded the helicopters, had done a last-minute check, and found a helicopter with a hydraulic pump glowing red and knew it would fail. He reported the situation to Colonels Beckwith and Kyle. Knowing that the helicopter was doomed to fail, Charlie Beckwith had the tough decision to abort the mission. He and Jim Kyle contacted Major General Vaught via satellite radio and advised him of the need to abort the mission. Vaught supposedly asked Beckwith whether it was possible to continue, and Beckwith responded that it was not advisable. Vaught then confirmed the need to abort. Vaught then contacted General David Jones, the Chairman of the Joint Chiefs, and advised him that the mission was aborted. Jones then informed President Carter. Dick Meadows and the others on the advance party were advised via satellite radio that the mission was aborted, and they began to make plans to leave Tehran the following day.

***

A plan was quickly devised at Desert One. The ground force boarded the three EC-130s and one MC-130 still on the ground and were to return to Masirah Island. The helicopters were to return to the USS *Nimitz*. The bus passengers would be left at Desert One. Jim Schaeffer was the first to lift off the ground. He proceeded forward over the EC-130 that had refueled his helicopter. For some inexplicable reason, his helicopter crashed into the port or left side of the EC-130 that had Delta's B Squadron on board. The helicopter rotor blades sliced into the forward cockpit of the EC-130 and its wing fuel tanks which immediately set off a huge fire followed by explosions when ammunition and explosives on board the helicopter were ignited. Five of the Air Force crew were killed almost immediately. Three enlisted Marines on the back of the helicopter also perished. Miraculously, Jim Schaeffer and his co-pilot were able to struggle out of the helicopter cockpit. They were severely burned but were recovered by the ground force and survived. Delta's B Squadron, led by Major Logan Fitch, began evacuating the EC-130 on the right or starboard side of the airplane. Some were burned, but all survived.

Even during tragedy, there was some humor. Frank McKenna, one of the operators, had been dozing off after he boarded the EC-130. He awoke after the crash and saw his comrades running towards the right rear door. For some reason, Frank thought he was on a HALO jump. He got to the door, flung himself out, spreading his arms and legs as one does on a HALO jump. He smacked face down on the desert floor and never lived that down afterwards. That was the only bit of humor on a tragic night. The crews of the other helicopters abandoned them rather than flying out and boarded the other fixed-wing planes on the ground. They left classified information on board as well as fully encrypted state-of-the art Vinson cryptographic radios.

I was oblivious to what was happening and the helicopter crash into the EC-130. At the time, I was walking backwards towards the planes and helicopters, maintaining security, and looking west while the helicopters and planes were behind me to the east. Because I was assigned only two motorcycles and had a total of 11 people, I was the odd man out as I began shuttling the others back to the helicopters and planes. Robert Rubio was supposed to return to pick me up. As I learned later, he had been yanked off his motorcycle and ordered onto a plane when the accident occurred.

My mind wondered where Robert might be as I continued to walk backwards. I started to formulate a plan for the eventuality that I be left behind. My plan was to commandeer the bus and get as far as I could. Little did I know that the bus had been disabled so I would not be able to drive it anywhere! I heard a vehicle coming up behind me. When I turned around it was Jesse Johnson in the driver's seat and Lieutenant Colonel Carl Savory, our Delta doctor, in the passenger seat. Johnson made a U-turn, slowed the jeep, but would not stop. I literally had to throw my rifle into the jeep and, while running, leapt onto the back. I saw the fire from the crash but wrongly assumed that the helicopters were being destroyed as I was unaware of the plan to fly them from Desert One to the USS *Nimitz*.

As I learned later, if it weren't for Carl Savory, I might very well have been left behind at Desert One. Carl had been informally trying to account for Delta's personnel and did not see me. He approached Jesse Johnson, who was supposed to be the Roadblock leader, and asked him where I was. Johnson reportedly shrugged his shoulders and never responded. Carl, then a lieutenant colonel and former infantry officer before becoming a doctor, pulled rank on Johnson and ordered him to get into the jeep and go back down the desert road to look for me. If not for Carl, I might still be a resident of Iran! I tease Carl continually about the Oriental tradition where once you save another's life, you are responsible for that person—I keep asking him for my monthly stipend, and he keeps telling me the check is in the mail! Thank God for people like Carl Savory. He showed what leadership is about.

***

When we got back to the aircraft, my first concern was to account for Rubio, McGirr, and Massey. The situation was chaotic, and I knew there was a rush to get people on the C-130s to fly out. Reluctantly, I got on board the plane piloted by Captain Jerry Uttaro. Sergeant Major Country Grimes was gesturing at people. I asked him what was going on, and he replied that there was a live grenade on board and we had to find it. I saw one of the helicopter crewmen about to light a cigarette while seated on a fuel bladder. Fortunately, the Air Force crew chief saw that and lashed out with his long microphone cord to keep the cigarette from being lit. The grenade was found and disposed of. Country and I sat next to each other on the web-seating on the right side of the plane. The clamshell doors closed, and we began taxiing for take-off. There was a loud thump and the plane bounced into the air. Jerry Uttaro did a masterful job in keeping control of the plane and getting it off the ground. The airplane reeked of fuel fumes. The crew opened the caps on the top of the plane and began flushing it with hot air to get rid of the fumes. I looked at the sky through the open cap and wondered when we would see an Iranian fighter shoot us down.

Country Grimes was seated to my right. On my left was Jeff Huber, one of our B Squadron operators, next to him was Kent Brown, one of our medics. Jeff had a proverbial thousand-mile stare on his face. I wanted to snap him out of his doldrums and slapped him on his thigh. Jeff gave out a loud yell, and Kent Brown gave me an evil look. I then learned from Country that Jeff had been burned. Country also filled me in on the crash of the helicopter into the EC-130. I really felt stupid. Mostly, it was a very silent flight back to Masirah Island. Country told me that he was thinking about retiring from the Army. I cajoled him and said he needed to stay on. Ironically, I ended up retiring before him.

We landed at Masirah Island, and Country proceeded to account for all of Delta's personnel from the three planes that had flown out of Desert One. I saw that Charlie Beckwith was on the same plane as Country and me. He looked like a broken man. I did an inspection of our plane to see if anything of value had been left behind. The only thing I found was a large bundle of laundry that the bus passengers had put on the plane when the plan was to fly them out of Desert One. A dejected ground force then moved to two C-141s to fly from Masirah to Wadi Qena. One of the C-141s had a mini-hospital that Carl Savory designed. That undoubtedly helped the severely burned to survive. Carl Savory's vision for advanced medical care in the forward battle area set the tone for what is happening today with forward medical treatment that has saved numerous lives. Carl Savory has lived his life in the spirit of *Intoku*—never seeking recognition, always humble and dedicated to helping others.

The flight to Wadi Qena was marked by silence. Clearly, everyone was disappointed at not being able to continue the hostage rescue mission. On landing, we were met by General Vaught and Dick Potter. Howard Bane handed a bottle of whiskey to Charlie Beckwith and he guzzled it down. We gathered our belongings and were getting ready to board the C-141s to return to the States. Charlie Beckwith, undoubtedly influenced by the whiskey, for some insane reason started to berate everyone for leaving weapons and money packages (the evasion and escape kit) behind at Desert One. Sergeant Major Don Simmons respectfully tried to say something about that. Charlie told him to shut up and had other words that he delivered to Don. I don't know anyone who wasn't offended by Charlie's actions. My boss and friend, Wayne Long, shouted, "We have to go back in." I reminded him that we had no helicopters to go back into Iran. Wayne was clearly emotionally upset at the failed mission. The sad fact was that we lacked the helicopter assets to immediately try another rescue. In addition, the Iranian government would undoubtedly do things to make a rescue attempt more difficult.

Back at Masirah Island, Colonel Jim Kyle assembled the MC- and EC-130 crews. They found a pallet of beer with a handwritten sign that said, "Thanks for the Guts to Try." Our British friends had provided the beer and the thanks. Jim Kyle would later write a book titled *The Guts to Try*, which is the definitive account concerning the fixed-wing air operations during Operation Eagle Claw.

At Wadi Qena, we packed our gear and boarded two C-141 planes for a long flight back to America. It was a somber group and most of us slept for most of the flight. I saw Charlie Beckwith seek out Don Simmons and they had a quiet talk. Neither would say what was discussed, but I hope that Charlie apologized to Don. I was so tired that I can't remember whether we landed at Ramstein AFB in Germany to refuel or did a mid-air refueling to return home. I think we landed at Ramstein and that the Detachment A mission members debarked to return to Berlin. We landed at an Air Force base and were transported by bus to the same CIA location where we had been in isolation in November and December 1979. I was asked to remain behind and greet the second C-141 that was due to arrive about one hour later and ensure that everyone would be put on a bus to the CIA facility. When the second group arrived at the CIA facility, I saw the Station Chief Ed Mitchell standing outside to greet us. When he saw me, he ran up to me, gave me a big hug and told me that he was worried about whether I was one of the casualties. I will always remember what Ed did and spoke. He was yet another of those I have been fortunate to know who embodied *Intoku*.

***

We remained at the CIA facility for about a week for operations security reasons. The White House issued a press announcement discussing the failed rescue attempt. In Fayetteville, North Carolina, the *Fayetteville Observer* descended on Fort Bragg to try and find out anything they could. They found out where Charlie Beckwith lived and irresponsibly published a picture of his house with the address prominently displayed. The national news media quickly picked up the story and discussed it on the late evening news. All of this transpired while we were still flying back from Wadi Qena. My extended family in California (Butch and Lei Fernandez) saw the news and got on the phone to call Mi Hye and ask her if I was all right. It was after midnight in Fayetteville when Mi Hye received the call. She was shocked and had no idea if I was okay, and that was another reason that she would develop depression. As a result of the press picture of Charlie Beckwith's house, it was decided that his family needed protection and that Katherine Beckwith would be brought to where we were staying. Country Grimes travelled to Fayetteville and drove Katherine to a 7-11 store where Bucky Burruss and I waited. We transferred Katherine to our car and drove her to Bucky's family home where she was reunited with Charlie.

One of the things on my mind was whether the four-person advance party was able to get out of Tehran. The day after we arrived at the CIA facility, I discovered that Clem Lemke, Scotty McEwan, and Dick Meadows had gotten out on the same flight on April 25. They related that the White House press release indicated there was Iranian help in the rescue attempt. That made it dangerous for Fred Arooji to get out the next day. He took Dick Meadows to Mehrabad International Airport and then returned to his hotel room. He was convinced that Iranian security services would come and get him. After hours of waiting and contemplating his fate upon being arrested, he came to his senses. He then devised a plan, left Tehran, and went to a location hundreds of miles away. After a week, and with some help from a businessman, he went back to Tehran and caught a flight to Frankfurt. He had a phone number and coded phrase to call the CIA base in Frankfurt. When Fred did so, the person who answered hung the phone up on Fred! On the second try, the CIA person came to his senses. Fred was picked up and flown back to the States.

A few days after we got to the CIA facility, we were told that President Carter would visit us and would be accompanied by Zbigniew Brzezinski, the National Security Advisor; Harold Brown, the Secretary of Defense; and Stansfield Turner, the Director of the CIA. Charlie Beckwith told me that I would be Stansfield Turner's escort and that he would arrive before the others. I told Charlie that Wayne Long should be the escort, and he told me to just do what he said! When Turner arrived, Ed Mitchell did the introductions and we had lunch together. Turner asked me to recount what happened at Desert One, and I did so. I was taken aback when he asked me, "What color was the fuel truck?" I wondered what kind of dumb question that was. I kept my cool and reminded him of his time in the Navy and that one could only distinguish shades of grey at night. I went on to say that I was not sure what color the truck was, but it was black after Rubio and I destroyed it.

We stood in formation in a hangar and awaited the arrival of the President, Secretary Brown, and Brzezinski. The President's Secret Service detail looked very nervous as they looked at a bunch of fit, evil-eyed, long-haired, bearded guys! For whatever reason, Charlie had me stand next to the Iranian drivers that the CIA had furnished for the mission. President Carter walked through the formation followed by the three other dignitaries and shook everyone's hand. Brzezinski was taken aback when he came up to Bruno Urbaniak, who said to Brzezinski, "I like your boots." Bruno spoke in Polish and that took Brzezinski by surprise. When President Carter came up to me, he had a quizzical expression on his face as here was the Oriental next to some Iranians. I quickly explained who I was and that the others were patriotic Americans and ex-patriates from Iran who had volunteered to be the mission's drivers. The President nodded his head and thanked me and the Iranians.

While still waiting to return to Fort Bragg, General Vaught summoned Charlie Beckwith to Washington, DC, to appear before the press. Unfortunately, there were some members of the media who implied that Charlie was responsible for the failure. Vaught never made a press appearance himself, nor did he order Colonel Charles Pitman, the ranking officer on board the helicopter that flew back to the USS *Nimitz*, to make an appearance.

We were given clearance to return to Fort Bragg. My intelligence team informed me that the press was constantly surveilling our headquarters. Based on the lesson I had learned from observing the aircraft hijacking in Illinois the previous year, I instructed my guys to implement the "dime" plan and told them when we were scheduled to arrive at Pope Air Force Base adjacent to Fort Bragg. The dime plan was to go to a pay phone, call the local media, and inform them that Delta would soon arrive at the Fayetteville regional airport. The media bought the tip hook, line and sinker and headed to the commercial airport! Ironically, when they got there, by coincidence members of the 82nd Airborne Division were returning from a training exercise. The media immediately assumed they were Delta operators, thrust microphones in their faces and, of course, the young soldiers in the 82nd thrust out their chests and acted like they were from Delta! Meanwhile, Delta arrived at Pope AFB, went to our headquarters, and then went home without attracting any media attention.

We were given a week off from work to help wind down and to attend to our families. Mi Hye was glad to see that I was okay as she had worried herself sick. I took the time to do things around the house. I was in the front yard weeding when I saw a shadow of someone. I slowly turned and saw our 74-year-old neighbor, Flora Felton, standing there with tears in her eyes and her hand outstretched. I stood up, shook her hand, and asked her why she was crying. She then sobbed and said how much she wanted to thank me. I looked at her and asked what she was talking about. She then proceeded to tell me not to lie to her, that she knew I was in Delta, and described the date I had left to go to Washington, DC, before the mission launch. She then gave me a big hug and kept crying. Flora had intuitively figured out these things on her own. She was the proverbial one-person neighborhood watch and greatly cared for her neighbors. Another humble person who embraced the spirit of *Intoku*. God bless people like Flora. I did learn one lesson from that event. It was that operations security couldn't get by an observant neighbor!

CHAPTER 15

Back to Business

After the week off, it was back to business. Intelligence told us that none of the hostages in Tehran had been killed, but that they had been scattered throughout the country. Nevertheless, planning for another rescue attempt continued, especially at the Joint Chiefs of Staff level. The plan was called Honey Badger. General Vaught continued as the Task Force Commander and Air Force Major General Richard Secord was appointed as the deputy. In Delta, there was little planning that could be done because of the lack of information on where the Iranians had relocated the hostages. However, time was spent refining weaponry and individual tactics and skills.

General David Jones, Chairman of the Joint Chiefs, convened a small commission to review Operation Eagle Claw and to provide their observations and recommendations for change. The commission was called the Holloway Commission because the head of it was retired Navy Admiral James Holloway, a former Chief of Naval Operations and Naval aviator. All the commission members were highly regarded. The two with the most Special Operations experience were retired Army Lieutenant General Samuel Wilson and retired Air Force Lieutenant General Leroy Manor. General Wilson had been a member of Merrill's Marauders in World War II, had many assignments with Special Forces, and, towards the end of his career, was the defense attaché to the Soviet Union, the Deputy Director of the CIA, and the Director of the Defense Intelligence Agency. General Manor was most noted for commanding the task force that attempted to rescue American prisoners of war in North Vietnam in 1970. Others on the commission were Army Major General James Smith, an aviator; Air Force Major General John Piotrowski, who had air commando experience; and Marine Major General Al Gray, who had Special Operations experience and would later become commandant of the Marine Corps. They began their review in May 1980 and published their report in August 1980. Interestingly, all six members of the commission approved the report's findings.

Admiral Holloway had these words to say at the beginning of the unclassified Holloway Commission Report, July 1980:

The concept of a small clandestine operation was valid and consistent with national policy objectives. It offered the best chance of getting the hostages out alive and the least danger of a war with Iran.

The operation was feasible. It probably represented the plan with the best chance of success under the circumstances, and the decision to execute it was justified.

The rescue mission was a high-risk operation. People and equipment were called on to perform at the upper limits of human capacity and equipment capability.

The first realistic capability to successfully accomplish the rescue of hostages was reached at the end of March.

OPSEC [Operational Security] was an overriding requirement for a successful operation. Success was totally dependent upon maintaining secrecy.

Command and control were excellent at the upper echelons, but became more tenuous and fragile at the intermediate levels. Command relationships below the Commander, JTF [Joint Task Force], were not clearly emphasized in some cases and were susceptible to misunderstandings under pressure.

External resources adequately supported the JTF and were not a limiting factor.

Planning was adequate except for a number of backup helicopters and provisions for weather contingencies. A larger helicopter force and better provisions for weather penetration would have increased the probability of mission success.

Preparation for the mission was adequate except for the lack of a comprehensive, full-scale training exercise. Operational readiness of the force would have benefited from a full-dress rehearsal. Command and control weaknesses probably would have surfaced and been ironed out.

Two factors combined to directly cause the mission to abort: Unexpected helicopter failure rate, and low-visibility flight conditions en route to Desert One.

These conclusions lead the Group to recommend that:

- a Counterterrorist Joint Task Force (CTTJTF) be established as a field agency of the Joint Chiefs of Staff with permanently assigned staff personnel and certain assigned forces.
- the Joint Chiefs of Staff give careful consideration to the establishment of a Special Operations Advisory Panel, comprised of a group of carefully selected high-ranking officers (active and/or retired) who have career backgrounds in Special Operations or who have served at the CINC or JCS levels and who have maintained a current interest in Special Operations or defense policy matters.

Before closing, let me make a couple of very important points.

First, the group unanimously concluded that no one action or lack of action caused the operation to fail—and conversely, no one of our identified alternatives or all the alternatives could have guaranteed success.

Second, as I mentioned earlier, we unanimously agreed that the people who commanded, planned, and executed the operation were the most competent and best qualified for the task of all available. There were none better.

The most significant result of the Holloway Commission's report was the creation of a standing Counterterrorist Joint Task Force, formally established in December 1980. However, other initiatives were spawned due to the lessons learned from the Eagle Claw Operation. Within the Army, General Edward Meyer revitalized a Special Operations planning element on the Army Staff. He also started a much more robust Army helicopter capability in what initially was a task force but later became the

160th Aviation Regiment, which continues to be a vital cog in Special Operations. General Meyer became the Army Chief of Staff in June 1980 and improved both Army Special Operations and counterterrorism capabilities. He created two intelligence organizations, the Intelligence Support Activity, and Yellow Fruit, to improve human intelligence and other Army intelligence capabilities. General Meyer also laid the groundwork for the expansion of Special Forces and the creation of the 75th Ranger Regiment. In the Navy, approval was given for the expansion of the SEAL community for the creation of a special mission unit dedicated to counterterrorism. Dick Marcinko commanded the unit, with Norm Carley as his deputy. Delta offered Marcinko help, but he was rather standoffish and wanted to set his own course. The Air Force moved to better resource the 1st Special Operations Wing and to set the stage for the growth of what would become the Air Force Special Operations Command.

The Defense Intelligence Agency had been criticized in the Holloway Commission report, and they took baby steps to improve their terrorism support capabilities. Wayne Long and I were summoned to DIA headquarters where we were met by an Army lieutenant colonel, who started to describe what DIA would do and how it would become much better. He struck me as having no experience and did not seem very smart. He kept saying, "The CRT is going to do this; the CRT is going to do that." It was obvious that he didn't know what he was talking about. I finally had enough of it. I played dumb and asked him, "Excuse me, sir, but could you tell me what a CRT is?" Of course, I knew that it meant cathode ray tube, which was the early monitor for computer systems. He looked at Wayne and me with a blank expression and tried to change the subject. So much for what DIA was doing to improve their terrorism support skills. Things at DIA only began to change positively in September 1981 when Army Lieutenant General Jim Williams became the director. He was an infantryman who was not only intelligent but knew what warfighter support was all about.

During the remainder of 1980, after the failed mission, the task force conducted several different exercises and experiments throughout the country. No actual planning could happen because of the lack of information concerning exactly where the hostages had been moved, coupled with the risks of attempting to rescue a small number of hostages which would undoubtedly place those who were not rescued at risk of death. The good thing that came out of the exercises and experiments was that new tactics and equipment were created that would help mold future Special Operations missions.

Prior to the April 1980 rescue attempt, Delta had been slated to participate in a major national counterterrorism field exercise that had a nuclear extortion scenario. This was the second major exercise, named Sundog, involving a nuclear scenario and the Department of Energy. It was conducted in the heat of summer at the White Sands Missile Range in New Mexico. The notional scenario had the event occurring in a fictitious overseas country. The United States Secret Service provided the terrorism actors and the Department of Energy, together with its National Laboratories, provided the hostage actors. Jerry Boykin had taken command of the squadron used in the exercise. Jim Coughlin and I were the Intelligence Section participants. I flew in as the lead of the advance party on a very rough terrain following a low-level flight on an MC-130. It was especially rough because of the heat which caused the airplane to bounce around. I walked into the mock U.S. Embassy Headquarters, introduced myself and immediately demanded that I be shown the accommodations for the incoming squadron. One of the exercise controllers was Bob Wilde, who I would later work for after retirement. He was quick to respond to my request and later told me that he was, on the one hand, impressed by my demeanor but on the other hand, scared by this evil-looking guy making demands!

The most challenging thing about Sundog for the operators was the vicious heat that exceeded 110 degrees. Bruno Urbaniak had crawled into a position and had to stay in the heat for hours to keep from compromising his location. We were worried about dehydration or heat exhaustion, but he kept indicating that he was fine. Rick Race was on the exercise control staff and thought he would test Delta's security. He was caught by our squadron operators. Because he was a friend, Bucky Burruss and I decided to play games with Rick. He was blindfolded, stripped down to his underwear, and had his hands secured behind his back. We then had him kneel on the hot road and started a mock interrogation. The other exercise controllers were concerned for Rick and called an administrative halt, and made us stop the interrogation. When the assault to free the hostages began, Don Purdy threw a flash bang at a window—somehow it bounced back and went off in the face of Don Simmons, who thought he might lose his sight. Don Purdy had a black cloud over his head during the time he was in Delta and was blamed for getting others hurt. As a result of this incident, Don Purdy was directed to leave the unit. He went on to become a well-respected sergeant major in the Ranger Regiment, which was good for his self-esteem. He gained a reputation as a great leader who cared for his soldiers.

As the assault was launched, Don Feeney's sub-machine gun jammed. He was at a dead run and just lowered his head and knocked one of the terrorist actors to the ground. That gave us a live notional terrorist to interrogate. In real life, he was a lieutenant in the Secret Service Uniformed Division providing security at the White House. Regrettably, I got carried away in the interrogation, causing him to have a mental breakdown. When I realized what I had done, I quickly got the CIA psychiatrist, Bob Bloomingdale, to render medical attention.

There was one other comical thing that happened. During the assault, the operators retrieved some written notes with a lot of numbers. The DOE Nuclear Emergency Search Team people thought that it was a code that, if broken, would allow the supposed nuclear device to be disarmed. They asked for Delta's help in breaking the code. Within 15 minutes, Jim Coughlin and I had it figured out. Paul

Kelly, a Secret Service agent, who played the lead terrorist on the exercise, made the notes. Jim and I determined that the notes referred to his time sheet to calculate the overtime payments due to him. Knowing that the numbers had no relationship to a code, we decided to play games with the NEST folks. After an hour they came frantically to Jim and me and asked if we had made any progress in breaking the code. We calmly looked at them and said that we had. They demanded to know what we had found and scolded us for not sharing it sooner. I looked at them and told them it was Paul Kelly's overtime calculations and that we didn't tell them because they needed more experience in analysis!

We spent the remainder of 1980 maintaining the ability to engage in another Iranian hostage rescue mission, but with little chance of being deployed because of the scattering of the hostages. More importantly, assessment and selection continued, and Delta's numbers began to grow. One of the more exceptional individuals to join Delta that year was Eldon Bargewell. Eldon joined as a captain, would later command Delta as a colonel, and as a major general, was General George Casey's operations director in Iraq. Charlie Beckwith was told it was time for him to relinquish command and that he would be assigned to the standing Counterterrorism Task Force which would be stood up at Fort Bragg. His replacement was supposed to be Colonel Bo Baker, who had served with Charlie in Vietnam and was a well-respected Special Forces officer and leader. Unfortunately, Bo Baker died of a heart attack before he could assume command. Charlie's replacement was then to be Colonel Rod Paschall, who had been assigned to the J3 Special Operations Division in the Pentagon.

My boss and friend, Wayne Long, was also reassigned. For a few months, I continued as Delta's intelligence officer. Paschall then told me that a replacement for Wayne was needed. I understood why, and it was a matter of rank. I asked to be allowed to select the new intelligence officer and was permitted to do so. Working with the Army's Military Personnel Center, I was given five record briefs to consider. The most qualified one had decided to retire. Three others were lieutenant colonels and one had Special Forces experience but did not have a good reputation. I selected Major Thomas W. O'Connell, who had worked as a district advisor in Vietnam and had been wounded in action. Tom was returning from an exchange assignment in the United Kingdom. I was able to reach him by phone, and he kept me on the phone for close to two hours. I finally told him to just get his butt to Fort Bragg and report for duty the following week.

Tom showed up the following week almost in a state of shock. I calmed him down and assured him, that if he trusted me, I would do my best to explain how the unit and the Intelligence Section operated and to help him learn the ropes. He agreed, and that began a 36-year friendship, which only ended with his untimely death in 2016. Tom was eager to learn, honest, dedicated, and without a self-serving bone in his body. Like myself, Tom had his faults, but his dedication and humility won me over. With Tom's arrival, I was faced with a dilemma. Colonel Jerry King was starting the Intelligence Support Activity and wanted me to join that unit, and I was sorely tempted to do so. Two things led me to decide to remain with Delta. The first was my promise to Tom O'Connell that I would help him as the Delta intelligence officer. In the spirit of *Intoku*, one's word is sacred. The other thing that kept me from leaving was my lack of faith in the leadership of the second Delta commander and his deputy. I felt that by staying on I could help overcome some of the poor decisions they were making.

In December 1980, the standing Counterterrorism Joint Task Force was formally established, and Delta was placed as a subordinate unit to that command. Major General Richard Scholtes was selected as its first commander. They began to operate out of World War II buildings on Butner Road at Fort Bragg which housed the Summer Camp headquarters for the ROTC Region; however, construction was proceeding to build a new headquarters on Pope AFB. Remembering that Joint Task Force 1-79 had less than 70 people assigned to plan and execute the Eagle Claw mission, it was amazing to see the size of the headquarters being formed. One of the lessons I learned was that when a new headquarters is formed, the organization will initially be staffed with many who have little or no experience in the mission of that headquarters. This was in stark contrast to the start of Delta. Whereas Delta started small and had a definitive selection process in place, this was not so for the new Counterterrorism Joint Task Force. Their start-up also contrasted how the Office of Strategic Services was created during World War II. I mean this as a factual statement and not a criticism. However, whenever you assemble a group of people from disparate backgrounds to address a new mission, a significant amount of time will have to be spent in determining how the mission will be accomplished and people organized to meet that requirement.

CHAPTER 16

Valuable Lessons

On January 20, 1981, the 52 remaining hostages in Iran were released, thus bringing an end to that crisis. The timing of their release coincided with the inauguration of Ronald Reagan as the President of the United States of America. Most people were of the opinion that the Iranian government deliberately timed that release in the hope of gaining relief from the sanctions that had been placed on Iran. That did not happen. The release of the hostages was a joyous time for them, and their families, and Americans celebrated their return. After flying from Iran to Algeria and Germany, they landed at Stewart Airport near West Point, New York. They were then transported to the Thayer Hotel outside the United States Military Academy entrance. Americans waving flags lined the route for 17 miles from Stewart Airport to West Point. It was a wonderful show of patriotism.

The sad part is that most, if not all, of the hostages suffered from post-trauma ailments. Some of the military hostages decided to leave and to find a new life as civilians. Two of them were Marines Rocky Sickmann and Billy Gallegos. Rocky became an executive with Anheuser Busch and supported many military offerings from that company. Billy Gallegos went on to become a detective in Colorado. One of the hostages that continued in his field was John Limbert. John, whose wife was born in Iran and had to live out his captivity in Saudi Arabia, rose to become an ambassador. He also became a professor at the U.S. Naval Academy. All three of these great Americans embody the spirit of *Intoku*. They have done much to care for other Americans without seeking recognition.

As the J2 or Intelligence Section of the counterterrorism task force stood up, all of us in the Delta Intelligence Section wanted to help them get off to a running start. We were prepared to introduce them to our contacts, and show them what we had been producing and how we provided intelligence support to the Delta operators. To that end, I scheduled an office call with Colonel Don Gordon, the Task Force J2. Gordon was a signals intelligence officer and stated that he had Special Forces experience. When I went into his office, he did not offer me a seat and acted like he was very busy. I courteously offered the help of Delta's Intelligence Section to brief and perhaps train his incoming personnel. He never commented on my offer. Instead, he looked up at me and in a condescending manner, asked me if I had ever heard of the Green Beret incident in Vietnam. This was the case involving Detachment B-57 and the killing of an ostensible double agent that I discussed previously in this book. I replied that I was somewhat familiar with the incident. In a dismissive voice, he said, "Well, I was there." I had to restrain myself from calling him an outright liar. He then dismissed me.

I left Gordon's office feeling that the relationship between Delta's Intelligence Section and the J2 was not going to go well. We had a few individuals from the J2 seek help from us, and we provided that help freely. However, it was apparent that they were told not to have anything to do with us, and contact was broken. In 1981, I never saw a single product that the J2 produced in support of Delta. Gordon had them scurrying around trying to build a computer network. Fortunately, they did not interfere with our relationships with the intelligence community, and we continued to do everything necessary to support Delta's operators. The only significant thing that happened within the J2 was when one of their members caused a wave of activity by reporting that he had spotted the terrorist, Carlos the Jackal, in a department store in Fayetteville. Ilich Ramirez Sanchez, also known as Carlos the Jackal, was the mastermind of the takeover of OPEC headquarters in Vienna, Austria, in 1975. All of us in the Delta Intelligence Section knew intuitively that it was highly improbable. Anyway, we had to waste our time to help Task Force J2 understand that the report was erroneous. One of the other inanities the J2 created was purchasing a large recreational vehicle that they would use as a mobile command post. We tried to point out that the vehicle would stick out like a sore thumb overseas, but they never listened. The vehicle was never used, and money was wasted. There are times when the spirit of *Intoku* cannot overcome arrogant people.

I had the honor (and extra work) to be the co-exercise director of three significant counterterrorist exercises during 1981. Two of them were focused on the FBI and the need for a hostage rescue team. The third was to be the first major field exercise involving the counterterrorism task force. That I led those exercises as a captain illustrates that knowledge, competence, and experience are more valuable than the rank one might hold. A very small staff helped me plan and direct the exercises, demonstrating once again the power of competence and experience. Those who assisted in the planning continued to do their regular duties. They just quietly did what needed to be done without fanfare and seeking recognition. They lived the spirit of *Intoku* as true professionals.

The two exercises designed to assist the FBI in evaluating the need for a hostage rescue team were called Masquerade I and II. The push for the exercises came from John Otto and Jim McKenzie. John had been the special agent in charge of the Chicago office and had to deal with two incidents involving Serbo-Croatian terrorism in Chicago. He was well acquainted with Delta and had ascended to become the executive assistant director of the FBI. Jim McKenzie was the assistant director for FBI training which, at the time, was Division VI and headquartered at the FBI Academy in Quantico, Virginia. Jim had learned about Delta shortly after taking the training division, when he was briefed by his predecessor, Ken Joseph. Both Joseph and McKenzie had a personal relationship with Charlie Beckwith.

Masquerade I was a field exercise conducted at Camp A. P. Hill in Virginia. The co-exercise director was John Simeone, an FBI agent who worked in the Special Operations Research Unit at the FBI Academy, was familiar with Delta. The scenario called for the invocation of the Insurrection Act to allow Delta to have to be called upon for help. Two targets had to be assaulted to conduct hostage rescues at both targets. One was assigned to Delta, and the other to the FBI. Because there was no hostage rescue team for the FBI, it called for a regional call out of different field office SWAT teams. For this exercise, the lead office was Washington with Ted Gardner, the special agent in charge of the Washington office, in charge of the other teams. Other SWAT teams came from Baltimore and Richmond, VA. Gardner was a former Marine known for his strong opinions. During the exercise, he came up to John Simeone and me and told us this exercise was bullshit. He was quite proud of the FBI and thought his teams could handle any situation.

The scenario called for a coordinated assault on both targets by Delta and the FBI with Delta initiating the assaults. The notional terrorists inside the FBI target were played by Delta operators, and the notional terrorists inside the Delta target were played by FBI agents, led by Tom Strentz, who was a psychologist and special agent at the FBI training academy. Delta initiated the assault using a non-lethal explosive device. They made their entry and quickly dealt with the notional terrorists and recovered the hostages. The FBI teams were stunned when the explosion went off and that delayed their assault. They were unable to make entry into the target, and as the co-exercise director, I had to tell the notional terrorists to surrender. At the end of the exercise, Ted Gardner came up to Simeone and me, stuck out his hand, and apologized for what he had said. He saw firsthand the difference between a dedicated unit (Delta) and part-timers (FBI SWAT). Gardner then became a supporter, along with John Otto and Jim McKenzie, for a dedicated FBI hostage rescue team.

Masquerade II was mainly oriented to allow the FBI to consider how they might employ a dedicated hostage rescue team and coordinate the overall effort. This was a command post exercise that did not involve any actual field activity. The scenario was made complex to have to address jurisdictional authorities. It involved a supposed foreign diplomatic facility in Washington, DC. The jurisdictional responsibilities included the FBI, the Washington Metropolitan Police Department, the U.S. Park Police, and the U.S. Secret Service. Senior officials from those organizations plus the Department of State were players in the exercise. The FBI was pleased with the exercise as it allowed them to examine their procedures to ensure better command and control and coordination of activities in a complex scenario. One of the observers of the exercise was Oliver North. He was relatively new to the National Security Council staff and was very interested in the interactions that would occur in the scenario depicted. There was a bit of amusement as the exercise progressed. At lunchtime, the Washington Metropolitan Police Department agreed that the FBI should have preeminent jurisdiction over the event. The department was represented by Chief Burtell Jefferson, their Deputy Chief Maurice Turner, who would succeed Jefferson in 1981, and George Bradford, their SWAT team leader who had been present at the Hanafi Muslim incident in Washington in 1977. Jokingly, Chief Jefferson, a Black American, literally was eating a chicken drumstick when he remarked, "You white boys sure got a problem!" Everyone broke out in laughter.

The third exercise was called Prince Sky. It was the brainchild of then-Captain Steve Wright. Steve was looking ahead to the 1984 Summer Olympics to be held in Southern California. It would give Delta and the Counterterrorism task force an opportunity to develop better relationships in the Southern California area and look for a potential base of operations should the military be called upon for support. Steve and I quickly came up with a scenario that would involve nuclear extortion on the part of a fictional terrorist group. I made an appointment with Troy Wade, the deputy director of the Department of Energy Nevada Operations Office, who oversaw the NEST activities. Troy was a great friend and agreed to meet. On the flight to Las Vegas, Steve and I brainstormed the features of the exercise and how it would benefit several interagency groups, including the Department of Energy. Troy Wade liked the concept we presented and agreed that DOE would participate. We then met with Jim Magruder, Troy's operations director, and began to iron out the details. While in Las Vegas, I contacted John Kolman with the Los Angeles Sheriff's Office and Mike Hillman of the Los Angeles Police Department to get their guy in. Upon returning to Fort Bragg, we briefed Colonel Bill Palmer, the J3 for the CT task force, and rapidly gained his approval along with Major General Scholtes.

The exercise went from Steve Wright's initial concept to actually conducting the exercise in less than four months. It was a tribute to great people like Troy Wade, Jim Magruder, John Kolman, and Mike Hillman and the tacit support we received from Colonel Bill Palmer. The entire planning staff for the exercise consisted of less than fifty people. In today's world, it would require a staff of hundreds and would take a minimum of one year to plan and execute. All the planners were exceptionally competent, understood the necessary steps to plan the exercise, and devoted themselves to making it happen without fanfare or seeking recognition.

The scenario involved a notional terrorist group that threatened to detonate a "dirty bomb" or radioactive dispersal device during a renowned street festival in downtown Los Angeles unless their demands were met. They also threatened to detonate the device if they saw the street festival being cancelled to put additional pressure on the decision-makers. John Kolman quickly found an ideal site for the scenario. It was the Hall of Justice on Temple Street in downtown Los Angeles and was the headquarters for the Los Angeles Sheriff's Office. The 12-story structure had previously been a jail, but the upper floors had been closed and the jail moved elsewhere. Mike Hillman rapidly found and recommended the Los Alamitos Reserve Air Base as an ideal spot for the CT task force and Delta to use as a staging base along with the NEST Team. John obtained permission from Peter Pitchess, the long-time sheriff of Los Angeles County. Mike Hillman got approval from Darrell Gates, the Los Angeles Police Department Chief. DOE tasked Sandia National Labs to build a notional dirty bomb. Planning sessions were held in Las Vegas and Los Angeles, and I got full cooperation for the planning agendas I had developed.

There was a rather amusing incident during one of the planning sessions held in Los Angeles. John Kolman had arranged for the planning group to have lunch at the Sybil Brand Institute, which was a jail for female prisoners. DOE had assigned two female planners; Sheila Schramm, who was like a daughter to me, and Sharon Fulwider. They were both apprehensive about having lunch at the female jail. I teased Sharon by telling her that she needed to keep a close eye on the inmates who were serving the meal as they would spit on the food for females. Sharon's eyes were glued on the servers, and she still was not sure about eating the meal. I traded trays with her and later told her I had pulled her leg.

The exercise went off like clockwork. The CT task force assigned Major Doug Shelton and Lieutenant Colonel Bob Jacobelly as exercise controllers. They were great people and had no problem taking direction from me even though they outranked me. For whatever reason, the FBI only offered one of their agents to play the entire FBI during the exercise. Unfortunately, I forget his name, but he did a tremendous job of playing the role of the FBI special agent in charge. There were many valuable lessons learned for all the organizations involved. The DOE NEST organization faced challenges in identifying the device due to the thick concrete and rebar in the Hall of Justice; the CT task force gained invaluable experience on how to coordinate activities and command and control of forces; Delta was faced with a new scenario of going against a hardened facility. We made the exercise more realistic by asking John Kolman to contact a Hollywood stuntman to build a system to place on the notional terrorists that would discharge fluid resembling blood. There was an unfortunate thing that happened during the assault to rescue the hostages and secure the dirty bomb. I briefed my good friend and A Squadron Commander Darrel Elmore that they would not have to breach jail bars and that a very small explosive charge would shatter the plywood façade. Darrell foolishly chose to ignore what I had said. They used a full-sized explosive device to make entry. Downstairs, a sheriff's deputy had a piece of ceiling tile fall on him. Outside, sheriffs' deputies who were deployed to provide security for the exercise heard a massive boom and swore that the building shook, and then saw smoke coming out of the upper floors. The Hall of Justice was two blocks away from the headquarters of the *Los Angeles Times*, and we were fortunate that no reporters were alerted. We were also lucky that none of the terrorist and hostage actors were hurt as there was debris thrown for over 50 feet in the corridor where the assault took place. John Kolman was livid and was prepared—as Sheriff Pitchess's special assistant—to get Delta thrown out of town. It was all I could do to convince John not to do so by profusely apologizing and calling on our friendship. I also had to apologize to Sheriff Pitchess who had tremendous political clout in Southern California. He was first elected as sheriff in 1958 and would retire in 1981.

On the operational side, Delta began receiving more requests from the Department of State to send operators in small numbers to provide discreet assistance to U.S. Embassy security. They would work with the embassy's regional security officer and the CIA chief of station in a low-visibility mode. These efforts did not conflict with the very capable Marine Corps Fleet Anti-Terrorism Security Teams (FAST), who were best deployed in large numbers to provide a visible deterrent to any attack against a U.S. embassy.

The one large-scale operation that Delta began planning for was an attempt to rescue American prisoners of war ostensibly held in Laos. The CT task force thought it was a big deal and established tight compartmentation over who could know about the planning. I was highly skeptical because of the lack of meaningful intelligence to support live American prisoners of war in Laos. Although there were many Americans declared as missing in action from the Vietnam conflict, there was no hard information that any of them were alive and prisoners. Two items of supposed intelligence were highly suspect. One was the belief that "B52" was stomped in the grass outside the supposed compound housing the prisoners. The other was the mensuration (measurement) of shadows that showed taller persons who had to be Caucasians. I reviewed both and thought that someone's imagination was running wild and that it was pure speculation. The other intelligence came from retired Special Force Lieutenant Colonel Bo Gritz who had convinced people that he could sneak into Laos and get corroborating intelligence. The Intelligence Support Activity was tasked with handling Gritz and providing him with support. Delta's communications warrant officer, Paul Zeisman, was made to hand receipt a long-range radio for Gritz's use. Gritz recruited a retired Special Force radio operator to accompany him on the mission into Laos. Gritz was launched from Thailand into Laos and, upon return, reported that he had confirmed Americans were indeed being held. Almost everyone wanted to believe Gritz. I was skeptical and arranged for a great friend, then-Lieutenant Colonel Jack McGuinness, to interview Gritz. Jack had spent four tours in Laos as a Special Forces and intelligence officer supporting the CIA.

Jack returned after talking with Gritz and quietly told me that Gritz was lying. Jack was intimately familiar with the area where Gritz described crossing into Laos from Thailand, as well as the area where the supposed prison camp was located. Gritz had described crossing into Laos at a known border crossing point and having to cross a raging river. Jack told me that he had been at that location many times, including during the worst recorded monsoon season in Laotian history, and that the water was no higher than his knees and certainly not a raging river. Jack also stated that the description Gritz gave of the terrain did not match his personal experience. Despite Jack's credibility, many wanted to believe the lies told by Gritz. In 1981, the Department of Defense relied on the Defense Intelligence Agency to oversee all POW/MIA affairs. The office was led by Rear Admiral Jerry Tuttle. Very discreetly, he was made aware of what Jack McGuiness had reported and took steps to shut the planning. Gritz was dropped as an asset of the Intelligence Support Activity. Regrettably, Gritz kept his lies alive and raised funds to go into Laos again. Reportedly, he bilked the actors William Shatner and Clint Eastwood out of large amounts of money to support his claims. The radio operator with him on the supposed crossing into Laos wrote a book denying that they had crossed into Laos, but no one paid attention to his account. When Gritz tried again, Thai officials arrested him and others that he had recruited. That ended his perfidy.

One of the interesting visitors to Delta was Rafi Eytan who was accompanied by an Israeli Defense Force senior colonel. Charlie Beckwith was very forthcoming and open. The Israeli colonel was appreciative and learned many things that could help the Israeli counterterrorist effort. Conversely, Eytan was aloof and arrogant and pooh-poohed much of what he was briefed on. Years later, Eytan was unmasked as the agent handler for Jonathan Pollard, the American who was caught spying for Israel and given a life sentence. William Casey, the Director of the CIA, also visited us. He was a remarkable person and a true intelligence professional. During the staff briefings to him, he kept nodding off, but he absorbed everything that was being said as witnessed by the questions he asked and the comments he made.

One of the most significant contributions to national counterterrorist capabilities was when Delta hosted five FBI members who would spend a month with the unit learning how Delta operated and many of its operational tactics, techniques, and procedures. The five were: Danny Colson, who would become the first leader of the FBI's hostage rescue team; John Simeone, who would become Colson's deputy; Jeff Wehmeyer, who had led the Washington Office SWAT team on the Masquerade I exercise and would later head the hostage rescue team; Tom Nicoletti, who for whatever reason would not join the HRT; and Jaime Atherton, who would become the main breacher for the HRT. The FBI hand-picked them after the FBI leadership had decided to form the HRT. The five bonded well with Delta's operators and the foundation for continuing cooperation was firmly established and has stood the test of time. From its inception in 1977, Delta had established excellent ties with the FBI and received help from the likes of Bill Koopman, who led their technical collection operation, and Barry Mones who was the unit chief for their special photography unit.

The Delta Intelligence Section was finally able to gain additional slots to help relieve the workload of the analysts. We got John Stanley and Willie Welsch promoted to warrant officer. I recruited a friend, Ted Finley, who I had served with in Vietnam and Okinawa. Ted had become a warrant officer and was coming from the 7th Special Forces Group in Panama. He told me about two others that he wanted to bring on board, Dennis Chew and Gary Sporer—I was able to get permission to add them to our assets. Both Dennis and Gary would later become the sergeant majors of the Intelligence Section. Adding those three on board allowed Larry Gabe to switch his focus from being an analyst to developing a much better technical intelligence capability for Delta. My workload had been reduced significantly and I thought things were going well. General Bob Kingston contacted me and told me I would be promoted the following year to become a major. Then in November I received a call from Dr Judith Daly, with whom I had worked very closely on several Defense Advanced Research Projects Agency programs. She confided in me and told me that Colonel Don Gordon, the Standing CT task force J2, was accusing me of trying to sabotage the terrorist database and predictive analysis project we had been working on. I was both flabbergasted and angry as his accusations were completely untrue.

***

The straw that finally broke my back and caused me to retire came in mid-December 1981. Brigadier General James Dozier had been kidnapped in Verona, Italy, by members of the Italian Red Brigades terrorist organization. The Red Brigades had kidnapped and then assassinated the former Italian Prime Minister Aldo Moro in 1978. I was slated to go on an advance party together with Jesse Johnson, whom Rod Paschall had made the deputy commander, even though Johnson was neither qualified as a Delta operator nor as a Special Forces officer. I walked into Johnson's office and saw him packing a black kit bag, a black helmet, a black uniform, and a tactical vest, along with an MP-5 sub-machine gun. I asked him what that was for and got a "You Know" response. I told him that I didn't know, and then berated him for not knowing what an advance party was supposed to do, namely assist the U.S. Embassy and the Italian government. I then went on to tell him that he was not a qualified operator but that he was a proverbial wannabe.

I stormed out of his office and quickly decided that I had enough. I walked to Delta's personnel section and filled out my retirement request. Thanks to the help I received from the likes of Angela Whitaker and Russ Vona, I was could retire in a couple of weeks. I immediately contacted Charlie Beckwith. Charlie was in Austin, Texas, where he had started a firm called SAS of Texas, Ltd. He had contacted me a couple of months previously to ask if I would consider joining his company. I now told him that I was ready, and he welcomed me on board. I was to receive two pieces of bad news as I prepared for my last day on active duty. The first was that I would be retired as a master sergeant instead of as a sergeant major. This was based on the fact that I had never officially pinned on the sergeant major stripes before being called to active duty as an officer. The second was that any move I made would have my household goods allowance computed as a master sergeant instead of as a captain. I didn't have time to argue but was angry at those decisions as they would cost me money.

On my last day on active duty, my retirement ceremony consisted of me walking through a sleet storm to collect my final pay. Then I headed to the headquarters of the CT task force and barged into Colonel Don Gordon's office. Typically, he was seated behind his desk and never offered to have me sit down. That was fine by me, because I walked up to him, poked my finger in his chest, and then called him less than an honorable man. I said that he was a liar about his supposed involvement in the Green Beret incident in Vietnam and that he was a worm for accusing me falsely of sabotaging the TRAP/TARGIT program. I hoped he would get up so I could smash his face in with my fists. Instead, he looked down and started to sob. I did an about-face and stormed out of his office thinking that his actions were a good affirmation of why I was retiring. What an end to my Army and Special Forces career.

DEPARTMENT OF THE ARMY
1ST SPECIAL FORCES OPERATIONAL DETACHMENT - DELTA (AIRBORNE)
FORT BRAGG, NORTH CAROLINA 28307

REPLY TO
ATTN OF: DF-SB

28 December 1981

SUBJECT: Farewell

TO: Ish, AKA MSG Wade Y. Ishimoto
AKA CPT Wade Y. Ishimoto

1. (U) We hate to see you leave. They were the best of times, they were the worst of times. (Apologies to no one).

2. (U) We are pleased that you will continue to serve "this great country".

3. (U) You have been an inspiration to all who have served with you. Each of us has learned a great deal from your example and we sincerely hope that we can apply those lessons in a manner which is consistent with the high standards you set.

4. (U) Awards and gifts cannot adequately express our appreciation upon the occasion of your departure. Therefore, leave with our greatest measure of respect and admiration. You will not be forgotten. We are better people for having known you. The Army is a better Army because of you. You are one hell of a man.

All Ranks
Intel Section

Farewell letter, 1981.

CHAPTER 17

A Second Career Begins

Mi Hye was shocked by my decision to retire, but she understood my anger and stood by me once again as a loyal wife. She was also somewhat ready to move as she never cared for the heat and humidity of North Carolina. I contacted my brother-in-law, Chong Il Choe, whom we had sponsored to immigrate to America the year before and asked him to help Mi Hye should she need any assistance. He willingly agreed to do so. He had lived with us for a few months, but then found work in the Raleigh, North Carolina, area as a welder and had moved there. Chong Il epitomized the hard-working immigrant who would succeed because of his work ethic and tenacity. He went from being a welder at an auto body shop to becoming a welder on a nuclear powerplant in Apex, North Carolina. He then bought a shoe repair shop and eventually moved to Baltimore, Maryland, where he continues to operate a grocery store. The value of an extended family once more came to light.

I packed my small Toyota station wagon and set out for Austin, Texas, leaving Mi Hye in Fayetteville tasked with selling our house. Once again, the spirit of *Intoku* came to bear as Nick Goresh very quietly and competently put our house on the market, got us a solid offer in a couple of months, and made us a profit on the sale. Once again, we packed up and moved to a different location. We searched for a house and decided to move into a newly built house in the Great Hills Country Club area with a great view overlooking Austin Hill country. The house was situated on Lost Horizon Drive, and that turned out to be a very propitious name.

The name of the company that Charlie Beckwith started was called SAS of Texas, Ltd. It showed his affinity for all things British and his fond memories of his time with the Special Air Service in Britain. The SAS stood for Security Assistance Services. The next two years were a great learning experience about what it takes to start a new business and succeed. In short, the company did not get off to a good start and was doomed to fail almost from day one. The company started with Charlie, a secretary, Cecil "Bud" Morgan, who had been in Delta and decided to leave the Army, and Doug Ramsay, a former Secret Service Uniformed Division officer who left before retirement. We each had different talents that could have led to a successful business. Bud was a talented close-quarter battle operator who also could plan and execute entry into a building or room, which could have been used by local law enforcement. Doug Ramsay held multiple National Rifle Association marksmanship records with rifles and revolvers.

The first problem was that there was no business plan. Charlie thought that we could succeed as a consulting organization; however, a marketing analysis had never been conducted to determine whom we might consult with and for what purpose. The location of the business in Austin, Texas, could have been better. There were no large companies that could use and pay for security consulting. This was before Austin grew to become a technology development center akin to Silicon Valley. Austin was the capital of Texas, but we had no contacts with significant politicians who could assist us in procuring business.

Charlie told me that Bill Blakemore, the owner of Alpha 21 in Midland, Texas, who was a multimillionaire making his money in the oil business, had recommended we locate in Austin. Charlie also told me that Blakemore had furnished seed money to start the company. As I found out later, neither the location nor the seed money were true. Charlie liked Austin because he had led a contingent of Special Forces to help train Mexican Army officers in how to coach sports in the mid-70s. He was invited to attend a University of Texas football game, and treated to a barbeque by the Texas football coach, Darrell Royal.

The location was not based on any analysis of business opportunities. Instead of seed money, a loan had been given by the First National Bank of Midland, Texas. At one time, that bank had some $1.2 billion in holdings. In October 1983, the bank failed and the Federal Deposit Insurance Corporation took over its assets. An investigation discovered the loan to SAS of Texas literally in the bank president's desk. They demanded that the loan be repaid—the death knell for SAS of Texas, Ltd.

The amount of income generated was paltry. Earl Lockwood of BETAC Corporation in Alexandria, Virginia, was a friend of Charlie's and myself, and he offered some consulting activities that were a major source of income. However, the total was not sufficient to make us a profit. Ben Schemmer, the owner of the *Armed Forces Journal International*, also provided some opportunities but they were few and far between. A gentleman in Austin whose name was Jim tried to find work for us. He arranged for us to provide security for Bob Hope at a golf tournament near Houston, Texas, but again, that was not a big income producer and basically a one-time shot. I was teaching infrequently for the Air Force Special Operations School and the California Department of Justice, but again the income was sparse.

We thought we had an excellent opportunity in 1983 when Tom Quinn, a former Secret Service agent, convinced President Ronald Reagan's Chief of Staff Michael Deaver, that an examination of security for the 1984 Summer Olympics in Los Angeles would be an excellent idea. The report we prepared was well received with over 70% of our recommendations adopted. Unfortunately, the promises we were made by the people who gained promotions because of our report were never followed up. We put much more effort into the report than what we were paid.

We did far too many things for free out of the goodness of our hearts. We assisted the Texas Department of Public Safety's Narcotics Division with explosives, firearms, and raid-planning for free in the hope that they would use us on a paying basis. That never occurred.

Bobby Shelton, who would sue the Exxon Corporation and win over $10 billion, talked us into doing an assessment of his property portfolio. A proposal for service was offered and nothing materialized. John Bianchi, the owner of Bianchi Leather, and a friend of Charlie and me, caught wind of our plight. John paid for a friend of his—who had been the security director of the Sahara Casino in Las Vegas, Nevada, and had left them to start his own security business—to visit us in Austin.

His frank assessment was that it was great to have a dream of making money consulting, but our business plan needed to be stronger. He also offered that we needed a foundation to keep the lights on and pay the bills. He saw opportunities in providing guard services or alarm services. I was the only one with any knowledge of alarm systems and monitoring but needed to be fully technically qualified to get into that business. On the other hand, I saw a great opportunity with guard services. When I presented that idea to Charlie, he revolted and said it would tarnish his name. Ironically, three years later, after SAS of Texas had failed, Charlie ended up running a guard service owned by a city councilman in Austin. I also mentioned to John Bianchi's friend that Charlie would get invited to have lunch or dinner with some high rollers from time to time. John's friend was blunt and said it was unlikely they were looking to offer business. Instead, they were just seeking bragging rights with their friends—Guess who I had lunch with?

There was one other idea that Charlie crushed. It was to offer an adventure over a few days or a weekend to people who were well-to-do. Bud Morgan and Doug Ramsay would introduce them to shooting techniques, driving techniques, and other things to get their adrenaline pumping. I would take them through a briefing on the Iran hostage rescue attempt and other terrorism case studies. We had the perfect spot in mind. Bill Blakemore owned a remote ranch near Marfa, Texas, and ideally suited for adventure training. Charlie refused to approach Bill Blakemore on the idea. Yet later, Charlie would approach Bill Blakemore and have him hire a former NCO of Charlie's as a caretaker at the ranch.

Let me not belabor the business failing. However, in the spirit of *Intoku*, I continue to advise aspiring entrepreneurs of the necessity of a business plan, of marketing analysis and strategy, seeding money to start, and having a clear understanding of the need for their product or service. They will need a timeline to assess whether to continue or fold the business. A dream alone is not sufficient to guarantee success in business. I learned those lessons the hard way, and wish to keep others from making the same mistakes. Failing in business was not that traumatic for me but it hurt me deeply to see Bud Morgan and Doug Ramsay leave. Fortunately, they both landed on their feet. Bud went back to school and became an engineer. Doug did well for himself with several different companies. Curt Hurst, Delta's first operations officer, came on board without pay. Curt, his wife Susan, and their son Eric were wonderful people. The harsh lesson once again was that being a nice person was not necessarily relevant to bringing in business. Curt met a wealthy couple who owned a sailing yacht and talked of doing things for youth. That was admirable, but it would not bring in income for the business.

After two years, I concluded that the business was going to fail. I had dipped heavily into our savings to try and keep the company alive. I was the only one bringing in any income, which was insufficient to pay my salary even after Charlie reduced my pay. Within two months I found another job. As I told Charlie and Curt, my income, along with that of Mi Hye working as an assembler for Texas Instruments, was insufficient for me to continue without the prospect for growth.

The two years in Austin were not wasted. Outside of the business failure, there were a few downs, but there were many good times and the opportunity to learn a lot. The two most significant "downs" were, firstly, learning the difference between the honor and word of those in the military versus those in the civilian world. The second was the treatment I received from the Veterans Administration. I had hoped to get a decent disability payment from the Veterans Administration. To that end, I applied for my benefits and was sent to Waco and Temple, Texas, to two different VA facilities for evaluation. The medical assessment was done by a doctor who spoke broken English, and whose certificates were all from the University of Mexico. He tried to humiliate me by having me stand before him naked and asking me to describe what ailments I had. I asked him if he wanted me to start from the top down or bottom up. He responded from the bottom up. I described having broken both ankles on active duty, then went on to describe the 14-degree bend in my left leg because of my parachuting accident in Okinawa which caused me pain and limited mobility in my left ankle. The doctor stopped me and in broken English told me I was born that way. His attitude made me furious, and I proceeded to swear at him and tell him that he had no right to treat a veteran that way. I doubt he even listened after that as I described other ailments. His shoddy report resulted in me receiving only a 20% disability. That meant my retired Army pay would be deducted by about $400 a month, offset by a similar tax-free amount from the VA. Essentially, that meant my net benefit was less than $50 a month.

The learning experiences and good times far outweighed the bad. Earl Lockwood at BETAC kindly taught me a lot about business and how to write business proposals, government contracting, and fiscal planning. One of the exciting projects that I did for Earl was to develop plans for the U.S. government's Continuity of Government and Continuity of Operations Program, which was revised in the early 1980s. Earl also had me work on a capabilities document some years later that became the model for the U.S. Special Operations Command Capabilities statement. Earl did this for free in the spirit of *Intoku*. John Bianchi and his friend from Las Vegas also gave me important lessons on business development.

I met Bob Hope and his wife Dolores when we provided security for him at a golf tournament in Port Arthur, Texas. At the same tournament I met Earl Campbell, the renowned running back from the Houston Oilers. I was amazed to learn what was being done at the Hughen Center and Bob Hope School, which took in severely handicapped youth and provided them with opportunities to get on with their lives. I witnessed a paraplegic communicating by typing with a stylus in his mouth. It tugged at my heart to see him and the others that the Hughen Center quietly supported in the spirit of *Intoku*. At Bobby Shelton's ranch outside Fredericksburg, Texas, I got a glimpse of how billionaires live. His driveway was paved with bricks imported from a Houston stockyard. He also owned the American Quarter Horse Association Horse of the Year, named Leonard Milligan. The horse had his own private stable and exercise field that would be checked daily for mole and gopher holes so he wouldn't get hurt. The stables for mares brought in for breeding were temperature-controlled, had misting machines to kill flies, and the mares were fed oats that were as good as Quaker oats sold for human consumption.

I became a close friend of Ben Schemmer. Ben was a powerful figure in Washington, DC, regarding defense matters and national security. Ben graduated from West Point and left the Army as a captain. He was the owner, publisher, and editor of the *Armed Forces Journal International*, which was the premier defense publication at the time. Ben asked that I visit him at his offices on M Street NW in Washington to pick my brain on the Iran hostage rescue attempt and the need for reforms in Special Operations. I walked into his office without knowing much about him. His secretary ushered me in, and Ben gestured for me to sit down as he was on a phone call. He placed his hand over the phone and asked me if I wanted a drink to which I replied, "No thank you, sir." He then said, "This is Ross Perot on the line." Ben was cussing and swearing, and I was thinking that this couldn't be real. As I found out later, it was real. Ben had known Perot when he was at West Point and Perot was at the Naval Academy. Ben had written a book about Perot's operation to rescue one of his employees from Tehran after the Ayatollah Khomeini ascended to power. Perot asked Ben not to write about the treatment that one of his employees on the rescue had received afterwards. Ben refused, and Perot would not allow the book to be published. Perot then contracted with Ken Follett to write about the event in a book titled *On Wings of Eagles*.

After Ben finished his call with Perot, he took another phone call and told me it was John Lehman, the Secretary of the Navy. Ben again cussed and swore and said that if Lehman didn't have his aide show up in 30 minutes, he would go public with some story. The thought was running through my mind that this can't be real, that Ben is a phoney.

Twenty minutes later, Ben's secretary opens the door and lets a Navy rear admiral into the office. The admiral was very respectful towards Ben and handed over several papers. I was shocked and quickly realized that Ben Schemmer was the real deal!

People had differing opinions about Ben Schemmer. Some saw him as a loud, heavy drinker. Others saw him as a talented writer, defense analyst, and a person not to be ignored. I saw both those sides of Ben, but I also learned about another side that not many people knew about. That side of Ben was one where he embodied the spirit of *Intoku*. As the owner of the *Armed Forces Journal International*, he ensured that about half of those receiving the publication got it for free. He wrote a definitive story of the Son Tay Raid—the attempt to rescue POWs in North Vietnam—titled *The Raid*. He used the profit from the book to assist charities focusing on Special Operations. He helped to start the Special Operations Warrior Foundation, which was created in the aftermath of the 1980 failure to rescue hostages in Iran.

Ben convinced wealthy businessmen to donate and join him on the board of that foundation. His affinity for Special Operations, which began with his book on the Son Tay Raid, led him to advocate for significant reform within the Department of Defense. He worked quietly with Senators William Cohen (R-Maine) and Sam Nunn (D-Georgia), to understand the issues, and write the legislation that was to create the United States Special Operations Command and the Assistant Secretary of Defense for Special Operations and Low-Intensity Conflict in 1986. He used his power and influence to gain support for that legislation. On one occasion at the exclusive Jockey Club in Washington, DC, I saw him convince Senator Howard Baker (R-Tennessee) to support the Nunn-Cohen Bill that led to major reform in American Special Operations. He also made Senator Baker buy my dinner! I saw Ben stage a coup in the Warrior Foundation in 1998. He acrimoniously resigned from the board of directors and told them they were stupid if they did not hire retired Air Force Colonel John Carney as the CEO. The board had failed to take action to remove the previous CEO for poor performance.

John Carney was selected to lead the Warrior Foundation. When he stepped in, the foundation had less than $200,000 in assets. When John stepped down as CEO in 2013, there was close to $70 million in assets for the foundation. Ben also worked with John Carney to publish a coffee table book on U.S. Special Operations. John Carney, the lead combat controller on the Eagle Claw mission in 1980, also convinced the Air Force to start the Special Tactics career field before he retired from the Air Force. John is another sterling example of *Intoku*. John Carney was one of Ben's favorite friends because of his spirit of *Intoku*. John and I mourned the loss of Ben at 71 years of age in Naples, Florida, of a cardiac incident. Ben had met his fourth wife, Elizabeth, a former flight attendant, when she found him unconscious on a sidewalk and got him medical attention. They just don't make many people like Ben Schemmer.

I also learned the insidious side of politics. I was asked to visit with two special assistants in a Cabinet department who were trying to get Charlie Beckwith to endorse their efforts for a commemorative pistol for the National Rifle Association. They were young lawyers who had helped in a presidential campaign for Ronald Reagan and used that involvement as leverage to gain their positions in government. They were trying to impress me and told me of a scheme where they would provide grants if they were given a percentage of the grant under the table. On one visit to their offices, they summoned me to a door that they cracked open. I peered through the crack in the door and saw the daughter of a Cabinet secretary having sex on a desk with another special assistant. I didn't say a word, but the thought ran through my mind about what good my time in the Army—and putting myself in harm's way—had accomplished in the light of this despicable behavior. What I witnessed was certainly not a good example of *Intoku*.

One of the best things that happened to me in Austin was the chance to get back into Aikido training. I looked at several offerings and found that Mark Leidig led the best group. Mark had learned most of his Aikido from Shizuo Imaizumi in New York. Imaizumi Sensei had been a so-called *shido-in* or live-in student with Morihei Ueshiba, the founder of Aikido, who was called OSensei. Ueshiba Sensei had stopped using the term *uchi-deshi* and replaced it with *shido-in*. Imaizumi Sensei, and a few others, had to tend to OSensei's needs as he became older and frail. When OSensei died, Imaizumi Sensei accompanied the family as a photographer on a trip through Japan. Imaizumi Sensei was a 7th Dan in Aikido. He chose to follow Koichi Tohei Sensei when Tohei left the Aikikai hombu dojo and started his own style known as Shinshin Toitsu Aikido. In 1975, Tohei instructed Imaizumi to open a dojo in New York City, where Mark Leidig met him. Mark Leidig was an excellent instructor and was assisted by Kim Caroland. David Hamilton, Terry Startzel, and I joined the group about the same time and helped Mark take his organization to a higher level. Aikido practice really helped me overcome the anger that I felt when I retired from the Army. As I would learn years later, I had Post-Traumatic Stress Disorder with anger being the principal manifestation. Aikido, with its close attention on blending with others, was most helpful to me.

Before I departed SAS of Texas, I was the recipient of an act of *Intoku* by Dick Potter, Delta's first deputy commander. Dick was in command of the 10th Special Forces Group at Fort Devens, Massachusetts, when he found out that I had been made to retire as a master sergeant rather than sergeant major. Dick tasked his Staff Judge Advocate to contact me and to help me prepare an appeal to the Army Board for Correction of Military Records. Thanks to Dick and his lawyer, my appeal was accepted a year later, and I was given back pay as a sergeant major. That helped our financial situation greatly.

CHAPTER 18

The Land of Enchantment—Albuquerque, New Mexico

From the time I decided I needed to leave SAS of Texas, it took me approximately two months to find a job. I had hoped to find work in Austin, but there was not much available. I had befriended the security director of the Austin National Bank, and he informed me of the modest salaries for bank security personnel. I reached out to my friend Wayne Adams, the director of security for the DOE Nevada Operations Office. Wayne did not have any vacancies but informed me about openings in the Albuquerque Field Office of DOE. He put in a recommendation for me and informed me how to apply. As I found out later, the Albuquerque DOE Office oversaw the nuclear weapons complex and that security for the complex had come under heavy Congressional scrutiny for being inadequate. I applied, and I was hired immediately.

Once again, I left Mi Hye alone in our house with the task of trying to sell it. It was not a great time to sell, and it took several months and one bad offer before we could sell our home. I would try to get to Austin from Albuquerque at least twice a month. It was over a 700-mile drive that would usually take 11 hours. Friends on the Texas Highway Patrol helped me plan a route where I could speed without much chance of getting a ticket. I could make the trip in eight and a half hours, going over 100 miles per hour for much of the way. I found an unfurnished apartment and would live lean and mean until Mi Hye joined me. My only piece of "furniture" was a folding Japanese mattress I had bought when I was a bachelor in Okinawa. That was not a hardship because of the time I would spend on the road doing inspections.

The Albuquerque Operations Office oversaw security at the main contractor and National Laboratory locations involved in the production of nuclear weapons. Los Alamos and Lawrence Livermore Laboratories were responsible for the design of the weapons; Sandia National Laboratories was responsible for the engineering portion including the arming, fusing and firing systems; the Pantex Plant in Amarillo, Texas, was responsible for final assembly and disassembly; Rocky Flats in Boulder, Colorado, was the main plutonium processing facility; the three other main operations were in Kansas City, Pinellas, and Mound, which was near Dayton, Ohio.

The security department at the Albuquerque Operations Office inspected physical security, guard force capabilities, accounting of nuclear materials, and personnel security. The Department of Energy issued Q clearances, which required special background investigations equivalent to those used in the rest of government for top secret clearances. Roy Crouch headed the Albuquerque security department. He would retire shortly after I signed on and replaced by Randolph Sabre, a former Army helicopter pilot.

When I reported for my new job as a physical security specialist, the Albuquerque Operations Office Manager, Ray Romatowski, called me in and placed me on a management Tiger Team that he had formed to address security preparations for the nuclear weapons complex. He had previously been with the National Aeronautics and Space Administration and had transferred to the Department of Energy when it was stood up in 1977 by President Carter. He was under a lot of pressure from Representative John Dingell (D-Michigan) who was very critical of the security at nuclear weapons facilities. Romatowski was happy to have me on the rolls because of my extensive security background, not often found in those assigned to the Albuquerque Operations Office. Being on the Tiger Team was an ideal opportunity to learn about the approach to security throughout the complex and to get a solid understanding of the capabilities and problems. The Tiger Team completed its report after an intense two months. Romatowski presented me with a manager's award and a cash bonus that was greatly appreciated.

After the Tiger Team, I fully joined the security department and began participating in inspections of the different facilities in the nuclear weapons complex. I quickly discovered several things of concern or that would affect me. The first was the lack of formal training for my counterparts. Everyone learned their job responsibilities through on-the-job training without any formal education and training. For example, the only two people other than myself with knowledge of physical security and guard forces were a former Army Military Police officer who only served a few years before leaving the Army, and a former nuclear weapons courier. Phil Burnworth was the former nuclear weapons courier and became a close friend. The second was that there was a definite clique, and I was not to be one of them. That didn't bother me much as there was meaningful work to do that I could accomplish despite not being one of the favored sons. I also learned that at all the weapons complex locations, there was only a single location where a DOE security person was responsible for overseeing security on the part of the contractors daily. Her name was Maggie Schumann, a wonderful person who was continually challenged because she was a female and did not have the full support of her DOE bosses. I also noted that security for the laboratories and contractors was seldom led by anyone with a strong security background. The exception was at Kansas City where Otto Handwerk, a former FBI supervisor and Frank Maudlin, a former police officer, were in charge. As with my DOE counterparts, there was no central training for those responsible for security at the laboratories and contract locations. The DOE later took steps to rectify that by creating a central training academy.

DOE had an excellent policy concerning the issuance of security clearances and the handling of classified information. However, the policy on physical security and guard force operations was inadequate, along with active counterintelligence programs to detect espionage. Representative Dingell was justified in his harsh criticism of DOE and its contractors. He was also realistic in his approach to improving security by ensuring that DOE received sufficient funding to do so. In my opinion, much of that money was squandered because of the absence of policy and training. I saw the contractor organizations independently hiring subcontractors to run unrealistic exercises and present dubious recommendations on security improvement. The two most egregious examples follow. A subcontractor had put forth an unrealistic scenario where they would steal nuclear material inside a tunnel complex by breaching vault doors with explosives. The amount and placement of the explosives, and also their timeline, was completely unrealistic, and showed their lack of operational experience and technical knowledge. The second bad example was a subcontractor insisting that helicopters could be assembled and used against a facility to steal nuclear materials. The chances of a terrorist group being able to steal or procure the number of helicopters proposed by the subcontractor were illogical for the area concerned. Worse yet, the subcontractor then proposed a defense in which the guard force would establish a cordon rather than directly engage the terrorist group. I suggested to the security force that they not follow that guidance and that they could use their armored vehicles to ram and destroy the helicopters if that unlikely situation were ever to occur.

Within DOE, there are some excellent initiatives that were not fully used because of the lack of policy and training. Sandia National Laboratories was well-funded to conduct research and develop physical security equipment, including personnel and vehicle barriers, sensor systems, entry control technology, and security monitoring operations. The expertise they developed could have been put to better use if DOE had developed a means of providing expert advice to the other contract locations to protect nuclear materials. Instead, each contractor was left to its own devices to determine what systems might work for them and then independently contract for their installation without seeking or receiving advice from real experts. Each of the contractor locations spent a great deal of effort on simulating different terrorist scenarios. Mostly, they were poorly designed due to the lack of training or bad advice from subcontractors. The DOE had also mandated using a system Sandia National Laboratories had developed for the U.S. Army, and that the DOE called the Multiple Integrated Laser Engagement System (MILES). The system consisted of eye-safe laser emitters mounted on weapons, with everyone wearing a vest with sensors on it. Should the laser beam hit one of these sensors, the person would be neutralized. All too often, I found that the desire to "win" led to cheating. Cardboard could stop the laser beam from engaging the sensors, and people were often caught using other methods to shield themselves from the laser beam. However, it would not stop a real bullet. On the plus side, security personnel responded well when DOE umpires on an exercise would take steps to stop cheating and to create realistic exercises.

I enjoyed my time with DOE. The work was rewarding, and I quietly influenced and mentored others both within DOE and their security contractors. The pay was good and, although I was not in the inner clique, I knew there were opportunities for growth and promotion. Mi Hye and I found an excellent realtor named Diane Green who would become a great friend. She helped us find a home built to specifications in a gated community adjacent to a golf club. Mi Hye found work with Honeywell as an electronics assembler, and our financial situation began to improve significantly. Life was also good on the personal side. I ran into Major Dick Broder and his wife. Dick had been of great help to me at the Army's Sergeants Major Academy. He had retired and his wife had opened a fast-food restaurant inside one of the malls, selling teriyaki bowls. Another significant event was that I met Steve Casalnuovo at an Aikido seminar in Boulder, Colorado. I convinced Steve and Jennifer Yazawa to start an Aikido club in Albuquerque. Steve was an engineer at Sandia National Laboratories, and Jennifer was a teacher and had moved from Austin where she practiced Aikido under Mark Leidig. We started to train in a public park but kept looking for opportunities to train indoors with mats. The break came through the University of New Mexico Community College system. I met with Linda Alsup and Dora Delgado who were intrigued by the prospects of an Aikido class. They were very helpful and arranged for me to meet with a YMCA branch that had an agreement with Hoover Middle School. That school had wrestling mats that we could use for Aikido classes. What started with three of us working out in a park would eventually lead to over 30 dedicated students.

***

In the summer of 1985, I was approached by the vice president for administration at Sandia Labs. He oversaw Sandia's security organization and offered me a manager's position at a significant pay raise. I asked him what I needed to do to apply. He told me that the only thing I needed to do was to gain the approval of my supervisors at DOE and that there would be no hard feelings on DOE's part. I told him I was prepared to do what he asked but that it would take me out of contention for a promotion at DOE. The VP told me not to worry and the job was mine. After a few weeks, I went back to the VP and told him I had done his bidding and that there were no hard feelings on the part of DOE. He told me that was great and that he was leaving. When I asked him when he was coming back, he told me he was being reassigned to AT&T, but had ensured that the director of security at Sandia was on board. I found out later that either he or the security director lied. My mistake was not getting anything in writing or in a recorded conversation. That was a hard lesson for me—and I lost out on a promotional opportunity at DOE.

My stubborn nature and wounded pride led me to make Sandia deliver on the VP's broken promise. All I got from the Sandia security director was hot air saying he was working on the matter, which I knew wasn't the case. I sought help from Bill Myre, a respected high-level technical director at Sandia who oversaw the Nuclear Emergency Search Team effort for Sandia, among other responsibilities. I had befriended Bill Myre when I was on active duty and working on nuclear terrorism matters. He remembered that I had helped Sandia's reputation on the Prince Sky exercise by making up for the lack of experience on the part of Sandia's lead on that exercise. Bill was yet another person who embodied *Intoku* and I was honored to be his friend. It took about a month before he called me and said that he could not negotiate a management position for me but could get me on the rolls with a pay raise. I thanked him profusely and accepted the offer.

I was brought into Sandia's security organization to work emergency management issues under Jim Kaiser. Jim Kaiser was a gentleman with little security experience but glad to have me on board. His boss was Bob Wilde who I had met when he was a member of Sandia's NEST organization. There were four of us working for Jim Kaiser. Of the other three, only one had any experience in emergency management. His name was Jim Altwies, a retired Marine Corps major, who became a very close friend along with his wife Janice and three daughters. Jim and I worked hard to build an emergency management program, an emergency operations center, and to conduct exercises for management to handle security incidents that might occur within Sandia.

The only challenging part of the job was getting Sandia management to learn how to make decisions during a crisis. I started a counterintelligence effort at Sandia, where I would brief those attending international events and debrief them afterwards. It came as no surprise to learn that foreigners were approaching many Sandia employees attending conferences to elicit information about the nuclear weapons program. Jim Kaiser decided to retire, and I was in charge of the department for a short period. Bob Wilde called for a meeting one day and came in to announce Jim Kaiser's replacement. Jim Altwies and the other two looked at me with the expectation that I would be promoted. Instead, Bob announced that it was another person. A person who had an administrative position and no experience in security. I was severely disappointed and made up my mind to seek a transfer. I felt that the security director missed an opportunity to make up for the promise made by the departed VP or at least compete for the position. He did neither, and I was determined not to work for his organization or him any longer.

Once again, Bill Myre came to my rescue. He brought me into his directorate to work on NEST matters, physical security research and development, and as a liaison with the military for projects that Sandia did on their behalf. I learned about the caste system at Sandia. Simply stated, there were three general categories of employees at Sandia. At the lowest end were technicians who did not have college degrees but who were master craftsmen and machinists. They were talented, paid decently, but would never get management positions. The next level was called Members of the Laboratory Staff (MLS), people who generally worked in support or administrative positions and had college degrees. The highest level was a Member of the Technical Staff (MTS), who were engineers and scientists. There was a pecking order within the MTS who were influenced by the level of college degree held, where it was obtained, and what one's grade point was.

My work with the technical staff members was rewarding. I brought practical experience to many of their projects and my advice was valued. I also devoted a goodly amount of time to the NEST program. Bill Myre had me representing Sandia with the senior NEST program managers at Los Alamos National Laboratory, Lawrence Livermore National Laboratory, EG&G in Las Vegas, and the DOE Nevada Operations Office. I worked on exercises and developed a key leader training course for NEST. I gained the respect of and became friends with the likes of Bill Chambers and Carl Henry at Los Alamos, Bill Nelson at Lawrence Livermore, Hap Lamonds and Gene Sasso at EG&G, and Troy Wade, Ernie Campbell, and Wayne Adams of DOE. They were all quiet professionals who wanted to do what was right for America and the NEST program. It was indeed a joy to work with them. Other interesting assignments included collaborating with Jim Rea and Sandia VP Bob Pureifoy to address a defect in a particular nuclear weapon design.

***

In 1988 I was asked to be the chief controller and scenario developer for Compass Rose, a major national terrorism exercise. It was held in the San Diego area and involved the Department of Energy, the FBI, local law enforcement, and the military's Joint Special Operations Command. Estimates were that the Department of Energy spent $10 million to conduct the exercise. I had the opportunity to meet two young FBI agents, Marene and Hank Allison. Marene was a graduate of the first female class at West Point. She and Hank were Military Police officers, got married, and decided to leave the military and join the FBI. Marene led the FBI planning effort for the exercise and gave me credit for helping to mentor her. In 2023, Marene retired as the security director for the large pharmaceutical firm Johnson & Johnson and was also inducted as a Distinguished Graduate of the United States Military Academy.

Another noteworthy project that I led was to work with the Defense Nuclear Agency (DNA) on Recapture/Recovery operations for stolen nuclear weapons. That assignment gave me the opportunity to travel overseas to locations where U.S. nuclear weapons were stored and to evaluate their security preparations. This project was instrumental in giving me firsthand knowledge of security against acts of terrorism. The lead for DNA was Lieutenant Commander Neil Ramsey and we became close friends as we traveled through Germany, Italy, and Turkey.

Among the many recommendations we made were ways to improve the deployment of response forces and their tactics, enhanced use of defensive weaponry, and planning improvements. There were some memorable personal moments on the project.

In northern Italy, Neil and I stayed at a villa as there was no hotel accommodation available. When we checked in, there was a wedding celebration and the wedding party invited us to participate in the festivities—we had a great time thanks to the Italian hospitality. When Neil and I left northern Italy, a major earthquake closed large portions of the autostrada leading to our next location. It added five hours to our trip, but we were able to see several castles as we took detours on surface roads.

In Turkey, our military escort did not show up. So, I rented a car and we drove through the Turkish countryside for over 100 miles and quickly learned the rules of the road—honk your horn, flash your lights, and then pass cars, people, and carts! Our military hosts showed us where we could buy some quality Turkish rugs. Art Trujillo from Sandia accompanied Neil and me on that trip. He and Neil bought several rugs which I fastened to the top of the rental car. We made quite a sight as we drove back to the airport after finishing our assessment.

Yet another fascinating assignment was to be part of a Nuclear Regulatory Commission effort to work with the Japanese Atomic Energy Research Institute and the Korean Atomic Energy Research Institute, to consider security preparations at nuclear reactors. Liz Ten Eyck led the NRC effort. She was the sister of my Secret Service friend Tom Quinn, and extremely competent. We found security adequate at the facilities we visited. In my opinion, the most secure facility we toured was the experimental breeder reactor that the Japanese were building in western Japan, called Monju located in Tsuruga, Fukui Prefecture. Although security was tight, the Japanese government closed the facility in 2016 due to mismanagement, high costs, and other problems.

Bill Myre retired from Sandia and was replaced by Jim Jacobs. Jim was a gruff person but with a heart of gold. He was a hard taskmaster and consumed by delivering the best product or service possible. A substantial change came to Sandia Labs after Admiral James Watkins became the secretary of energy. Overnight, he declared that all maintenance and operating contractors of the DOE would be liable for both civil and criminal activities related to nuclear security. He declared that all DOE elements would be in full compliance with Environmental Protection Agency and Occupational Safety and Health Administration standards. My thoughts were that this was an ill-thought-out decision. With the advent of the nuclear weapons program, there was a steep learning curve concerning safety as many developments were based on brand-new concepts and experiments.

As a result of the Watkins decision, the cost of doing business increased enormously for the contractors. AT&T, which had operated Sandia Labs for $1 a year, decided that was enough and gave up the contract. Martin Marietta Corporation initially took over the contract and was later bought out by Lockheed Martin. A wholesale change in leadership occurred, particularly on the administrative side. Jim Jacobs was lured to the administrative side to run the facilities organization for Sandia. He had a management position open that I applied for and was selected for. It was a joy working for Jim Jacobs—just as it was working for Bill Myre. For Jim, I initially ran a customer service department responsible for helping the line organizations with facilities projects. I then moved to another department that was responsible for facility standards and quality improvement. I was very fortunate to have a wonderful person as my secretary, Carol Wilson. She had a heart of gold and cared about everyone she worked with.

When I initially took the Customer Service Department, morale was low. The folks I had working for me didn't have college degrees and subsequently were on the low end of Sandia's caste system. Yet, they were good-hearted people that wanted to add value through their work. I helped them develop procedures and processes and then moved towards a self-directed work team. I had one of the representatives be responsible for our weekly department meeting. I intended to help them gain confidence and grow. That proved to be very insightful, as I was called upon to be part of the Branch Davidian review by the Department of Treasury and had to make several trips to Washington, DC.

CHAPTER 19

The Branch Davidian Incident Review

The Secret Service asked me to participate in the 1993 review of the Branch Davidian incident at Waco, Texas, because of my reputation. The review examined the actions taken by the Bureau of Alcohol, Tobacco, and Firearms to investigate and attempt a warrant service against Vernon Wayne Howell (aka David Koresh) for the illegal conversion of weapons to fully automatic capability and illegal manufacture of explosive devices. I went to Jim Jacobs and he gave me his full approval to participate in the investigation, knowing the importance and the value of my contributions to the country.

When it was first decided to have an internal government review of the incident at Waco, it was supposed to be a joint review of ATF and FBI actions. The Department of Justice requested that the reviews be separated due to an ongoing FBI investigation. When the review was to be a joint review, Jeff Wehmeyer from the FBI stood up for me, and Lew Merletti from the Secret Service, along with Secret Service agent Joe Masonis, sought my participation. I had first met Jeff when he was the FBI SWAT leader for the Washington Field Office. Lew Merletti headed the treasury review team. He was a former Special Forces officer in Vietnam and both he and Joe Masonis knew me well from my work with the Secret Service both on active duty and later. The Treasury review team reported to the Undersecretary of Treasury for Law Enforcement Ron Noble. Ron was a former assistant U.S. attorney with an excellent reputation. He would later become the secretary general of INTERPOL for many years.

The teasury team included several lawyers; Bill Bradley and Beth Jones were the two most outstanding members of the team. Another key member was John Battle who came to the team from the Federal Law Enforcement Training Center at Glynco, Georgia. John did a tremendous job of organizing and digitally filing the thousands of pages of interviews and evidence used to reach the report's conclusions. Other than me, other consultants were brought in to provide independent expert opinions. My friend, John Kolman from the Los Angeles Sheriff's Department, was the most notable and best qualified. An assistant chief of police from the New York

Police Department and the lieutenant responsible for NYPD SWAT operations were also good contributors. The last was retired Colonel Rod Paschall, the second commander of the Delta Force, who added little but kept angling for future work, which he never received!

The team conducted interviews, reviewed numerous documents, and scrutinized photographs and videos to reach its conclusions. We heard that the investigation of the Branch Davidians began when a delivery service had some boxes addressed to the Branch Davidians break open with gun parts and grenade casings spilling out. The McLennan County Sheriff's Office, which covered Waco, Texas, received the report. The ATF was then notified, initiating a year-long investigation. During their investigation, they established an undercover house across the road from the Branch Davidian compound with the agents posing as college students. They heard explosions and automatic weapons fire that helped establish probable cause for a search warrant as the Davidians did not possess the proper authorization for automatic weapons or explosives. The Houston Field Office of ATF took the lead in the investigation and the warrant service. ATF determined that entry into the compound was necessary to seize evidence for weapons and explosives violations. Second-guessers often asked why ATF did not arrest David Koresh outside the compound. The simple answer is that such an arrest would not have resulted in the seizure of evidence for weapons and explosives violations.

ATF did not have a nationwide SWAT team like the FBI's Hostage Rescue Team. They had to assemble agents from other ATF offices, including Dallas, Albuquerque, and Little Rock. The ATF assistant special agent in charge of the Houston office was working on a national response plan for sweeping warrant services and the decision was made to use that plan even though it had yet to be tested. A U.S. Army advisor to the Texas National Guard recommended that ATF seek training from the Army's Special Forces. A request was made, and personnel from the 3rd Special Forces Group were sent to Fort Hood, Texas, to train the ATF agents on room entry and hostage rescue. A court order was obtained for the warrant service based on probable cause, and the date for the raid was planned for early March. ATF learned that the *Waco Tribune-Herald* was planning a major article concerning the Branch Davidians. ATF feared that the publication of the article would lead to an uproar by the Davidians that would trigger violence. ATF approached the newspaper and asked for their cooperation not to publish the article. The newspaper was part of Cox Communications headquartered in Atlanta, Georgia. The Cox security director was a retired U.S. Secret Service agent, and ATF hoped he would understand and assist in securing permission not to publish the article until after the raid. Cox decided not to delay publication of the article, that was published with the front page taken by the article and a large picture of Koresh.

ATF then decided to move the date of the warrant service to February 28 rather than March. The plan was to hide agents in the back of two cattle trailers towed by pick-up trucks to enter the compound property and then launch their raid. They followed the bad advice of the Texas National Guard advisor, who recommended that National Guard helicopters be flown at the back of the compound, diverting attention from the effort at the front. One of the critical factors to success and to minimize casualties, both on the part of the Davidians and ATF, was to separate the men from where ATF believed there was a central arms storage room. The undercover operation determined the regular routine during the day was for the men to go outside the main building and continue working on an underground structure. The Davidians were not seen carrying weapons to that work location by the undercover agents. ATF was set to conduct the raid except for one last step that would ultimately lead to the compromise of the raid. During their training by Special Forces at Fort Hood, the SF medical sergeant highly recommended that they have a medical evacuation plan. That required ATF to contract for an ambulance and medical evacuation. However, due to a limited budget, the contract specified a time frame that, regrettably, would reveal the timing of the raid. Our investigation showed that the contracted ambulance service dispatcher's boyfriend was a television cameraman. She told him about the contract, and he notified his colleagues of the plan.

The newspaper and television station then planned to divide into two groups with one group going to the back of the Davidian compound and the other to the front. Both groups left early in the morning of February 28 to position themselves. Because they were early, they avoided being stopped by Texas Highway Patrol officers, who would establish roadblocks later. The media group headed for the front of the compound got lost. They saw a rural postal carrier coming down the road and asked him for directions. The postal carrier asked them why they wanted to know where the compound was. The media advised him to stay away from the compound as the ATF and National Guard were going to raid it. The postal carrier's name was Perry Jones, and he was a member of the Branch Davidians. He left the media and went straight to the compound. One of the ATF undercover agents had entered the compound for a last-minute reconnaissance. He was greeted by Koresh who led him into a private room and was attempting to convert the agent to join the Branch Davidians. As the agent recounted during the investigation, Koresh's followers came to the room twice to ask him to take a telephone call. Koresh waved them off. On the third attempt, the followers physically pulled Koresh out of the room. Koresh came back to the room a short time later. His hands were shaking. He dropped his Bible, and then told the undercover agent that he should leave because the ATF and National Guard were coming to raid the compound. The agent immediately left and crossed the street to the undercover house, where he called the assistant special agent in charge of the Houston office, Chuck Sarabyn. Sarabyn asked the agent whether he saw the Davidians getting prepared and whether he saw them in the windows. The answer to both questions was no. The question Sarabyn should have asked but didn't was whether the agent saw the men working outside the main building, as that was critical to success. Sarabyn should have also recognized that the raid was compromised. Instead, he drove at a high rate of speed to a community center where the SWAT personnel were assembled. He ran into the building and shouted to the team, "Let's go, they know we're coming." The agents had a great deal of respect for Sarabyn and immediately headed out to the cattle trailers and headed to the compound.

ATF entered the compound and exited the cattle trailers. One of the agents ran towards the front door where Koresh was standing. The agent was shouting, "Police, Police." Koresh shut the front door and the agent kept running towards it. The door erupted with gunfire from within and the agent lost his thumb. ATF agents climbed a ladder and headed for Koresh's bedroom, suspecting it held the weapons. Automatic weapons fire repulsed them. A standoff then took place. Four ATF agents were killed, all shot in the head attesting to the marksmanship of the Davidians, while 19 others were wounded. One of the wounded was Agent Kenny King, a former U.S. Marine officer, who lay injured and wounded after falling off a roof for some four hours. ATF agents were outgunned and received wounds from grenades. Six Branch Davidians were killed on the first day of what turned out to be a 51-day siege. Allegedly, two of the Davidians were killed by other Davidians. One of the Davidians killed was Perry Jones, the rural postal carrier. After about four hours, ATF Agent Jim Kavanaugh and a McLennan County sheriff's deputy negotiated a cease-fire. ATF was allowed to retrieve their wounded and dead and left the compound in abject defeat.

ATF asked the FBI to assume jurisdiction for the event, and they deployed their hostage rescue team to lay siege to the compound and attempt to negotiate a settlement. Koresh allowed 21 children and two elderly people to be released. Negotiations were going nowhere. Janet Reno, the Attorney General, authorized the FBI to enter the compound using riot control gas and armored combat engineer vehicles to bring an end to the siege. On the last day of the siege, nine Branch Davidians left the compound and were later tried and convicted of different offenses. Over 70 Branch Davidians, including children, perished on the last day. After some 20 Congressional hearings and legal reviews, it was determined that the Branch Davidians were responsible for setting fire to the compound. Autopsies later conducted also revealed that there were Branch Davidians who either shot or stabbed each other to death. It was truly a tragic ending.

My involvement in the investigation—published as the Report of the Department of the Treasury on the Bureau of Alcohol, Tobacco and Firearms investigation of Vernon Wayne Howell in September 1993—had a personal aspect. I received two death threats from unknown individuals. Additionally, several Branch Davidians from Hawaii lost their lives. One individual, who survived but was convicted of voluntary manslaughter while using a firearm during a crime, was the son of a close friend and former Criminal Investigation Division agent. His father refused to talk to me after my involvement in the investigation. I found it difficult to understand why he had animosity towards me.

After the review was completed, Ron Noble asked me to advise him on creating an All-Treasury SWAT team that would call upon the ATF, Secret Service, IRS, and U.S. Customs and Border Patrol to form a unit. On April 19, 1994, I was presenting an account of the Branch Davidian incident at the U.S. Air Force Special Operations School, when my class was interrupted by an announcement that the Murrah Building in Oklahoma City had been bombed. As it turned out, the bombing conducted by Timothy McVeigh and Terry Nichols was partially out of retribution for the Branch Davidian incident.

After completing my work for the Department of Treasury, I returned to work at Sandia Labs running the Customer Service Department. Just before Christmas of 1993, I accompanied Nettie Jones, one of my great customer representatives, and Jim Jacobs to a meeting with a new Sandia VP from Martin Marietta. Jim Jacobs had been asked to attend to an issue that concerned the VP. The VP had promised Jim that he would be allowed to make some organizational changes in return. Jim reported that the issue had been taken care of, and asked when he would be able to institute the promised changes. The VP would not look Jim in the eye, kept shuffling papers on his desk, and then said that he had changed his mind, and dismissed the three of us. Jim was astounded and deeply disappointed. He wished Nettie and I a Merry Christmas, and we left feeling bad about how he was treated and the failure of the VP to honor his word. Jim was an honorable person whose handshake and word meant everything. On December 29, 1993, Jim died of a heart attack. I attributed his heart attack to a broken heart from being lied to by the VP. This was a portent of things to come.

When Jim Jacobs first became the director of facilities, he made two excellent choices for his front office. Martha Cesarano was his secretary, and Carol Harrison was his administrative assistant. Both were very competent and humble people. With the passing of Jim, they both left. Jim's replacement was not of the same caliber, but was okay to work for. He asked me to take the Standards and Quality Improvement Department, and I did as he requested. The senior VP that Lockheed Martin had brought in was Jim Tegnelia. He announced that all future management promotions would use a participative management selection board.

There were two director openings that I applied for, one being the director of security and the other being a newly created position as the director of ethics for Sandia National Laboratories. Both selection boards told me informally that I was their preferred candidate. Several weeks passed after the two boards had met without an announcement of who had been selected. I was finally approached by the vice president for safety and security, who had come from Oak Ridge. She wouldn't say if I was the person selected by the selection board but asked if I was still interested in becoming the director of security. I told her I was, but I was also waiting to hear about the director of ethics position, and asked if she could wait a week or so. She never commented on my request.

Frankly, I preferred the ethics position because of the unethical behavior that shown by some of the new management team that had come in with Lockheed Martin. I was also not enthused about working for the person who called me in, as I had witnessed several incompetent decisions on her part. One of these decisions was the excessive cost and lack of common sense that I viewed one day in my facilities management role. I came across an operation to remove two floor tiles for asbestos testing. I saw two people in full protective clothing, including respirators inside an area marked by yellow tape. Only one was removing the floor tiles. Outside the tape were two others—in full protective gear—standing and watching inside another yellow taped area. Outside of the second yellow taped area stood one Sandia safety employee and one from the Department of Energy, both in street clothes. I was astounded by this overreaction to safety, which was at high cost to the taxpayer.

The announcements were made shortly after my meeting for the two director positions, and I was stunned and flabbergasted. The selection for the security director was a Hispanic with absolutely no background in security. Worse yet, Sandia Labs had settled out of court with an employee who was being sexually harassed by the selectee. To me, this choice smacked of affirmative action and selection based on race. The director of ethics was announced as a retired Air Force brigadier general who had previously been on the Air Force Thunderbird demonstration team. I discreetly inquired about the ethics position and was dismayed to discover what had happened. Apparently, I was the clear choice for the position, and head and shoulders above anyone else. Tegnelia asked the board if they had considered the Air Force general and was told that they had, but his application hadn't been received in time. Tegnelia told the board to reconsider. They did and ranked him sixth with me still as the preferred candidate. Tegnelia made the decision to hire the general regardless of what the board recommended. I heard that two board directors chose to retire because of what they considered to be a violation of ethics.

I was furious and consulted with a lawyer, who later became the Bernalillo County District Attorney. He advised me that it would likely be a four-year process, enumerated the costs to me, and discussed the composition of judges who would not be prone to decide in my favor. I appreciated his candor and decided not to pursue legal action. At the same time, I decided that I was done with the administrative side of Sandia and would go back to a research and development organization. My only regret in leaving the facilities organization was that I would miss the wonderful people in the two departments I managed. They worked hard and were team players. I would especially miss my secretary, Carol Wilson.

My time in the facilities organization also gave me the opportunity to get my master's degree and to build my Aikido dojo as my travel was considerably reduced. Mi Hye and I had invested in a second house that we leased back to the builder who was using it as a sales office and model home. I received a call from Diane Green, our realtor friend, who told me that she sensed something was wrong, but didn't have any details. I went to check and found the sales office abandoned with papers strewn around, and fixtures from two of the bathrooms had been removed. I surmised that the builder had taken them out to use in other homes. I went to their main office and saw tool marks on the door and the door ajar. The office was in disarray, and I knew something was wrong. I picked up some records and then called the State Attorney General's Office. Their investigation showed that the owner of the company was defrauding people in New Mexico, Colorado, and California. He was later convicted. I called on my Aikido student, Phil Parkinson, who repaired the damage, and we rented the home.

From 1994 to 1996, I was back to working on security and intelligence projects, mentoring others, and was involved with the Nuclear Emergency Search Team (NEST). One of the rewarding projects I led was when the Department of Energy requested that Sandia Labs sponsor a symposium to showcase DOE and their contractor work regarding counterterrorism. DOE provided a small amount of financial support, but I was confident that we didn't need much to put on a good symposium. I was very fortunate to have the support of Karen Shane who had exceptional planning abilities. She and I compiled a program that invited the various DOE contractors to display their counterterrorism efforts. DOE was very pleased with our accomplishments and decided to rotate the symposium in the following years. As mentioned, Karen and I had put the program together with very little funding. We were shocked to learn that another DOE entity was given over $1 million the following year to host another symposium. Using my contacts, we successfully got attendance from various law enforcement and military organizations. One of the rewarding things to me was to meet three majors who represented the U.S. Special Operations Command. They were Jim Holloway, Gus Taylor, and Shelley Bennett. They were bright and eager to do a good job. I took them under my wing from that point forward. Jim Holloway retired as a colonel and became the honorary colonel of the Special Forces Regiment. Gus Taylor retired as a lieutenant colonel and went on to a highly successful position providing support to Special Operations through the Naval Surface Warfare Center in Crane, Indiana. Shelly Bennett retired as a colonel and also did well after retirement.

In March 1996, I was on the way back to Albuquerque, flying out of Dulles Airport. I thought I saw General Wayne Downing getting on the plane. We stopped in Cincinnati for a plane change, and I saw that it was General Downing. I caught up with him and learned we were on the same flight out of Cincinnati going first to Colorado Springs and then Albuquerque. We got the airline to rearrange our seats and spent the flight to Colorado Springs catching up with each other. General Downing had retired earlier that year and was residing in Colorado Springs with his wife Kathy. That proved to be an auspicious meeting.

At Sandia Labs in early June 1996, I was tasked by two Sandia vice presidents to start a combating terrorism program to offer Sandia's services and expertise to the interagency community. This was a daunting task as I was expected to coordinate the activities related to countering terrorism of some eight directorates at Sandia. I was given no personnel other than being blessed with a super secretary in Sherry Wright to work with and no budget. Yet I was confident that I could put a program together.

CHAPTER 20

The Khobar Towers Review

My planning for a new program came to a screeching halt after the terrorist bombing of the Khobar Towers complex in Dhahran, Saudi Arabia, on June 25, 1996. A sewage truck loaded with explosives was detonated on the perimeter of the complex killing 19 U.S. Air Force personnel and wounding a reported 500 other Americans. On June 28, 1996, Secretary of Defense William Perry convinced General Wayne Downing, who had retired earlier in 1996 as the Commander of the United States Special Operations Command, to accept an appointment to lead a task force to examine the Khobar Towers event. General Downing immediately formulated a plan and contacted Colonel Steve Wright, who was on leave, to return to the Pentagon and start assembling the task force team. He gave Steve a list of names to contact, and I was one of those. Steve, who had served in the Delta Force and was a close friend, called me on July 4, 1996. I obtained permission from Sandia VP Roger Hagengruber to join the effort. The idea was that my involvement would contribute positively to the start of the combating terrorism program at Sandia Labs.

I hastily made my travel arrangements and got to the Pentagon where the task force had assembled on July 6, 1996. There was a flurry of activity to decide what to examine, where to look and to prepare to deploy. It was an amazing effort with Steve Wright as the Chief of Staff assembling people and issuing instructions. Astonishingly, we were ready to deploy on July 11, 1996. We had a plan to conduct the review, checklists, reference material, passports, visas, uniforms, and equipment for over 60 persons who had gathered from various locations and organizations to be on the task force. Other than General Downing and Steve Wright, some of the others included Lieutenant General James Clapper, who had retired in 1996 as the Director of the Defense Intelligence Agency; Marine Colonel Gordon Nash, who would run the operations shop; Army Colonel John Smith and Lieutenant Colonel Wayne Price, who were noted lawyers; Air Force Colonel Rocky Lane, who would lead the physical security review; two Air Force Office of Special Investigations agents, including Bob Pecha; Air Force Major Patricia Merrill, a medical doctor; an FBI Agent; Delta operators Sergeant Major Don Simmons, Lieutenant Colonel Doug Norvell, Sergeant Major Mike Vining (bomb expert); Lieutenant Colonel

Frank Newell; and Marine Captain Barry Neulen. The other unnamed persons on the task force were superb contributors, and all of them played as a team and were more than qualified to contribute.

Our first stop was at U.S. Central Command Headquarters at MacDill Air Force Base in Tampa, Florida. General Downing and the task force were met by General Binford Peay, the Central Command commander. Peay was not happy to see us and stated that he didn't know why we needed to be there. In the few days we spent at Central Command, we found ample reason for the task force to review what Central Command had done—and it was open to a lot of criticism. Their support for anti-terrorism and force protection left much to be desired along with their knowledge and support of the Air Force 4404th Wing (Provisional), which was the main unit at Khobar Towers. Part of the task force split off to visit Patrick and Eglin AFB where there were survivors from Khobar Towers and where several airmen who died at Khobar had been stationed.

On our second day in Tampa, General Downing had set up a secure video teleconference with Brigadier General Terryl Schwalier, the commander of the 4404th Wing (Provisional). When the task force was first formed, we believed our mission was to conduct an after-action review. Per instructions from Secretary of Defense Perry, that changed to become an investigation. When the teleconference opened, Schwalier was in a room surrounded by his staff believing that there would be questions that his staff would be able to answer. General Downing asked Schwalier to excuse his staff from the room. Schwalier did so but had a quizzical look on his face. He was floored when General Downing announced that he was under investigation and then had John Smith read him his rights. Schwalier's facial expressions showed his shock, but he cooperated fully and answered all questions that were posed to him.

We left Tampa on board a dedicated C-141 that would stay with us for over a week. The Air Force had put in business class seats, a command module, and a galley to cook meals. The crew was the epitome of professionalism. Our air planner was a Navy lieutenant commander and P3 pilot who ensured that our travel went off without a hitch. We landed in Riyadh, the capital of Saudi Arabia, where the Saudis made a big deal of checking passports and visas. I believe that was because some American politicians were attempting to attribute the events at Khobar Towers to the Saudis. After a few hours, we could board the C-141 and fly to Dhahran where we were greeted by our AFOSI agent, who had been sent ahead of the task force to make billeting and working space arrangements. We were also met by the new commander of the 4404th Wing (Provisional) and given a tour of the Khobar Towers complex and the buildings where the 19 airmen were killed. Khobar Towers had been built by the Saudi government in the hope that nomadic Saudi tribes would move into the complex, but that idea did not fit with the lifestyle of the nomadic tribes. The complex was then offered to the U.S. Air Force and U.S. Army.

Eight-story buildings were scattered throughout the compound, and there were huge apartments with multiple bedrooms, a spacious kitchen, and living room areas in each apartment. Many of the buildings were sparsely populated, and the task force was billeted in several apartments. There was more than enough room, and I slept in a bedroom by myself that was a good 400 square feet in size. It dawned on me that the occupants of Building 131, where 18 of the 19 deaths occurred, could easily have been moved either to the side of the building away from the perimeter or into other buildings. Such a move would have saved many, if not all, of the lives of those killed in the attack.

Work began in earnest the following day. We were presented with over 100 security improvements that the 4404th Wing had undertaken after a car bomb had killed seven people at the Office of Program Manager, Saudi Arabian National Guard, in Riyadh on November 13, 1995. Unfortunately, very few of those improvements helped with the security of the perimeter adjacent to the building where 18 deaths occurred at Khobar Towers. Many of the improvements were eye wash. For example, a two-and-a-half-ton truck was placed at the main entry point with the intention that it could be driven to halt an intruding vehicle. However, there was uncertainty as to who would operate the vehicle, implying that it might not be deployed promptly. Instead of becoming embroiled in assessing the supposed improvements, the task force looked for more fundamental factors that contributed to the casualties at Khobar Towers.

Pre-incident intelligence was a key. We found that there was but one human intelligence report from a source of unknown reliability that stated some 50,000 pounds of explosives were being smuggled into Saudi Arabia. It did not specify the group, what the explosives were to be used for, or any other meaningful details. On the other hand, we discovered eight reports of suspicious activity adjacent to Building 131 that were not properly analyzed by intelligence assets or the Air Force Security Police squadron. We also found that the Security Police squadron and the Wing intelligence personnel lacked the training to analyze terrorist activity. In addition, the Air Force OSI detachment was inadequately staffed and tasked with numerous other responsibilities. The lead OSI agent, Rick Redecliff, had conducted an assessment that pointed to the vulnerability of Building 131. However, no one paid much attention to his finding.

The Security Police Squadron was led by Lieutenant Colonel James Traister, who had an impossible job. He was faced with 10% work force turnover every week! In some cases, security policemen were sent for a few days' temporary duty. Due to the turnover, many security police had to be put on duty within hours of arriving at Khobar Towers after a long flight. They did not bring their own weapons, and were handed the weapon of the person they were relieving. On the night of the attack, Staff Sergeant Alfredo Guerrero was stationed on the roof of Building 519. He saw the sewage truck and a car approaching the perimeter fence, the occupants of the truck getting into the car, and departing. Guerrero immediately sensed what was going to happen. He radioed an alert and then began running through Building 131, pounding on doors and telling people to evacuate. His actions saved many lives.

The FBI had sent an investigative team to collect evidence and to conduct a detailed forensic examination of the bombing. They were working very hard and suffering from heat-related medical issues. Major Merrill from the task force assisted them with ways to avoid and cope with the heat and diarrhea. Mike Vining worked closely with the FBI to determine the approximate size of the bomb. Their estimate was that it was 4,000–6,000 pounds. This led to some controversy as the Defense Special Weapons Agency (DSWA) estimated that the bomb was 20,000–40,000 pounds, claiming a scientific analysis and recreation of the bomb. Months later, I made myself unpopular when I stated that a 50% error factor (the difference between 20,000 and 40,000) was not very scientific. I found out that they had never tried to pack that quantity of explosives into a sewage truck like the one used at Khobar Towers. Instead, they placed explosives on pallets to conduct their experiments and analysis.

There was also controversy over which terrorist group was responsible for the bombing. No group claimed credit for the bombing. Many intelligence analysts believed the bombing was the work of al-Qaeda, a Sunni-based organization led by Osama bin Laden with supporters in Saudi Arabia. The FBI, after months of investigation, concluded that Hezbollah, an Iranian Shia-backed terrorist group, was responsible.

In short, the task force concluded that the number of deaths could have been reduced by relocating occupants of Building 131 away from the side facing the perimeter of Khobar Towers. Accordingly, there was command responsibility on the part of the 4404th Wing (Provisional). On the other hand, the wing could have—and should have—been better supported by the Joint Task Force Southwest Asia to whom the 4404th Wing (Provisional) reported, the U.S. Central Command, and the Air Force component of the U.S. Central Command.

The task force had a secondary mission to evaluate anti-terrorism and force protection in the Middle East. Accordingly, members of the task force also went to Jeddah and Riyadh, Saudi Arabia; Bahrain; the United Arab Emirates; Qatar; Kuwait; and Egypt. Before leaving Dhahran, General Downing arranged a meeting with Prince Muhammad bin Fahd, the governor of Saudi Arabia's Eastern Provinces. Tom Quinn, formerly of the U.S. Secret Service, had helped to facilitate the meeting because of his connections with the Saudi royal family. Sheikh Muhammad maintained a certain distance as there were those in the Reagan administration who were trying to blame the Saudis for the bombing. The meeting was held in the Governor's Palace, and it was like stepping back in time. The palace guards looked like they were from the era of Lawrence of Arabia with bandoliers of ammunition across their chests and silver revolvers. There was a carpet at least 200 feet in length in the meeting room.

When the task force got to Kuwait, we were told that the Kuwaitis were paying for everything out of gratitude for the U.S. liberation of Kuwait in Operation Desert

Storm in 1991. Don Simmons and I had signed up for a 1st Special Forces Group reunion that we were unable to attend because we were on the task force. We took advantage of Kuwaiti hospitality by having a substantial meal of sushi and sashimi that cost over $200 for each of us. We toasted our friends who were at the reunion! In Egypt, the task force returned to the Pentagon to start drafting the investigative report. General Downing directed that Doug Norvell, SEAL Master Chief Kevin Farrell, and myself accompany him to visit several other countries to gain insights on anti-terrorism.

The day the team departed from Cairo, the four of us were invited to lunch by an Air Force major general who oversaw foreign military sales out of the U.S. Embassy. We were taken on a tour of the Pyramids and Great Sphinx, followed by an Air Force VIP jet flying above the Nile River Delta and landing at Tel Aviv. We were met by a young Navy officer who acted as if his job was to monitor us and report to the defense attaché. General Downing had me pull the young officer aside and tell him that we didn't need someone to meddle in our business and that we were acting at the direction of the Secretary of Defense. We were taken to a hotel where a Russian prostitute approached General Downing. Kevin, Doug, and I had a good laugh at that event. On the other hand, the task force scheduler had declared me as an intelligence officer—the Israelis had a female officer shadow me. That proved to be quite interesting! We paid a visit to the U.S. Embassy to meet with Ambassador Indyk and the CIA station chief. We were sitting in the "bubble" (a secure room shielded from electronic surveillance) when Big Bill Dickey, who was so helpful during Operation Eagle Claw, walked into the room. His jaw dropped as he saw people from different times in his life, having met me in 1980, General Downing later, and then Doug Norvell. He had no idea that we were visiting Israel and asked what we were doing. I piped up, saying that we were there to have him take us to dinner that night. Bill was a great sport and promptly agreed. That night he picked us up and drove us to Jerusalem for a great meal and camaraderie.

The next day we met with the Israeli Defense Force, then headed for Amman, Jordan. Our host was General Tahseen Shurdom, the director of public safety. He was a mountain of a man and a most gracious host. Additionally, Prince Abdullah wanted to meet with General Downing, whom he had known previously. Prince (now King) Abdullah took us to visit his special forces unit, which he had formed and previously commanded. We were given a tour and viewed demonstrations of their capabilities. Again, the task force scheduler had declared me as an intelligence officer, and I was being followed by a Jordanian officer. On the day we were to leave Jordan, I told Doug Norvell that I was going to shake the officer following me, which I did. Doug and General Downing had a good laugh as the officer was running around, asking where Mr "Hashimeto" was? General Downing nicknamed me the King of the Hashemites after that.

We left Jordan, flew over the Red Sea, and then to Cairo for a refueling. From there it was on to Naples, Italy, where we transferred to a Beech King Air aircraft.

Leaving Naples at sunset was a beautiful sight, and then we headed to Paris. We landed at Orly Airport, where Charles Lindbergh had completed his transatlantic flight years earlier. Paris was lit up and we saw the Eiffel Tower and the Champs-Elysées. A glowing McDonald's sign spoiled those wonderful sights as we approached Orly Airport. The following morning, we were hosted by the French National Gendarmerie, at their headquarters in Paris, where they shared their thoughts on Islamic terrorism. We left in the afternoon and headed for London. The following day, we met with the defense attaché and State Department regional security officer at the U.S. Embassy. Meetings were to take place with the British Ministry of Defence and MI-5. General Downing received a message from Secretary of Defense Perry, asking Downing to return for an important meeting. We had already scheduled a commercial flight for the following day, but General Downing insisted that he needed to get back earlier. The defense attaché's office located a scheduled C5 Galaxy flight out of Mildenhall headed for Andrews Air Force Base. I advised him to wait and take the commercial flight the next day, but he was adamant about leaving sooner. He allowed me to stay behind but made Doug Norvell and Kevin Farrell go with him. I had a pleasant dinner at the Intercontinental Hotel, slept well, met the State Department regional security officer for breakfast the following morning, and then made my way to Heathrow. When I got back to the Pentagon early that afternoon, I found out that the C5 had mechanical problems and Downing, Doug, and Kevin had to hustle to Lakenheath Air Base, where they got onto a military flight. They had arrived in Washington about an hour before I got back. General Downing told me not to rub it in!

It was now early August, and the pressure was on to publish the final report. General Downing tasked retired Army Colonel John McDonald to be the editor, and I was assigned to assist John. John did most of the editing and writing. In accordance with their specialties, the remainder of the task force prepared their input for the report. John had developed an excellent outline for the report that, with a few modifications, met Wayne Downing's approval. I would review the input for content and accuracy, then John would edit the input to improve clarity and fluency. Wayne Downing's goal was to finalize the report by the end of August. The previous week had been hectic for John and me. We would work until 2 AM, preparing the latest edit for Wayne Downing's review early the next morning. We would get back to work before 8 AM. John would make the changes to align with Wayne's preferences, and I would return to the task force elements to obtain clarifications or additional information requested by General Downing. Thanks to John McDonald, the deadline was met and the "Memorandum for the Secretary of Defense, Subject: Report of the Assessment of the Khobar Towers Bombing" was published on August 30, 1996. The unclassified portion exceeded 60 pages with a classified supplement that mainly dealt with intelligence matters.

Downing Assessment Task Force
NMCC Room 2C890, The Pentagon
Washington, DC 20310

OCT 2 1 1996

OCT 0 9 1996

MEMORANDUM THRU Mr. Roger Hagengruber, Sandia National Laboratories,
PO Box 5800, Albuquerque, NM 87185

SUBJECT: Letter of Commendation -- Mr. Wade Ishimoto

1. On 28 June 1996, the Secretary of Defense chartered the Downing Assessment Task Force to examine the facts and circumstances surrounding the 25 June 1996 bomb attack on the Khobar Towers complex in Dhahran, Saudi Arabia.

2. Within this charter, we were also tasked to assess the security infrastructure, policies, and systems in Dhahran and other U.S. Central Command facilities in the Area of Responsibility (AOR), and recommend measures to prevent similar attacks or minimize casualties and damage.

3. Please accept my sincere appreciation for Mr. Ishimoto's superb support as a member of the Downing Assessment Task Force. He was the consummate professional and was an essential member of the Task Force from the onset. His tremendous experience in intelligence, physical security, force protection and knowledge of the Middle East was simply invaluable to the completion of the mission. His insights into governments, their officials, and policies brought a much needed perspective to the entire assessment. Many of the U.S. military officials were either personally acquainted with or knew Mr. Ishimoto by reputation. Because of the respect they held for him, the work of the Task Force was often expedited or made more smoothly. His unique experience and understanding of the area was also put to excellent use in a Red Team effort which critically examined the Task Force report for accuracy and consistency. He directed and coordinated the effort to archive all report data, making this report an automated model for others to emulate. His knowledge of technologies and their potential utilization in force protection measures were essential to the report. Finally, Mr. Ishimoto's fine sense of humor and lack of ego often brought relief to otherwise tense situations during the many long and arduous hours under trying circumstances which surrounded the Task Force effort. His professionalism and dedication have contributed significantly to the report, which will further the national security interests of the United States.

4. I would also like to thank you for making Mr. Ishimoto available for this important work. On behalf of the Department of Defense and the Task Force, please accept my sincerest thanks.

WAYNE A. DOWNING
General, U.S. Army (Ret)
Director, Task Force

Downing Task Force commendation.

Talking about intelligence, Jim Clapper, who had retired as the Defense Intelligence Agency director earlier in 1996, came to my place of work one day and asked me what my problem was. He was quite upset as he felt that I was being overly critical of the Defense Intelligence Agency (DIA). Somehow, I calmed him down and we had a meaningful discussion. The first thing I mentioned was that there was but one true intelligence report from a human source, the report was not very detailed, came from an unproven source, and that the lack of intelligence collection against terrorist groups needed to be improved. Secondly, I discussed a term I had created called "analysis by mouse," where a supposed analyst would use a computer mouse to cut and paste portions of an intelligence report, and then speculate—rather than analyze—what the reporting could mean regarding specific targeting. As an example, I used the DIA *Military Intelligence Digest* article that some felt predicted the Khobar Towers incident. In my opinion, it was a classic example of "analysis by mouse." The article lacked analysis of potential targets, the identity of the group who would be responsible for the attack, provided no details of the modus operandi to be used, and did not specify when the attack might occur. Therefore, the article was almost useless. The last thing I emphasized was that the DIA had been granted additional analytical slots by Congress ever since the 1980 Iran hostage rescue failure specifically to address terrorism There were now over 500 analysts. General Clapper asked me how many in DIA were working on terrorism—and I responded that the DIA Joint Intelligence Task Force Combating Terrorism had roughly 125 people assigned. General Clapper was astounded and asked me what happened to all the slots. I gave him my opinion—he had been undermined by several people in DIA who had transferred slots to their own pet projects—most with only a peripheral bearing on terrorism. I could tell by his facial expressions that Jim Clapper was upset that people he had trusted had hoodwinked him.

The release of the report led to a wave of activity in the Department of Defense. The U.S. Air Force challenged some of the findings, to no avail. Brigadier General Schwalier was denied the promotion that he had earned and, in many ways, became a scapegoat while others in his chain of command escaped criticism. The Department of Defense changed its policy directives on anti-terrorism and force protection, and the Joint Chiefs created a position called J34 under the J3 Director of Operations. After the publication of the report, I assumed I would be free to return to Sandia Labs. However, General Downing asked me to stay on for several reasons, including ensuring that all the task force records were organized and turned over to the Defense Department. I enlisted the help of John Battle, who had been of great value in the Branch Davidian investigation in 1993. John helped to categorize and develop computer files to store the task force records.

I accompanied General Downing at a somber Senate Armed Services Committee hearing chaired by Strom Thurmond (R-SC) with John Warner (R-VA), also a leading player. Senator Thurmond quoted the philosopher Santayana, whose contention was that those who cannot remember the past are condemned to repeat it. Secretary of Defense William Perry and Chairman of the Joint Chiefs, General Shalikashvili, were grilled extensively and Secretary Perry accepted responsibility and spoke almost in a whisper. I also accompanied Wayne Downing to a meeting with Ike Skelton (D-MO), a powerful figure on the House Armed Services Committee.

Colonel Steve Wright and I closed the task force and I returned to Albuquerque and Sandia Labs in late October 1996. While I was on the task force, I regularly communicated opportunities for Sandia Labs to the director I reported to, only to discover that she had not followed up on any of these opportunities. Consequently, I began planning on how I would get the combating terrorism project at Sandia revived. A few weeks later, the director called me into her office to inform me that I should collect my salary and that of my secretary, Sherry Wright. I told her that I could do that, but I would then not be able to comply with the wishes of the two vice presidents to start a combating terrorism program. She insisted that I could, and I disagreed. She had never given me monetary resources or people to get the program started. It was pointless to argue. I left her office, returned to mine, and pondered how I would get out of this mess. As luck would have it, my phone rang, and it was Wayne Downing calling. He succinctly told me that I would be getting a call from an Air Force general. Without any further details, he told me, "You make up your mind on what to do."

Shortly thereafter, my phone rang again. It was Major General Gary Curtin, the Director of the Defense Special Weapons Agency (ODSWA) in Virginia. He informed me that DSWA had received a mission to establish Joint Staff Integrated Vulnerability Assessment Teams (JSIVAs), that he needed help, and wanted to discuss the matter with me. Suddenly I saw the way out of my predicament with my director. I obtained permission to travel and meet with Curtin. When I met with him, I discovered that Wayne Downing had highly recommended me to provide expertise for the new DSWA mission. Curtin told me that he had less than five months to reach an operational capability to conduct worldwide anti-terrorism and force protection assessments and really needed help. I quickly formulated a plan and gained Gary Curtin's approval. The plan would have me receive an Intergovernmental Personnel Act (IPA) assignment to DSWA for a period of at least three years. I sought out the DSWA general counsel, Bob Britigan, whom I had known previously along with the personnel director, Paul Morgan. They both heartily endorsed the plan and set things in motion to prepare the agreement for the assignment. I returned to Sandia Labs and obtained approval for the assignment. My predicament was over and a new career chapter was about to happen! I told Mi Hye what the plan was and why it was best for us to take the assignment. She was concerned, but once again was very supportive, even though she knew it would mean another temporary separation.

CHAPTER 21

Anti-terrorism

I reported to DSWA headquarters located at 6801 Telegraph Road in Alexandria, Virginia. Ironically, this was the same location that I had been to in 1965 to help clear the caseload of security investigations that I inherited. My IPA assignment was to be a special assistant to General Curtin, but I was asked to be the deputy director of the division that was being created to conduct the JSIVAs. In the interest of teamwork and getting the organization started I agreed to do so. Air Force Colonel Rick Kingman had been assigned as the director. Rick was a B-52 Stratofortress navigator and had no experience in anti-terrorism. The agreement with the Joint Staff was that the JSIVA effort would be allocated about 50 personnel with five drawn from existing DSWA personnel. Gary Curtin didn't have much experience to draw on but had faith in Kingman. Kingman, an Army lieutenant colonel who planned to retire early the next year; a temporary secretary, Dianne Fortunato; and myself had a monumental task. The decision was made to establish five teams, and job descriptions were developed to be filled by active-duty military and civil service civilians.

The five teams would each comprise a colonel or Navy captain as the team chief; a structural engineer to examine building resilience against bombs; an infrastructure engineer to assess electrical power, water supply, and other infrastructure necessary for emergency response; two physical security specialists to scrutinize protection operations, alarm and sensor systems, and terrorism response plans; a Special Operations (Army Special Forces or Navy SEAL) to assess intelligence preparations and propose realistic terrorist scenarios against a specific facility; and an operations readiness specialist to examine medical response, recovery plans, and other measures to ensure operational readiness to deal with an act of terrorism. The Joint Staff mandated that the teams be stood up and fully operational by April 1997, which didn't leave time to waste.

The JSIVA effort was to receive initial help from a contracted effort conducting Balanced Survivability Assessments (BSAs), which included helping to develop a training program. I believed it was essential to develop a training and certification effort based on the individual skills of the team members. This approach was based on the lessons I had learned with the Nuclear Emergency Search Team and the key leader training I had developed, along with my experience in the Delta Force. Certification was critical to demonstrate that the teams were well-trained and capable. In early January, I set out to discover exactly what the contracted BSA effort was all about. I made a hurried trip to Moffett Field, California, to see how they did business. When I inquired about their schedule for the following day, I was informed that they did not have one. They would just figure out what they were going to do without a plan, and there was no schedule to complete their assessment.

The next thing I discovered was that none of the team had any significant experience dealing with terrorism, and that their qualifications were questionable. For example, the two team members assessing physical security consisted of a former Army chemical officer and a former Army artillery officer. When I asked them where they had received their training on physical security, I got less than a desirable answer. The next thing I unearthed was that they were the proverbial PowerPoint Rangers, concentrating on a voluminous PowerPoint presentation that epitomized a shotgun approach rather than focusing on the most critical vulnerabilities. It smacked of what I had seen at Khobar Towers. The leader was totally consumed with preparing PowerPoint slides. I watched him try to wordsmith the presentation, and noticed well over a ream of paper under his desk where he had discarded slides. I queried whether there was classified information on the slides, and did not get a clear response. The last question I asked before leaving was who would present the out-briefing to the installation commander. They informed me that the presenter would be a very pretty young lady with an associate degree and no assessment experience. I shook my head and left in disgust, concerned that the JSIVA effort would not be well served by the BSA contractors.

Upon returning to DSWA headquarters, I shared my unease with Rick Kingman, along with emphasizing the need to proactively hire the right people, and to engage the newly formed J34 Anti-terrorism Division on the Joint Staff. I mentioned where I had contacts and who I could approach to get the right people. The Joint Staff agreed that two team chiefs would come from the Army, two from the Navy, and one from the Air Force. I had hoped to get Marine Colonel Carlos Hollifield as one of the team chiefs. He was interested and had the right background. I approached Jim Conway—who had been frocked as a Marine colonel to a brigadier general to lead J34—to have Hollifield assigned. Conway informed me that the Marine Corps was not supportive and that the Joint Staff agreement called for the Navy—rather than the Department of Navy or Marine Corps—to provide two of the team leaders. Because of my friendship with Peter Schoomaker, who was in command of the U.S. Army Special Operations Command, I requested his help with an Army team leader and two Special Forces NCOs. Pete suggested I contact his personnel officer, Colonel Mike Cummings, who was tremendously helpful in getting the right folks. Colonel Jack Dibrell, an Army aviator who had been the Air Operations officer in the Delta Force, was selected. Jack proved to be an excellent team leader because of his demeanor, experience, and leadership abilities. Sergeant 1st Class Pat Kelleher turned out to be the best terrorist specialist assigned to the JSIVA teams.

My only Navy contacts were with the SEAL community, and I approached Master Chief Greg Philpott, the SEAL detailer. Greg fully understood the requirement, and recommended that I select one East Coast SEAL, one West Coast SEAL, and one from the development group. He screened records and allowed me to select three outstanding SEALS, Eric Hill, Pat Trey, and Barry (whose last name I can't recall). I approached Brigadier General Coleman, head of the Air Force Security Police before it became Security Forces, and he directed that his senior chief master sergeant assist with finding the right security policemen for the assignments. Thanks to Major Matt Branigan, who had been on the Khobar Towers task force, I could travel to Hurlburt Field, Florida, and recruit Master Sergeant Marion Andrews. Coleman's senior master chief agreed to that assignment. I selected one other, Ismael Pagan, who was about to return from an assignment in Japan. The payback was that I was asked to accept a major and a chief master sergeant that Coleman and his senior NCO wanted to be assigned to the JSIVA effort. Marion Andrews and Ismael Pagan were outstanding performers and the salt of the earth. Both were knowledgeable, team players, and hard workers. Without any involvement from me, the Army assigned Colonel George Abraham as one of the team leaders, as well as providing two Military Police NCOs, of whom Fred Struber was an absolute gem and sterling performer.

The Navy assigned Captains Mike Hlywiak and Marty Leghart as team chiefs. They were both amphibious ship commanders with no experience in terrorism but put in the effort to do well. DSWA provided two engineers; we were very fortunate to get Lieutenant Colonel Ken Knox assigned. Ken proved to be our best structural engineer by far. He was always seeking new information on ways to protect buildings and the effects of explosives.

Fifteen civilian slots had to be filled, comprising eight being engineers, two physical security, and five operational readiness personnel. DSWA did not have the authority to hire those individuals directly and had to go through the Washington Headquarters Service (WHS). WHS had a bad reputation for taking a long time to post openings and then conducting the selection process. DSWA's personnel director, Paul Morgan, was of great help. They found the name of the person in WHS responsible for the posting and hiring. I then picked up some candy and flowers, visited the person, and convinced her of the urgent need for the hires. I helped in refining the job descriptions and selecting the right people. Being nice and treating people with respect certainly paid off. The lesson learned was not to bemoan another organization's response, but to make them part of the team and the solution. Working closely with WHS definitely paid off. Of the 15 civilian hires, only one turned out to be an inadequate performer. That meant the success rate was over 93%! We got some real stars. Engineers like Young Son, Paul Styre, Ramesh Sheth; security specialists like Carl Franquet and Jeff Edwards; and operational readiness specialists like Don Neale.

There were two other critical aspects to standing up the JSIVA effort and to performing the mission in a quality way. One was the need to have an operations and planning effort, and the second was to develop standard procedures and a training program for the incoming hires to mold them into functional teams. With the operations and planning effort, there was some good luck involved in standing up what would be a two-person effort. Mary Ann Bennett was a long-time DSWA employee who understood the organization well, was well-liked, and knew how to arrange travel. She welcomed the opportunity to do something new and exciting and was quick to arrange a transfer to the JSIVA effort. The really lucky stroke was to get Major Curt Brandt.

At a staff meeting one day, the person leading the meeting announced that he had a West Point Special Forces officer that he didn't know what to do with. I jumped at the opportunity and declared that I knew how to use him to the benefit of DSWA. The senior person had backed himself into a corner and agreed to have Curt assigned to the JSIVA team. Curt had been assigned to DSWA because his military secondary specialty was in nuclear operations. As he told me later, he had never served a day on nuclear operations or in a nuclear unit! I convinced Rick Kingman that we needed Curt and brought him aboard post haste. He and Mary Ann had a daunting task. They would have to coordinate with the Joint Staff to determine where inspections would be held worldwide. They then had to design a schedule for those inspections, coordinate with the installations to be inspected, and make work-related travel arrangements. The plan was to keep a team on the road for two weeks straight and conduct two separate inspections within those two weeks. Time had to be allocated for travel and five days at an installation. Upon returning from a two-week trip, the teams would prepare their reports, and prepare for their next deployment. I cannot thank Curt and Mary Ann enough for the superb job they did for the first few years that the JSIVA effort existed.

Developing team standards and a training program proved to be a real challenge. Kingman told me that the contractors conducting the so-called Balanced Survivability Assessments (BSAs) were preparing a training program. Based on my observation of their performance at Moffett Field, I was highly skeptical. Following one of the early leadership principles that I learned in the Army and the words of the philosopher, Santayana ("Skepticism, like chastity, should never be relinquished too readily,") I kept asking to see where they stood on preparing the training program. The leadership principle was to "ensure the task is understood, supervised, and accomplished."

I constantly asked the contractors for a status report and got the runaround. Finally, at the beginning of February 1997, I had enough. I went to their location and demanded that they show me their preparations. They produced two large three-ring binders. One of the binders was the U.S. Navy manual on how to conduct training that they had obtained from Mike Guarracino, a lieutenant commander assigned to DSWA before retiring and signing on as a contractor. I would later hire Mike for the JSIVA team. Mike was most capable, but the contract organization never involved him in preparing the JSIVA training program—other than providing the Navy manual on how to conduct training. The other three-ring binder had a handful of scribbled notes without any semblance of structure or detail. I was livid, told them they were fired and went back to inform Kingman. Kingman was petrified. I told him I had a plan in mind. He was uncertain what to say or do, so I proceeded to launch my plan.

The key person to win over was the head of DSWA resources and contracting. He had a reputation of being hard-nosed, a nay-sayer, coupled with a dour personality. I scheduled a meeting with him and did some homework beforehand. I walked into his office and was greeted in a gruff manner. He saw me staring at the wall behind him in silence. He asked me what I was looking at. I pointed at the wall, and asked, "Is your son still in the 82nd Airborne Division?" He turned towards the wall and saw me pointing to a picture of his son in Army uniform. He replied that his son was still with the division. Of course, my homework had told me that his son was still on active duty! That broke the ice, and he asked what I needed. I breathed a silent sigh of relief and informed him I needed money to create a training program for the JSIVAs, pointed out how incapable the contractors were, and then convinced him of the importance of the effort. In short, he went out of his way to show support! This was yet another example of how to make a supposed problem person part of the solution.

***

There was still plenty of work to be done. A concept of operations for the JSIVA trams had already been developed, along with the team composition. Most of the job descriptions were adequate, but a description of tasks needed by each of the team skills (team leader, structural engineer, infrastructure engineer, physical security, operational readiness specialist, and terrorism specialist) was needed, together with reference material. The time I spent on the Khobar Towers task force was highly beneficial as I had a list of reference material that applied to virtually all the JSIVA skills. The other challenge was to write a Statement of Work for a contract to develop the training and to get that issued with a selection made of the vendor in short order. The DSWA contracts people were again of great help. They advised me that we could legally do a limited competition to choose the vendor. Based on my knowledge, I produced the names and contacts of five companies that I knew were qualified. I had friends and professional contacts with all the companies but would make an unbiased selection. Time was of the essence as it was now mid-February and we needed to launch the training in April. I had to make a trip—for a reason I can't remember—and went to Curt Brandt and told him what needed to be done. Curt gave me this incredulous look, as in "What the fuck!" and told me he had never done anything like that before. I told him "Curt, you're Special Forces; you are an intelligent graduate of the United States Military Academy; and you can do it." Curt, knowing how crazy I was, shrugged his shoulders and got on with what I asked him to do! And he pulled it off! God bless people like Curt Brandt! Ironically, years later as a colonel, he was assigned to the United States Special Operations Command J8 (Resources) organization from which he retired.

There was little time to waste. The request for proposals was sent to five capable companies under the rubric of a limited competition. I was familiar with all five and knew they could do the work. Beta Analytics, headed by Art Hutchins, who had been on the O&I Committee with me at the Special Forces School, won the competition. They did a remarkable job in gathering reference material, compiling lesson plans, and how to certify the different skill sets that comprised the JSIVA teams. There is little doubt in my mind that Art and Beta Analytics lost money doing the work, but they did it willingly because they knew the importance of the work they delivered. Their efforts were truly appreciated.

Thanks to the tremendous support from the military services, the DSWA personnel section, and the Washington Headquarters Service, the initial complement of personnel was on board by April 1997. An intense training effort commenced and the teams were ready to deploy by June 1997. Curt Brandt, Mary Ann Bennett, and Dianne Fortunato worked long hours to compile a schedule of visits and to make the travel arrangements for the teams, including passports, and procuring laptop computers and software for the team members. The J34 section of the Joint Staff specified the sites to be visited, but it was up to DSWA to develop the visit schedule. The teams assessed installations in Europe, Central America, in the Pacific area, and domestic military installations. The operations tempo was fierce and very trying on the team members. They would spend two weeks on the road doing back-to-back assessments, return home to prepare their reports, and then have down time for a week before going out again.

***

The state of anti-terrorism and force protection throughout the Defense Department was not very good. The most significant gaps were a lack of good planning coupled with a lack of exercises and tests to see if the plans were viable. Another noticeable gap was the lack of training for those designated to oversee anti-terrorism and force protection at different installations and to certify them in their duties. There were two other major shortcomings: the capability of installation commanders to understand what was necessary for a good plan, and the absence of a central point for obtaining expert advice on physical security equipment and construction.

To address these gaps, I proposed to DSWA and the J34 section that several programs be initiated. The first was to create a centralized training program for anti-terrorism/force protection personnel to ensure quality standards across the Department of Defense. DSWA had classroom space on Kirtland AFB where they taught various classes on nuclear subjects. The classrooms were not fully utilized, and collaborating with Sandia National Labs' physical security test bed to provide students with firsthand knowledge of barriers and security systems, they would provide ideal training locations. The second idea was to create an "811" hotline where people in the field could call the number and receive specific advice on physical security systems and equipment that were best for the terrain and climate suitable for those requesting help. My belief was that the Physical Security Action Group, combined with the Army Corps of Engineers and Sandia National Labs, could have provided an essential service. I often saw people in the field make bad decisions on equipment and procedures simply because of a lack of knowledge. A third idea was to create a template and explanatory manual on how to create and test anti-terrorism/force protection plans. The last idea was to devise a policy wherein an installation and its commander would be subject to a special inspector general investigation should major gaps found on a JSIVA not be corrected. All these ideas fell on deaf ears and were never addressed.

On the other hand, there was a wave of activity throughout the Defense Department to address improvements in anti-terrorism with mixed results. Each of the military services took a different course of action. Overall, the policy for anti-terrorism was addressed by the Office of the Assistant Secretary of Defense for Special Operations. There were some improvements made to the previous policy, but the revised policy left many gaps in how the Services should construct their programs. The stand up of the J34 section on the Joint Staff was a significant move. The challenge arose when the section was established, there were too few highly qualified people to support their efforts. From my perspective, only four of their staff brought significant experience to anti-terrorism. The Army contributed Major John Alexander, a former Delta operator, and Captain Jeff Hill. The Air Force contributed a superb Air Force Office of Special Investigations Major Mary Peterson, and Tom Barrale, a very competent Security Policeman. Four were simply not enough. It affirmed in my mind that experience is a vital ingredient for success in any endeavor. There were some excellent officers in J34, but that did not mean they had anti-terrorism or force protection experience. Jim Conway would later become commandant of the Marine Corps, John Sattler would be promoted to lieutenant general and the director of the J7 on the Joint Staff, Bill Burke would retire as a vice admiral, and Tom Waldhauser would be promoted to general and command Africa Command.

A Defense Science Board study was convened to examine force protection measures. The number of study members with bona fide experience in terrorism and force protection was minimal. Unfortunately, the study did not bring needed changes to the Defense Department. Once again, the lack of true experience showed in the published report. There was one funny moment during the study. A small group had been asked to meet in Rosslyn, Virginia. The meeting began with people introducing themselves by talking about their experience in physics and engineering but not terrorism or force protection. There were only three of us with such experience, including Lieutenant General Emil "Buck" Bedard and Marine Captain Steve Reese. I felt that I was wasting my time in the meeting. When it was time for me to introduce myself, I pulled out a knife, stuck it in the conference table, and proclaimed that my degree was in chasing and killing terrorists. General Bedard and Steve Reese had a hard time suppressing their laughter!

The Air Force created a Force Protection Battle Laboratory in San Antonio, Texas, and began researching better ways to provide physical security, as well as a course to train anti-terrorism and force protection personnel. They also created a new squadron specifically designed to deploy to high-threat areas to deal with terrorism. They also included intelligence personnel in the squadron. This was the start of changing the Security Police field in the Air Force to become Security Forces.

The Marine Corps added to its headquarters Marine Corps staff in Plans, Policies, & Operations under the leadership of Ray Geoffroy. The Corps also emphasized that force protection was integral to mission accomplishment and that command responsibility could not be ignored. The Army Staff also added personnel to focus on force protection and did a six-month study to determine their way forward. One of the Army's better contributions was to hatch the idea for an annual anti-terrorism conference. On the other hand, they mandated a four-hour annual instruction course on anti-terrorism that was video- and computer-based, and lacked the personal touch of informing people of the specific threat to units. Four hours of instruction was a waste of time. The Navy added personnel to their Master of Arms program but did little else. In October 2000, the Navy was embarrassed by the attack on the USS *Cole* in Aden, Yemen. Through the efforts of Admirals Thomas Fargo and Robert Natter, a mandatory one-week anti-terrorism course was designed for those slated for promotion to captain. Admiral Natter had the U.S. Pacific Fleet at the time. Admiral Fargo had commanded the Navy's Fifth Fleet in Bahrain shortly after the Khobar Towers bombing and took anti-terrorism very seriously. While at Fifth Fleet, his two trusted anti-terrorist experts were Marine Colonel Paul Cahill and Lieutenant Commander Gordon Sheek. They were called to action by Admiral Natter to originate an anti-terrorism course and did so superbly.

***

The three years that I spent with DSWA and subsequently with the Defense Threat Reduction Agency that replaced DSWA were a period of continual travel. We were short of a team chief, so Rick Kingman and I would lead teams. I would also accompany new team chiefs to guide them on their first assessment. The travel was tiring but rewarding. I saw firsthand the problems that the post-Vietnam military was encountering and could visit places that I had never been to before or had not seen for some time. My trips took me to Seoul; Pusan; and Chinhae, Korea; Pearl Harbor; and Kaneohe Marine Corps Base in Hawaii; Soto Cano, Honduras; Vicenza and La Madalena in Italy; Hamburg, Bitburg, Spangdahlen, Wiesbaden, Garmisch, and Stuttgart, Germany; Bahrain; Ecuador; Tazar, Hungary; Bosnia; Guantanamo, and numerous stateside installations.

There were three special assessments of note. One was an assessment to look for alternative air bases for counternarcotics because Howard AFB in Panama was closing. Mike Guarracino, who would replace me as the JSIVA deputy and later become the deputy marshal of the Supreme Court, accompanied me to Quito and Manta (Eduador), Aruba, and Curacao. We had planned on driving from Quito to Manta, but major demonstrations blocked the route. So, I got tickets on a local air carrier and flew via an old DC-3 to Manta. We returned to Quito and then had to fly to Caracas to transfer to a flight going to Aruba. We had to exit security and re-enter it again in Caracas. There was a fee to be paid to get back through security. Mike started arguing with the lady collecting the fee. The only words of English she could speak were "Twenty-five Dollars." Mike kept arguing to no avail. I pulled out $25 and paid the lady to get Mike to shut up! Our assessment was that Manta, Ecuador, would require significant work as American forces had not used that location to any significant degree. Aruba was to be an emergency location and did not require much effort. Curacao already had U.S. Air Force aircraft operating there. In Aruba and Curacao, the Dutch provided excellent intelligence support to America.

The second special assessment was in Pristina, Kosovo. Colonel Hal Johnson from the J34 staff accompanied me on that trip. It was my introduction to coalition operations. We flew from Washington, DC, to Ramstein AFB, Germany, and took a C-130 into Macedonia. A British coalition air operations officer arranged for us to fly to Pristina on a Russian-built Mi-7 HIP helicopter piloted by Ukrainians. On landing in Pristina, we noted that UAE Apache helicopters were used for security. The coalition operation in Kosovo was being commanded by a German general. Hal and I were met by a U.S. Army intelligence officer who had requested an assessment of a new Sensitive Compartmented Intelligence Facility being built for American use. We had a good meal, then went to bed. I awoke the following morning woozy and nauseous. I looked to my left and saw that I had been sleeping next to a Japanese kerosene heater, and immediately knew I had carbon monoxide poisoning. Hal escorted me to the medical facility, where a Greek doctor examined me, then transported via a Dutch ambulance to a British field hospital in a former prison, where I was tended to by an Irish doctor and Scottish nurse. They cleared me to return to the headquarters and I was transported in a Belgian ambulance. I was dehydrated and stood in line behind several Russians to buy some Gatorade and Rehydrat. It was amazing to see coalition operations at work! The reason for the special assessment was a concern that one of our allies was aiming antennas at the security facility being built. I assured them that if the facility were built to standards, there would be no potential for electronic intercepting of our intelligence.

The third special assessment was to Bosnia in the aftermath of an attack by Serbs against an American Special Forces Joint Commission Observer (JCO) team located in Bijeljina close to the Serbian border. I was fortunate to have Doug Norvell, a former Delta operations officer and operator, accompany me on the trip. We were asked to assess security at four Special Forces locations in Bosnia, to include Brcko, Banja Luka, and Tuzla. The JCO teams were controlled by the Combined Joint Special Operations Task Force out of Sarajevo. Each team consisted of a Special Forces A Detachment living on the economy rather than on a military base. Their role was to act as peacemakers by interacting with factions in the area where they were located, getting those factions to talk with each other, and resolving differences peacefully. The teams enjoyed great success and were a tribute to the work that Special Forces personnel can demonstrate in various situations. The teams were rotated on a six-month basis and had a procedure whereby excellent continuity in their operations was maintained when a new team replaced the outgoing team. A month before the transfer, a ranking member of the incoming A Detachment would spend time with the outgoing team, learning who to work with, and the intricacies of working with different factions. When the incoming team arrived, they would spend a week with the outgoing team. Why this same process was not used in Afghanistan and Iraq in the 2000s is beyond me. It just goes to show that valuable lessons learned are often forgotten.

The CJSOTF provided two vehicles, two Special Forces personnel, and one SEAL to accompany Doug and me. Frankly, I was not impressed with them. Before departing Sarajevo, I insisted they get handheld radios to communicate with each vehicle, as well as maps. The only map they could find was a 1:250,000 scale which was not suitable for clearly tracking our location. My premonitions were correct. On the way to Bijeljina, the lead vehicle got lost, crossed a small river, then proceeded down a dead-end street. The driver panicked and backed into a civilian vehicle. He jumped out along with his partner and the SEAL and began arguing with the civilian who didn't speak English. It was reminiscent of Mike Guarracino in Caracas! Worse yet, they left the doors of the vehicles open with their rifles exposed. Doug Norvell and I were unarmed, but Doug moved towards one vehicle, and I stayed with the vehicle I was riding in to keep anyone from snatching the weapons. I kept trying to tell the idiot to just pay the civilian $50 so that we could leave. He didn't listen and was bent on arguing with the civilian. Luckily, three Humvees on patrol from the 1st Infantry Division saw what was happening and came to our assistance. They had an interpreter who resolved the situation and we were on our way.

We arrived at the JCO team location in Bijeljina close to four hours after leaving Sarajevo. The team greeted us warmly and briefed us on the attack wherein Russian light anti-tank weapons were fired into the house where the team was living. Fortunately, no one was wounded. As with the three other locations we would visit, the teams were vulnerable to attack because they were not on a guarded military base. However, it was clear that the risk was necessary for them to conduct their peace-keeping operations. At all four locations, Doug and I recommended that they attempt to procure ballistic blankets to provide better protection on exterior walls. At two locations, we also recommended that they move their communication antennas away from the operations room as the antennas were a tip-off as to where the operations center was located. The most rewarding part of the trip was seeing the professionalism and dedication of the Special Forces A Detachments. They epitomized the "Quiet Professionalism" that is the hallmark of Special Forces.

Concerning the regular JSIVA assessments, the teams saw all too many examples of poor leadership at the installation level, coupled with the lack of planning for a terrorist event, and many questionable security practices. A few examples follow. A commander refused to attend the out-briefing because she had dyed her hair the night before and it turned purple; another commander ordered the gate guards to wear pistol belts and holsters but instructed them not to carry weapons; one commander wanted the JSIVA team to declare the Officers Club as a vulnerability so he could request funds to build a new club next to the base golf course; one Naval Base had no guards at the entrance, and one could easily drive to where several nuclear-powered submarines were berthed, with the only potential obstacle being a sentry armed with a handgun at a gate that was always open; at an Air Force base, F-16 fighters were parked less than 100 yards away from a tourist lookout point and were vulnerable to attack from small arms or rocket-propelled grenades. I lost my temper on one assessment when the commander swiveled his chair and told his people that if the JSIVA didn't bring money, then all they had done was another study. I rebuked him and said to him that a 90% improvement could be made through procedural remedies that didn't require any money. He was about to take command of a Defense Agency with a $5 billion-dollar annual budget. I asked him if he was prepared to take a one-percent reduction and allocate that money to the installation. The staff was shocked, and the general just shut his mouth.

The excuses that the JSIVA teams were given for not being able to improve their force protection programs were rampant and pathetic. One of my best physical security specialists, John Fowler, came to me one day and asked if I had heard of mantras. When I replied that I had, he then asked me if I knew what a cantra was, to which I replied that I did not. John then vented his frustration by telling me that all he was hearing was "I can't, you can't, we can't, etc." in response to improvements against terrorist attacks. John coined the term "Cantra!" Unfortunately, the Cantra mindset also applied to most of the JSIVA team leaders. I urged them to help the installation commanders by rank-ordering the vulnerabilities that were noted during an assessment. They passively ignored me as it was easier to simply list every vulnerability without prioritizing them.

In October 1998, the Defense Special Weapons Agency was replaced by the Defense Threat Reduction Agency (DTRA). Both agencies were designated as combat support agencies, but the first director of DTRA was a physicist from Lawrence Livermore National Laboratory, who had never served a day in uniform. The support that the JSIVA effort had enjoyed under DSWA began to wane. Rick Kingman retired in 1999. I requested that I be considered to lead the JSIVA effort but never received a response. Kingman's replacement was another Air Force Colonel who had been a weapons system officer on F4 Phantoms and had no force protection experience prior to coming to DTRA as a team leader. I was disappointed in what was happening and decided that it was time for me to move on. I ensured that Mike Guarracino would take the deputy director position and then started looking for my next adventure. While at DSWA and DTRA, Dennis Miyoshi became my supervisor at Sandia Labs. Dennis tried to find me a job back at Sandia. He was apologetic when he told me that the only position was to work in security for the despicable person and sexual harasser who had been selected instead of me—despite the recommendation of a selection panel. Had I gone back to Sandia for six months, I would have been eligible to receive full retirement. It simply was not worth working for an incompetent person, and I began to look for something in the Washington, DC, area.

I left DTRA the same way I had come into DSWA, quietly, without fanfare. I knew in my heart what I had accomplished and the people I had mentored in my three years working the JSIVA process. Mi Hye and I made great progress on a personal level. Mi Hye did not have to work because of the boost in income I received by taking the DSWA assignment. She found a church and became an evangelical born-again Christian. Her years of dealing with anxiety and depression came to an end. Thanks to my friend, Larry Reiman, we were introduced to the Morris family who built over 90 custom homes of excellent quality, one of which we still live in after 25 years. We moved into a great neighborhood with neighbors that cared and looked after each other. Life was good!

CHAPTER 22

Fighting Terrorism in the Corporate Sector

I quickly found out two things. One was that my experiences and skills were in demand by so-called Beltway Bandit companies doing contract work for the federal government. The other was that I refused to work for people of questionable ethics and competence. My first opportunity came from Major General Bill Garrison, whom I first met in 1977 at Fort Bragg, North Carolina. Among his notable assignments were his time as an intelligence special mission unit, as a commander of Delta, commander of the Joint Special Operations Command, and commander of the Special Warfare Command. I had the utmost respect for him. Bill was working with SAIC, he had obtained an intelligence support contract and recommended me as the project manager. I reported to Joe Soukup who was a great person and manager. Everything was great on the SAIC end, but I ran into problems with the government contract manager, who I believed was incompetent, inexperienced, and unethical. It was clear to me that he was threatened by my background and pushed to have me replaced by a female psychologist, who had a hard time spelling intelligence. He offered to give me several months to find a different job and said he would pay for my travel. I found that both disgusting and unethical. Joe Soukup wanted me to stay with SAIC, but I felt that it was in the best interest of the company for me to resign.

In less than a week, I received an offer from Titan Corporation, which had received a multimillion-dollar contract to develop an automated anti-terrorism threat-assessment tool from the Technical Support Working Group (TSWG). I was familiar with the project and the TSWG, so it appeared to be a great fit. I was asked to lead the project and take on other responsibilities to obtain more work associated with security assessments. The threat-assessment tool was subcontracted to a start-up company that was behind schedule with the development of the tool but had received an extension from the TSWG and additional funding. The subcontractors were sold on using Bayes theory as the major algorithm for the tool and had difficulty getting the program to work without crashing. Because of the potential for the tool, I continued to be supportive until after the al-Qaeda attacks on 9/11. I was also approached by a member of the Bush Administration transition team and asked to submit my résumé for me to be considered for the Principal Deputy Assistant Secretary for Special Operations and Low-Intensity Conflict or for a deputy assistant secretary's position. I did so and met with Michelle van Cleave who was the choice to become the Assistant Secretary. Months went by without my being called for an interview. Upon enquiring about it from the transition team, the person who had asked and encouraged me to apply was very apologetic and implied that the positions would be filled by political appointees, who did not have much experience, if any. I was disappointed, but shrugged my shoulders and marched on with my Titan work.

On September 11, 2001, I saw the television coverage of the attack on the World Trade Center and was about to depart for a meeting with the Marine Corps to pursue an anti-terrorism contract. My secretary came to me with tears in her eyes and implored me not to go to the Pentagon. When I asked her what was happening, she gestured to a TV where breaking news showed the attack on the Pentagon. I immediately called my contacts at Headquarters Marine Corps, but the phone kept ringing and was unanswered. Two weeks later I learned that my contacts had survived the attack. We were sent home early from work on September 11. It usually took me 40 minutes to drive home from the Reston, Virginia, office; that day it took me four hours. My wife and I had planned a trip to Hawaii the following week but had to cancel because of the disruption in air travel. One of the unsung heroes of 9/11 was the secretary of transportation, Norman Mineta, who made the decision to bring commercial airliners out of the sky to land at the closest airport to preclude any further use of commercial aircraft for a terrorist attack. In the few months that followed 9/11, Secretary Mineta was tasked with creating the Transportation Security Agency (TSA) and hiring 190,000 people. As he related to me later, he was sorely disappointed when the White House offered former Secret Service and Bureau of Alcohol, Tobacco, and Firearms Director John Magaw to lead TSA. Mineta related to me later that the day Magaw came on board, he was excited to have Magaw and informed Magaw that they would have a planning session that evening. Magaw told Mineta that his work hours were 9 to 5, and he did not show up for the planning that evening. Mineta was disillusioned by Magaw's performance and eventually had to plead with Andrew Card, the White House Chief of Staff, to ask Magaw to leave. One of the people that Magaw brought on board was my friend Tom Quinn, who who was asked to improve the Air Marshal program. That appeared to be the only positive decision Magaw made.

I became really busy in the aftermath of the 9/11 attacks. I was sought out as a pundit on terrorism issues by the media. Fox News was the first to reach out to me and I was invited to their headquarters in New York City for an interview a few days after commercial air traffic was allowed to resume operations. Only a few people were on board what usually was a packed flight from Washington to LaGuardia Airport, and there was almost no traffic from the airport to Fox News. It was chilling to see the devastation of the World Trade Center from the air. I met Linda Vester, who would host an hour-long program with three other contributors located away from the studio. One of the interviewees tried to belittle Linda. She promptly put him in his place by briefly describing her experiences overseas, especially in Rwanda. She appreciated that I was concise and focused on answering her questions in layman's terms without acronyms or terminology that the public could not understand. She liked my style and after the interview took the time to introduce me to her husband, Hank Greenberg, Jr., whose father was a noted baseball player and executive.

Over the next three years, I did close to 200 interviews, most of them for Fox. One of the main reasons I did so was to counter other pundits who knew not of what they spoke, yet wanted to come across as experts. Many of them were getting paid. I refused any compensation and only asked that when appropriate they identify me as associated with the company I worked for. I did this to help gain recognition for the company. I was often pushed to answer questions that would have revealed classified information and techniques and steadfastly refused.

With Titan Corporation, we undertook various assignments. These included conducting assessments for the Corps of Engineers at Cape Cod, Massachusetts; overseas with for the Abu Dhabi emirate on their fleet of aircraft; for the Port Authority in New York and New Jersey; and teaching a class on anti-terrorism planning and operations to the National Guard Bureau. On the other hand, two things got me upset. The first was that Titan bought a company that irradiated food to kill fruit flies and pathogens. With the media fueling fear about anthrax and the call for mail-screening equipment, there were those in Titan who believed food irradiation technology was a perfect fit. They wanted to advertise it as mail-screening equipment. I tried to explain the difference between mail screening to detect anthrax and technology that would neutralize it. I further attempted to explain the effects of radiation on electronic components and other materials, like plastic, if the radiation levels were too high. My advice fell on deaf ears in the interest of greed. In its haste to field any solution, the federal government paid Titan and other firms tens of millions of dollars for mail-screening equipment. They soon discovered that the Titan equipment and others were not suitable for mail screening. In the end, the anthrax panic killed five Americans and sickened 17, but panic on the part of government officials, coupled with media hype and greedy contractors, resulted in hundreds of millions of dollars being wasted. The rush to address the threat of anthrax resulted in expenditure on solutions that had costly side effects, such as destroying electronic media and legitimate biological samples sent through the mail, warped plastics, paper degradation, and weakened pharmaceuticals.

The second thing that happened was that the subcontractors for the threat-assessment software were behind schedule and a field test was scheduled by the Technical Support Working Group. I made a stupid mistake and took the subcontractor's word that the software was working. I did not personally check whether the program worked reliably. The software failed to perform, and the software kept crashing during the tests, including on an overseas trip to Kuwait. I was highly embarrassed but accepted responsibility as I should have personally checked the software prior to the tests. I was accompanied during the tests by one of the principals in the subcontractor organization who was unapologetic for the failure, while insisting that it could be fixed. After the failed field testing, I became more demanding of the subcontractor to live up to the terms of the contract. They finally got the software to go through an assessment without any major crashes of the program. I then ran a test using an actual military facility as the test bed. The software assessed that the serious threat to this installation was an armed attack against a water reservoir. At the same time, the subcontractor asked for more money and time. My assessment was that the software design was deficient in its reliability and ability to achieve meaningful results. I advised the subcontractor that I would not seek additional government funding or time, but they still had time left on the contract to correct the deficiencies in the software and program. Unfortunately, they were unable to do so.

At about the same time, I was approached by the person I reported to at Titan who informed me that he needed me to pick up the salaries of two people he had hired. He had agreed to allow them to work remotely, with one in Montana and the other in California, paying them each over $100,000 a year. I asked how much time I had to find them work and what percentage of their salaries was covered by existing work. The answer I received was two months, and that they were covering 30% of their salaries. I knew the chances of making that happen were slim to none. I was peeved at my boss for asking me to correct his error and not giving me enough time to rectify it.

Once again, good fortune blessed me as I received a call from a friend at ACS Defense named Owen Greenblatt, who pitched me hard to join that company. ACS Defense had bought BETAC corporation, which was owned by my friend Earl Lockwood, with whom I had previously worked in the early '80s. I knew many of the people and felt that it would be a good fit for me. I accepted the offer and gave two weeks' notice of resignation to Titan. There were some outstanding people on the Titan staff that I regretted leaving. However, my disdain for their leadership made it easy for me to resign.

The transition to ACS was effortless. I knew many of the people working there, and my commute to work was reduced by 40 minutes. I was asked to assist in writing proposals for new business and to provide subject-matter expertise on existing projects. My role changed dramatically with the formation of the Office of the Assistant Secretary of Defense for Homeland Defense in December 2002. ACS was approached to provide contract-planning support to that office. The government contact insisted on seeing and approving the people who would be contracted. She was not satisfied with the initial people that were offered to work on the contract. It was decided that my résumé would be offered for review on a part-time basis. The government representative insisted that she wanted my services on a full-time basis, along with Gregg Jones, a great friend and retired Special Forces officer. Reluctantly, ACS agreed based on securing additional work. In November 2002, Gregg and I began working in the Pentagon on a full-time basis.

As I had learned from previous experience, it is challenging to find genuinely experienced people when you start a new endeavor in government. However, you will likely also get some all-stars who will carry the day. One of those was Lieutenant Colonel Craig Costello, a Special Forces Reservist who was brought on active duty. Craig knew what he was doing, worked tirelessly to get reference material, and to develop policy for the organization. Other stars were Bob Salesses, a former Marine who became the Chief of Staff and later a Deputy Assistant Secretary; Tom Kuster, a retired Special Forces lieutenant colonel; Lloyd Phillips, assigned as the military assistant to the assistant secretary; and an active-duty Marine whose name I unfortunately cannot recall. Pete Verga was assigned as the principal deputy, and his knowledge of the ins and outs of the Pentagon bureaucracy was of great value. The Bush Administration hit a home run when they nominated Paul McHale to be the assistant secretary. Paul was a former Democratic congressman from Pennsylvania who had served on the House Armed Services Committee and was also a colonel in the Marine Corps Reserves. He had the requisite background knowledge of the subject he was to oversee and of how the Department of Defense and interagency work. He sailed through the Senate nomination and came in with a strong vision and excellent leadership.

In late November 2002, al-Qaeda operatives in Mombasa, Kenya, attempted to shoot down an Israeli charter airplane using man-portable air-defense missiles (MANPADS). Although the attack was not successful in shooting down the airliner, a wave of activity began in the USA because of the threat to commercial aviation. The National Security Council and Homeland Security Council convened a high-priority meeting at the FBI headquarters in Washington, DC. I was assigned to be the representative from the Homeland Defense Office. At the first meeting, there were over 150 attendees. The meeting was led by Coast Guard Rear Admiral Brian Peterman, who was assigned to the Homeland Security Council. Peterman was well organized and announced that there would be four committees formed, announced the date of the next meeting, and informed everyone that assignments would be given at that meeting. In fact, Admiral Peterman distributed assignments to various agencies/departments at the second meeting, which drew half the number of attendees as the first. At the third meeting called by Admiral Peterman, fewer than 35 people were in attendance! All the people that I dubbed as members of the PMGS (Professional Meeting-Goers Society) had disappeared when it came time to do real work! The leadership that Admiral Peterman provided was superb. A small working group consisting of Lieutenant Colonel Steve Weiler from the SO/LIC

Office, myself, and Nick Rasmussen from the State Department's Political-Military Bureau met and rapidly formed a strategy to help deal with the threat. The strategy was straightforward and consisted of trying to eliminate the MANPADs that could be bought or otherwise provided to terrorist groups. The intelligence community provided us with estimates of what countries were likely to supply MANPADS missiles and the strategy was to place diplomatic pressure against their sale to terrorist groups along with a buy-back program. It was decided that the primary country to focus on buy-backs was Nicaragua. I was very impressed with Nick Rasmussen. Years later he became the director of the National Counterterrorism Center. Working with Rasmussen and Admiral Peterman reaffirmed to me the value of experienced people with excellent planning and leadership skills when it comes to dealing with complex problems. Nothing beats leadership and experience.

General Wayne Downing was appointed by President Bush as the director for combating terrorism on the National Security Council. He assembled a strong team to work with him on creating the first national strategy to combat terrorism. His team included Army colonel and Special Forces-qualified Joe Rozek; Army colonel and psychological-operations expert Jeff Jones; FBI special agent Ken Piernick, who had been an Army helicopter pilot in Vietnam; and Navy Captain Bill McRaven who would later command the United States Special Operations Command as an admiral. Michelle Malvesti, the daughter of Wayne's Ranger friend Dick Malvesti, who died in a parachute accident, also contributed to the strategy. The first four brought extensive experience in combating terrorism and wrote a robust strategy that had achievable goals and objectives. I asked Wayne if there was a way that I could help. He advised me that it would not be a good idea. After he resigned, I learned why. Within a week of his taking the director's position, he was undermined by the bifurcation of the combating terrorism effort, by the appointment of former Pennsylvania Governor Tom Ridge to have an equal position to look at homeland security and terrorism. Wayne was deeply disappointed but continued until the strategy that he and his team had created was adopted. The 2003 National Strategy showed again the value that leadership and experience can bring when addressing serious matters.

When Greg Jones and I joined the Homeland Defense organization we were assigned to work, under the supervision of a GS-15, with 10 others to help develop policy and strategy regarding technical developments for homeland defense. Within three months, I was the only one left of the 12. The government civilian that I reported to would not allow me to leave. For the most part, that was okay with me, as she valued my work and contacts. The problem was that she had a bipolar personality, which made her unpredictable and prone to flying off the handle when she was unmedicated. I spent most of my time introducing her and Secretary McHale to other government organizations that were involved in homeland defense and security technologies. These included the Technical Support Working Group and the

DOD Combating Terrorism Technical Support Office, the DOD Physical Security Equipment Action Group, the Corps of Engineers and their physical and electronic security operations, and the Department of Energy and its national laboratories. I helped in understanding developments to counter weapons of mass destruction, emergency operations, and intelligence support to domestic operations. An interesting short-term project was to participate in a bilateral visit to Israel with members of the Defense Department Acquisitions, Technology and Logistics organization. I briefed the Israelis on the Combating Terrorism Technology Support Office and rapid prototyping. We attempted to help the Department of Homeland Security with their technical development, communications, and emergency management. Still, we found that the DHS was in disarray without genuinely experienced people working in those areas along with intelligence. I felt that there was so much more I could offer in other offices within the Defense Department, especially in intelligence or Special Operations.

***

Early in 2003, two things happened that would lead to my departure from the Homeland Defense organization. The first was the creation of the Office of the Undersecretary of Defense for Intelligence and the appointment of my friend Lieutenant General William (Jerry) Boykin to be the first principal deputy assistant secretary in that office. The second was a call I received from Tom O'Connell, who asked my advice on accepting a nomination to become the Assistant Secretary of Defense for Special Operations and Low-Intensity Conflict. I had stayed in touch with both from the time I first met them in the Delta Force. Tom was the one I selected to take my place as the Delta intelligence officer. I advised Tom to accept the nomination. He asked if I would give him help and I agreed to do so with the proviso that he would allow me to develop a strategic plan for the SO/LIC Office. I decided to help Tom O'Connell rather than asking Jerry Boykin to bring me into the USD for intelligence organization or seeking a government position with Homeland Defense. Tom was not sure how to bring me on, and I told him that the easiest way would be to have me take another Intergovernmental Personnel Act assignment. Fortunately, retired Delta Force Colonel Lee Van Arsdale was starting a program at the University of Nevada Las Vegas for Security Studies. Lee was happy to assist me in getting hired by the university and allowing me to take an assignment with SO/LIC.

It took several months to get everything in place to join SO/LIC. In February 2004, my father called me and stated that it was time for him to go into a hospice care facility. I quickly arranged to travel to Hawaii. On the day I arrived, representatives from the St. Francis Hospice visited my father and stated that they had a vacancy, and they were not sure when the next opening would be if he did not take this one.

He accepted the opening. It was evident that he had thought through his options beforehand. He packed a bag, and walked on his own with his oxygen supply to the car I rented. I asked him if there was anybody he wanted to see or anything he wanted to do. He answered that he just wanted to go to the hospice in Nuuanu Valley adjacent to the Boy Scout Aloha Council Offices where he had worked. By coincidence, when we checked into the hospice, I noticed that a male nurse had the last name of Morrett. I asked him if he was related to the Reverend John Morrett, and he replied that he was his father. I was an acolyte for Reverend Morrett at Holy Nativity Church where my parents were parishioners. The nurse told me his dad retired in Florida. I later contacted Reverend Morrett and he was kind enough to send me a copy of a book he wrote, *Soldier Priest*. He wrote about dropping out of seminary and going with his National Guard unit to the Philippines just before the outbreak of World War II. He was captured, did the Bataan Death March, escaped when the Japanese ship he was being transported on was sunk by a torpedo, and managed to link up with Filipino guerrillas, who arranged his escape to Australia.

***

My dad was told by his primary care physician that he had a few months to live. I was in a quandary about how long I should stay in Hawaii to be with him. I slept in his house and discovered that he was a hoarder and that it would be a daunting task to clean the house and dispense of everything he had accumulated. My old bedroom had boxes literally stacked to the ceiling, and the one-car enclosed garage was the same. I intended to spend a week with my dad believing that he would be in hospice for several months. During the day, I would sort through his hoard and take items to be donated, and would then visit my dad during the evening. Among the things he had hoarded were over 100 large bottles of hand cleaner and hundreds of rolls of toilet paper. I concluded that he had plenty of disposable income and that his social life consisted of going to Longs Drug Store, where all the employees knew him by name—the same with Costco! Among other things, there were stacks of magazines and newspapers. I knew I could not adequately clean the house in a week. On the third day my dad was in the hospice, he asked to be moved to a room where he could see his old office at the Boy Scouts. That night he fell into a coma. I believe that he had accomplished the last thing on his bucket list—being able to see his old office, and then decided it was time to go. The hospice staff could not predict how long he would continue to live. I reluctantly decided to return to Virginia as I was not able to communicate with him. During the last two days in Hawaii, with the help of my cousin's wife, Isabel Brighter, I looked at his estate documents and planned for his cremation. Two days after I got back to Virginia, Isabel called me to tell me my dad had passed away. With a flurry of activity, I signed out of Homeland Defense, resigned from Lockheed Martin that had bought ACS

Defense, and decided to sign on with the University of Nevada and sign into SO/LIC after I took a month's leave in Hawaii with Mi Hye.

It was a hectic month in Hawaii. I did all the paperwork to get death certificates, pay my dad's taxes, stop his social security and pension, and the myriad other things required when a person passes away. Mi Hye and I arranged for his funeral and inurnment, wrote an obituary, and then started the process of cleaning my dad's house. I received a good deal of help from my extended family—my nephew Andrew Pascoe and Andrew's father-in-law, Wayne Parker. We decided what needed to be repaired at the property and Andrew began working on it. His sister, his niece Kristie, and Kristie's husband Bert were of great help in cleaning things up. My niece Heidi helped me sell some things of value. I had to laugh at their father, Billy Pascoe, my lifelong friend, who didn't do anything to clean up but spent his time browsing for things he wanted to ask me to give to him! Mi Hye was a real champion and worked tirelessly to sort through all the belongings. Every night we would return to our hotel room dirty and sweaty. I had to ask her to slow down as she inadvertently threw away things of value simply because she didn't know the value. We made many charitable donations and gave away a lot of valuables. My cousin Ginny asked me to give her some rare and valuable koa wood furniture and I did so in requital for the help that she and my aunt had given to my dad. A year later, I was sorely disappointed to see the furniture stored outdoors at their home, and not being used. But life goes on. It took two-and-a-half construction dumpsters to get rid of all the trash. Thanks to Andrew and Wayne, the house and garage looked new by the time we left. He had changed wiring, plumbing, replaced termite-eaten floors and walls, and painted. I could never have done all that needed to be done without the help of Mi Hye and my extended family. The value of an extended family can never be overstated.

CHAPTER 23

Life in the Pentagon

On my return to Virginia, I began serving as the senior advisor to Tom O'Connell. The Principal Deputy Assistant Secretary was Marshall Billingslea. Marshall had been the acting Assistant Secretary after the Undersecretary of Defense for Policy, Doug Feith, had fired Robert Andrews, who was acting as the Assistant Secretary. There was a distinct contrast between O'Connell and Billingslea. Marshall had worked for Senator Jesse Helms and became a senior staff member on the Senate Foreign Relations Committee. He came to SO/LIC after being the Deputy Assistant Secretary of Defense for Negotiations Policy. He was young, energetic, and not afraid to go directly to the Secretary of Defense, Donald Rumsfeld. His sister, Rachel, was a special assistant to Rumsfeld who helped him gain insight on the secretary.

Although Marshall had no military experience, he was well versed in foreign affairs, Congress, defense funding matters, and how to deal with the Pentagon bureaucracy. During his time as acting Assistant Secretary he aggressively pursued more involvement in the SO/LIC Office to combat terrorism globally and to develop a strategy for Operation Iraqi Freedom. He was aware that his confirmation as Assistant Secretary was unlikely, given that his aggressive manner had resulted in many adversaries in the Senate. Yet he was absorbed in Special Operations and wanted to contribute as the Principal Deputy Assistant Secretary after Tom O'Connell's confirmation.

In contrast, Tom O'Connell was the proverbial nice guy. He was well-liked by many but despised by others who saw him as weak. He had retired as a colonel in charge of the USSOCOM Washington Office and then worked for Raytheon. In 1980, I selected and groomed him to be my successor as the 1st SFOD-D intelligence officer. He went on to command the military intelligence battalion for the 82nd Airborne Division during the invasion of Grenada; served as the J2 for the Joint Special Operations Command; commanded a special mission unit intelligence organization; and served with the CIA's Office of Military Affairs. He had minimal experience in dealing with Congress and the Pentagon bureaucracy. As I was to learn later, his nomination to become Assistant Secretary came about because a four-star general, who had Secretary Rumsfeld's ear, learned of Tom through a female—with whom he was having an affair—who knew and liked Tom.

I soon noted the contrast in experience and style between Tom O'Connell and Marshall Billingslea. I also sensed that Billingslea was frustrated in his dealings with O'Connell. Billingslea confided in me that he was looking for another position. He became the Assistant Secretary General of NATO for Defense Investment and accomplished much in the three years that he was in NATO. Two of his notable accomplishments were: firstly, getting NATO to adopt an intelligence-sharing system known as the Battlefield Information Collection and Exploitation System (BICES); and, secondly, forming a NATO Special Operations Forces Coordination Center to be led by an American three-star general or admiral.

I also realized that Tom O'Connell was having a hard time dealing with Doug Feith and Ryan Henry (respectively the Undersecretary of Defense for Policy and the Principal Deputy Undersecretary for Policy) along with Steve Cambone, the Undersecretary of Defense for Intelligence, and other assistant secretaries. He should have been actively engaging with them to further enhance the contribution of the SO/LIC organization to defense strategy and policy. The role of an assistant secretary is to engage in strategy, policy formation, planning, and oversight of organizations under the purview of that office. The most successful assistant secretaries bring vision, have a plan to accomplish the mission of their office, engage with Congress, and actively communicate with other Defense Department organizations. Unfortunately, those were not Tom O'Connell's strengths. His strength was caring about those who worked for him. From the time in 1980 that I chose him to replace me in the Delta Force, Tom had become a younger brother to me. The next three years were frustrating times for me. I wanted Tom to succeed and for the SO/LIC organization to contribute to what President Bush referred to as the Global War on Terrorism. At the same time, I wanted to be loyal to him and respect him as he was my boss. Tom's heart was in the right place, but he acted more like he was commanding a military organization than an assistant secretary's office.

There were three deputy assistant secretary positions within SO/LIC. One for combating terrorism; another for stability operations; the third for counternarcotics. The SO/LIC Office was exceedingly well-served by Mary Beth Long, the DASD for counternarcotics, and Jeb Nadaner, the DASD for stability operations. They both brought vision and energy to their work and needed no supervision. They were also adept at working with Congress to get the requisite authorities and funding for their activities. As DASD for counternarcotics, Mary Beth oversaw a budget of close to one billion dollars that provided military support to interagency and allied partners in the war against drugs. She was a lawyer who had served as a case officer with the CIA for 12 years and was fluent in Spanish. Two of her many achievements as DASD stood out for me. One was to create a joint intelligence-sharing program with the United Kingdom that openly shared classified and sensitive information on narcotics. The other was the work she brought about to help the Afghan National Police create an anti-narcotics special unit which was also used against the Taliban and terrorism groups in Afghanistan. While profit-minded American defense companies were trying to push American helicopters and contracted maintenance on the Afghans, she calmly provided Russian-designed helicopters that the Afghans already knew how to fly and maintain. She would later become the Assistant Secretary of Defense for International Security Affairs and was highly regarded by the State Department.

Jeb Nadaner graduated from Yale University and was an exceptional person to run stability operations and humanitarian affairs for the Defense Department. He was an excellent leader and mentor to those who worked with him. He and his staff created two critical pieces of legislation to allow and provide funding for military support to the Department of State, as well as assist with the reconstruction of Afghanistan and Iraq. Under his leadership, a new Defense Department directive was created (3000.05) to guide DOD's efforts to establish security, stability, transition, and reconstruction efforts overseas. He was singled out for praise by Secretary of Defense Robert Gates who clearly saw the value of that directive. Too few bureaucrats and Americans genuinely understand the value of the efforts led by Jeb Nadaner, which continue to be overlooked in our foreign policy. It is one thing to cause regime change, but the hard work comes afterwards in rebuilding good governance in a nation. Jeb was also very astute in mentoring those working for and with him. As a leader, he both encouraged and challenged others and was able to have them excel at policy and strategy. Among the excellent people he led were Dave Mitchell, Vikram Singh, Heather Panitz, and Bailey Hand. Janine Davidson, another member of his staff, would later become the Undersecretary of the Navy.

The Deputy Assistant Secretary for Combating Terrorism should have played a more prominent role in forming strategy and policy for the Global War on Terrorism. I was disappointed to see how little was being done in that office. The Deputy Assistant Secretary for the office was Mike Westphal. Mike was, like Tom O'Connell, a nice person but he lacked a strong vision and did not have any tangible experience in Special Operations or combating terrorism. Mike inherited two personnel issues involving GS-15 employees. One instance involved a GS-15 having an affair with another employee, while his wife was deployed in Iraq as an Army warrant officer. It was discovered that he and his female paramour were involved in travel fraud while supposedly providing Defense Department support for the 2004 Olympic Games in Greece. Other employees were loath to report their behavior, except for then-Major Don Bolduc, who dared to provide information that led to the male GS-15 and his female friend leaving their positions. Don was one of the few outstanding performers in the CT Office and would later command a battalion in Afghanistan with the 3rd Special Force Group and retire as a brigadier general after leading the Special Operations Command Africa. He epitomized the ethics and morality that military officers and government employees should possess. The other GS-15 was a retired Air Force colonel who had a good reputation in the psychological operations community. Unfortunately, he was not very effective as he had become an alcoholic.

Another problem was with a Special Forces colonel who was in a director's position. He told a good story, but never did anything of merit. He had two piles of papers on his desk—each over a foot high—and he would proclaim that it showed how hard he was working. I discreetly placed a Post-it at a marked spot in one of his two piles—when I checked over a month later, the Post-it was in the same place.

Yet another problem in the CT Office was with the anti-terrorism program. It was led by a Navy captain with an explosive ordnance disposal background, with no practical experience in anti-terrorism. He knew that I was very critical of what he was not doing and one day he confronted me in the halls of the Pentagon. He declared that he didn't have to be a mechanic to know when a car wasn't running correctly. His analogy was meant to convey that he didn't need detailed experience with anti-terrorism to do his job. My reply to him was that he was not hired to know that there was a problem. He was hired to fix or deal with the problem which required in-depth experience. To his credit, he acknowledged the point I made. I recommended to Tom O'Connell that the captain be transferred to other duties where he could use his EOD experience and that the program be given to Lieutenant Colonel Margie Garrison, a Military Police officer with experience and leadership in anti-terrorism. Tom did not act on my recommendation. SO/LIC would later lose the anti-terrorism program for DOD to the Homeland Defense Office, based on the ridiculous argument that there were more installations to protect inside the U.S. than overseas. My contention was that although that was true, the bulk of terrorist incidents against America would occur overseas with much greater loss of life. Margie would later lead anti-terrorism efforts for the Multi-National Force Iraq, serve as the installation commander for the headquarters of the Army's Forces Command, and after retirement became the deputy inspector general for the Department of Defense. She was a great mentor for those that worked with her in the CT Office.

Apart from Margie, there were other outstanding people in the CT Office. They included Dorsey "Ed" Rowe, Thori Wolfe, Kweilen Kimmelman, Jana Kay, and Stephanie Dang. Ed Rowe had been the military assistant to Jim Locher, an early assistant secretary for SO/LIC (and the most outstanding one in my opinion), retired as an Army colonel, and became a GS-15. He was an excellent mentor for the younger people in the CT Office and offered over 15 years of experience in SO/LIC. One of the projects he started was to scan and digitize years of documents that had accumulated in the office from 1987 to 2006. He realized the value of being able to retrieve historical information to keep from repeating past mistakes. He could not complete the project due to the shortsightedness of SO/LIC leadership which cut funding for the project. Ed moved to Birmingham, Alabama, after retiring from civil service and continues to mentor university students as an adjunct faculty member of the University of Alabama at Birmingham.

Thori Wolfe joined the CT Office as a Marine Reservist on active duty. He had been furloughed as a United Airlines pilot during the airline's challenging economic time after the 9/11 attacks. Thori had no previous experience in Special Operations but was a quick and eager learner and excellent writer. He was able to gain civil service status, became the director of the National Counterterrorism Center's Watch Center, and as of 2023 was a deputy director for a cyber operation with the Central Intelligence Agency.

Kweilen Kimmelman and Jana Kay joined the CT Office as presidential management fellows. Both were very bright, eager and quick to learn about Special Operations and terrorism, and excellent writers and planners. Kweilen later became a director of policy for the office of the deputy undersecretary of the Navy, married Knut Hatleskog, moved to the United Kingdom, scaled the corporate ladder to become a vice president, and is now a partner in a defense firm. Jana Kay became the director of Iran Policy and as of 2023 is in a senior position with Amazon Web Services on Cloud security issues. Stephanie Dang and her family escaped from Vietnam in 1979. She graduated from the College of William & Mary and Georgetown University before joining the Defense Department. She was also an eager learner and an excellent planner and writer. She married Sean Murphy, moved to Florida, became the first Vietnamese woman to become a member of Congress, was the vice chair of the House Subcommittee on Intelligence and Special Operations, the chair of the Special Operations Caucus, and a key member of the January 6 congressional investigation. She left Congress in 2023 and became an executive with Sungate Capital in Florida. It was a pleasure to work with people like Thori, Kweilen, Jana, and Stephanie and to help them learn. They demonstrated the value of hard work, humility, eagerness to learn, and genuinely caring about responsibility rather than ego.

David Radcliff was another outstanding contributor to the CT Office. David, with the contracted help of retired ranger Colonel Jeff Ellis and his wife Lexi Alexander, had created a program known as the Defense Counterterrorism Fellowship Program. The aim of the program was to build an international network of allies working against terrorism using educational efforts as the basis for building the network and continuing relationships. The program had great potential which was never realized due to poor management and leadership after Radcliffe decided to leave SO/LIC and the CT Office. I felt that Radcliffe should have been promoted and the program raised to a higher level of management, but that did not happen. Under the program, funding was dispensed to the Marshall Center, the Asia-Pacific Center for Security Studies, the Joint Special Operations University, the National Defense University, and the Naval Postgraduate School. The Defense Security Cooperation Agency (DSCA) was asked to play a significant role in the program. I believed that three of the keys to success were to develop a centralized database of students, maintain contact with them after they had attended a course, and to conduct alumni activities that would cross regions of the world.

After Radcliffe's departure, I participated in a review to ascertain DSCA's continued support for the program; I was both shocked and dismayed at what I discovered.

DSCA was charging a ridiculous 25% administrative fee to participate in the program, whereas in the private sector administrative charges range from 5% to 10%. DSCA could not show that they had a viable database of students, were not obtaining information from the funded organizations providing instruction under the program, nor had they or the CT Office reviewed what was being presented, and they had no plans for follow-on activities. I raised my concerns to the CT Office and Tom O'Connell; nothing was done. A few years later I suffered my biggest disappointment while in the SO/LIC Office. O'Connell had promised that he would allow me to run the program and scheduled a meeting to announce it. I had discussed expansion of the program with Congressional staffers and had informal agreements to double the amount allocated to it. Before the meeting, a flustered O'Connell came to me and said that a powerful Congressional staff director, with whom Tom had just had a meeting, needed a ride back to Capitol Hill. Tom was beside himself, so I offered to drive the gentleman. When I returned, I discovered that Tom had given the program to his military assistant. I was livid. The unfortunate thing is that the program has been flat-funded at $30 million annually ever since 2007 and that the original objectives have never been achieved.

***

The front office of ASD SO/LIC was in turmoil. The PDASD position had not been filled after Billingslea's departure, the two military assistants were about to leave for other assignments, the administrative assistant was about to go, and the ASD's confidential assistant was also about to resign. I sat down with Tom O'Connell to help him plan replacements and even offered to give up my IPA agreement and become the PDASD. His mind was set on offering the PDASD position to Mike Westphal or his deputy in the CT Office. Neither wanted the position and they both advised Tom of their lack of desire. Tom never took me up on my offer and directed Westphal to become the PDASD. O'Connell also never took me up on my offer to become the DASD for CT. Within months, Westphal resigned and left for a private sector job. I again offered to become the PDASD but Tom again ignored my offer. Instead, he went to his boss, Doug Feith, the Undersecretary of Defense for Policy, and asked for permission to bring Bob Andrews back into Defense and SO/LIC. Feith had fired Andrews for poor performance after the 9/11 attacks. Feith told Tom to do what he wanted, but it was apparent that Feith and his deputy, Ryan Henry, lost faith in his decision-making ability. The day Andrews reported back into SO/LIC, he presented a poorly thought-out white paper which essentially called for America to declare a religious war against Islam. No wonder Doug Feith had fired him previously. Andrews was a nice person, but he did not show leadership qualities or the ability to think strategically along policy lines. He proved again to be ineffective and within a year left for another job.

I advised Tom to go to the military services to get nominees to replace his military assistants. Instead, he chose to select Army Intelligence Colonel Sylvia Moran, who had worked for him when she was a lieutenant, and Lieutenant Colonel Steve Weiler, who was in the CT Office. Sylvia was in the first female class at West Point and participated in judo while at the academy; she would be reassigned within a year and Tom would have to find another senior military assistant. Sylvia took copious notes at the meetings she attended with Tom. Unfortunately, she did not get along with Weiler and the new confidential assistant and was not good at interfacing with other military assistants in DOD. She meant well but had some curious thoughts such as directing Weiler and the confidential assistant to recycle Post-it notes! Tom did go to the services for her replacement and was very fortunate to have Marine Colonel Giles Kyser assigned. Giles was promoted to colonel by General Peter Pace and was a Naval Academy graduate who had been part of the early efforts to form the Marine Special Operations Command. He had a great personality, worked hard, and interfaced well with other military assistants.

Tom and the SO/LIC Office really lucked out with the new confidential assistant, Anne Meree Morehead. She had a great personality and charm along with many other talents. She had graduated from Wofford College, got her master's degree from Middlebury College, played soccer, played the piano, spoke fluent Spanish, and was working on her doctorate at the University of Georgia when she decided to answer the call after the 9/11 attacks. Short of stature (Steve Weiler nicknamed her "the Midget"), but with boundless energy and people smarts, one could not ask for a better special assistant. Although she had no experience in defense or Special Operations, she was an exceedingly quick learner. I was glad to mentor her and adopt her as one of my extended family. I nicknamed her "Bunctious" for her rambunctious style and indomitable spirit. She tried her best to keep Tom O'Connell out of trouble, by giving him sound advice. She may well have saved Tom's life on one occasion when Tom was sweating profusely, red-faced, and with labored breathing. When he refused to go to the Pentagon medical clinic, Anne Meree went directly to the wife of Steve Bucci, a Special Forces Colonel, who was a nurse on the Air Force staff. She immediately came to Tom's office. His systolic reading was over 200 and his diastolic reading was 140, and she immediately took emergency measures. One of the things that Anne Meree had to learn was how to deal with criticism and less-than-optimal outcomes. She had always excelled at whatever she did, and it was hard for her to be criticized. One of the semi-comical times that occurred was on a trip to the United Kingdom. Tom blamed her for sitting in a pool of hydraulic fluid on a helicopter flight (not her fault at all) and then choosing a bad hotel. Then, we were taken to the wrong hotel and had to walk a few blocks to get to the right one. Tom kept threatening to fire her. Anne Meree wasn't sure how to react. I finally told Tom to shut up and be grateful for her loyalty to him and all she had done to keep him out of trouble! Anne Meree, now Craig, has done well in the years after SO/LIC. One of her great achievements was founding the COMMIT foundation that offers help to military persons to transition back into civilian life. She is now a senior partner with Airbnb in Montana.

I never dwelled on Tom O'Connell's failure to act on my offers to be the PDASD or DASD for CT, as there were many other things to do in SO/LIC, where my experience was sought and valued. One of these was a request from General Dick Cody to help with the Improvised Explosive Device (IED) Task Force that he had formed in 2003. Dick selected then-Colonel Joe Votel to head the task force and secured $25 million to get it off the ground. Joe Votel had a small staff and little money but envisaged that the way ahead was to plan counter-measures against IEDs. Both Dick Cody and Joe Votel valued my advice. I got Rich Higgins involved from the CTTSO, who also provided valuable guidance. More on Rich Higgins later.

One of the more outstanding members of the IED Task Force was Marine Captain Mike Livingston. Despite his rank, Mike understood what needed to be done and how to do it, especially with regard to intelligence support for the task force. He showed the importance of experience and sound planning, reinforcing the fact that one's rank should not determine the value a person can add to an organization. It was obvious to me that the task force could use top cover from the ASD SO/LIC Office to achieve defense-wide acceptance of their work, provide oversight, and obtain the required funding.

I recommended that Tom O'Connell appoint someone to oversee and assist the IED Task Force and that his two best choices would be myself or Ed McCallum, who headed the CTTSO. Curiously, he chose the SO/LIC bean counter (resource director), a retired Army artillery colonel with no experience in IEDs. That individual did nothing to provide advice or oversight to the task force. Joe Votel was promoted to brigadier general and left as the head of the task force. Paul Wolfowitz, the Deputy Secretary of Defense, decided to discontinue the Army as the executive agent for the task force and to place it directly under his office. Wolfowitz selected retired Army General Montgomery Meigs to head what became the Joint IED Organization JIEDDO. JIEDDO took on the appearance of being a defense agency with a budget that rapidly grew to billions of dollars annually. Typically, defense agencies are overseen by an undersecretary or assistant secretary in the defense department. This was not the case with JIEDDO, and the DEPSECDEF's staff was incapable of providing oversight.

From the task force led by Joe Votel, with less than 50 people assigned, JIEDDO grew to thousands of military personnel, civilians, and contractors. What Captain Mike Livingston had done on his own was replaced by over 1,200 people. Instead of looking at tactics and how to reduce the number of IED incidents, JIEDDO focused on technology and squandered billions of dollars on electronic jammers and mine-resistant ambush-protected (MRAP) vehicles. There was no consistency with the type of electronic jammers, no effort to maintain them or provide good training, and no consideration given that the insurgents would revert to command-detonated devices. The MRAPs were also a costly addition. Interestingly, the design of the MRAPs grew from the innovation of Special Forces in Iraq, who placed armored plates around a two-and-a-half-ton-truck with a .50-caliber machine gun on top! A cheap alternative to the $600,000+ MRAP! Over $45 billion was spent on MRAPs—unbelievable!

***

In the summer of 2004, I received a call from Andrew Provorse, a National Security Council staff member who requested a meeting with me. Andy was working for Colonel Jeff Jones and Jeff recommended that Andy talk with me about a program that Jeff had conceived and had obtained permission from Condoleezza Rice, the National Security Advisor, to start. The program's name was well-crafted by Jeff to prevent naysayers from stopping the program. It was named the Interagency Counter-Propaganda Panel. The "interagency" aspect meant that it would be harder to stop by a single government agency. The "counterpropaganda" made it seem like it would only counter enemy efforts. The "panel" wording was meant to get around the formation of another program of record. The program was designed to wage information warfare, the target being al-Qaeda in Iraq. I had just moved offices in the Pentagon and could not find a writing pad. However, I had plenty of napkins from my visits to the snack bars in the Pentagon! Andy also did not have a writing pad. So, we drafted a plan on a couple of napkins.

Within months, Andy had assembled an interagency group and hatched a plan for their first operation. He had managed to get approval from the Joint Staff, the State Department, the CIA, and the DIA. The plan was straightforward. An announcement would be made lowering the reward for the capture or death of Abu Musab al-Zarqawi. Zarqawi was the leader of al-Qaeda in Iraq at the time. The interagency team had conducted a psychological profile on Zarqawi. They believed his ego would be affronted by the lowering the reward, and he would do something to prove his worth that would get him captured, killed, or for his movement to lose favor in Iraq. The plan was reviewed by Stephen Hadley, who had replaced Condoleezza Rice as the national security advisor. Hadley stopped the plan from being executed, but gave no reason. It should be noted that none of the principal members of the National Security Council chose to overturn Hadley's unilateral decision. The net result of Hadley's decision was that al-Zarqawi had over a year and a half to form the Islamic State of Iraq (ISIS) before he was killed in an airstrike.

Hadley's decision was only one of hundreds of high-level decisions made after the 9/11 attacks that were questionable. They all pointed towards the lack of a coherent strategy for dealing with Afghanistan, Iraq, and global terrorism that still continues. What has posed as strategy has lacked a well-defined end-state that is measurable with the right metrics and accomplishable. I could easily write over a hundred pages about what I consider to be mistakes in Afghanistan and Iraq, but that is not the purpose of this book. Rather, the purpose is to share lessons I have learned, and to extol those with whom I have worked, and who embody the spirit of *Intoku*.

My attempts to create a strategic plan for the ASD SO/LIC Office failed. I was slow-rolled by the SO/LIC financial manager, and it took me months to finally get the funding, thanks to Mary Beth Long, the DASD for counternarcotics at the time. Two of the three DASDs (Mary Beth and Jeb Nadaner) clearly saw the value of a strategic plan. I was fortunate to find a company willing to take on the work at a loss because of their desire to help. A day-long session was scheduled to finalize the plan. Tom O'Connell was in favor of the plan during the morning session. Something happened to him over lunch as he came back totally negative and started attacking Jeb Nadaner and Mary Beth Long. Tom's actions killed the strategic plan that was aimed towards helping him quell the criticisms he was receiving from the two top people in the Undersecretary of Defense for Policy Office (Doug Feith and Ryan Henry).

Rather than dwell on that setback, I put my head down and weighed in on other matters that had an impact. I started speaking at every course for the Joint Professional Military Education Phase II held at the Armed Forces Staff College in Norfolk, Virginia, to help the students better understand the contribution of Special Operations to military strategy and the fight against terrorism. I lectured at the U.S. Special Operations Command Pre-Command Course to impart the value of interagency operations to Special Operations, to lieutenant colonels/commanders and colonels/captains about to assume command of Special Operations units. There was one session that was particularly rewarding for me. Colonel Bill Coultrup was in a bad mood as he had been picked for assignment to the Joint Task Force Philippines. He felt that he should have command of the Delta Force. He was also angry because then-Colonel Don Bolduc had convinced people that he should be reassigned to Afghanistan, rather than take command in the Philippines. Bill was a superb squadron commander in Delta and, in my opinion, should have taken command of that unit. Without seeking recognition, he had a major role in finding Saddam Hussein's two sons and Saddam himself. I understood Bill's anger and frustration and felt the need to get his mind straight. I called him out into the parking lot outside the classroom and began to counsel him. I asked him what color beret he was wearing. He answered, "Green." I then told him that he was indeed Special Forces and was about to take command of an organization that would allow him to fight Islamic militants in the Philippines, to deal with interagency partners, the Filipino government and military, and the U.S. ambassador. I also explained that he would have a remarkable life experience. He wasn't quite sure whether he should take my word or not. The following year, I saw him and his wife at the Pacific Special Operations Conference banquet in Hawaii. As I approached him, he held up his hand and said, "Don't say it!" He had a smile on his face and described how much he appreciated being able to command the Joint Task Force! Bill extended for a year in the Philippines and returned to be the head of the USSOCOM Legislative Liaison Office where he again did a superb job. He should have made general officer. Sometimes life is not fair. Bill retired and is doing well in the private sector. He should be proud of what he accomplished in the spirit of *Intoku*.

***

I participated in several Pacific Area Special Operations conferences representing ASD SO/LIC, doing presentations and working quietly to encourage increased partnerships. At one conference, I got traditional enemies to talk with each other—representatives from the People's Republic of China, South Korea, and Japan with the help of the Australian Special Air Service delegation. The Australians, then under the leadership of General Mike Hindmarsh, certainly had a grasp on how to build relationships with other nations. Hindmarsh would later retire and then be snapped up by Sheikh Mohammed in the UAE as an advisor.

At another conference—thanks to a friend teaching at the Asia Pacific Center for Security Studies—I assisted in reestablishing relations with the Hong Kong Police Service and the Special Operations Command Pacific, along with the 1st Special Forces Group, facilitated through Frank Kwok who led the Hong Kong SWAT organization. I accompanied General Doug Brown, then commanding the USSOCOM, when he announced the decision to curtail the development of an advanced SEAL delivery vehicle to the SEAL Delivery Team 1 at Pearl Harbor, due to cost escalations and poor performance and design by Northrop Grumman. Another highlight was participating in a panel where Maria Ressa made an insightful presentation on how the internet and cell phones were changing information flow and how the military needed to adapt to those changes. The term disinformation was not used in those days, but she clearly referred to that phenomenon. Unfortunately, 90% of the audience did not comprehend what she was saying. Ressa later became head of a major Filipino media network, was seen as a threat by President Duterte, survived those threats, and won the Nobel Peace Prize in 2021.

I was fortunate to meet Chandi Duke Heffner, the adopted daughter of tobacco heiress Doris Duke. Chandi was doing philanthropic work in India, understood the insurgent challenges inside India, and had become very good friends with a retired Indian Police Service official, named KPS Gill who, as a Sikh, was noted for his leadership in quelling an insurgency in Punjab. After retirement, Gill started the Institute for Conflict Management in Delhi, a think tank that produced many insights into India's internal problems, along with relations with Pakistan and China. He was pro-American but retained a strong sense of Indian nationalism. He was the head of the Indian Field Hockey Association and believed that association was beneficial in building better relationships with Pakistan. Our State Department was reluctant to deal with him as he was falsely accused of human rights violations by left-wing elements in India. I was able to help Chandi obtain State Department approval for a visit to Washington, DC, and to open the doors at what is now Indo-Pacific Command, and with law enforcement in Hawaii. When General Bryan Fenton had command of the Special Operations Command Pacific, he saw the value of improving relationships with India and visited with KPS Gill. General Fenton became the deputy commander of Indo-Pacific Command and played a prominent role in solidifying our relationship with India in his role as the commander of the U.S. Special Operations Command. My most memorable trip to India was when KPS Gill took me to Chhattisgarh National Forest where the Maoist Naxalite movement had its headquarters and conducted insurgent and terrorist activity throughout India.

During my time in the SO/LIC organization and later working as a special assistant to the Deputy Undersecretary of the Navy, I saw the need for educational efforts to help others better understand Special Operations, terrorism, crisis management, collaborative partnerships, and leadership. The students or audiences that I taught included U.S. and foreign military, federal agencies, civilians, and university students. The university programs were led by David Silverstein, a great American who clearly saw the need to provide America's future leaders with accurate and meaningful information on terrorism.

The leading organization I supported was the Joint Special Operations University (JSOU), an element of the U.S. Special Operations Command, initially located at Hurlburt Field, Florida, and later moved to MacDill Air Force Base in Tampa, Florida, adjacent to the U.S. Special Operations Command Headquarters. JSOU was created in 2000 by General Peter Schoomaker, who was one of the original members of the Delta Force. JSOU went through three reserve generals as its president before selecting retired Air Force Colonel Brian Maher. Brian was the commandant of the Air Force Special Operations School before retirement and was the deputy at JSOU from its inception. He was the glue that kept JSOU on the right path. Regrettably, before his retirement, he made some bad decisions, but that did not diminish the value he added to JSOU over a 15-year period. He was ably assisted by two outstanding individuals: Major Barabara Stearns and retired Special Forces Lieutenant Colonel George (Hal) McNair. Maher and Hal McNair were instrumental in awarding me the designation of Distinguished Senior Fellow for the JSOU. They based their selection on my dedication to helping JSOU achieve its goals, to nurture students, and to share lessons learned throughout my life.

Barbara was an Air Force Special Ooperations maintenance officer who was a superb planner and organizer. She was the course director for the crisis management course and for the pre-command course. She was also the lead to establish the move of JSOU from Hurlburt Field to MacDill AFB. Barbara and her husband had a bagel shop near Hurlburt Field but sold that when she retired and they set off in their sailboat to sail the seven seas! She organized the courses she was responsible for ensuring that the proper subjects were taught, and the right instructors were selected to support those courses. She sought to expand offerings designed to encourage interagency cooperation with the FBI, law enforcement, Homeland Security, State Department, and others. Barbara was ahead of her time and recognized the value of such cooperation well before the advent of terms like "whole of government" or "whole of society." In the spirit of *Intoku*, Barbara never sought recognition and remained humble.

***

Hal McNair graduated from the University of Georgia with a degree in finance. How he became a Special Forces officer is a story on its own. Brian Maher relied on Hal for the fiscal planning for JSOU, but Hal was more noted for his brainstorming role in developing an international program. Special operations have long understood the need to work with global partners, but relatively little was being done to advance their skills in unconventional warfare. Hal was determined to fill that gap. He was fortunate to secure Blake Edwards as his right-hand man. Blake was a Special Forces master sergeant who retired and gained a civil service position with JSOU. Blake was not only an excellent instructor but also one to adopt different methods of teaching to better the student's ability to not only comprehend, but to apply what was being taught.

One of their initial successes was to educate both conventional and Special Operations personnel at the North Atlantic Treaty Organization (NATO) School in Oberammergau, Germany. Hal and Blake worked diligently to establish programs in other countries. Through their efforts, I was fortunate to be able to instruct in Germany, Poland, the United Kingdom, Sweden, Norway, Estonia, Lithuania, Hungary, Slovakia, Romania, Albania, and Belgium. Other countries where they developed programs included Saudi Arabia, the United Arab Emirates, the Philippines, Bangladesh, Thailand, Indonesia, Taiwan, Uruguay, Brazil, and Colombia. They understood the value of maintaining relationships with past students who would rise to a higher rank and responsibility in their countries. One of the best examples is Magne Rodahl, who attended one of the early NATO School courses as a captain and ultimately retired as a general officer in the Norwegian Army. He was a key player in the formation of the Norwegian Special Operations Command. No two people have done more to build international partnerships than Hal McNair and Blake Edwards. They embodied the spirit of *Intoku* in everything they did and how they did it.

Away from JSOU, I also taught at the Joint Force Staff College, the Naval War College, the Marine Corps University, the National Defense University, the Marine Special Operations Command, the Naval Special Warfare Command, the Air Force

Special Operations Command, and the Army's Special Warfare Center. I felt that it was absolutely necessary to share lessons learned, encourage others to continue their learning efforts and to improve themselves, the units they were assigned to, and the men and women working for or with them. I always sought to get people to know how to think rather than what to think. Ultimately, they would have to make their own decisions, and they would profit more from being able to analyze a problem rather than follow a set solution. During a course at the Naval Special Warfare Center, I was confronted by a young Navy lieutenant who had just completed BUDS who stated that he disagreed with something I had said. Instead of getting into a confrontation with him, I stated that I did not care that he disagreed with me—what I cared about was that he was thinking through an issue, had the courage to disagree, and what I hoped for was that his disagreement was based on solid research and analysis coupled with facts. I then conjectured that at some point he might be in a SEAL platoon, and his chiefs might object to something he instructed them to do. I then asked him to think about how he would respond. After the class, he came up to me and thanked me for a great lesson in leadership.

One of the significant roles I played in the SO/LIC organization was to screen individuals wanting to present ideas to Tom O'Connell. There were some brilliant ideas and other ideas that were useless and presented by people without experience. One of the more inspirational ideas was hatched by a Reserve Army captain who conceived the idea of cultural engagement teams to assist efforts in both Afghanistan and Iraq to help American and allied forces relate to and understand the indigenous population. Unfortunately, his superiors gave the program to an inexperienced contractor only interested in making money and a name for herself. Working with Rich Higgins from CTTSO gave me infinite pleasure. Rich had been an enlisted explosive ordnance disposal soldier who left the Army, got a degree from Tufts University, and became a project manager to rapidly prototype and field ways to counter terrorists. He brought boundless energy and brilliant ideas to his work. On the mundane side, he developed booties for dogs to keep their paws from burning in the heat of Afghanistan and Iraq. On the esoteric side, he developed analytical techniques to identify key terrorist bomb-makers; methods to collect crucial evidence from terrorist safehouses, either clandestinely or in the aftermath of a raid; psychological warfare projects to undermine terrorist leaders; tools to disrupt terrorist financing; and developed unique training methods for Special Operations personnel. Rich met an untimely death caused by heart failure at the age of 47. America truly lost a hero with his passing. He was strong-willed, but humble and dedicated in the spirit of *Intoku*.

In stark contrast to great Americans like Rich Higgins, there were far too many people with little to no experience who proclaimed that they had identified problems that needed to be addressed and solutions that were nonsensical. The problems they raised were in large measure not based on intelligence or common sense, but on mere speculation. One person insisted that major water reservoirs would be poisoned using chemical agents and the solution was to fence every reservoir in America. He could not describe the type of chemical agent, the amount required to lethally poison large reservoirs, nor did he understand that a fence was meaningless unless there was monitoring of the fence to detect incursions and a response force available to react. Others frequently used the term "game-changer" and created acronyms to make them look smart. One person stated that HMEs (home-made explosives) were a game-changer. When I pointed out that most of the bombs used in Afghanistan and Iraq by the insurgents/terrorists were made from large stocks of standard explosives or military ordnance, he could not bring himself to face reality. Another set of instant experts proclaimed that ENEs (Enhanced Novel Explosives) were another game-changer that would kill thousands. The so-called ENEs were commonly described in Special Forces as flyer plates which were deadly against vehicles but could not match the lethality of standard explosives detonated in a crowd. On one hand, no one wanted to squash new ideas, but there was also a responsibility to put things in perspective and base decisions on facts rather than speculation.

***

During my time in SO/LIC, I made two trips to Iraq. The first was a fact-finding trip in 2005 and was also taken to introduce a new GS-15 director in SO/LIC to the reality of the conflict in Iraq. The trip began in Qatar where I was met by Lieutenant Colonel Reese Rogers, a Marine Corps Reservist and special operator. Reese took me to visit the Combined Forces Special Operations Command and to meet an Air Force medical team dedicated to supporting Special Operations. Reese ensured that I had a helmet and protective vest before heading to Iraq. It was a whirlwind trip. I met with my friend Eldon Bargewell, the director of strategic operations for General George Casey and Multinational Force Iraq; then Lieutenant General Martin Dempsey, who commanded the Multinational Security Transition Command Iraq, responsible for training the Iraqi Army and National Police. My cousin, Joe Peterson, was Dempsey's deputy to train the Iraqi National Police. I met with Rick Zaner who was Casey's intelligence officer, who disillusioned me when he declared that the main threat in Iraq was organized crime, not the ongoing insurgency and terrorist activity. I visited the Abu Ghraib prison that had come under intense scrutiny, and found that major improvements had been made but that there was still work to be done with respect to interrogations and stopping the prisoners from continuing to recruit for terrorist organizations.

I then met with Colonel Kevin McDonnell who commanded the 5th Special Forces Group and the Combined Joint Special Operations Task Force Arabian Peninsula. Kevin was responsible for the equivalent of 79 Special Forces Operational Detachments in Iraq, including SEALs and coalition partners. During Kevin's briefing I nodded off from being tired. At the end of the briefing, with a skeptical look on his face, Kevin asked me if I had any questions. I asked him to bring up PowerPoint slide #25. He had an incredulous look on his face, and when he brought the slide up, I asked him where his assigned air assets were. He told me that they had to beg, borrow, and steal air assets and that the 160th Aviation Regiment was totally in support of the Joint Special Operations Command. I also discovered that his headquarters was not invited to the immense JSOC operations center daily which made no practical sense as his forces represented a wealth of intelligence, along with conducting more operations than the JSOC. I also met with Lieutenant General John Vines who commanded the Multinational Corps Iraq. His aide was Louis Zeisman, the son of my great friend Paul Zeisman, who was so instrumental in creating the Delta Force communications organization and system. The corps was headquartered at Saddam Hussein's former Water Palace. Louis put me up in the bedroom of Saddam's son. It had a huge bed the size of two king beds and gold shower fixtures.

During the last part of the trip, we encountered bad weather and had to move by vehicle. I was accorded an 18-man security detail comprising Texas Army National Guardsmen, led by First Lieutenant Trooper Smith. They impressed me with their professionalism, attention to detail, and planning. I bonded well with them and thoroughly enjoyed my time with them. One day, I asked First Lieutenant Smith whether he would allow me to man the .50-caliber machine gun on the top of a Humvee vehicle. He looked me in the eye and said he didn't think it was a good idea. I chided him by asking if he thought I was too old or incapable of firing the machine gun. Without hesitation he told me that it was neither, but that he thought I would cause trouble if I manned the machine gun! We both had a good laugh, and I took a seat in the passenger compartment. The detail escorted me to board a C-130 headed for Kuwait. I shook their hands and hugged them and wished them well. I really felt that I could count on them in battle, and it was an emotional farewell for me. Upon landing in Kuwait, I was headed to a dining facility when I heard a voice call out, "Uncle Ishi!" I turned around and was greeted by then-Major Ben Dennis, my nephew. We had a great reunion and he convinced Major General Lloyd Austin to allow me to give a speech on Veterans Day.

The other trip to Iraq was in 2007. I accompanied Tom O'Connell to hopefully change his perspective on Iraq and Special Operations. Anne Meree also went on the trip, and it was her first to Iraq. Tom had made two previous trips to Iraq to visit only JSOC. As was the case on this trip, he refused to meet with the MNF-I leadership. He should have done so as an assistant secretary but felt uncomfortable doing so. He agreed with the agenda I arranged, which commenced with visiting an augmented battalion from the 10th Special Forces Group that was responsible for merging different Iraqi counterterrorist units into one organization. The battalion was led by Sean Swindell and Command Sergeant Major Mitch Conway, two superb Special Forces warriors and leaders. O'Connell witnessed the Iraqis plan their own operation and execute it with precision while the SF soldiers remained in the background. Tom also witnessed how the insurgents instantly prepared a press release declaring that the Iraqi unit had committed atrocities—which was a total lie. Swindell and Conway pointed out that they anticipated the false information and had a prepared public announcement, but MNF-I would not approve it.

From Baghdad International, we flew on a Navy Reserve helicopter squadron UH-60 instead of a 160th Aviation Regiment helicopter to Balad. The Navy crew was highly competent, but their aircraft lacked the sophistication of those of the 160th. For example, I pointed out to Tom that the door gunner was sitting on a camp stool that he probably bought out of his own pocket, and was firing an M-60 machine gun attached to a sling rather than a more capable M249 machine gun on a fixed mount. In Balad, I had arranged for us to stay at the CJSOTF-AP headquarters where Ken Tovo presented a detailed briefing to Tom along with a quick trip to al-Asad Airbase where a Navy SEAL platoon was based.

We spent the last night at the JSOC huge operations center that was being overseen by Scotty Miller, who would later become a four-star general. The operations center was truly impressive with much of the design and communications done by Paul Zeisman as a chief warrant officer. JSOC had clearly advanced the art of immediately exploiting intelligence gathered on a raid through an interagency effort involving everything from interrogations to analysis of captured material. Stan McChrystal was a gracious host as usual and attempted to gain my support to declare a CIA official as his deputy. I recommended that Stan choose another title as the CIA person did not have Title 10 authority to handle several matters.

I also made two trips to Japan in the interest of increasing Japanese Special Operations capability and encouraging Japan to take on an increased role in the regional defense of Asia. Frank Clark, the assistant army attaché to the U.S. Embassy in Japan, arranged both trips. He was a fine officer who understood the necessary steps to achieve the goals I had set. I met with high-level officials from the Japan Self-Defense Force Headquarters prior to establishing their Ministry of Defense, the Army Special Operations Group at Camp Narashino outside Tokyo, and the Navy Special Boarding Unit on Eta Jima Island near Hiroshima and Iwakuni Air Base. On both trips, I also coordinated participation from the 1st Battalion, 1st Special Forces Group in Okinawa to solidify their relations with the Japanese. Aki Cibulka, a civilian working for the U.S. Navy, was of great assistance as an interpreter on these trips. On the second trip, I took a few days of vacation to visit my grandparents' relatives in Yanai, Japan.

***

One of the interesting aspects of my role in SO/LIC was to engage with the media and journalists. The goal was to help them cast accurate stories that did not reveal classified information. The better ones included David Martin and his producer, Mary Walsh from CBS; Jim Miklaszewski from NBC; and writers like Mark Bowden, Linda Robinson, and Jeff Stein. There is an amusing story concerning Linda Robinson who wrote two books about Special Forces and one about David Petraeus. I was in my Pentagon office when the phone rang with Linda calling from Iraq. She was desperately seeking help from Uncle Ish as the Iraqi government was refusing to allow her to leave the country unless she complied with two medical requirements that she had no idea how to accomplish. I calmed her down, contacted Command Sergeant Major Mitch Conway, and connected the two of them. Mitch quickly took care of the matter and Linda could depart Iraq. Mitch again showed his *Intoku* spirit!

During my time in the Pentagon, there were four people who truly embodied the spirit of *Intoku* and I would be remiss if I did not mention them. The first is my adopted niece Karen Theobald Conlin. Karen had been a successful sports publicist in Canada and moved to the Washington, DC, area to work for an architectural firm. She became interested in supporting the military, and the Army in particular. With compassion for our wounded coming out of Afghanistan and Iraq, she formed the Helping Our Heroes Foundation. The foundation sought to assist wounded military members and their families with advocacy, financial support, and activities to reduce the trauma of the wounded and their families. She also supported the staff of the Walter Reed Medical Center by arranging spa treatments for the overworked nursing staff. As a public affairs expert, she was successful in getting political figures to meet with those at Walter Reed on a bipartisan basis, including Senator Jeff Sessions (R-Alabama), Secretary Norman Mineta (Department of Transportation), and Representative Madeleine Bordello (D-Guam). For several years, she helped to sponsor weekly events at Walter Reed to help with building morale and providing support to the wounded.

Karen also made a trip to Iraq, and her mother was greatly concerned with Karen's safety. Her mother called me with her concern. I told an outright lie that I had received personal word from the U.S. central commander and the commanding general in Iraq that she would be safe. That relieved her mother's concerns! (I did know that she would be well-protected.) Karen was extolled by General Dick Cody who was the Army's Vice Chief of Staff and a true humble warrior in his own right. After Dick Cody's retirement, the Army began to institute a large measure of bureaucratic red tape, which made the provision of assistance very difficult.

Coupled with her marriage and the birth of two children, Karen closed the foundation. Her love for the Army did not stop—she was appointed as a civilian aide to the secretary of the Army for the Northern Virginia area. As a CASA, she worked hard to establish better relationships and an appreciation for the Army. Karen never sought recognition for her efforts. She did it out of patriotism, compassion for our military's sacrifices, and a desire to do her part for America. It was a joy to support her in her efforts.

The second person is William G. "Jerry" Boykin. I first met Jerry in 1978 when he was one of the originals to pass the selection course for the Delta Force. After my retirement I stayed in contact with him and watched him grow in knowledge and responsibility. He was severely wounded during the invasion of Grenada and at Mogadishu, Somalia, shortly after the Black Hawk Down incident. I heard that his treatment in Somalia was overseen by Dr. Rob Marsh who himself was severely wounded at the time.

He would later be assigned to the CIA and then as commander of the 1st Special Forces Command and thereafter as the commander of the Special Warfare Center. In 2003, Secretary Rumsfeld selected him for promotion to lieutenant general and assignments as the first deputy when Rumsfeld formed the Undersecretary of Defense for Intelligence Office. In every assignment he had, Jerry helped to empower his subordinates and mentored them to improve their capabilities. He was a superb planner who showed a clear grasp of the right objectives for an organization to achieve. In the USD Intelligence role, he spearheaded many innovations aimed at providing support to warfighters.

In late 2003, the *Los Angeles Times* and an NBC reporter accused Jerry of making anti-Islamic comments. Accusations were also made that he did not have permission to wear his uniform during several speeches he delivered, nor permission to make those speeches. Jerry personally requested the opening of a Department of Defense inspector general's inspection. After 10 months, the IG report found that he did have permission to wear his uniform and to make speeches. The investigation found that on one occasion, he failed to deliver a disclaimer stating that he was presenting his personal views rather than those of the Defense Department and that he had failed to file a senior official form regarding travel reimbursement from outside sources. The report did not find that he cheated the government regarding the reimbursement. All the other allegations, including his supposed anti-Islam comments, were not substantiated.

Despite everything, the accusations and attempts to smear Jerry Boykin continued. He finally decided to retire in 2007. I later met with James Clapper who had taken Steve Cambone's post as Undersecretary for Intelligence. Clapper told me that he was initially concerned about Jerry Boykin, but after meeting Jerry, Clapper wished that he could have spent nine years with Boykin rather than the nine months before Jerry retired. After retirement, Jerry was hired by the President of Hampden Sydney College, the legendary retired Lieutenant General Samuel V. Wilson, to be a chair. After nine years, Jerry left to become the executive director of the Family Research Council. He continues to mentor many in all walks of life with great humility and human compassion.

The next *Intoku* warrior is retired General Norton "Norty" Schwartz. I first met Norty when he was newly assigned to the 1st Special Operations Wing at Hurlburt Field, Florida. I witnessed his rise through the ranks, including being the J3 for the Special Operations Command Europe, where he was employed by another unrecognized *Intoku* warrior, Dick Potter. Norty also commanded the Special Operations Command Pacific, the Alaska Command, and became the director of operations for the Joint Staff in 2002. His two vice-directors were Stan McChrystal and Joe Peterson. When McChrystal left to become the JSOC commander, Joe Peterson was selected to follow. I sent Norty an email saying that Joe deserved close watching. Within an hour, Norty sent me a return email in his typically polite fashion asking me to tell him more. I responded that Joe was my cousin, that I used to change his diapers, and poke him with a safety pin when he cried. Norty got a laugh out of that.

He was then promoted to director of the Joint Staff, the commander of the U.S. Transportation Command, and then became the Air Force Chief of Staff. His selection was unusual as he was Jewish, which not many Special Operations pilots of C-130s and helicopters were. Shortly after he became Air Force Chief of Staff, he was invited to the 50th wedding anniversary of Dick and Annie Potter. Norty took the time to drive himself from the Pentagon to Gettysburg, Pennsylvania, to attend the ceremony out of respect for Dick and Annie, as well as how Dick had mentored him previously. At my retirement ceremony in 2012, he took the time as Chief of Staff to attend the ceremony. After retirement, Norty led the Business Executives for National Security and then became the president of the Institute for Defense Analyses. Throughout his life, Norty has been humble, dedicated, hard-working, and a mentor to those working for and with him. A true patriot.

The fourth *Intoku* warrior is Joe Peterson, my cousin, but it is not our relationship that leads me to write about him. Instead, it is his leadership and character that epitomize doing good in secret. He has shown a passion for serving America and a compassionate leadership style that nurtures those under his command. In the late 1990s, he commanded the 3rd Infantry Division. I visited with then-Major General James Thurman and my Santa Clara protégé, Colonel Florian Rothbrust, at the National Training Center, Fort Irwin, California. Thurman and Florian told me that Joe was the only division commander to be with all three of his combat brigades as they completed their training at Fort Irwin. Joe did that to offer advice and encouragement to his troops and to let them know that the division commander supported them fully.

The three brigade commanders were still in place when the 3rd Infantry Division led the charge into Baghdad in 2003, after Joe moved to command the 1st Cavalry Division. After he took command of the 1st Cavalry Division, I was walking in the courtyard of the Pentagon on a dreary and cold day. He reluctantly told me that he was there to be interviewed to be the corps commander for the corps that would lead the Army's efforts into Iraq. I asked him where his aide was, and he told me he had instructed his aide and staff to remain in a hotel because of the lousy weather. He always cared for the soldiers he served with.

In 2003, he had two Apache helicopter pilots taken prisoner by the Iraqis. On their return to America, Joe arranged a welcome home where he took a back seat so that the focus of the ceremony would be on the two pilots. Norty Schwartz thought that Joe would have a tough time filling the shoes of Stan McChrystal on the Joint Staff, but after a few months, Norty told me that Joe was doing a superior job, in a different way from Stan McChrystal but equally as effective. Norty and Joe worked 16 hours a day on the Joint Staff without complaint. After the Joint Staff, he became the commanding general responsible for training Iraqi police. Martin Dempsey, who would later become the Chairman of the Joint Chiefs, extolled Joe's work.

Joe developed strong friendships and camaraderie with two Iraqi interior ministers who appreciated his approach to helping shape Iraq's future. His wife, Ann Moix, was equally caring for the families of the units that Joe commanded. They continually showed their compassion and concern for soldiers and their families. They did it humbly and without seeking recognition.

Many others worked selflessly towards achieving national security or to care for the men and women in uniform making sacrifices in defense of our country. I apologize for not mentioning each of them by name or in some detail. I had the honor and pleasure of dealing with hundreds of incredible people, and regret that I have not mentioned them all.

***

In April 2007, Tom O'Connell announced that he was resigning as the Assistant Secretary of Defense SO/LIC. Lieutenant Colonel Preston Plous, his military assistant, and I collaborated to present Tom with a farewell gift at his departure ceremony. I presented him with a wooden humidor lined in green felt with a fleur-de-lis carved on the top. It had belonged to my father. The small metal plaque attached to it read, "Tom O'Connell, the Last Boy Scout." This was a double entendre. As I presented the humidor, I remarked that the fleur-de-lis is one of the symbols of the Boy Scouts. I went on to say that the Boy Scout motto starts out by saying, "On my honor, I will do my best ..." I then remarked that those words epitomized the way Tom led his life. He was an honorable person who always gave his best. He genuinely cared about those who worked with and for him. Tom was very appreciative of the humidor, but then came the real surprise. I opened the box and brought out the .45-caliber pistol that I carried into Iran on the 1980 hostage rescue attempt. He was floored! He couldn't understand the double entendre, and I explained to him that there was a 1991 movie starring Bruce Willis called *The Last Boy Scout*. In the last stages of the movie, Willis is handed a stuffed toy by his daughter which conceals a handgun which he retrieves and uses to deal with his captors.

Tom O'Connell could be criticized for many things, but in the spirit of *Intoku*, no one could ever question his honor, humility, and care for others. Out of respect for his accomplishments while on active duty in the Army, I wrote his nomination for the U.S. Army Military Intelligence Hall of Fame, which resulted in his induction in 2008.

Shortly after Tom O'Connell's departure, Marshall Billingslea, who had returned from being an Assistant Secretary of NATO and was now the Deputy Undersecretary of the Navy overseeing intelligence, Special Operations, and policy, called me. He asked me to be his special assistant, and I willingly agreed, knowing that he had also brought on board Giles Kyser as his miliary assistant, adopted niece Kweilen Kimmelman, and LeAnn Borman. All of whom I had the utmost respect for. My role was essentially the same that I had in the SO/LIC organization. I provided support to the SEALs and the Marine Special Operations Command, assisted with intelligence oversight and policy, and continued my teaching engagements. I was instrumental in getting Secretary of the Navy Don Winters to approve the use of females for the Navy SEAL counterterrorist unit, where they would be in dangerous situations but not used as assaulters. I assisted with the formation of Cultural Engagement Teams for Naval Special Warfare Command. I also provided support to Captain Pete Wikul to stand up the Trident organization in the Office of Naval Intelligence to support the SEAL community. Trident became the Kennedy Maritime Intelligence Center and is a major sub-organization for Navy Intelligence.

Billingslea was seeking to have the Navy declared as the executive agent to support the U.S. Africa Command that Secretary Rumsfeld had sought to create. He thought it was an excellent opportunity for the Navy to take on a role like the lead they had in the Pacific Command. The problem stemmed from his reliance on false information being issued by the USD (Policy) organization, which asserted that the Department of State had committed well over 100 personnel to support AFRICOM. Marshall had committed that Secretary Winters would make a decision within a week from when I found out. I told him that the numbers were atrociously inflated for State Department support. He believed me but said that he needed verified information to get to Secretary Winters. I called Kweilen, explained the situation, and she jumped in with both feet. Within days, she reported that she had talked with a Navy admiral on the transition team, who stated that they had fewer than 20 State Department slots, and Theresa Whalen, who was the principal person working with the State Department. Whelan stated that the agreement was for only two State Department personnel! Marshall quickly changed his mind and did a pre-brief to Secretary Winters. Secretary Winters invited Theresa Whalen to the meeting and asked her to confirm the number of State Department personnel committed. She replied honestly that it was two. Further discussion also revealed that the supposed agreements to establish regional headquarters throughout Africa were also false. Secretary Winters wisely decided not to pursue becoming the executive agent for AFRICOM.

Billingslea also sought to revise Department of Navy policy regarding certain intelligence operations. For two years, the director he had tasked with revising the policy did not deliver anything. I again called Kweilen Kimmelman for help. In two weeks, she had drafted an outstanding policy. Unfortunately, Billingslea could not get it fully approved before the change of presidential administration and his departure. Kweilen never received the accolades she so richly deserved. She decided to get married and to move to the United Kingdom where she has excelled in business.

There are two other individuals who embodied *Intoku* who I need to recognize. The first is Mark Donald. Mark grew up in Albuquerque, New Mexico, and enlisted in the Marine Corps after graduating from high school. He served in Force Reconnaissance, but had a deep desire to pursue medicine, so he transferred to the Navy to become a corpsman. In 1987, he completed BUD/S and became a Navy SEAL. In 1996, he was accepted to become a physician's assistant, and after graduation the Navy commissioned him as an ensign.

In 2003, while assigned to the Navy's special mission unit, he won the Navy Cross, which is the second-highest decoration for valor. In a separate action, he won the Silver Star. On a later tour in Afghanistan, he won the Bronze Star for valor. I first met Mark when he was assigned to the Deputy Undersecretary of the Navy's (DUSN's) Office. Among his projects were assisting the Kennedy Maritime Intelligence Center and working towards better ways of collecting and analyzing DNA samples to identify terrorists and insurgents. Mark was quiet, dedicated, and hard-working.

He helped anyone in the DUSN's Office who had a medical issue, helping them to understand and analyze the issue, as well as receive treatment. Mark suffered from PTSD but never let that interfere with his work or his relationships with others. Unfortunately, there were those who were jealous of his competence and combat record and sought to undermine him by implying that his PTSD should disqualify him from working in the DUSN's Office. I rose to his defense and stopped any action to remove him from the DUSN's Office. After he retired from the Navy, he continued his involvement in charitable work to assist others through education and medical treatment.

I first met Lea Potts, now known as Lea Gabrielle, in late 2008. After graduating from the U.S. Naval Academy in 1997, she became an F/A 18 pilot and flew combat missions. In 2006, she changed to intelligence, completed the CIA's Field Training Course and was certified as a case officer. She subsequently deployed to Afghanistan where she supported the Navy's special mission unit as a case officer. The Navy then assigned her to the Navy's N2X organization. Marshall Billingslea asked me to recruit her for the DUSN's Office.

When I met Lea, it was to receive a briefing on a proposal to build a human intelligence capability within the Navy. Her boss briefed me on his proposal which I found lacking in practicality and detail. Lea sat silent during the briefing, and her body language told me that she was not in full concurrence with the proposal. I later had lunch with her and discussed the offer to work for the DUSN Office. We both agreed that it would not be a good fit because of the person she would be working for. A classmate from the Field Training Course and one of her instructors contacted me previously—both thought that she was an exceptional person.

I sensed that Lea was not happy with her current job but wasn't keen to go to the DUSN's Office, I asked her what she would like to do. She told me that she was going to leave the Navy and wanted to study broadcast journalism. With that, I offered to arrange meetings with Jim Miklaszewski, the NBC Pentagon correspondent, and David Martin and his producer Mary Walsh from CBS. Jim offered her a job as an NBC reporter. She told Jim that she wanted to go to the New York Film Academy beforehand. After leaving the Navy and having completed the course in New York, Jim again offered to immediately put her on the air. Again, she declined because she wanted to learn the business thoroughly. After a year, she finally accepted the offer to go on the air and became the military correspondent for an NBC affiliate in San Diego. Subsequently, she became Shepard Smith's main reporter on Fox News. Then she was approached by Secretary of State Mike Pompeo to become the special envoy for global engagement in the State Department.

As of 2023, she was a Sloan Fellow at the MIT Sloan School of Management. Lea has continually displayed the courage of her convictions, a willingness to serve America, and the courage to tackle new challenges, and do so with great humility. Another great example of *Intoku*.

***

In late 2010, I presented with symptoms of colon cancer. I had committed to attend another Pacific Area Special Operations Conference and to also attend the funeral of my childhood hero, James "Aki" Fuchise, who had fought in the battle of Taejon during the Korean War and was awarded for heroism. In March 2011, I was diagnosed with colon cancer between Stages 3 and 4. I went through a regimen of radiation, chemotherapy, and two surgeries. I was not sure if I would survive. There were four people, along with my wife, who gave me the will to live. Good friends Larry Reiman and Rod Azama visited me in the hospital. Colonel Bryan Fenton and his Command Sergeant Major Dave Gibbs visited me at my home. They spent a couple of hours with me building my morale and will. These four clearly showed *Intoku*. In March of 2012, I resigned from the DUSN's Office to rebuild my health and life.

THE ASSISTANT SECRETARY OF DEFENSE
WASHINGTON, D.C. 20301-2500

SPECIAL OPERATIONS/ LOW-INTENSITY CONFLICT

Mr. Wade Ishimoto
Alexandria, VA

Subj: Retirement from Federal Service

"Ish",

On the occasion of your departure from an exceptionally outstanding life of service to the nation, I wish to extend my most sincere and heartfelt appreciation.

You have served with exemplary courage and selflessness. You have become a true Special Operations and Intelligence legend. From the jungles of Vietnam, to the sands of the Iranian desert, to the halls of Washington, DC, you have truly "done it all." You leave a stable of dedicated and talented followers and peers who have excelled under your demanding leadership. The nation owes you a debt we can never re pay: VR, OC

— Tom O'Connell
Asst. Secretary of Defense

Letter on retirement from federal service.

Epilogue

My bout with cancer ended my full-time work, but it never deterred me from continuing to care about others and to live the spirit of *Intoku*. I continued to teach for the Joint Special Operations University, participate in leadership professional development activities for our Special Operations forces, and mentor others. As I conclude writing this book, I intend to do so as long as I am able to, and offer value to others.

The cancer, along with a hip replacement and chronic back pain, also meant an end to my practice of Aikido. I was well on the way to being promoted to 7th Dan, but that was not to happen. I was not disappointed in not achieving the promotion but I was sad that I could not help others through the practice of Aikido.

I have never sought recognition for what I did and my support for others. However, I was recognized for my efforts. Among other awards, I was inducted in 2017 to the U.S. Special Operations Command Commando Hall of Honor. At the ceremony, instead of perfunctory handshakes, I got hugs from Generals Tony Thomas (USSOCOM) and Joe Votel (USCENTCOM), Lieutenant General Brad Webb (AFSOC), Lieutenant General Mike Nagata, Major General Jim Linder, and others. It was because I had either mentored them or supported their commands and personnel. Those hugs rather than handshakes were truly more meaningful than receiving an induction into the Hall of Honor. It affirmed for me that my doing good for others made a difference, which is what I sought to do above all else.

My life has been blessed with many super mentors and with opportunities to mentor others who, in turn, care for and mentor others. Again, I apologize for not naming all of you. You know who you are! Many of you cannot be formally recognized because of the sensitivity of the work you do. I honor and respect you all. You have names like Victor, Jae, Monica, Adriana, Rick, Joshe, Stu, Joe, and Matt. Continue to hold your standards high and to make a difference in military, national, and public service. You are the future of America and the world.

Remember that life is full of challenges and opportunities. Everyone needs to deal with reality by understanding that one can overcome setbacks, mistakes, and supposed failures, by having a resilient outlook on life and dealing with a path that may be bumpy and full of curves. Be steadfast, be resolute, and continue to care about others. Never lose your desire, your determination, or your courage.

Remember and practice the tenets of *Intoku*—doing good without seeking recognition—and the world will be a better place. I hope the lessons in this book help you to help others.

God bless you.